DATE DUE

DEMCO 38-296

POLITICAL THOUGHT

AND

POLITICAL THINKERS

Judith N. Shklar

Political Thought
and
Political Thinkers

Edited by
Stanley Hoffmann

Foreword by
George Kateb

THE UNIVERSITY OF CHICAGO PRESS / CHICAGO AND LONDON

...owles Professor of Government at Har-
... was the author of nine books, includ-
...justice.

...therine Buttenwieser University Professor at Harvard.

GEORGE KATEB is professor of politics at Princeton University.

The University of Chicago Press, Chicago 60637
The University of Chicago Press, Ltd., London
© 1998 by The University of Chicago
All rights reserved. Published 1998
Printed in the United States of America
07 06 05 04 03 02 01 00 99 98   1 2 3 4 5

ISBN: 0-226-75344-1 (cloth)
ISBN: 0-226-75346-8 (paper)

Library of Congress Cataloging-in-Publication Data

Shklar, Judith N.
    Political thought and political thinkers / Judith N. Shklar ;
edited by Stanley Hoffmann ; foreword by George Kateb.
        p.   cm.
    Includes bibliographical references and index.
    ISBN 0-226-75344-1 (cloth : alk. paper). — ISBN 0-226-75346-8
(paper : alk. paper)
    1. Political science—History.   I. Hoffman, Stanley.   II. Title.
JA83.S52   1998
320′.09—DC21   97-27074
                                                        CIP

CONTENTS

FOREWORD
by George Kateb

nyone familiar with Judith Shklar's books knows how wide her range is. The essays collected in this volume, together with those in *Redeeming American Political Thought*, amply confirm the sense that her achievement is large in its scope, that it is various and marked by little repetition. We could see her collected essays as an introduction to her thought as a whole, and a distillation of it. Yet it would be better to say that these essays add up to a separate work. They not only fruitfully supplement the discussions in the eight books she published, they also address new subjects. Fresh arguments, insights, and considerations continuously appear. It must be stressed, however, that Shklar was not an especially opportunistic writer. She did not write on one subject after another, as mood or occasion dictated. Rather, her thought has a kind of unity. There is no absolute need, of course, to insist on that unity, but one can nevertheless point to certain elements that, from the start of her career, seem to constitute her writing, to stamp and define it, and also to account for its great worth. The collected essays have these elements in profusion. They are an integral part of her achievement.

What do we find in this volume, as in the rest of her writings? Shklar unmistakably dislikes excess: political excess, everyday excess, excess of imagination, of aspiration, of exertion. Correspondingly, she favors restraint, moderation, in politics as well as in all the transactions of life. The sensibilities of Montaigne and Montesquieu guide her in her reflections and in the books and essays that these reflections yield. But the moderation is hard-earned. It is not a quality attained by automatically assuming a middle position; it is not invariably associated with compromise or splitting the difference. Much less is

Shklar's sensibility lukewarm or neutral; she is not diffident. Shklar is strenuous in her defense of moderation. If she does not adopt some version of the Aristotelian idea of the mean—an idea that is too lofty for her, too nondemocratic, too intimately implicated in privilege, habituation, and self-display—she does clearly sympathize with Aristotle in his "contempt for the utopian imagination" and for his general aversion to extremism of any kind.[1]

Her commitment to moderation makes her a member of the party of memory rather than of the party of hope. She borrows these categories from Emerson's essay "The Conservative" (1841). One use of this distinction is found in "Politics and the Intellect," where she sees John Adams as standing for the party of memory and Thomas Jefferson for the party of hope.[2] Adams studied the past for its lessons: "He looked back with the disenchanted eye of a social scientist."[3] Jefferson, on the other hand, was bored and irritated by history; he valued progress and looked ahead to continuous improvement, especially in the arts and sciences. Shklar is on Adams' side, even though, like Adams, she is far from being hopeless.

The lessons of the past must be kept to mind because they chasten hope; they reduce expectation concerning the possibility of reaching an ideal society. Memory, however, is not only studious knowledge of the turmoil and frustration of the past; it is also a felt knowledge of recent events. Shklar belongs to the party of memory primarily because of the evils systematically perpetrated in this century. These evils not only circumscribe expectation, they are invincibly there, part of the permanent record of what human beings are capable of. To hope too much is to be guilty of forgetting the unspeakable, which happened in our lifetime, and will doubtless happen again, if it is not already taking place somewhere or other.

Shklar reverts to the distinction between the party of memory and the party of hope in perhaps her most famous essay, "The Liberalism of Fear." The grimness of the twentieth century dominates it. Shklar never undertakes a systematic inquiry into such phenomena as totalitarianism, extermination of whole populations, and savage, technologically enhanced warfare. But the terror of these events comes out, if only indirectly for the most part, everywhere in her writings. From her earliest days as a scholar, beginning with *After Utopia* (1957), she is mindful of the way ideologically inflamed people, possessed by hope for a radically changed world, can make a hell on earth. That she herself was driven out of her native country by political persecution simply counted as just one illustration of an infinitely wider fate. It can be said, therefore, that an unlurid pessimism, sometimes subdued and sometimes modified, characterizes Shklar's whole body of work.

As a political theorist, Shklar seeks to understand oppression and injustice and then to defend time-tested ways of reducing, if not completely eliminating, their occurrence. There is no way of absolutely or forever preventing them: to think otherwise is to be lost in utopian delusion. But to think that oppression and injustice can be reduced is sensible and realistic. There are, after all, societies in which the worst political manifestations are warded off, the worst tendencies are held in abeyance. She quotes the poet C. Day Lewis: we must "defend the bad against the worse."[4] Shklar devotes herself to the project of understanding why social life is so often terrible and why amelioration is uncommon and precarious. In her twofold role as a student of political theory and as a political theorist in her own right, she thus aspires to penetrate to the sources of human misconduct and to defend the imperfect barriers that may be erected against them.

The essays in this volume show Shklar at work as a student of political theory. Actually, only in her last two books—*The Faces of Injustice* (1990) and *American Citizenship* (1991)—does she theorize directly. For the most part she works on the texts of other writers and elicits from these texts either truths about politics or suggestions that may provoke or stimulate. In reading her essays, we see that in case after case, she stages a strenuous confrontation with the work of others and does not rest until she has won something valuable from them—something valuable in itself or something cautionary. The reader has the constant impression of a passionate mind that is most fully responsive when the mind it faces is itself also passionate. Shklar's passion is thus spent on behalf of moderation and restraint in politics and in the rest of life. The sum of Shklar's readings do not, of course, yield a systematic political theory, but they do contribute immeasurably to the reader's political education.

By concentrating on the sources and alleviations of oppression and injustice, Shklar is a selective student of political theory. Her incomparably wide range is thus actually quite determined in its purpose. Shklar speaks only occasionally about the very nature of political theory. In *Ordinary Vices* (1984), she defines the "job" of political theory: "to make our conversations and convictions about our society more complete and coherent and to review critically the judgments we ordinarily make and the possibilities we usually see."[5] But this formulation is rather bland, and therefore out of character. Elsewhere she is more true to her own practice: "Political theory is inherently contentious and persuasive."[6] A fuller conception can be found in "What Is the Use of Utopia?" written in the 1980s and published for the first time in this volume. It nicely complements the discussion of the uses of political theory and the learning and the techniques needed to read it that she presents in the postscript to *Men and Citizens: A Study of Rousseau's Social Theory* (1969). In the essay in this volume, she frankly acknowledges that in her earlier years she thought that when utopian ideas had been discredited in the 1950s, "we had run out of political ideas as well."[7] Furthermore, she was premature in announcing the death of utopia and other "transformative ideas" about a substantially better world. This kind of thought revived in the 1960s. The crucial point, however, is that political theory does "not depend entirely on the survival of future-oriented ideologies."[8] She had been mistaken in thinking that "we had nothing more to say."[9]

What more was there to say? Whatever the shape of Shklar's own work, she describes the sorts of political theory that she respects. She knows that with her there will always be "fear of hope and of change."[10] That means that she will always oppose serious utopianism: perfectionist speculation that becomes dangerously intoxicating when it goes beyond the function of holding up existing society to severe criticism. She will also always oppose ideological thinking in its "relentless future-directed, prophetic, activist and all-encompassing pretensions, its pseudoscientific aspirations and its dogmatic ways."[11] The nineteenth century was "the age of ideology," but the political theory that preceded the nineteenth century provides models for contemporary political theory. Shklar offers two recent theoretical approaches of which she approves: the skeptical worldliness of Michael Oakeshott and Isaiah Berlin and the "normative" political theory of John Rawls and Jürgen Habermas. Especially noteworthy is that the normative theory shows a resolute avoidance of such ideals as fraternity or solidarity; it does not envisage "the creation of a new man"; it does not offer "a total critique of the actual."[12] Shklar does not prefer the skeptical model to the normative one, as perhaps once she would have. Instead, she praises Rawls and Habermas for producing theories that "are not fictions but formal and critical models immanent in constitutional democracy, embedded in it but not realized."[13] Still, let it be remarked that she does not endorse with a full acceptance either political skepticism or Rawls or Habermas.

Shklar observes with satisfaction the revival of political theory amidst the decline of utopia and the (Western) abandonment of ideology. But this revival, whether skeptical or normative, really leaves Shklar comparatively untouched. As always, she moves in her own direction, even when she formulates a theory of injustice in *The Faces of Injustice*. She concentrates her attention first and foremost on those texts that will help her understand the sources of wickedness and wrongdoing. From *After Utopia* onward, Shklar is a student of moral psychology (a term she uses as the title of the second chapter of *Men and Citizens*). Moral psychology, rather than a systematic theory of the state and its powers and purposes, is, for her, the heart of political theory. At least that is the matter that dominates her work. She is interested in—indeed, she is obsessed by—moral psychology wherever it can be found in its most instructive delineation. She looks first to the reputable texts of political theory for assistance; but not finding enough, she exploits the riches of the great moral essayists, the poets, and the writers of drama and fiction. Not everything she discovers is put to a political use. Shklar is not embarrassed to be a thinker about the human condition—to use a phrase made memorable by her beloved Montaigne. Her emphasis is nevertheless political. The human record of humanly inflicted suffering defeats the mind's effort to encompass it, much less to make sense of it. Surely, however, clues are waiting for the patient reader?

As Shklar works with the concept, moral psychology in general is the untechnical or unscientific effort to specify the main pervasive human motives, sentiments, and desires that are present everywhere; to show how they affect and shape the practices and relations of life; to see whether they typically work themselves out in a definite pattern or logic; to observe how the motives, sentiments, and desires conflict with or reinforce or even grow out of one another; to determine whether any of the desirable ones may be trained or educated into virtues, and any of the deplorable ones, which are prone to vice, curbed, discouraged, or sublimated; and hence to suggest—no more emphatically than that—what is and what is not profoundly and unalterably human, for good and for bad.

It turns out that just as Shklar has no worked-out theory of the state and its powers and purposes, so she gives no cumulative account of the sources in society and human nature of wickedness and wrongdoing. She believes, to the contrary, that although humanity can know many things, it cannot know itself very well. Perhaps this smallness of self-knowledge is incurable. She says that:

> social explanation is insuperably dependent upon psychology. Unless we really know what the motives of social agents are, we cannot get it perfectly right. That does not mean that psychology is all one has to know. It is group, not individual, conduct and change that are at stake, but there is no answer to the question "Why?" without a scientifically

adequate psychology. Nothing of that order is now available . . . We
do not even have an idea what such a psychology might look like.[14]

Yet Shklar persistently seeks to know what moves or drives people,
especially what moves or drives them to inflict oppression and injustice. What she seems to ignore or disavow is psychological explanation that aims to plumb depths. It is possible to think that though
she is aware of the overall opacity that permeates life in society, she
does not seem to believe that human nature is essentially mysterious.
People are what they are; we can see or infer what they do and more
or less why they do it; true knowledge does not add up theoretically
but is instead a matter of quantity. The more the better.

It is only when an ambitious scheme like that of neo-Marxist Karl
Mannheim tries to capture all of history in one theory that Shklar
turns reproachful and asks for a psychological explanation. She says
that "the most serious deficiency of Mannheim's sociology of knowledge was its failure to concern itself with the psychological mechanisms by which social conditions are translated by groups and individuals into doctrines."[15]

In regard to the several vices she considers at length in *Ordinary
Vices*—cruelty, hypocrisy, snobbery, betrayal, and misanthropy—
she says that they are "the sort of conduct we all expect, nothing
spectacular or unusual."[16] Shklar is never surprised by terrible occurrences, but always fascinated by them. If no deep explanation of them
is possible or needed, we are nevertheless obliged to continue to think
about them. Shklar is content that Orwell's *Nineteen Eighty-Four* is
a powerful picture of brutal political power and does not offer much
speculation about the subtleties of deference or the "inherent attractions of authority."[17] She renders Rousseau's explanation of cruelty
with a deliberate flatness: "Cruelty is a response to fear and weakness."[18] Rousseau, Orwell, and others help us to remember the end-
lessness of wrongdoing but they never become reconciled to it. Protest
is rightly inspired by an indelible impression of the terribleness of
wrongdoing, yet the struggle against wrongdoing must be restrained
by the conviction that only limited gains are possible. Rousseau's proposed remedies for the pathologies of radical inequality "may well
have been worse than the disease."[19]

The point is not to reveal or unearth motivation but to assemble
as many persuasive descriptions and characterizations as possible.
Shklar can be taken as saying that the worldly observation found in
the best political theory and imaginative literature exposes the indefinite scope of human possibility. The finest achievement of political theory is to help fill out our sense of human possibility—for good,

but, more important, for bad or even evil. And the quality of description that counts is evocativeness, vividness. Great writing lodges pictures of human motivation in our minds, whether in the form of analysis, "subversive genealogies," or fictional stories.

Shklar's general sense of the nature of moral psychology is expressed in her treatment of "subversive genealogies." These genetic accounts include creation myths and conjectural histories of the human race, as well as narratives of founding a society and of its historical experience. Obviously not all the work of moral psychology is done in genealogies, but they are its epitome. Of myths of origins, she says:

> They are meant to make evident and clear what is often merely felt. Actuality is to be revealed, shown, and shown up by a review of its origins that does not delineate the causes, but the awful character of this aging world. This is neither pseudo-history nor pseudo-etiology nor primitive science. It is neither the rival nor the precursor of more rigorous forms of thought. It is psychological evocation, an appeal, with the aid of very familiar memories, to others to accept a picture of social man as a permanently displaced person.[20]

These words capture the essence of the best moral psychology as it is contained in the texts that Shklar studies.

Another valuable formulation of the purpose of moral psychology comes when Shklar defends her practice of relying on novels and plays to further her own explorations. She says of these stories:

> They are told in order to reveal something directly. These illuminations are not meant to prove anything or to make it easier to grasp some general idea. They are there for their own sake, for their ability to force us to acknowledge what we already know imperfectly. They make us recognize something as if it were obvious.[21]

As a student of political theory, Shklar presents to her readers in the form of scholarly treatises and lectures the moral psychology she finds most compelling in the work of others, especially political theorists, moral philosophers, and writers of fiction and drama. To repeat: she wishes not so much to explore the depths of the human propensity to oppression and injustice, but to bring home to us, in her own way, what greater writers when properly read have brought home to her and to other interpreters. Shklar is a kind of mediator between worthy texts and readers, young and old, who are perhaps disposed to naiveté or a too urgent hopefulness or an overpowering disgust or, on the other hand, to a self-serving forgetfulness of the historical record or of the abundant evidence of everyday life that stares us in the face, or to plain dishonesty. She mediates with the intention of discouraging radical or reactionary political projects and shoring up those political and cultural institutions that tend to the reduction of wickedness and wrongdoing. She is an advocate of the Enlightenment purged of its zeal. Living two horrible centuries after the *philosophes*, she knows things about success and ruin that they could not have known. Her understanding of moral psychology helps her to confine the aspirations of the Enlightenment. Or, at least, she returns her readers and herself to Montesquieu's practically cautious but inwardly radical Enlightenment, the Enlightenment already enlightened by "doubt, pessimism, and self-criticism."[22]

Shklar mediates between texts and readers by means of interpretation. She practices this art with consummate skill. A tactful reader, she is nevertheless determined to carry lessons out of a text. There certainly are lessons even though there is no theoretical system to be made of them. To learn from a writer, he or she must be interpreted—that is, a writer must be worked on. An indefinite number of implications are lodged in any worthwhile text. Much experience and the experience of many readers are needed to unpack it. At the same time, when Shklar interprets a text she does not simply report on its contents. She is a master of the art of interpretation as restatement. It is not that she substitutes her own thought for the thought of the writer she studies; she does not wish new meaning into existence by taking advantage of a writer's prestige and pretending that the writer is saying what she in fact has invented. No, her restatement helps to bring a text to life, just as, to begin with, a worthwhile text helps to give life to some undeniable but obscured truth about human nature or the human condition. "If we interpret a man's thought in order to be directly instructed by him,"[23] we must restate him, we must as it were rewrite him, in order to be instructed. Interpretation does not happen merely by reading an author with attention. And interpretation is endless because worthwhile texts are overflowingly rich, too much for any single reading or reader to take in. Concerning Plato and Aristotle—but the point can be extended to others—Shklar says that "they educate us and that is why they are interpreted and reinterpreted."[24] Not only diversity but uncertainty marks interpretations, and that is an irremediable situation that we should enjoy, not bemoan.[25]

The importance of the example set by Shklar's interpretations of what turns out to be an amazingly large number of writers in her books and essays is that she teaches us not to be ingenious. She takes issue with the self-described hermeneuticist who is disposed to look for "some teleology or some external or hidden social purpose and slips it into the interpretive moment of understanding."[26] This admonition is directed, in the first instance, to those who try to understand whole societies or historical periods. But her practice as an interpreter of texts scrupulously avoids intimating that she knows better than those whose ideas she sets down and restates. If we did not think an author "a greater man than his readers, we would not undertake the labors of interpretation in the first place."[27] Of course, the interpreter may know things the original writer could not have known, and have had experiences unavailable to that writer. Yet we cannot understand what is before us as interpreters, whether the subject is a society or a text, unless we look at it first from the intention or point of view of the subject.[28] (It must be noticed that Shklar found dubious "the analogy between reading a text and recording social acts.")[29]

Shklar's labors of interpretation are principally on behalf of moral psychology. But as a political theorist she cannot help but be interested in political power, in methods of influence and control, and in forms and procedures of government. To be sure, she loved the subject of moral psychology for its own sake and pursued knowledge wherever she thought she could find it. She went so far as to say that Rousseau was such a great psychologist that to "have read Rousseau with some care is to have thought about all that is most relevant to political philosophy and to the intellectual imagination in general."[30] The two essays on Rousseau in this volume give eloquent testimony to Shklar's respect for Rousseau and her ability to be instructed by him and thus to instruct us. The study of moral psychology, however, has also a major practical use. It serves Shklar as the basis for her substantive political views. Her politics of moderation and restraint and her moral psychology are tightly joined; each sustains and strengthens the other.

Politics often arouses or systematizes the human propensity to wickedness and wrongdoing. (She uses the word "evil" sparingly, but late in her work she refers to her "preoccupation with political evil.")[31] The only acceptable politics is that which restrains or somehow neutralizes that propensity. The ordinary name for such politics is constitutionalism; Shklar's political theory is a defense of constitutionalism. Her emphasis is characteristically on avoiding or reducing or preventing the worst things that people do to one another. She is famous for asserting that physical cruelty and mental cruelty define the worst.[32] "The Liberalism of Fear" is a passionate espousal of constitutionalism on the grounds that it prohibits the government's use of physical cruelty and correspondingly aims at preventing government from establishing a condition of sharp or endemic fear—fear of governmental cruelty—among the population.[33] (Her lecture on Pope's *An Essay on Man* speaks movingly of human cruelty to animals. In her horror she approaches the vice of misanthropy.)[34] Constitutionalism puts cruelty first; that is, it is concerned above all with facing up to it and ridding political society of its ravages.

The emphasis on avoidance, reduction, and prevention of the worst brings out the negativity of Shklar's political theory—at least until her last two books, in which government is entrusted by her theory with energetic reformist activity. But again such activity does not promote any end beyond avoidance or reduction of physically or mentally painful circumstances: in the last two books, social injustice and demoralizing unemployment are to be corrected by governmental action to the fullest extent possible. But let us see that even when Shklar assents to active government, her purpose is still negative. It is to make life less crushing or burdensome for individuals, not to promote happiness or self-fulfillment. She endorses a "negative egalitarianism," which is really a somewhat tempered social inequality copresent with equal political status.[35] Shklar does not love the market economy; she does, however, reconcile herself to its existence as something tolerable and less harmful, on balance, than a state-run economy. She does not love the state at all, despite speaking with approval of "the positive potentialities of existing forms of government."[36]

To place and defend limits on all kinds of suffering that come from political wickedness and wrongdoing: that is Shklar's highest hope, her deepest commitment. Writing in 1959, early in her scholarly life, she refers to the "survivalist" tradition in political theory. The phrase is that of her colleague Carl J. Friedrich, but the meaning is enlarged by her. She says of this tradition:

> Amoral, and a-ideological, it rests on the assumption that government cannot make men good, but that it can keep them from violent action. The strict adherence to the letter of the law is demanded not as just, but as the one means of stopping violence and resentment among the governed; mixed-government, as the way to prevent acts of hostility from rulers. That, in fact, *is* justice. The end of government is at the most civic harmony; at the very least it is to prevent clashes of interest and conviction from becoming violent.[37]

With time, Shklar carries this concept in a less antipopular direction, but it contains the essential elements of her constitutionalism. She fears elites, and she also fears ordinary people when they are massed together in action or mobilized to act. She fears the power of the powerful and the concerted irrationality of the many. Yet she does not want the few to disappear or the many to be dominated. She is a pessimist, but she is a moderate. She is a moderate because she is a particular kind of pessimist: not sour, not cynical, but shrewd and, where possible, forbearing.

If she fears power, she dreads irrationality. The many can be whipped up into irrationality, but it usually requires a doctrine of some kind to instigate their passions, and such doctrines are always originated by members of the few. Her early essay on Henri Bergson shows a well-developed aversion to all those doctrines that depart from reason on principle and encourage people to act out their fantastical perceptions and ambitions. The worst social effects come from an ideologically manipulated mass of people, but Shklar also dislikes the romanticism or aestheticism of the few. She goes so far as to put individualism under suspicion, because she holds that the romantic worship of individuality tends to involve a hatred of the masses.[38] But even as an ideal for oneself or the chosen few, individualism tends obnoxiously to the "aesthetic ethics" of "exhibitionism."[39] Freedom, for Shklar, is not the unpredictability and spontaneity of the creative individual. Freedom depends "not on the possibility of creating a new, future self out of nothing, nor on the occasional moment of self-expression," but instead on the presence of alternatives, between which one may choose.[40]

If there has to be individualism, she seems to prefer Rousseau's "individualism of the weak" to Locke's "individualism of the strong."[41] And though Shklar defends the doctrine of individual rights, she sees them as legal rights that governments must create and enforce so that the liberalism of fear be institutionally adequate. Rights are not naturally or divinely ordained or endowed.[42] They have no metaphysical sponsorship. Individuals have no aura; they are creatures with needs and fears. The needs must be met and the fears assuaged. Government does not create the needs, but must try to meet them where necessary; but government can be the greatest source of fear, and its structure and mentality must give insurance against itself. Shklar's effort to defend the creatureliness of human beings, as distinct from their individuality, also shows itself in her conceptualization of the difference between obligation and loyalty. She says: "The emotional character of loyalty also sets it apart from obligation. If obligation is rule driven, loyalty is motivated by the entire personality of an agent."[43] On the one hand, obligation is owed to the right institutions in the right circumstances, but it is more a debt paid by good sense than a requirement of conscience; on the other hand, loyalty should be deserved, even though those who exact it do so ravenously and demand that it be blind, and even though a person's feelings of loyalty begin too early in life ever to be completely under one's control.

In one respect, then, Shklar asks for a great deal: a society rid of the worst, rid of fear, rid of physical cruelty and moral humiliation. In another respect, Shklar asks for little: no transformation, no perfection, no grandeur, nothing spectacular or especially well defined. Constitutionalism, democratically maintained, is enough, far more than we can ever take for granted, given human proclivities and the record of human history.

To read these essays, then, is to encounter a political theorist of rare gifts. Shklar has a voice and a vision. She unintentionally summarizes the qualities of her own mind in fine words that she uses about two political writers of the twentieth century. About George Orwell she says that he had "an uneasy, doubting, self-assertive mind."[44] About Hannah Arendt she says that her essays are "bold without becoming dogmatic," and that Arendt's mind "explores, it tries and it expects."[45] These phrases about Orwell and Arendt suit Shklar herself perfectly.

Notes

1. "What Is the Use of Utopia?" p. 187.
2. "Politics and the Intellect," p. 96.
3. Ibid., pp. 98–99.
4. *Ordinary Vices* (Cambridge, Mass.: Harvard University Press, 1984), p. 226.
5. Ibid.
6. *Men and Citizens: A Study of Rousseau's Social Theory* (Cambridge: Cambridge University Press, 1969), p. 221.
7. "What Is the Use of Utopia?" p. 186.
8. Ibid., p. 187.
9. Ibid., p. 188.
10. Ibid., p. 190.
11. *Political Theory and Ideology*, ed. Judith N. Shklar (New York: Macmillan, 1966), p. 19.
12. "What Is the Use of Utopia?" p. 189.
13. Ibid.
14. "Squaring the Hermeneutic Circle," p. 89.
15. *Political Theory and Ideology*, p. 13.
16. *Ordinary Vices*, p. 1.
17. "Nineteen Eighty-Four: Should Political Theory Care?" p. 347.
18. *Men and Citizens*, p. 35.
19. "Jean-Jacques Rousseau and Equality," p. 282.

20. "Subversive Genealogies," p. 154.

21. *Ordinary Vices*, p. 229.

22. "Politics and the Intellect," p. 95.

23. *Men and Citizens*, p. 219.

24. Ibid., p. 218.

25. "Squaring the Hermeneutic Circle," p. 93.

26. Ibid., pp. 90–91.

27. Ibid., p. 83.

28. Ibid., pp. 90–91.

29. Ibid., p. 84.

30. *Men and Citizens*, p. 231.

31. "Obligation, Loyalty, Exile," p. 38.

32. *Ordinary Vices*, chap. 1, pp. 7–44.

33. On the liberalism of fear, see also *Ordinary Vices*, pp. 237–38.

34. "Poetry and the Political Imagination in Pope's *An Essay on Man*," especially pp. 196–201.

35. *Ordinary Vices*, p. 28.

36. "What Is the Use of Utopia?" p. 187.

37. "Ideology Hunting: The Case of James Harrington," p. 230. See also *Ordinary Vices*, p. 4.

38. "Bergson and the Politics of Intuition," p. 334.

39. Ibid., pp. 333–34.

40. Ibid., p. 325.

41. *Men and Citizens*, p. 41.

42. "Political Theory and the Rule of Law," p. 32; "The Liberalism of Fear," pp. 8, 18–19; *Ordinary Vices*, pp. 237–38.

43. "Obligation, Loyalty, Exile," p. 41.

44. "Nineteen Eighty-Four: Should Political Theory Care?" p. 348.

45. "Rethinking the Past," p. 360.

EDITOR'S PREFACE
by Stanley Hoffmann

I

It is hard not to be overwhelmed by Judith Shklar's work; it was hard not to be overwhelmed by her personality. The range of the essays collected in the two volumes published by the University of Chicago Press is extraordinary—even more so if one keeps in mind that these essays are the major part, but not the totality, of what she wrote in addition to her books. I have left out, after consulting with many colleagues, essays that seemed to duplicate what she put into her books on Rousseau, Hegel, and Montesquieu, many book reviews, and a few unpublished pieces she would probably have revised extensively.

This volume, which deals with those of her writings that do not focus on the United States, shows, in its variety of themes, that she was both a fox and a hedgehog—to use the distinction made by her friend Sir Isaiah Berlin, whose scholarship, intelligence, humane liberalism, and immense culture she admired, even though she reached conclusions far removed from the relativism he sometimes displays. The fox, here, pursues a fascinating menagerie of profoundly different thinkers, from the ancient Greeks to Hannah Arendt, from her Enlightenment favorites to the romantic Bergson, from famous Athenian exiles to Michael Walzer, from Harrington to Orwell. A fox always on the alert against the dangers of utopian thinking (should one try to realize the utopias despite the resistance of reality), she nevertheless celebrated "the political energy required to think both critically and positively about the state we are in and how to improve it," and she hoped "that the inspiration for so imaginative and fascinating a form of literature might enlighten us again"—or at least warn us against the kind of "cognitive nightmare" that Orwell described in *1984*. Utopias à la More or Fourier may have disappeared, but, in her view, contemporary normative theory, à la Rawls, performs a similar function.

The hedgehog—being Judith Shklar—knew not just one thing, but two. Methodologically, she was, to use her own term, a mandarin. Knowledge has to be pursued for its own sake. Not all ways of reading texts are equally valid. Historians too much concerned with being useful and drawing lessons, and willing, unlike d'Alembert, to sacrifice accuracy, as happens in Arendt's kind of "monumental history," are retreating from the obligation "to study mankind carefully and scientifically." Political science, about which she cared greatly, insofar as she never thought that ideas about good and bad government could be divorced from the study of institutions which embody them, was, she believed, inseparable from the knowledge of history. "Memory is passive, a mere attic, but without it all our other knowledge is useless to us. Remembering is active . . . an activity of the human mind without which there could be no human understanding." A historically informed discipline, the study of politics must therefore be sensitive "to intangibles, and to qualitative considerations," unlike Harrington, and unlike so much of "20th century academic ideology," with its pretensions to science.

Normatively, from the beginning to her premature end, she knew what had to be avoided, because it was, in her view, the central, common experience of twentieth-century men and women, and had been the common experience of so many human beings in the past: the politics of cruelty and fear. Her studies of political thought were steeped in history. Her normative thoughts about politics were steeped in the values of the Enlightenment, which, she said, were still ours. "If one . . . begins with the fear of violence, the insecurity of arbitrary government and the discriminations of injustice one may work one's way up to finding a significant place for the Rule of Law, and for the boundaries it has historically set upon these the most enduring of our political troubles."

The originality of her liberalism lies in the fact that it not only is without illusions, that is, severed from the philosophy of historical progress that had sustained it since the eighteenth century, but also is derived not from a philosophical conception of human reason, as in Kant or (despite his attempt at differentiating his approach from Kant's "comprehensive" conception) in Rawls, but from an existential experience of fear and cruelty. It lies also in the perspective which this primordial concern of hers dictates. I would call it (doubly) sub-versive liberalism. Most thinkers in the pantheon of liberalism looked at society from above, and at the state from the top down. Most of them, like J. S. Mill and his friend Tocqueville, described in great detail the kinds of political and social institutions they deemed essential for the protection of liberty. Judith Shklar looked at society and the state from the perspective of the losers: the poor, the outcast, the slaves, America's blacks, the exiles, all the victims of injustice and neglect (she sees in Rousseau, of whom she remains the subtlest analyst, "the Homer of the losers").

Moreover, she was more interested in warning us about the varieties of bad and cruel government than in telling us what good government would entail. In the last years of her life, she became more explicit about the requirements of good government, about the need for a vigilant citizenry making sure both that the state respects individual liberties and that the common tasks are performed by civic-minded representatives. She proposed that exiles be granted citizenship rights in their countries of refuge. But she continued to spend more energy attacking conceptions she deemed dangerous for her passionate liberalism of the losers. From her first book on, she criticized the political effects of Romanticism, with its focus on heroes and geniuses (Bergson, she wrote, was the only democratic Romantic, but she finds him devoid of "any viable proposals for the reconstruction of political thought"). In her last years, she concentrated her fire on the warm confusions of communitarianism, admonishing Walzer against the idealization of often pettily oppressive voluntary or local associations, pointing out the difference between these (based on loyalty) and the state (a legal construct buttressed by obligations); "clubby life" is the enemy of rights, and "shared understandings" are the last thing one finds among the citizens of a modern state, "disparate culturally and often deeply hostile to one another as individuals and especially as members of ascriptive groups." Hence her (in my opinion successful) attempt to show that a communitarian reading of the *Social Contract* is quite wrong.

Judith Shklar, the refugee from Latvia, was an intellectual descendant of Montaigne and Montesquieu. A convert to America, an admirer of America's democratic aspirations, she nevertheless always reminded her American readers of their country's original and unredeemed sin—slavery—and of the victims crushed by its occasional excesses of patriotism and prejudice, and by its enthusiasm for an unfettered capitalism.

II

Dita Shklar was a second-year graduate student in Government when I came to Harvard for a year as a visiting graduate student in September 1951. We were in many courses and seminars together. She dominated every one of them, in a group of classmates that contained many future stars of the American academic and political stages. We quickly became friends. We were both, in different ways, survivors from the European catastrophe in which public horrors had shaped our private lives. We were both awed by Jean-Jacques Rousseau and enthralled by *Così fan tutte*. We were both liberals without illusions, addicted to the study of Power in order to understand what had hit us, and to think about how to resist both its seductions and its perversions. We had the same conception of our role as teachers, and the same distaste for the murderous simplicities of ideology.

She was a perfect blend of polar opposites. As one of her students put it, she offered "the challenge of complete skepticism uncontaminated by the slightest trace of cynicism." She combined an ebullient fondness for intellectual combat with a passionate desire to avoid conflict in human relations, as was shown by her initiating a pseudo half-time permanent lectureship when my colleagues were still too full of male prejudice to grant her the tenured professorship she so obviously deserved. Occasional intellectual ferocity was offset by constant emotional generosity, just as her impatience with fakes, bores, and mediocrities was balanced by incredible indulgence and delicacy toward friends and a glowing tenderness toward her children, her grandchildren, and her husband.

No one was a more accomplished professional, but nobody had a more extended culture in every conceivable domain, however remote from her field. She defended the individual and his rights, but she insisted on our responsibility toward others, on our obligation to avoid cruelty, above all, but also snobbery and the kind of indifference to misery and misfortune which constitutes political injustice. She was pessimistic about human nature, as a refugee from the Holocaust and a student of slavery, but she had a fine Enlightenment faith, if not in progress, at least in the virtues of education and consciousness—especially in this country.

The blend these opposites produced was all of one piece. She was at twenty-three as she was at sixty-three. Her prose reflected her personality, and her ideas expressed her character. There was no gap between her beliefs and her behavior—how rare, even among political theorists! If I had to describe this blend in six words, here they are.

The first is *curiosity*. Hers, driven by the need to "make sense," was unlimited. She could never find out enough about the intricacies of the human mind and the human heart or about the origins, the effects, the multiple interpretations, of a thinker's ideas.

The second word is *clarity*. Her dazzling conversations, her painstakingly prepared lectures, her carefully wrought essays threw piercing shafts of light into confusions, cant, conventions, and cliches.

The third word is *self-assurance,* or *ease.* She could detour, but she never waffled or wobbled. Whether buying a handbag in a store, walking all over Paris, counseling a student, or discussing events and ideas, she knew exactly what she thought and wanted. She knew how bright and gifted she was, and she knew that her male colleagues weren't always so happy about her brilliance. But she had no vanity, no affectation, and no need to boast or preen.

The fourth word is *energy*. She was a whirlwind. When she entered a room, the level of intensity jumped. In the last dozen years, after her children had reached or moved beyond adolescence, the scope and number of her activities, at Harvard and outside, became phenomenal. She rarely talked about them. Her efforts for racial justice at Harvard, her support for young faculty women (despite her firm, if quiet, nonfeminism: she disliked *isms*) were as constant as they were discreet.

The fifth word is *honesty:* not only that of an immensely erudite and scrupulous scholar for whom work was almost sacred, but also that of a teacher who despised the posturings of pompous gurus and the complacent collecting of disciples. With her students, she displayed a unique combination of intellectual toughness and quasi-maternal warmth and concern. With her colleagues (I don't say "her peers"—she had no peers), she practiced candor and wit. She wrote the way she talked: directly and straightforwardly (thus achieving a tour de force in explaining Hegel in short sentences).

And the last word is *fidelity*. Considering herself privileged, she wrote for and from the perspective of the victims and the excluded. Her loyalty to her friends, indeed her cult of friendship, equaled that of her hero Montaigne. She wrote, in *Ordinary Vices,* "A person incapable of friendship would be not only miserable, but incomplete." When we taught jointly a course on political ideologies, she read me her lecture drafts months ahead of time. I prepared mine the day before. Thus, we terrorized one another, but as friends, we carefully refrained from revealing, respectively, her fears and my awe.

Montaigne, long after the death of his friend La Boétie, stated: "If one should ask me to say why I liked him, I could only give this answer: because it was he, because it was me." She always gave, and asked for nothing. She was a life force. Her example kept us honest, and her affection kept me going.

Note: The second part of this essay is based on my remarks at the Harvard Memorial Service for Judith Shklar, November 6, 1992.

PART ONE

Learning about Politics

CHAPTER ONE

The Liberalism
of Fear

B efore we can begin to analyze any specific form of liberalism we must surely state as clearly as possible what the word means. For in the course of so many years of ideological conflict it seems to have lost its identity completely. Overuse and overextension have rendered it so amorphous that it can now serve as an all-purpose word, whether of abuse or praise. To bring a modest degree of order into this state of confusion we might begin by insisting that liberalism refers to a political doctrine, not a philosophy of life such as has traditionally been provided by various forms of revealed religion and other comprehensive *Weltanschauungen*. Liberalism has only one overriding aim: to secure the political conditions that are necessary for the exercise of personal freedom.

Every adult should be able to make as many effective decisions without fear or favor about as many aspects of her or his life as is compatible with the like freedom of every other adult. That belief is the original and only defensible meaning of liberalism. It is a political notion, because the fear and favor that have always inhibited freedom are overwhelmingly generated by governments, both formal and informal. And while the sources of social oppression are indeed numerous, none has the deadly effect of those who, as the agents of the modern state, have unique resources of physical might and persuasion at their disposal.

Apart from prohibiting interference with the freedom of others, liberalism does not have any particular positive doctrines about how

This chapter was previously published in *Liberalism and the Moral Life*, edited by Nancy Rosenblum. Copyright © 1989 by the President and Fellows of Harvard College. Reprinted by permission of Harvard University Press.

people are to conduct their lives or what personal choices they are to make. It is not, as so many of its critics claim, synonymous with modernity. Not that the latter is a crystal clear historical concept. Generally it does not refer to simply everything that has happened since the Renaissance, but to a mixture of natural science, technology, industrialization, skepticism, loss of religious orthodoxy, disenchantment, nihilism, and atomistic individualism. This is far from being a complete list, but it covers the main characteristics of modernity as it is perceived by those who believe that the word stands for centuries of despair and that liberalism is its most characteristic political manifestation.

It is by no means necessary to engage in disputes about the quality of the historiography or factual validity of this sort of discourse in general, but for the student of political theory at least one point must be noted. That is that liberalism has been very rare both in theory and in practice in the last two hundred odd years, especially when we recall that the European world is not the only inhabited part of the globe. No one could ever have described the governments of eastern Europe as liberal at any time, though a few briefly made a feeble effort in that direction after the First World War. In central Europe it has been instituted only after the Second World War, and then it was imposed by the victors in a war that we forget at our peril. Anyone who thinks that fascism in one guise or another is dead and gone ought to think again. In France liberalism under the three Republics flickered on and off and is only now reasonably secure, though it is still seriously challenged. In Britain it has enjoyed its longest political success, but not in the vast areas, including Ireland, that England ruled until recently. Finally, let us not forget that the United States was not a liberal state until after the Civil War, and even then often in name only. In short, to speak of a liberal era is not to refer to anything that actually happened, except possibly by comparison to what came after 1914.

The state of political thought was no more liberal than that of the reigning governments, especially in the years after the French Revolution. And we should not forget the deeply illiberal prerevolutionary republican tradition of which John Pocock has reminded us so forcefully. It is in any case difficult to find a vast flow of liberal ideology in the midst of the Catholic authoritarianism, romantic corporatist nostalgia, nationalism, racism, proslavery, social Darwinism, imperialism, militarism, fascism, and most types of socialism which dominated the battle of political ideas in the last century. There was a current of liberal thought throughout the period, but it was hardly the dominant intellectual voice. In the world beyond Europe it was not heard at all. It was powerful in the United States only if black people are not counted as members of its society.

Why then, given the actual complexity of the intellectual history of the past centuries, is there so much easy generalizing about modernity and its alleged liberalism? The reason is simple enough: liberalism is a latecomer, since it has its origins in post-Reformation Europe. Its origins are in the terrible tension within Christianity between the demands of creedal orthodoxy and those of charity, between faith and morality. The cruelties of the religious wars had the effect of turning many Christians away from the public policies of the churches to a morality that saw toleration as an expression of Christian charity. One thinks of Sebastien Castellion among Calvinists, for example.[1] Others, torn by conflicting spiritual impulses, became skeptics who put cruelty and fanaticism at the very head of the human vices; Montaigne is the most notable among them. In either case the individual, whether the bearer of a sacred conscience or the potential victim of cruelty, is to be protected against the incursions of public oppression.

Later, when the bond between conscience and God is severed, the inviolability of personal decisions in matters of faith, knowledge, and morality is still defended on the original grounds that we owe it to each other as a matter of mutual respect, that a forced belief is in itself false and that the threats and bribes used to enforce conformity are inherently demeaning. To insist that individuals must make their own choices about the most important matter in their lives—their religious beliefs—without interference from public authority, is to go very far indeed toward liberalism. It is, I think, the core of its historical development, but it would be wrong to think of principled toleration as equivalent to political liberalism. Limited and responsible government may be implicit in the claim for personal autonomy, but without an explicit political commitment to such institutions, liberalism is still doctrinally incomplete. Montaigne was surely tolerant and humanitarian but he was no liberal. The distance between him and Locke is correspondingly great. Nevertheless, liberalism's deepest grounding is in place from the first, in the conviction of the earliest defenders of toleration, born in horror, that cruelty is an absolute evil, an offense against God or humanity. It is out of that tradition that the political liberalism of fear arose and continues amid the terror of our time to have relevance.[2]

There are of course many types of liberalism that remain committed to the primacy of conscience, whether in its Protestant or Kantian versions. There is Jeffersonian liberalism of rights, which has other foundations; and the Emersonian quest for self-development has its own liberal political expression. Liberalism does not in principle have to depend on specific religious or philosophical systems of thought. It does not have to choose among them as long as they do not reject toleration, which is why Hobbes is not the father of liberalism. No theory that gives public authorities the unconditional right to impose beliefs and even a vocabulary as they may see fit upon the citizenry can be described as even remotely liberal. Of all the cases made against liberalism, the most bizarre is that liberals are really indifferent, if not openly hostile, to personal freedom. This may follow from the peculiar identification of *Leviathan* as the very archetype of liberal philosophy, but it is a truly gross misrepresentation which simply assures that any social contract theory, however authoritarian its intentions, and any anti-Catholic polemic add up to liberalism.[3]

The convoluted genealogy of liberalism that insists on seeing its origins in a theory of absolutism is not in itself interesting. More common is a sort of free association of ideas that perceives a danger to traditional revealed religion in toleration and hence assumes that liberalism is of necessity atheistic, agnostic, relativistic, and nihilistic. This catalogue of accusations is worth mentioning, because it is commonplace and because it is easily and usefully refuted. The original mistake is the failure to distinguish psychological affinities from logical consequences. As a result, these critics cannot grasp that the liberalism of fear as a strictly political theory is not necessarily linked to any one religious or scientific doctrine, though it is psychologically more compatible with some rather than with others. It must reject only those political doctrines that do not recognize any difference between the spheres of the personal and the public. Because of the primacy of toleration as the irreducible limit on public agents, liberals must always draw such a line. This is not historically a permanent or unalterable boundary, but it does require that every public policy be considered with this separation in mind and be consciously defended as meeting its most severe current standard.

The important point for liberalism is not so much where the line is drawn, as that it be drawn, and that it must under no circumstances be ignored or forgotten. The limits of coercion begin, though they do not end, with a prohibition upon invading the private realm, which originally was a matter of religious faith, but which has changed and will go on changing as objects of belief and the sense of privacy alter in response to the technological and military character of governments and the productive relationships that prevail. It is a shifting line, but not an erasable one, and it leaves liberals free to espouse a very large range of philosophical and religious beliefs.

The liberalism of fear is thus not necessarily tied to either skepticism or to the pursuit of the natural sciences. There is, however, a real psychological connection between them. Skepticism is inclined toward toleration, since in its doubts it cannot choose among the competing beliefs that swirl around it, so often in murderous rage. Whether the skeptic seeks personal tranquility in retreat or tries to calm the warring factions around her, she must prefer a government that does nothing to increase the prevailing levels of fanaticism and dogmatism. To that extent there is a natural affinity between the liberal and the skeptic. Madison's discussion in the *Federalist* of how to end sectarian and similar factional conflicts through freedom is the perfect example of the fit between skepticism and liberal politics.[4] Nevertheless, a society of believers who choose never to resort to the use of the agencies of government to further their particular faith is imaginable, though not usual.

The intellectual flexibility of skepticism is psychologically more adapted to liberalism, but it is not a necessary element of its politics. A society governed by extremely oppressive skeptics can be easily imagined if, for example, they were to follow Nietzsche's political notions energetically. That is also true of the natural sciences. These tend to flourish most in freedom, quite unlike the fine arts and literature in this respect, but it is not impossible to imagine a science-friendly dictatorship. The publicity and the high standards of evidence, as well as the critical cast of mind which the natural sciences ideally require, again may suggest a psychological bond between the inner life of science and liberal politics. That is, however, far from being necessarily or even normally the case. There are many thoroughly illiberal scientists, in fact. The alliance between science and liberalism was one of convenience at first, as both had much to fear from the onslaughts of religion. With this shared enemy of censorship and persecution in abeyance, the identity of attitudes tended to fade. Science and liberalism were not born together; the former is far older. Nothing, however, can erase the chief difference between the two. The natural sciences live to change, while liberalism does not have to take any particular view of tradition.

To the extent that the European past was utterly hostile to freedom and that the most ancient of Indo-European traditions is the caste society, liberals must reject particular traditions. No society that still has traces of the old tripartite division of humanity into those who pray, those who fight, and those who labor can be liberal.[5] To turn one's back on some or even most traditions does not, however, mean that one must forego all tradition as a matter of intellectual honesty. Liberalism need not decide among traditions that are not hostile to its aspirations, nor does it have to regard the claims of any traditions as inherently false, simply because they do not meet scientific standards of rational proof. It all depends on the content and tendencies of the tradition. Clearly representative government is impregnated with traditions in Britain and in the United States. The habits of voluntarism depend on a variety of traditions. These are surely more than merely compatible with liberalism.

Intellectual modesty does not imply that the liberalism of fear has no content, only that it is entirely nonutopian. In that respect it may well be what Emerson called a party of memory rather than a party of hope.[6] And indeed there are other types of liberalism that differ from it sharply in this respect. First of all there is the liberalism of natural rights which looks to the constant fulfillment of an ideal pre-established normative order, be it nature's or God's, whose principles have to be realized in the lives of individual citizens through public guarantees. It is God's will that we preserve ourselves, and it is our own and society's duty to see that we are protected in our lives, liberties, and property and all that pertains to them. To that end we have a duty to establish protective public agencies and the right to demand that they provide us with opportunities to make claims against each and all.

If we take rights seriously we must see to it that principles such as those of *The Declaration of Independence* be made effective in every aspect of our public life. If the agencies of government have a single primary function it is to see to it that the rights of individuals be realized, because our integrity as God's or nature's creations requires it. Conceivably one might argue that a perfect or optimal society would be composed solely of rights-claiming citizens. In all cases, therefore, the liberalism of natural rights regards politics as a matter of citizens who actively pursue their own legally secured ends in accordance with a higher law. The paradigm of politics is the tribunal in which fair rules and decisions are made to satisfy the greatest possible number of demands made by individual citizens against one another individually, and against the government and other socially powerful institutions. The liberalism of natural rights envisages a just society composed of politically sturdy citizens, each able and willing to stand up for himself and others.

Equally given to hope is the liberalism of personal development. Freedom, it argues, is necessary for personal as well as social progress. We cannot make the best of our potentialities unless we are free to do so. And morality is impossible unless we have an opportunity to choose our courses of action. Nor can we benefit from education unless our minds are free to accept and reject what we are told and to read and hear the greatest variety of opposing opinions. Morality and knowledge can develop only in a free and open society. There is even reason to hope that institutions of learning will eventually replace politics and government. It would not be unfair to say that these two forms of liberalism have their spokesmen in Locke and John Stuart Mill respectively, and they are of course perfectly genuine expressions of liberal doctrine. It must be said, however, that neither one of these two patron saints of liberalism had a strongly developed historical memory, and it is on this faculty of the human mind that the liberalism of fear draws most heavily.

The most immediate memory is at present the history of the world since 1914. In Europe and North America torture had gradually been eliminated from the practices of government, and there was hope that it might eventually disappear everywhere. With the intelligence and loyalty requirements of the national warfare states that quickly developed with the outbreak of hostilities, torture returned and has flourished on a colossal scale ever since.[7] We say "never again," but somewhere someone is being tortured right now, and acute fear has again become the most common form of social control. To this the horror of modern warfare must be added as a reminder. The liberalism of fear is a response to these undeniable actualities, and it therefore concentrates on damage control.

Given the inevitability of that inequality of military, police, and persuasive power which is called government, there is evidently always much to be afraid of. And one may, thus, be less inclined to celebrate the blessings of liberty than to consider the dangers of tyranny and war that threaten it. For this liberalism the basic units of political life are not discursive and reflecting persons, nor friends and enemies, nor patriotic soldier-citizens, nor energetic litigants, but the weak and the powerful. And the freedom it wishes to secure is freedom from the abuse of power and intimidation of the defenseless that this difference invites. This apprehension should not be mistaken for the obsessive ideologies which concentrate solely on the notion of totalitarianism. This is a shorthand for only the extremity of institutionalized violence and almost implies that anything less radically destructive need not concern us at all.

The liberalism of fear, on the contrary, regards abuses of public powers in all regimes with equal trepidation. It worries about the excesses of official agents at every level of government, and it assumes that these are apt to burden the poor and weak most heavily. The history of the poor compared to that of the various elites makes that obvious enough. The assumption, amply justified by every page of political history, is that some agents of government will behave lawlessly and brutally in small or big ways most of the time unless they are prevented from doing so.

The liberalism inspired by these considerations does resemble Isaiah Berlin's negative liberty, but it is not exactly the same. Berlin's negative liberty of "not being forced" and its later version of "open doors" is kept conceptually pure and separate from "the conditions of liberty," that is, the social and political institutions that make personal freedom possible. That is entirely necessary if negative liberty is to be fully distinguished from what Berlin calls "positive liberty," which is the freedom of one's higher from one's lower self. It cannot be denied, moreover, that this very clear demarcation of negative liberty is the best means of avoiding the slippery slope that can lead us to its threatening opposite.

Nevertheless, there is much to be said for not separating negative liberty from the conditions that are at least necessary to make it possible at all. Limited government and the control of unequally divided political power constitute the minimal condition without which freedom is unimaginable in any politically organized society. It is not a sufficient condition, but it is a necessary prerequisite. No door is open in a political order in which public and private intimidation prevail, and it requires a complex system of institutions to avoid that. If negative freedom is to have any political significance at all, it must specify at least some of the institutional characteristics of a relatively free regime. Socially that also means a dispersion of power among a plurality of politically empowered groups, pluralism, in short, as well as the elimination of such forms and degrees of social inequality as expose people to oppressive practices. Otherwise the "open doors" are a metaphor—and not, politically, a very illuminating one at that.

Moreover, there is no particular reason to accept the moral theory on which Berlin's negative freedom rests. This is the belief that there are several inherently incompatible moralities among which we must choose, but which cannot be reconciled by reference to a common criterion—paganism and Christianity being the two most obvious examples.[8] Whatever the truth of this metapolitical assumption may be, liberalism can do without it. The liberalism of fear in fact does not rest on a theory of moral pluralism. It does not, to be sure, offer a *summum bonum* toward which all political agents should strive, but it certainly does begin with a *summum malum,* which all of us know and would avoid if only we could. That evil is cruelty and the fear it inspires, and the very fear of fear itself. To that extent the liberalism of fear makes a universal and especially a cosmopolitan claim, as it historically always has done.

What is meant by cruelty here? It is the deliberate infliction of physical, and secondarily emotional, pain upon a weaker person or group by stronger ones in order to achieve some end, tangible or intangible, of the latter. It is not sadism, though sadistic individuals may flock to occupy positions of power that permit them to indulge their urges. But public cruelty is not an occasional personal inclination. It is made possible by differences in public power, and it is almost always built into the system of coercion upon which all governments have to rely to fulfill their essential functions. A minimal level of fear is implied in any system of law, and the liberalism of fear does not dream of an end of public, coercive government. The fear it does want to prevent is that which is created by arbitrary, unexpected, unnecessary, and unlicensed acts of force and by habitual and pervasive acts of cruelty and torture performed by military, paramilitary, and police agents in any regime.

Of fear it can be said without qualification that it is universal as it is physiological. It is a mental as well as a physical reaction, and it is common to animals as well as to human beings. To be alive is to be afraid, and much to our advantage in many cases, since alarm often preserves us from danger. The fear we fear is of pain inflicted by others to kill and maim us, not the natural and healthy fear that merely warns us of avoidable pain. And, when we think politically, we are afraid not only for ourselves but for our fellow citizens as well. We fear a society of fearful people.

Systematic fear is the condition that makes freedom impossible, and it is aroused by the expectation of institutionalized cruelty as by nothing else. However, it is fair to say that what I have called "putting cruelty first" is not a sufficient basis for political liberalism. It is simply a first principle, an act of moral intuition based on ample observation, on which liberalism can be built, especially at present. Because the fear of systematic cruelty is so universal, moral claims based on its prohibition have an immediate appeal and can gain recognition without much argument. But one cannot rest on this or any other naturalistic fallacy. Liberals can begin with cruelty as the primary evil only if they go beyond their well-grounded assumption that almost all people fear it and would evade it if they could. If the prohibition of cruelty can be universalized and recognized as a necessary condition of the dignity of persons, then it can become a principle of political morality. This could also be achieved by asking whether the prohibition would benefit the vast majority of human beings in meeting their known needs and wants. Kantians and a utilitarian could accept one of these tests, and liberalism need not choose between them.

What liberalism requires is the possibility of making the evil of cruelty and fear the basic norm of its political practices and prescriptions. The only exception to the rule of avoidance is the prevention of greater cruelties. That is why any government must use the threat of punishment, though liberalism looks upon this as an unavoidable evil, to be controlled in its scope and modified by legally enforced rules of fairness, so that arbitrariness not be added to the minimum of fear required for law enforcement. That this formulation owes something to Kant's philosophy of law is evident, but the liberalism of fear does not rest on his or any other moral philosophy in its entirety.[9] It must in fact remain eclectic.

What the liberalism of fear owes to Locke is also obvious: that the governments of this world with their overwhelming power to kill, maim, indoctrinate, and make war are not to be trusted unconditionally ("lions"), and that any confidence that we might develop in their agents must rest firmly on deep suspicion. Locke was not, and neither should his heirs be, in favor of weak governments that cannot frame or carry out public policies and decisions made in conformity to requirements of publicity, deliberation, and fair procedures. What is to be feared is every extralegal, secret, and unauthorized act by public agents or their deputies. And to prevent such conduct requires a constant division and subdivision of political power. The importance of voluntary associations from this perspective is not the satisfaction that their members may derive from joining in cooperative endeavors, but their ability to become significant units of social power and influence that can check, or at least alter, the assertions of other organized agents, both voluntary and governmental.

The separation of the public from the private is evidently far from stable here, as I already noted, especially if one does not ignore, as the liberalism of fear certainly does not, the power of such basically public organizations as corporate business enterprises. These of course owe their entire character and power to the laws, and they are not public in name only. To consider them in the same terms as the local mom and pop store is unworthy of serious social discourse. Nevertheless, it should be remembered that the reasons we speak of property as private in many cases is that it is meant to be left to the discretion of individual owners as a matter of public policy and law,

precisely because this is an indispensable and excellent way of limiting the long arm of government and of dividing social power, as
well as of securing the independence of individuals. Nothing gives a
person greater social resources than legally guaranteed proprietor-
ship. It cannot be unlimited, because it is the creature of the law in
the first place, and also because it serves a public purpose—the dispersion of power.

Where the instruments of coercion are at hand, whether it be
through the use of economic power, chiefly to hire, pay, fire, and
determine prices, or military might in its various manifestations, it
is the task of a liberal citizenry to see that not one official or un-
official agent can intimidate anyone, except through the use of well-
understood and accepted legal procedures. And that even then the
agents of coercion should always be on the defensive and limited to
proportionate and necessary actions that can be excused only as a
response to threats of more severe cruelty and fear from private
criminals.

It might well seem that the liberalism of fear is radically consequen-
tialist in its concentration on the avoidance of foreseeable evils. As
a guide to political practices that is the case, but it must avoid any
tendency to offer ethical instructions in general. No form of liberalism has any business telling the citizenry to pursue happiness or even
to define that wholly elusive condition. It is for each one of us to seek
it or reject it in favor of duty or salvation or passivity, for example.
Liberalism must restrict itself to politics and to proposals to restrain
potential abusers of power in order to lift the burden of fear and
favor from the shoulders of adult women and men, who can then
conduct their lives in accordance with their own beliefs and preferences, as long as they do not prevent others from doing so as well.

There are several well-known objections to the liberalism of fear. It
will be called "reductionist," because it is first and foremost based
on the physical suffering and fears of ordinary human beings, rather
than on moral or ideological aspirations. Liberalism does not collapse
politics into administration, economics, or psychology, so it is not
reductive in this sense. But as it is based on common and immediate
experiences, it offends those who identify politics with mankind's
most noble aspirations. What is to be regarded as noble is, to be sure,
highly contestable.

To call the liberalism of fear a lowering of one's sights implies that
emotions are inferior to ideas and especially to political causes. It
may be noble to pursue ideological ambitions or risk one's life for a

"cause," but it is not all noble to kill another human being in pursuit of one's own "causes." "Causes," however spiritual they may be, are not self-justifying, and they are not all equally edifying. And even the most appealing are nothing but instruments of torture or craven excuses for it, when they are forced upon others by threats and bribes. We would do far less harm if we learned to accept each other as sentient beings, whatever else we may be, and to understand that physical well-being and toleration are not simply inferior to the other aims that each one of us may choose to pursue.

There is absolutely nothing elevated in death and dying. Even if that were the case, it is not the task of public authority to encourage, promote, and enforce them, as they still do. Self-sacrifice may stir our admiration, but it is not, by definition, a political duty, but an act of supererogation which falls outside the realm of politics. There is nothing "reductive" about building a political order on the avoidance of fear and cruelty unless one begins with a contempt for physical experience. The consequences of political spirituality are, moreover, far less elevating than it might seem. Politically it has usually served as an excuse for orgies of destruction. Need one remind anyone of that truly ennobling cry: "Viva la muerte!"—and the regime it ushered in?

A related objection to the liberalism of fear is that it replaces genuine human reason with "instrumental rationality."[10] The meaning of the former is usually left unclear, but as a rule it is not a version of Platonic idealism. "Instrumental rationality" refers to political practices that pursue only efficiency or means-ends calculations, without any questioning of the rationality or other possible worth of their aims or outcomes. Since the liberalism of fear has very clear aims— the reduction of fear and cruelty—that sort of argument appears to be quite irrelevant.

More telling is the notion that "instrumental reasoning" places all its confidence in procedures, without adequate attention to the rationality of the conduct and discourse of those who participate in and follow them. It trusts the mechanisms for creating consent and ensuring fairness, without any attention to the character of the individual citizens or to that of the society as a whole. Even if a pluralistic political system under the rule of law were to yield a free and relatively peaceful society, it would not be genuinely rational, and not at all ethical, unless it also educated its citizens to a genuine level of political understanding and with it gave them the capacity to be masters of their collective life. This is supposed to be "substantially" rational in a way that the liberalism of fear, with its attention to procedures and outcomes, is not. But in fact the argument is not about rationality at all, but about expectations of radical social change and of utopian aspirations. The accusation of "instrumentality," if it means anything at all, amounts to a disdain for those who do not want to pay the price of utopian ventures, least of all those invented by other people. It refuses to take risks at the expense of others in pursuit of any ideal, however rational.

It cannot be denied that the experiences of politics according to fair procedures and the rule of law do indirectly educate the citizens, even though that is not their overt purpose, which is purely political. The habits of patience, self-restraint, respect for the claims of others, and caution constitute forms of social discipline that are only wholly compatible with personal freedom, but encourage socially and personally valuable characteristics.[11] This, it should be emphasized, does not imply that the liberal state can ever have an educative government that aims at creating specific kinds of character and enforces its own beliefs. It can never be didactic in intent in that exclusive and inherently authoritarian way. Liberalism, as we saw, began precisely in order to oppose the educative state. However, no system of government, no system of legal procedures, and no system of public education is without psychological effect, and liberalism has no reason at all to apologize for the inclinations and habits that procedural fairness and responsible government are likely encourage.

If citizens are to act individually and in associations, especially in a democracy, to protest and block any sign of governmental illegality and abuse, they must have a fair share of moral courage, self-reliance, and stubbornness to assert themselves effectively. To foster well-informed and self-directed adults must be the aim of every effort to educate the citizens of a liberal society. There is a very clear account of what a perfect liberal would look like more or less. It is to be found in Kant's *Doctrine of Virtue*, which gives us a very detailed account of the disposition of a person who respects other people without condescension, arrogance, humility, or fear. He or she does not insult others with lies or cruelty, both of which mar one's own character no less than they injure one's victims. Liberal politics depend for their success on the efforts of such people, but it is not the task of liberal politics to foster them simply as models of human perfection. All it can claim is that if we want to promote political freedom, then this is appropriate behavior.

This liberal prescription for citizenship, it is now often argued, is both a very unhistorical and an ethnocentric view that makes quite unwarranted claims for universality. That it arose at a given time and place is, after all, inevitable, but the relativist now argues that the liberalism of fear would not be welcomed by most of those who live under their traditional customs, even if these are as cruel and oppressive as the Indian caste system.[12] To judge inherited habits by standards that purport to be general, even though they are alien to a people, is said to be an arrogant imposition of false as well as partial principles. For there are no generally valid social prohibitions or rules, and the task of the social critic is at most to articulate socially immanent values. All this is not nearly as self-evident as the relativistic defenders of local customs would have us believe.

Unless and until we can offer the injured and insulted victims of most of the world's traditional as well as revolutionary governments a genuine and practicable alternative to their present condition, we have no way of knowing whether they really enjoy their chains. There is very little evidence that they do. The Chinese did not really like Mao's reign any more than we would, in spite of their political and cultural distance from us. The absolute relativism, not merely cultural but psychological, that rejects the liberalism of fear as both too "Western" and too abstract is too complacent and too ready to forget the horrors of our world to be credible. It is deeply illiberal, not only in its submission to tradition as an ideal, but in its dogmatic identification of every local practice with deeply shared local human aspirations. To step outside these customs is not, as the relativist claims, particularly insolent and intrusive. Only the challenge from nowhere and the claims of universal humanity and rational argument cast in general terms can be put to the test of general scrutiny and public criticism.[13]

The unspoken and sanctified practices that prevail within every tribal border can never be openly analyzed or appraised, for they are by definition already permanently settled within the communal consciousness. Unless there is an open and public review of all the practical alternatives, especially of the new and alien, there can be no responsible choices and no way of controlling the authorities that claim to be the voice of the people and its spirit. The arrogance of the prophet and the bard who pronounce the embedded norms is far greater than that of any deontologist. For they profess not only to reveal a hidden popular soul, but to do so in a manner that is not subject to extratribal review. That orgies of xenophobia just might lie in the wake of these claims of hermeneutical primacy is also not without historical example. The history of nationalism is not encouraging. But even at its best, ethnic relativism can say little about fear and cruelty, except that they are commonplace everywhere.[14] War also, though not perhaps in its present nuclear possibilities, has always existed. Are we to defend it on that ground? Actually, the most reliable test for what cruelties are to be endured at any place and any time is to ask the likeliest victims, the least powerful persons, at any given moment and under controlled conditions. Until that is done there is no reason not to assume that the liberalism of fear has much to offer to the victims of political tyranny.

These considerations should be recalled especially now, as the liberalism of fear is liable also to being charged with lacking an adequate theory of "the self." The probability of widely divergent selves is obviously one of the basic assumptions of any liberal doctrine. For political purposes liberalism does not have to assume anything about human nature except that people, apart from similar physical and psychological structures, differ in their personalities to a very marked degree. At a superficial level we must assume that some people will be encumbered with group traditions that they cherish, while others may only want to escape from their social origins and ascriptive bonds. These socially very important aspects of human experience are, like most acquired characteristics, extremely diverse and subject to change. Social learning is a great part of our character, though the sum of all our roles may not add up to a complete "self." For political purposes it is not this irreducible "self" of the peculiar character that we acquire in the course of our education that matters, but only the fact that many different "selves" should be free to interact politically.

To those American political theorists who long for either more communal or more expansively individualistic personalities, I now offer a reminder that these are the concerns of an exceptionally privileged liberal society, and that until the institutions of primary freedom are in place these longings cannot even arise. Indeed the extent to which both the communitarian and the romantic take free public institutions for granted is a tribute to the United States, but not to their sense of history.[15] Too great a part of past and present political experience is neglected when we ignore the annual reports of Amnesty International and of contemporary warfare. It used to be the mark of liberalism that it was cosmopolitan and that an insult to the life and liberty of a member of any race or group in any part of the world was of genuine concern. It may be a revolting paradox that the very success of liberalism in some countries has atrophied the political empathies of their citizens. That appears to be one cost of taking freedom for granted, but it may not be the only one.

Liberalism does not have to enter into speculations about what the potentialities of this or that "self" may be, but it does have to take into account the actual political conditions under which people live, in order to act here and now to prevent known and real dangers. A concern for human freedom cannot stop with the satisfactions of one's own society or clan. We must therefore be suspicious of ideologies of solidarity, precisely because they are so attractive to those who find liberalism emotionally unsatisfying, and who have gone on in our century to create oppressive and cruel regimes of unparalleled horror. The assumption that these offer something wholesome to the atomized citizen may or may not be true, but the political consequences are not, on the historical record, open to much doubt. To seek emotional and personal development in the bosom of a community or in romantic self-expression is a choice open to citizens in liberal societies. Both, however, are apolitical impulses and wholly self-oriented, which at best distract us from the main task of politics when they are presented as political doctrines, and at worst can, under unfortunate circumstances, seriously damage liberal practices. For although both appear only to be redrawing the boundaries between the personal and the public, which is a perfectly normal political practice, it cannot be said that either one has a serious sense of the implications of the proposed shifts in either direction.[16]

It might well seem that the liberalism of fear is very close to anarchism. That is not true, because liberals have always been aware of the degree of informal coercion and educative social pressures that even the most ardent anarchist theorists have suggested as acceptable substitutes for law.[17] Moreover, even if the theories of anarchism were less flawed, the actualities of countries in which law and government have broken down are not encouraging. Does anyone want to live in Beirut? The original first principle of liberalism, the rule of law, remains perfectly intact, and it is not an anarchistic doctrine. There is no reason at all to abandon it. It is the prime instrument to restrain governments. The potentialities of persecution have kept pace with technological advances; we have as much to fear from the instruments of torture and persecution as ever. One half of the Bill of Rights is about fair trials and the protection of the accused in criminal trials. For it is in court that the citizen meets the might of the state, and it is not an equal contest. Without well-defined procedures, honest judges, opportunities for counsel and for appeals, no one has a chance. Nor should we allow more acts to be criminalized than is necessary for our mutual safety. Finally, nothing speaks better for a liberal state than legal efforts to compensate the victims of crime rather than merely to punish the criminal for having violated the law. For he did injure, terrify, and abuse a human being first and foremost.

It is at this point that the liberalism of fear adopts a strong defense of equal rights and their legal protection. It cannot base itself upon the notion of rights as fundamental and given, but it does see them as just those licenses and empowerments that citizens must have in order to preserve their freedom and to protect themselves against abuse. The institutions of a pluralist order with multiple centers of power and institutionalized rights are merely a description of a liberal political society. The society is also of necessity a democratic one, because without enough equality of power to protect and assert one's rights, freedom is but a hope. Without the institutions of representative democracy and an accessible, fair, and independent judiciary open to appeals, and in the absence of a multiplicity of politically active groups, liberalism is in jeopardy. It is the entire purpose of the liberalism of fear to prevent that outcome. It is therefore fair to say that liberalism is monogamously, faithfully, and permanently married to democracy—but it is a marriage of convenience.

To account for the necessity of freedom in general, references to particular institutions and ideologies are not enough. One must put cruelty first and understand the fear of fear and recognize them everywhere. Unrestrained "punishing" and denials of the most basic means of survival by governments, near and far from us, should incline us to look with critical attention to the practices of all agents of all governments and to the threats of war here and everywhere.

If I sound like Caesare Beccaria, or some other refugee from the eighteenth century, it may well be that I have read the sort of reports they read about the ways of governments. The foreign news in the *New York Times* suffices, as do its accounts of the prevalence of racism, xenophobia, and systematic governmental brutality here and everywhere. I cannot see how any political theorist or politically alert citizen can possibly ignore them and fail to protest against them. Once we do that, we have moved toward the liberalism of fear, and away from the more exhilarating but less urgent forms of liberal thought.

Notes

I would like to thank my friend George Kateb for good advice and encouragement in writing this paper.

1. J. W. Allen, *A History of Political Thought in the Sixteenth Century* (London: Methuen, 1941), pp. 89–97, 370–377. Quentin Skinner, *The Foundations of Political Thought*, 2 vols. (Cambridge: Cambridge University Press, 1978), II, 241–254.

2. See Judith Shklar, *Ordinary Vices* (Cambridge, Mass.: Harvard University Press, 1984).

3. See, for instance, Laurence Berns, "Thomas Hobbes," in Leo Strauss and Joseph Cropsey, eds., *A History of Political Philosophy* (Chicago: Rand McNally, 1972), pp. 370–394. C. B. Macpherson, *The Political Theory of Possessive Individualism* (Oxford: Clarendon, 1962). These interpretations depend on seeing Locke as very similar to Hobbes, as Leo Strauss did in *Natural Right and History* (Chicago: University of Chicago Press, 1953), pp. 202–251.

4. Alexander Hamilton et al., *The Federalist Papers,* ed. Clinton Rossiter (New York: New American Library, 1961), nos. 10, 51.

5. Georges Duby, *The Chivalrous Society,* trans. Cynthia Postan (Berkeley: University of California Press, 1977), pp. 81–87.

6. Ralph Waldo Emerson, "The Conservative," *Essays and Lectures,* ed. Joel Porte (New York: Library of America, 1983), p. 173.

7. Edward Peters, *Torture* (Oxford: Basil Blackwell, 1985), pp. 103–140.

8. Isaiah Berlin, "Introduction" and "Two Concepts of Liberty," *Four Essays on Liberty* (Oxford: Oxford University Press, 1982), pp. xxxvii–lxiii, 118–172. Isaiah Berlin, "The Originality of Machiavelli," *Against the Current* (New York: Viking, 1980), pp. 25–79.

9. *The Metaphysical Elements of Justice,* ed. and trans. John Ladd (Indianapolis: Bobbs-Merrill, 1965).

10. For the best account of the notion of instrumental rationality and its implications, see Seyla Behabib, *Critique, Norm and Utopia* (New York: Columbia University Press, 1986).

11. George Kateb, "Remarks on the Procedures of Constitutional Democracy," *Nomos, xx, Constitutionalism,* ed. J. Roland Pennock and John Chapman, pp. 215–237.

12. Michael L. Walzer, *Spheres of Justice* (New York: Basic Books, 1983), pp. 26–28, 312–316.

13. See Thomas Nagel, *The View from Nowhere* (Oxford: Oxford University Press, 1986), for the philosophical panorama from that nonposition.

14. This is a critical response to Michael Walzer, "The Moral Standing of States," in Charles R. Beitz et al., eds., *International Ethics: A Philosophy and Public Affairs Reader* (Princeton: Princeton University Press, 1985), pp. 217–238.

15. Nancy L. Rosenblum, *Another Liberalism* (Cambridge, Mass.: Harvard University Press, 1987), for romantic liberalism, and Michael J. Sandel, *Liberalism and the Limits of Justice* (Cambridge: Cambridge University Press, 1982), for communitarianism, respectively.

16. Charles Taylor, "The Nature and Scope of Distributive Justice," in Frank S. Lucash, ed., *Justice and Equality Here and Now* (Ithaca, N.Y.: Cornell University Press, 1986), pp. 34–67.

17. Alan Ritter, *Anarchism* (Cambridge: Cambridge University Press, 1980).

CHAPTER TWO

Political Theory and the
Rule of Law

It would not be very difficult to show that the phrase "the Rule of Law" has become meaningless thanks to ideological abuse and general over-use. It may well have become just another one of those self-congratulatory rhetorical devices that grace the public utterances of Anglo-American politicians. No intellectual effort need therefore be wasted on this bit of ruling-class chatter. There is much to be said for this view of the matter. From the perspective of an historian it is, however, irrelevant. The Rule of Law did, after all, have a very significant place in the vocabulary of political theory once, so important in fact that it may well be worth recalling. Moreover, since legal theorists still invoke and argue about it, there may also be some point in comparing its present intellectual status with its original meaning. This may turn out to be not only an exercise in recollection, but also a diagnostic experiment. In the following pages I shall try to show that there are two quite distinct archetypes of the Rule of Law and that these have become blurred by now and reduced to incoherence because the political purposes and settings that gave them their significance have been forgotten. With some interpretive license I shall attribute the two models to Aristotle and Montesquieu respectively. Then I shall suggest that contemporary theories fail because they have lost a sense of what the political objectives of the ideal of the Rule of Law originally were and have come up with no plausible restatement. The upshot is that the Rule of Law is now situated, intellectually, in a political vacuum.

The Rule of Law originally had two quite distinct meanings. It

This chapter is reprinted with permission from *The Rule of Law*, edited by A. Hutchinson and P. Monahan (Toronto: Carswell, 1987).

referred either to an entire way of life, or merely to several specific public institutions. The first of these models can be attributed to Aristotle, who presented the Rule of Law as nothing less than the rule of reason. The second version sees the Rule of Law as those institutional restraints that prevent governmental agents from oppressing the rest of society. Aristotle's Rule of Law has an enormous ethical and intellectual scope, but it applies to only very few persons in the polity. Montesquieu's account is of a limited number of protective arrangements which are, however, meant to benefit every member of the society, though only in a few of their mutual relations. It is not the reign of reason, but it is the spirit of the criminal law of a free people. Aristotle's Rule of Law is, in fact, perfectly compatible not only with the slave society of ancient Athens, but with the modern "dual state." Such a state may have a perfectly fair and principled private law system, and also a harsh, erratic criminal control system, but it is a "dual state" because some of its population is simply declared to be subhuman, and a public danger, and as such excluded from the legal order entirely. They are part of a second state, run usually by different agents of the government, but with the full approval of those who staff the "first" of the two states. Such was the government of the United States until the Civil War and in some ways thereafter. Such also was Nazi Germany and such is South Africa today. I mention only these states because they are part of "the Western tradition" and are included in its legal development. There are no remnants of a Byzantine past to confuse the historical picture here.

In contrast to Aristotle's rule of reason, Montesquieu's Rule of Law is designed to stand in stark contrast not only to simple "oriental" despotism but also to the dual state with which he was well-acquainted, as his remarks on modern slavery show. If it is to avoid these conditions, the Rule of Law must take certain types of human conduct entirely out of public control, because they cannot be regulated or prevented without physical cruelty, arbitrariness and the creation of unremitting fear in the population. Coercive government must resort to an excess of violence when it attempts to effectively control religious belief and practice, consensual sex and expressions of public opinion. The Rule of Law is meant to put a fence around the innocent citizen so that she may feel secure in these and all other legal activities. That implies that public officials will be hampered by judicial agents from interfering in these volatile and intensely personal forms of conduct. The judicial magistracy will, moreover, impose rigid self-restraints upon itself which will also enhance the sense of personal security of the citizenry. They will fear the office of the law, not its administrators. Commerce, unlike religion, was not among the areas immune to governmental control. That is because Montesquieu's justification for limited government was grounded in a psychology, not in a theory of public efficiency or natural rights. His view of limited government could be called the rule to control criminal law. Contemporary legal theory still relies quite heavily on these two original models, but they have tended to ignore every political reality outside the courtroom or hurled the notion of ruling into such abstraction that it appears to occur in no recognizable context.

In Aristotle's account the single most important condition for the Rule of Law is the character one must impute to those who make legal judgments. Justice is the constant disposition to act fairly and lawfully, not merely the occasional performance of such actions. It is part of such a character to reason syllogistically and to do so his passions must be silent. In the course of forensic argument distorted syllogisms will of course be urged upon those who must judge. That indeed is in the nature of persuasive reasoning, but those who judge, be they few or many, must go beyond it to reason their way to a logically necessary conclusion. To achieve that they must understand exactly just how forensic rhetoric and persuasive reasoning work, while their own ratiocination is free from irrational imperfections. For that a settled ethical character is as necessary as is intelligence itself.

The benefit to society of judgments made by men of such character is considerable. Without such justice no one is secure in his material possessions and even in his social values. Moreover, in the structure of politics the presence of men with such a mind-set, most usually middle-class moderates, has the effect of inhibiting the self-destructive proclivities that tend to afflict most regimes. The rule of reason depends decidedly on the capacity of the same to persuade others to practice some degree of self-restraint and to maintain the legal order that best fits the ethical structure of a polity. To have a stable system of restraining rules would seem to put enormous burdens on just men in their daily conduct. They are required, in addition to their ratiocinating and political skills, to possess the psychological ability to recognize the claims of others as if these were their own. The just man sees the merits and deserts of others exactly as if he himself were making a claim on those grounds. He draws no difference between himself and another or between two other opposed claimants. He can see all the demands of others and his own on a perfectly equal footing. When he is asked to decide a dispute or punish a wrong he sticks as closely to the rules as possible, because that is how he would want to be treated as a litigant. His task is simply to restore the previous balance and no irrelevancy may disturb his determinations. Without Aristotle's confidence in syllogistic reasoning this picture of perfect judgment would not make sense, nor would its claim to rationality stand. It is, however, part of a very powerful psychology as well. The powers of reasoning are part of the whole mentality of a man who has the capacity and inclination to see all claims impartially. That is not only required for judges, but of anyone who engages in fair exchanges, but it is clear that the supremely just activity on which everyone in society depends is epitomized by judging in courts of law. For it is there that justice is activated into legality. The rationality of this procedure is made especially plausible since it is a form of social control that applies to only a very limited part of the population and then to only some human relationships. Women and slaves are not governed by the norms of either justice or law. These people like children are part of a domestic economy that is ordered on more personal lines. Moreover, there are relations of friendship and magnanimity which may involve other aspects of the best male character than its justice, which does not distinguish between friend and foe. The point that seems to me to matter most for Aristotle's understanding of the Rule of Law is its concentration on the judging agent, the dispenser of legal justice, the man or men of reason and of syllogism put to work in the arena where everyone else is driven by physical or political appetite. On their shoulders rests the responsibility for preserving the basic standards of the polity in their daily application, and for maintaining reasonable modes of discourse in the political arena. The picture is one of mediation, far more than of social control with all its uncertainties. Control is left to the masters of the domestic sphere.[1]

For an altogether different picture of the Rule of Law one cannot do better than to look at Montesquieu's version. While Aristotle's Rule of Law as reason served several vital political purposes, Montesquieu's really has only one aim, to protect the ruled against the aggression of those who rule. While it embraces all people, it fulfills only one fundamental aim, freedom from fear, which, to be sure, was for Montesquieu supremely important. Its range is thus far narrower than Aristotle's Rule of Law, but it applies to far more people, to everyone to be precise. To realize the objectives of this kind of Rule of Law does not require any exceptional degree of virtue. The English, among whom Montesquieu saw it flourish, were far from admirable in many respects in his view. All that was needed for the Rule of Law in Europe, given its many fortunate historical and geographic circumstances, was a properly equilibrated political system in which power was checked by power in such a way that neither the violent urges of kings nor the arbitrariness of legislatures could impinge directly upon the individual in such a way as to frighten her and make her feel insecure in her daily life. With religious opinion, consensual sex among adults and the public expression of public opinions decriminalized, the only task of the judiciary was to condemn the guilty of legally known crimes defined as acts threatening the security of others, and to protect the innocent accused of such acts. Procedure in criminal cases is what this Rule of Law is all about. That is what makes the imperative of the independence of the judiciary also comprehensible. The idea is not so much to ensure judicial rectitude and public confidence, as to prevent the executive and its many agents from imposing their powers, interests, and persecutive inclinations upon the judiciary. The magistrate can then be perceived as the citizen's most necessary, and also most likely, protector. This whole scheme is ultimately based on a very basic dichotomy. The ultimate spiritual and political struggle is always between war and law. Rome chose war and lost everything. If France were to choose world monarchy and war instead of the English path to liberty and law, it too would be doomed to a deadly despotism. That is the fate that the Rule of Law, as the principle of legality in criminal cases fortified by a multitude of procedural safeguards, was capable of averting. It is very much "made," indeed, planned law. For all his respect for mores and customs, "inspired" rather than invented, as instruments of social control, Montesquieu was far too aware of the need for conscious political action to trust history to take care of Europe. He knew that judicial systems did not grow. They serve known purposes and are chosen and defended.[2]

This version of the Rule of Law is evidently quite compatible with a strong theory of individual rights. Indeed, in America that was to be the case. It is not, however, in the first instance a theory of rights. The institutions of judicial citizen protection may create rights, but they exist in order to avoid what Montesquieu took to be the greatest of human evils, constant fear created by the threats of violence and the actual cruelties of the holders of military power in society. The Rule of Law is the one way ruling classes have of imposing controls upon each other. Even so passionate a critic of the English ruling classes of the eighteenth century as E. P. Thompson, after all, agrees with him on that point. England was not a gulag society and its political classes had to some degree shackled themselves.[3] That is what was then meant by the Rule of Law.

The most influential restatement of the Rule of Law since the eighteenth century has been Dicey's unfortunate outburst of Anglo-Saxon parochialism. In his version the Rule of Law was both traditionalized and formalized. Not entirely without encouragement from Montesquieu, but wildly exaggerated, he began by finding the Rule of Law inherent in the remote English past, in the depth of the early Middle Ages. Its validity rested on its antiquity, on its having grown, rather than being badly made, as was the case among the unfortunate countries of the Continent, especially France and Belgium. Its second pillar was that all cases were judged by the same body of men, following a single body of rules. The judges of the common law courts had slowly developed a suitable system, so that England had escaped that threat to liberty, administrative law, in which legally qualified tribunals dealt specifically with cases involving civil servants. Of the criminal law only habeas corpus mattered to Dicey, but the political arrangements of the English constitution did concern him. They were part of the Rule of Law. The Rule of Law was thus both trivialized as the peculiar patrimony of one and only one national order, and formalized, by the insistence that only one set of inherited procedures and court practices could sustain it. Not the structure or purposes of juridical rigor but only its forms became significant for freedom. No wonder that Dicey thought England's law and freedoms were already gravely threatened. If its liberty hung on so slender a thread as the avoidance of new courts to deal with new kinds of cases, the end was indeed at hand. The one political issue that worried him very little was the consequences and the nature of war and the militarization of politics.[4] That was, of course, Montesquieu's overriding concern, and the events of our century have amply justified him. Nevertheless, it is Dicey's shadow that hangs over both the libertarian invocation of the Rule of Law and the radical attack upon it. One need think only of Friedrich von Hayek and Roberto Unger, for example, at present.

The other current adaptation of the Rule of Law also has roots in the last century. Its origins are in the court-centered American jurisprudence of Gray, but divorced from his positivism. The Rule of Law remains the rule of judges, but collectively and potentially individually, their decisions amount to a rule of rationality. It is not perhaps as coherent as Aristotle's rule of logic, but the resemblance is clear. Without some sort of political and philosophical setting such as Aristotle had provided, however, this new rule of courts floats in a vacuum. That is one of the frequently noted weaknesses of the late Lon Fuller's "inner morality" of law, and it afflicts those early essays of

Ronald Dworkin in which Herculean judges maintain the Rule of Law single-handedly. Nor does the private law bias of these theories help theories help to integrate into the Rule of Law those aspects of social control that Aristotle's rule of reason had originally left to the masters of claimless people.

No defender of the Rule of Law has inherited more of Dicey's apprehensions than Hayek, but unhappily he has abandoned the latter's not inconsiderable historical learning.[5] In its place we get a theory of knowledge. The Rule of Law is necessary in Hayek's view, not because there are recurrent dangers of oppression and persecution, such as Montesquieu and even Dicey feared, but because of mankind's irreducible ignorance. Since it is impossible for us to predict the consequences or the form of the actions of each one of the members of society at any given time, it is also utterly impossible for us to plan our collective existence. Fortunately, if we set up general guidelines that attempt no more than to keep us from colliding as we go about our own projects, we will prosper in spite of our limited knowledge. These governing guidelines are what Hayek calls the Rule of Law. Their main achievement is to facilitate the free market, but there are other benefits as well. By internalizing these minimal rules of social conduct we become more intelligent. Far from being anarchical a "spontaneous order" can be expected to emerge as individuals freely adjust their personal choices to these essentially "right of way" rules. Indeed, there is an evolutionary process that is set in motion by these numberless personal acts or adaptations. A natural selection of rules and traditions can be expected as the result of aggregate individual mini-experiments. This is, however, possible only as long as the rules are purposeless, that is, as long as they have no social end in view. They adjust, they do not order. They must only direct activities in order to avoid unnecessary conflict, collision and unwanted damage. Moreover, they must not be too rigid. For though predictability is the main end of such law, it must not stifle technological change, but rather, help people to adapt to its demands. Why that is not purposive political action is not clear. It is also difficult to see why we are able to plan the vast enterprises that have created modern technologies and the business and manufacturing organizations that realize them, if we are so ignorant of the probable future. Nevertheless, it is Hayek's belief that a "constructive rationalism" has since the early modern era misguided us into believing that we could plan our social future, and even regulate the market. It has inspired attempts to impose artificial legislation upon society which never realizes its stated ends, but does much to disturb and impoverish the "spontaneous order." This does not, however, seem to apply to the regulation of criminal conduct and law, about which Hayek is extremely vague. There we can no doubt predict, plan and even legislate. Of our ability to wage war we hear even less.

Originally Hayek thought that the Continental legal code system was more suitable as a social facilitator, but eventually he came to see the common law as more likely to be slow but sure in developing those few but necessary rules to an ever-advancing economy. It was at one time capable of setting those formal and impersonal guidelines which allowed the "spontaneous order" of the market to advance without impediment. Public planning for social purposes is not, however, the only threat to this Rule of Law. Intellectual arrogance is joined by primitive feelings of tribal loyalty and communal attachments that express themselves in nationalism to hamper the rational evolution of the "spontaneous order." The latter is not the work of mindless or affective individuals. On the contrary, it is the outcome of the choices made by the most rational members of society. For these do not exercise their intelligence upon public objects which no mind can encompass in any case, but limit their calculations to their own plans, which they can realize. They can do this presumably in spite of all those other agents of whose activities they must remain ignorant.

Hayek is quite right in refusing to think of himself as a conservative. He is no defender of authority or hierarchy, nor does he pine for those familial and communal traditions that the conservative critics of liberalism accuse it of having destroyed. His "spontaneous order" is in no sense related to these emotional bonds. His Rule of Law is not meant to unite society, or to give it common aspirations. Quite the contrary. It exists to prevent inefficiency, irrationality, irregularity, arbitrariness and ultimately oppression. For once the "constructive rationalists" who try to reform society discover that their artificial policies are doomed to failure, they invariably resort to totalitarianism in order to maintain their power and to continue their disastrous rule. This is not, in fact, how the fascist, Nazi or Soviet regimes of our century came about. Without war, ideology, the survival of military classes and values, and much more, these phenomena cannot even begin to be explained. But then Hayek offers no historical proof for any of his theories. They are the working out of his unfalsifiable assumptions about human ignorance and its necessary political consequences.

For legal theory the significant feature of this version of the Rule of Law is not just its abstractness, but its scope. General and impersonal rules are not there to protect rights, which Hayek regards as too rigid, nor does it serve the modest ends tied to an institutional order that Montesquieu had in mind. It does far more than to make the citizen feel secure from the agents of coercive government. It sustains the free market economy, and that "spontaneous order" is itself the foundation that all other aspects of the society as a whole rest upon. Everything else is derivative. This construct has not only no relation to any historical society, it basically implies that justice has been impossible under any other circumstances. At some remote time in the last century it is said to have prevailed, but as Dicey already claimed it was already in decline in Britain and in America.

The negative mirror image of the Dicey-Hayek model of the Rule of Law can be found among the radical legal critics of liberalism, most notably Roberto Unger.[6] For him also the Rule of Law is the entire legal order of the liberal state. It was in force until the coming of the welfare state, and its purpose and character were as Hayek describes them, but instead of functioning to protect a spontaneous order of any kind, it served to mask hierarchies and exploitation, and the destruction of the pre-capitalist communities. The overt inspiration of the liberal rule of law, according to Unger, is what Hayek takes to be its reality, generality of rules with uniformity of application, enforced by a judiciary separated from the rest of the government. And, like Hayek, moreover, Unger thinks that this system has failed and indeed never could have lasted. Indeed, it never was "real." It begins in early modern Europe as a bad bargain between the merchants and the monarchical bureaucrats who are already operating a stable legal code in order to stabilize royal rule. The merchants would have preferred to establish their own order of rules apart from this state apparatus, which would have been more responsive to their real needs, but they were unable to escape the embrace of the pre-existing bureaucracy. It was not a good deal for them, but it was the best bargain they could get. Their second failure was that they were never able to infuse society with the spirit of liberalism, so that their legal order could not achieve any degree of legitimacy. The pluralism of interest groups and the free market never could arouse the sorts of attachments that the religious and communal loyalties that liberalism had undermined could so easily summon. The Rule of Law was, therefore, from the first deprived of any basis of social support. Not that it deserved to be defended, since from the first it was a mere mask. This reading of Max Weber passes for history, but, in fact, it is no less abstract than Hayek's account of the Rule of Law. It, moreover, agrees with Hayek's view of the incompatibility of primitive loyalties and the Rule of Law. Nor would there be any differences about the consequences of the judiciary being forced to choose between competing interest groups in the course of its procedures. Hayek would, of course, require them to stay out of such disputes, since it is not the function of his kind of legal order to get involved in making political choices. Unger thinks that this is inevitable, however, while Hayek merely thinks that it was a dreadful mistake that need not have happened. Interest groups could, in his view, have been left to work out their own problems. The result of the failure to leave them to it is what Unger calls "particularistic judgments." With that the fiction of judicial generality and neutrality are exposed for what they always were, shams, and any remaining public trust in the liberal Rule of Law must and should go. Nor can the governments of welfare states maintain the pretense that they are limited by rules. They do not merely serve one or another faction, they do so quite openly. In any case, the possibility that the Rule of Law might still be self-validating is destroyed by the realities exposed by both pluralism and the welfare system which reveal all the hierarchies and injustices of civil society. This is Hayek's lament and Unger differs from him only in regarding the collapse of the liberal order as a hopeful step to a far better political future. That the efficiency-minded and pragmatically open-minded policies of the welfare state spell the end of the Rule of Law was in fact already Dicey's message. The one question his heirs ought to answer is why citizens of Anglo-American and other welfare states are not as oppressed as he predicted they were bound to be.

In his later writings Unger has come to adopt an even more indignant tone in denouncing the Rule of Law. He now sees it, as he did not in his earlier analysis, as a pure ideological cloak that must be ripped off to expose the fraudulence of the entire ideology of the Rule of Law. As one of the spokesmen for "Critical Legal Studies," he now regards formalism, the belief in a gapless, impersonal legal system as the chief ideological screen behind which a "shameless" liberalism hides. In fact it is the servant of sinister interest groups, and its talk of rights is merely hypocrisy. That emerges as its most reprehensible public vice. The word ideology is moreover used here as a term of abuse that is meant to reveal the hypocritical and egotistical character of legal liberalism. A hierarchical and atomizing policy is the reality of liberalism, fairness and legal impartiality. The object of legal scholarship is to find the weak spots in the system and to put forward claims and to demand ever-new personal rights that will destabilize the whole system. The field of battle is to be the law school, where a co-operative union of teachers and students will set an example of how a more fraternal society would look. They would also suggest how less individualistic solutions to current legal cases might be devised.

That the reform of the law-school curriculum might alter American law is not a new idea. Case by case social renewal does imply a recognition that the legal system has a certain autonomy from the liberal political society in which it operates, an assumption that this critical and denunciatory analysis of the Rule of Law does not support. It is a protest that is in any case entirely within the tradition of American inter-generational conflict, which Samuel Huntington has recently described so well. It takes the form of a Manichean contest between the actuality of American politics and its promise.[7] And given the general cultural value attached to sincerity, especially among the young, the chief accusation is always hypocrisy. The call is for purity and there is a deep anti-institutional strain, recalling the creedal traditions of sectarian Protestantism. The hierarchies will eventually tumble and the American dream will be vindicated. It will also be a relatively painless transformation, since it will be conducted mainly through the existing legal structures. The success of this project is guaranteed by a simple faith in moral progress. From a functionalist social perspective one could argue that critical legal student-teacher ventures have served to sustain the existing legal profession by helping radical new college graduates to adjust to the alien and disliked culture of the law school and eventual professional world slowly and without too great a psychological cost. They have thus been eased into integration rather than hurled into it, which might have been far more disruptive for them and other people around them.

There is of course nothing new or odd in seeing courts and lawyers as members of the political society in which they perform both mediating and control functions as parts of a single political continuum on which other public agencies are also placed according to their degree of court-likeness or "tribunality."[8] It does not follow that courts do not have their own characteristic procedures or roles, nor that these constitute some sort of fraudulent charade to hide the actuality of oppression. The bench and bar have political tasks to perform and their practices constitute an integral part of an ongoing order. To judge one must obviously consider the viable alternatives and possibilities. This can be scorned as a craven "objectivism," devised to squelch the radical ardor of the pure. But why should one not estimate the current cost of innocence? That is not the utopian way of proceeding, and indeed Unger's vision, with its explicit rejection of historical argument, is not falsifiable or subject to deliberation. It is, like all faiths, a take-it-or-leave-it proposition. In that it also resembles Hayek's view of the Rule of Law as a cure-all. For on the basis of his belief in universal ignorance it is just as impossible to know the consequences of *not* pursuing a given line of action as of pursuing it. The fact that X seems to have failed as a social policy does not mean that doing non-X is bound to be a beneficial course of action. That belief is also grounded on blind faith and oddly it also is a belief in human progress. It is, however, scarcely cynical in the latter years of our century to find such beliefs aberrant. This consideration ought not to be taken as a complacent assurance that the Rule of Law need not concern us, or that America is beyond reform. It does imply that destabilizing the existing system of civil liberties and rights, and the individualistic ethos that sustains them, in the hope of building a truly fraternal order does not make sense. It shows little grasp of the fragilities of personal freedom which is the true and only province of the Rule of Law.

If Montesquieu's model has suffered at the hands of a historical theory, Aristotle has been abused no less. In his case also political and philosophical abstraction has done the damage. The rationality of judging, divorced from the ethical and political setting in which he described it, becomes as improbable as the liberal archetype when it is ripped out of its context. No two writers illustrate these difficulties better than America's two most representative legal theorists, the late Lon Fuller and Ronald Dworkin.

Both Fuller and Dworkin concentrate entirely on the rationality of judging, and especially as it is done by judges in the highest courts. The Rule of Law as the rule of reason is for both very much the expression of the authoritative judgments of appeals court judges, or often, of the justices of the United States Supreme Court. It has little to do with the realities of our municipal court system, especially as it operates in our cities. It is, however, not designed to describe the way the legal order actually works, but to demonstrate its rational potentiality, although this is not clear in Fuller's book, which often claims to be an account of the historical character of legal institutions. The point of significance for the notion of the Rule of Law here is, however, that rationality is to be found entirely in the arguments that judges must and do offer in defense of their decisions. While the emphasis on the rationality of arguments is Aristotelian, the divorce of the judge from the normative and political context within which his ratiocinations take place is not. The result is a level of abstraction so high as to make these models politically irrelevant.

In Fuller's version the legal order seems to cover the entire governmental process in its scope. It does more than merely protect the free market as it does in Hayek's ideal world. Fuller's definition is far more encompassing. His Rule of Law is designed to cover all social conduct. And its "inner morality" is due entirely to its defining characteristics. Law must be general, promulgated, not retroactive, clear, consistent, not impossible to perform, enduring, and officials must abide by its rules. Unlike Aristotle, Fuller did not specify what sort of society would be ruled by such a legal system, nor did he offer a very clear picture of its other historical institutions for social control and coercion. One may guess that he had not thought very deeply about any polity other than the United States. And as a legal ideal for us there is little to either accept or reject in this conventional list of lawyerly aspirations.[9] It is its moral status that, in the total absence of an ethical argument, seems unsure. Aristotle, after all, gave us reasons for the ethical and rational character and functions of the Rule of Law. In itself Fuller's inwardly moral law not only may, but has been, perfectly compatible with governments of the most repressive and irrational sort. The very formal rationality of a civil law system can legitimize a persecutive war-state among those officials who are charged with maintaining the private law and its clients. That was certainly the case in Nazi Germany, whose legal caste were perfectly ready to ignore the activities of the new court, police and extermination system as long as "the inner morality" of their law could remain unaffected.[10] The paradox of slavery, that made the slave both a human person, and the property of another, created a "dual state" in the pre-Civil War America as well, and it was just as irrational. No one can be three-fifths of a human being and two-fifths of a thing as the "federal ratio" had it in the original Constitution. Nor is the prohibition against murdering slaves, since they were people, compatible with their non-person status before the rest of the legal system, not to mention the exclusion from the guiding principles of the political order as a whole.[11] Such a legal system is as rational as the political order that it sustains. It may be a model of "inner morality" by virtue of the consistency and other marks of morality of the decisions of its judiciary, but it is still irrational. In a liberal society in the modern age slavery is irrational no matter how rigorously and impartially it is imposed upon the black population, and however free and secure its white citizens may be under a partial Rule of Law.

The "inner morality" of the law, far from imposing the rule of reason that it is supposed to create, may well serve to render political irrationality more efficient and more attractive to those who benefit from it. The "dual state" remains, moreover, a constant possibility in our century. Encouraged no doubt by its gradual disappearance in the United States, Fuller came to believe that law was bound in time to rationalize politics generally. Politics, he believed, is about purposes of the electorate and its officials and law structures these. There is here a theory of moral progress no less profound than Hayek's. It is, to be sure, difficult to imagine what else could sustain the notion of the Rule of Law as the proven agency of reason.

To an increasing degree the more recent essays of Ronald Dworkin absolve him from similar charges of political and historical fantasizing. It is clear that only a polity that has made a public and enduring commitment to something like the Declaration of Independence can be said to sustain his model of a legal rule of reason. He has not, in fact, singled that document out explicitly, but the primacy of equal rights, which is his basic norm, has no more enduring or better known public grounding. The Declaration may not be the law of the land, but it is surely not just any old pamphlet either. And when one considers the enormously reviving and invigorating role that it has played in the drama of political rights in America from the Revolution, through Jacksonian democracy, to Abolitionism and the implementation of constitutional rights since then, it is not fanciful to say that its function is to be an unalterable supra-legal source of justification for equal rights. It stands for a constant attention to the preservation and enhancement of equal rights by courts and citizens alike. It is not, therefore, the equal rights aspect of Dworkin's theory that is at issue here. It is his vision of the rule of reason generated solely by Herculean judges, in a political and ethical vacuum that is as troublesome as Fuller's "inner morality" of the law. Even with the justifiable assumption that in America, at least, though not in other political societies, rights are the dominant ethos, it is clear that the rule of reason cannot be sustained simply by the rational arguments that judges must offer in deciding both hard and easy cases.

The supremely competent judge in Dworkin's model of the rule of legal reason does not look, and his inventor does not look, at the political context within which he decides cases or that indeed generates the cases that come before him. He may live amid that mass of irrationality that is our tax and immigration law, the decadence of administrative agencies and the perpetual threat of and preparation for war, but the Rule of Law and the rule of reason will reign if judicial decisions are grounded in appropriate rules, principles and standards and rationally defended. The province of judicial action is indeed a very wide one. In choosing which of the two parties before him is right the truly knowing judge need not only look to rules to come to a rational decision, he may also ground his argument on the principles inherent in the political order of which he is a member and to its implicit standards of political morality. In doing so he does not legislate or exercise discretion, because his arguments are derived from a hierarchy of norms, not from considerations of policy, efficiency, or public welfare. Dworkin, of course, knows that policy choices can easily be translated into the language of principles. Indeed legislators and private persons do it all the time. The rationality of judicial discourse, nevertheless, does depend on this formally normative characteristic. As long as it remains within the limits of normative logic its rationality cannot be impugned.[12] Applied to a very limited group, and given the very specific ethical functions that Aristotle assigned to the Rule of Law, syllogistic judicial logic could well be said to have been the model for ruling by reason. But can it do so in the world into which Dworkin has pitched it, especially considering the kinds of controversies and political struggles in which his program must inevitably embroil the judiciary? The judiciary is not alone in claiming a rational standing; other agencies of government also have their share of "tribunality," that is, principled reasoned decision making. Even in terms of normative justification they may have rationally argued standards as grounds for not deferring to judicial decisions on rights or on anything else. Moreover while, indeed, every judicial decision grants and denies a claim, so do most political, and many private domestic ones. All these have a claim to rationality, but not to precedence. And few political struggles are more bitter than those that are fought over the question of "who decides?" Once the members of the judiciary are involved in this sort of political struggle their claim to a special and higher rationality dissolves, however elegant and principled their decisions in specific cases may be. Indeed the erosion of public trust that such political struggles must bring with them is likely to prove far more debilitating to the judiciary than to other institutional agents, and so to diminish any rational strength they might bring to the political system as a whole. But that is only a policy-course decision. The rationality of the system as a whole is, however, crucial. The only political order in which the kind of principled reasoning that Dworkin attributes to the rational judge is possible at all, is of necessity a representative democracy, and as such it is particularly given to jurisdictional and open-minded interminable disputes. The ability of Hercules to prevail in such a polity depends less on the rationality of his specific style of argument than on his power, which is in any case what his name implies. The rationality of his office depends not merely on the rational quality of his decisions, but far more on his relatively aloof place in the political order as a whole. Moreover, others may well propose not only policies but principled arguments that are as rigorous as his own. The final decision between them cannot ultimately be settled by anything other than political conflicts of uncertain outcome. Even if Dworkin were to identify reason and syllogistic argument as closely as Aristotle did, he could not without a comparable account of the process of persuasion in politics and of coercive social control show that the rationality of judicial decisions promotes the rule of reason throughout society, or even the legal rule of equal rights.

Is there much point in continuing to talk about the Rule of Law? Not if it is discussed only as the rules that govern courts or as a football in a game between friends and enemies of free-market liberalism. If it is recognized as an essential element of constitutional government generally and of representative democracy particularly, then it has an obvious part to play in political theory. It may be invoked in discussions of the rights of citizens and beyond that of the ends that are served by the security of rights. If one then begins with the fear of violence, the insecurity of arbitrary government, and the discriminations of injustice, one may work one's way up to finding a significant place for the Rule of Law, and for the boundaries it has historically set upon these the most enduring of our political troubles. It is as such both the oldest and the newest of the theoretical and practical concerns of political theory.

Notes

1. See especially *Nichomachean Ethics*, Book V, *Rhetoric*, Book I, ss. 1366b–1370a, 1373b–1377b, and *Politics*, Book III, ss. 1285b–1287b, and Book IV, ss. 1295a–1296b.

2. *De l'Esprit des Lois*, Chs. VI, XI, ss. 3, 4, 6, 18, 19; XIX, ss. 12, 14, 16; XXVI, s. 20.

3. E. P. Thompson, *Whigs and Hunters* (London, 1975), pp. 258–269.

4. A. V. Dicey, *Introduction to the Study of the Law of the Constitution* (London, 1927), pp. xlii–xlviii and 324–401.

5. See specifically, F. A. Hayek, *Law, Legislation and Liberty* vol. 1 (Chicago, 1973); vol. 2 (Chicago, 1974), pp. 133–152; and vol. 3 (Chicago, 1979), pp. 104, 155–169. John Gray, *Hayek on Liberty* (Oxford, 1984). J. W. Harris, *Legal Philosophies* (London, 1980), pp. 128–139 and 245–251.

6. Roberto M. Unger, *Law in Modern Society* (New York, 1976), pp. 52–

57, 66–76, 166–181, 192–216 and 238–242. "The Critical Legal Studies Movement" (1983), 96 *Harvard Law Review* 563–675. See also Duncan Kennedy, "Form and Substance in Private Law Adjudication," (1976), 89 *Harvard Law Review* 1685–1778. David Kairys ed., *The Politics of Law* (New York, 1982).

7. Samuel P. Huntington, *American Politics and the Promise of Disharmony* (Cambridge, MA, 1981).

8. Among political theorists see Judith N. Shklar, *Legalism* (Cambridge, MA, 1964), and more recently Martin M. Shapiro, *Courts* (Chicago, 1981), which again takes up the notion of a continuum.

9. Lon L. Fuller, *The Morality of Law* (New Haven, 1964), pp. 33–94 and 152–170. "The Forms and Limits of Adjudication" (1978–79), 92 *Harvard Law Review* 353–409. Robert S. Summers, "Professor Fuller's Jurisprudence and America's Dominant Theory of Law," *ibid.,* pp. 433–449.

10. Ernst Fraenkel, *The Dual State* (New York, 1940), one of the few older studies of the Third Reich that remain valid. See also, Martin Broszat, *The Hitler State,* introduction by John W. Hiden (London, 1981), pp. 328–345.

11. Willie Rose Lee, *A Documentary History of Slavery in North America* (New York, 1976), pp. 175–223.

12. Ronald M. Dworkin, *Taking Rights Seriously* (Cambridge, MA, 1977), pp. 14–45, 81–130, and 291–368.

CHAPTER THREE

Obligation, Loyalty, Exile

This is a work in progress. Not even a respectable title. I began work on political obligation and loyalty with a view to getting away from my preoccupation with political evil, but I soon found out better. It began harmlessly enough as a project to figure out the differences between political obligation and political loyalty. I turned to exiles only thanks to a chance conversation, which made me recognize that exiles because their situation is so extreme constitute a perfect limiting case for illustrating the nuances and implications of all the notions related to both obligation and loyalty. That is how I got to the topic.

To be sure, I have long been interested in betrayal, and exiles are often created by governments that betray their own citizens. Governments also frequently abuse residents under their jurisdiction by denying them membership in the polity and other rights, not as a matter of legal punishment but because they belong to a group that is thought to be inherently unfit for inclusion. These people are also exiles. In fact, the more one thinks about them, the more numerous the forms of exile turn out to be. Exile itself is but a part of a larger social category, ranging from the forcibly excluded to people who exile themselves without moving by escaping into themselves, as it were, because their world is so politically evil. I came to look all the way from coerced exiles to inner emigrants.

In spite of the difficulties and scope of the topic, I remain certain that exiles not only offer us a concrete way of examining the meaning

This chapter was previously published as "Obligation, Loyalty, Exile," in *Political Theory* 21, no. 2 (May 1993): 181–97. © 1993 Sage Publications, Inc. Reprinted by permission of Sage Publications, Inc.

of obligation and loyalty but also a chance to rethink some of the arguments made on behalf of the obligation to obey or disobey the laws and specifically the diverging claims of personal conscience and of group loyalty.

To that end I must first fit the special condition of exiles into the more general topic of the relations between obligation and loyalty. Let me begin with the current state of the literature on the subject, as I see it. The two dominant ways of discussing obligation and loyalty at present deal with benign ways of thought. Currently the discussion is often deeply apolitical as it tries to demonstrate the differences between universalistic morality and local, inherited, and more partial attachments. Occasionally this is a spin-off from the communitarian debate, but by no means always. Indeed the discussion often begins with a rejection of political obligation in favor of some form of anarchism, possibly Godwin's or odd versions of Kant. So while moral obligation and personal attachments are certainly set apart there is little effort to put either one of them in specific political contexts.

The second and more political form of discussion is only too deeply tied to recent events and disappeared with them. It arose out of the civil rights movement in the USA and later out of the protests against the Vietnam War and it died as soon as these conflicts ceased to dominate the front page and the TV screen. It was not a great literature. Given its deeply American setting it never really rose above the particular character of the American legal system, or the American Dilemma, our greatest and enduring moral and social burden, black slavery and its legacy. The brief protest against the war in Vietnam soon got bogged down in the issues of conscientious objection and just war theory. The result is that very little remains that is not tied to specific events. What is left is a rather tepid debate about whether one has or has not a prima facie duty to obey the law of a relatively just state. Little follows from this, since no one argues for unconditional obedience in response. It has been noted that one of Hitler's services to political theory has been to do away with theories of unconditional obedience to all and any ruler. Among his disservices is that he haunts every discussion of the subject.

If the discussion of obligation is tethered to events, so is the debate about loyalty. It usually comes up in the USA when there is an effort to extract test oaths from people suspected of subversion and a general anxiety about foreigners, dangerous radicals, and the like. This is now known as McCarthyism, but there have been far worse episodes of enforced loyalty in our history, especially during the First

World War, of which Senator McCarthy's rampage was the last outburst. In any case when McCarthyism died down so did the volume
of published material on loyalty.

As a rule these two discussions of obligation and loyalty have had
little to do with one another. But in ordinary talk the two words
loyalty and *obligation* are generally used interchangeably as if they
were identical. What then is their relation and are there significant
differences between loyalty and obligation? It will be my argument
that it is important not only to keep them apart but to go on to make
clear the distinctions between obligation, commitment, loyalty, allegiance, and fidelity. I shall say nothing about piety, the devotion that
is felt by religious persons for their deity, for my subject is politics,
in which loyalty to a church is very relevant, but which is not directly
affected by inward faith.

By obligation I mean rule-governed conduct, and political obligation specifically refers to laws and lawlike demands, made by public
agencies. This comes out very clearly in most of our obligation talk.
We are called to obey because it is right to do so according to natural
law and reason, or utility, or the historical mission of the modern
state. The reasons for accepting or rejecting political obligations in
liberal democracies are said to derive from consent, explicit or tacit,
while the modern state that merely enforces the rule of law is legitimated by the security and fairness that it gives its citizens. The very
word legitimacy reminds us of the law-bound character of political
obligation. And whatever else tyrannies are and have been, they are
always lawless regimes that we may resist.

I do not need to choose between these grounds for political obligation here, for I merely want to underline their rational rule-related
character. We are told that we have a duty to comply with the rules
of the political society in which we live because it is rational to do
so, even though the definition of rationality may be disputed. It is
rational to follow or reject rules because it is prudent to do so when
all consequences to oneself and others are considered. It is rational
to obey or not because there is a universal moral law we recognize
when we consider impartially and impersonally what duty as such
or justice imply. It is rational to obey because we have in some sense
promised to do so and promises must be kept for reasons of coherence, or because that is what promising *means*, or because promise
breaking is to lie and lying is against the universal law. These are all
examples of rational, rule-immersed thinking. Natural law, utilitarianism, deontology: all agree there are rational rules to guide us. They
may not agree about the meaning of rationality, but they do know

that obligation is a matter of rational rules and based on rule guided grounds. That is what defines it.

We do not, however, talk only about political obligations. Even if we limit ourselves to politics, which I do, we hear terms like commitment, fidelity, and most of all loyalty. Commitment seems to be the broadest term and it refers to chosen obligations. The term implies a voluntary engagement to do something in the future. It seems a lot looser than a promise and it can cover a vast range of actions. What is stable in its usage is that it is an engagement made voluntarily and is fully accepted by the person who is said to be committed to doing something. Political commitments usually imply the intention to support a party, a political agent, a public cause, or a political ideology. At that point feelings of loyalty may, but need not, be involved. The reasons for commitment may indeed be crassly self-interested and calculating. The dictionary speaks of pledges, and that seems right.

Commitment is my broadest category, but it has its limits. Commitments are meant to be enduring, and they imply choice. That would be as true of nonpolitical cases, such as commitment to the Society for the Prevention of Cruelty to Animals, or to a political cause, such as Amnesty International. I use these examples to show that not all our commitments are directly political or need have a direct bearing on human affairs, hence the broadness of the notion. I would suggest that both political obligation and loyalty are more specific than just any commitment and, above all, they may be less than voluntary.

What distinguishes loyalty is that it is deeply affective and not primarily rational. For the sake of clarity we should take loyalty to be an attachment to a social group. Membership may or may not be chosen. Belonging to an ascriptive group to which one has been brought up, and taught to feel loyal to it, since one's earliest infancy is scarcely a matter of choice. And when it comes to race, ethnicity, caste, and class, choice is not obvious. The emotional character of loyalty also sets it apart from obligation. If obligation is rule driven, loyalty is motivated by the entire personality of an agent. Political loyalty is evoked by nations, ethnic groups, churches, parties, and by doctrines, causes, ideologies, or faiths that form and identify associations. When it is a result of choice loyalty is a commitment that is affective in character and generated by a great deal more of our personality than calculation or moral reasoning. It is all of one that tends to be loyal.

If loyalty is given to groups, individuals may and do receive our fidelity. We remain true to them and to ourselves. We think of fidelity to our friends and this must include spouses and lovers. Causes, be they moral, political, or aesthetic, demand loyalty; friendship calls for fidelity. Of the two, fidelity is the most personal of all, the most expressive of our personality and emotional life. We are faithful to our spouses and to our friends; we are committed to those relationships in which there is, at least in principle, an element of choice. Once chosen we expect fidelity. That is why one can speak of a commitment to fidelity, as in marriage vows.

Fidelity does play a part in politics. Political leaders often expect and receive fidelity and are expected to show it to their followers. Harry Truman was renowned for both the fidelity he inspired and showed his supporters. Loyalty is the word used, but it seems wrong, because personal dynamics persist in all political systems. There are, I believe, good Freudian reasons for this. But in any event, leadership for better or worse involves fidelity.

Loyalty to groups, as I noted, is not, and often is not meant to be, a matter of choice. Very often we have no choice at all whether we belong to a group or not. Most of the memberships people have in groups are taken out at birth. You do not choose to be black, you do not fully choose to be Jewish, and you certainly do not choose your parents. And whether or not you choose your nationality is a very conditional and tricky question, but you are stuck with your race. And the language in which you learn to talk at all at two has a different bearing upon you than all the others you may master in later years. Now you have a choice to be either loyal or disloyal to these groups, but you do not have the choice of being neither. That is a pretty severe limitation. Fidelity can come to a stop: two people cease to care for each other, and there's an end to it. In a free society your commitments to parties and causes are expected to alter over a life span. But we characteristically demand loyalty to groups where the assumption of limited choice prevails. Selling out is the great crime of persons who have gone over to the "other side" but who by some definition still belong to the group.

In the days when a lot of people were interested in class politics there was always the distinction between workers, who had no choice about who they were as part of a class, and intellectuals who had made a choice. The reason for distrusting the latter was obvious: they could not give full and unselective loyalty, only a chosen commitment.

When we look at politics there is yet another bond: allegiance, a relationship that I think is clearly derived from feudal bonds. If you too have been deeply influenced by Bloch's *Feudal Society,* then you will recognize that in the anarchy after the collapse of Charlemagne's empire, the only way to reestablish political cohesion among armed men was to bind them through personal bonds, in which the inferior becomes "the man" of his superior, his vassal in due course. Eventually as oaths became an additional means of gluing the baronage together a religious element entered the bond as well. It was a very significant ritual that has not entirely disappeared. Not only do promises play a great role in creating political obligations, but, in spite of Hume's efforts, it has been very difficult to get God out of them. An oath is not an interpersonal bond, but in the first instance a promise to obey God. It is a covenant as much as a contract and entails both personal fidelity and social loyalty. So allegiance stands between fidelity and loyalty. The totally irrational habit of extracting oaths to which the USA is addicted has its roots in these rituals, and they are assumed to retain some of their ancient meaning, at least to the extent that they are not test oaths designed to entrap people into perjuring themselves.

I think I have now drawn a shaky intellectual map. It is meant less to be accurate than to throw a lurid light upon the difficulties of my project. One thing ties all of these notions together: They all invite conflict; trouble is their middle name. Conflicts are common between obligations, commitments, loyalties, fidelities, and allegiances. Moreover, each of these has to endure internal conflicts as well. Loyalties clash and so do obligations. However sincere we may be in our commitments, however rational our sense of political obligation, however devoted to our country, cause, and spouse, we will have diverse claims on our feelings and calculations. Probably the most severe tensions are between fidelity and all the others, but both fidelity and loyalty are most likely to collide with political obligation because they are different in kind not just in extent and intensity. They are not rule-bound imperatives. Personal fidelity and group loyalties have always put political obligation into question. Literature, especially the tragic drama, is a storehouse of examples of individuals torn between their obligations as public figures and their personal feelings for family and friends. Creon (backed by Hegel) had a rational point when he said to Antigone that authority saves lives. From Agamemnon to Cinna we have the clash of public roles and personal fidelity to child, sweetheart, and parents. The defenders of obligation, like Socrates, have told their friends to go away, while those who clung to them could look forward to anything from martyrdom to accusations of irrationality. At one time there was a flourishing literature about the conflict between fidelity to persons and loyalty to the Communist party when its line changed. "Dirty hands" was a serious problem. That may seem a long time ago, but it is not.

Because groups are the sites of most political action they are also the locus of conflict, and part of their language of combat is about loyalty, especially now. For the age of ideology has left us with only one survivor able to make claims upon primary loyalties: nationalism. It is all the more powerful because it has no serious rivals. That nationalism can and does conflict with personal fidelity is painfully clear. Think of all those wretched couples in Croatia, one of whom is Serb and the other Croat! Not to mention much that is closer to home. As for loyalty and obligation it is evident that nationality and state structures must conflict, because there is no single territorial state, except perhaps Iceland, that is not multiethnic and multinational or could ever be or have been.

Of course, this brief list certainly does not exhaust the possibilities. There are conflicts also within each form of attachment, such as conflicts of fidelity, say, to two friends who are at odds with one another, as when couples divorce. Then there are genuine conflicts of loyalty, say, between one's church and one's political party, such as many socialist Catholics faced in America in the thirties. More recently, members of the democratic political organizations have had to give up their membership in exclusive golf clubs. And most important of all are conflicts of obligation, as when two constitutional rights conflict, for example, the right to free press and the right to a fair trial, which has long been a sore point in American constitutional law. And then there is the perennial conflict in constitutional states between the demands of military security and the obligation to the laws, which presidents since Jefferson have bent, to say the least. Illegality, disloyalty, and infidelity are sometimes unavoidable, and they are witness to the conflict between our incompatible attachments.

I do not wish to imply that conflict between loyalty and obligation is inherent and inevitable, though it is very likely. Loyalty can and does sustain obligation, often. If state and nationality coincide, national loyalty will do much to reinforce obligation to the state and its laws. The ancien régime owed much to caste ties and interests. And party loyalty is necessary to maintain representative public institutions. When Max Weber claimed, quaintly it now seems, that devotion to a cause gave politics its ethical substance he was pointing to the dependence of loyalty and obligation on one another. Unreflective citizenship is often habitual and not really an expression of obligation. Once the question of whether one should or should not obey is asked, however, the difference between loyalty and obligation emerges. Then we cannot ignore the difference and the ways in which loyalty can both sustain and undermine public rules.

Having recognized that conflict is only part of the story, I do now want to return to it. In the conflicts between obligation, loyalty, and fidelity a decision one way or another will be a betrayal of the loser. While conflicts between loyalties and fidelities are particularly likely to induce a deep sense of betrayal among individuals, personal relationships are not the only ones that invite betrayal. States and groups also betray each other and states may betray some of their individual members by treating them unjustly and illegally, in some cases by exiling them. One advantage of looking closely at such exiles is that they help one to illustrate how obligation, loyalty, and fidelity support and undermine each other. The second interest of exiles is that they have been viewed very differently at various times and these differences reveal changes in attitudes to obligation and loyalty, especially in classical as contrasted with modern political theory, but also by different modern political theorists. Lastly, I think that exile can throw some light on the justifications we offer for our choices, specifically the claims of personal conscience.

What is an exile? I despair of ever completing my list. An exile is someone who involuntarily leaves the country of which he or she is a citizen. Usually it is thanks to political force, but extreme poverty may be regarded as a form of coercive expulsion. I will stick to the classic exile, involuntary emigrés who leave under threat of harm to themselves and to their family. I put aside ordinary criminals who are on the run and limit myself to persons who have good grounds to claim that the state has treated them unjustly by excluding them from its borders. They are the injured party. What are their political duties now? Consider a pair of famous ancient exiles, Themistocles and Aristides, who both appear in Plutarch and the former memorably in Thucydides.

Themistocles was ostracized because he had become too powerful and because he was not trusted. Ostracism was not a punishment. It was a public policy designed to prevent a too powerful individual from threatening democratic rule. There was no guilt or shame involved. Themistocles certainly felt neither; he just went over to the Persians, became an adviser to their king, dressed in Persian styles, and never seems to have given Athens a second thought. Thucydides who tells us of his career has nothing but admiration for this man. He was intelligent, prudent, and adaptable, a perfect survivor who never threatened the internal peace of either Athens or Persia. He served each state capably and did well for himself as well. If you think, as Thucydides did, that civil war is the most horrible thing that can happen, that civilization is very thin ice and that savagery and murderous rage are just below the surface of society, then loyalty and obligation are not to be regarded as nearly as important as adaptability, moderation, and prudence. And so Thucydides tells us that Themistocles was the most admirable politician he had known. Of him it could be said that he scrupulously met his political obligations and had no loyalties at all.

In his lack of affective political attachment Themistocles was quite unusual. Loyalty to the city was intense among the Athenian people at least, though perhaps not among the aristocrats. The practice of ostracism did nothing to make the latter more tractable and eventually the practice was dropped. In terms of Aristotelian notions of justice ostracism was certainly unjust, although Aristotle accepted its necessity under certain circumstances: as a matter of political prudence, not justice. Even some exiles seem to have taken that view, for there were great men who did not behave like Themistocles, nor was he universally admired in antiquity. Plutarch did not think much of him and praised the Roman Camillus in contrast, who, although banished and then recalled by most of the citizens, would not return until his sentence had been legally revoked. And then, even more notoriously, there was Aristides, who was Themistocles' contemporary and constant rival. He also was ostracized, but at no time did he contemplate going over to the enemy and in due course he was invited to come back. When he did, he did nothing to revenge himself on his enemies. He was in due course universally known as "the just." Clearly, this was a man who met all his obligations, no less than Themistocles, but there must have been an element of loyalty as well. We do not know.

It is not insignificant that Aristides in order to meet his obligations had no political friends, and he avoided all those actions and preferences which could disturb the frail civil peace of Athens. In this he was unlike Coriolanus, my third character out of Plutarch. Here is a story of personal fidelity triumphing over both loyalty and obligation. Coriolanus was noble, brave, and a great general. What was unique about him was that having lost his father as a child he was intensely devoted to his mother with whom he lived even after his marriage. In politics, out of aristocratic arrogance he did everything he could to insult the people and in this, gained the support of many young men from families like his own. Everything he did was designed to bring about a civil war until he finally left the city after losing a trial. He went right over to Rome's worst enemies to help them to destroy the city. So the women of Rome implored his mother to plead with him, which she did successfully. What Plutarch found so utterly objectionable in Coriolanus was not that Coriolanus had betrayed Rome but that first he threatened it with civil war and then returned out of love for his mother, a private and personal fidelity, not a political or military act. Plutarch was, in fact, following a long line of thinking about the political implications of personal friendship. As far as he was concerned, personal fidelity was a threat to the republic because it concentrates on particular individuals not on the city as a whole. And so, to top it all off, Plutarch compares him unfavorably to Alcibiades, after having painted a truly horrible portrait of the latter, because at least he did not bring Athens to the brink of civil war. He was consistently egotistic.

I mention these examples from classical political theory because they present a view of political obligation and loyalty that is gone. Even when, like Plutarch, treason is regarded as a crime and the fact that it is particularly excoriated by the people is recognized, serious political theory does not make much of an ado about it. The obligations and loyalties of the individual agent are entirely subordinated to the necessity of avoiding civil war. The single most important political aim is to avoid the carnage of internal war. That is the supreme evil. Everything is destroyed when that happens. It is the political equivalent of the bubonic plague. What else is Aristotle's *Politics* about? There is bound to be tension between justice and political prudence and that is a practical difficulty, rendered dangerous by the impetuosity of unruly aristocrats and an edgy people. It is wholly a question of policy. That is in fact what is meant by the priority of the city over its individual members. If biblical religiosity had been compatible with this view, my story would be over, but it is not so. It is also not the way modern political theory has thought of exiles and other excluded people. In fact it has not said as much as it should about the rights and obligations of exiles.

For modern exiles illuminate loyalty and obligation no less than their very different ancient counterparts. If we stick to relatively just regimes as Athens and Rome had been, the most interesting cases occur when fundamental public principles are disregarded and the legally defined and protected rights are violated, by subjecting an individual or a group to exile or by excluding them from citizenship. What happens when legally created expectations, based on a public and published system of rights and duties, are cast aside in this way? The excuse is usually that these regrettable measures were a matter of dire necessity. In fact, they rarely are. In retrospect there are few cases of governmental criminality that can be justified on grounds of unavoidable necessity. Moreover, governmental illegality is not a disregard for casual understandings, such as exist in many private quasi-contracts, but a disruption of the law as it stands and is known. It violates trust in a way that renders the very basis of public life unreliable and vitiates the chief reasons for our obligation to obey the law. Political loyalty may survive, but not obligation to obey the law. That is why I assume that exiles have no obligations to the country that expels them illegally and unconstitutionally.

Official illegality may also create a nonterritorial form of exile, internal exclusion from citizenship, which afflicts slaves, unwelcome immigrants and ethnic groups, and morally upright people trapped within the borders of tyrannical states. The excluded, or internal exiles as they have sometimes been called, even sometimes appear in constitutional regimes on those occasions when these engage in exceptionally unjust and immoral policies. The morally isolated individual may be reduced to living in accordance with no rule other than his private conscience, and I shall try to say something about the arguments that such people make, as part of my review of the obligations and loyalties of politically excluded persons.

Given that legality is the core of the legitimacy of the modern state, unjust exile evokes responses quite unlike those of the classical political scientists with their concern about civil war. Exile is subject to judgments based on the claims of the individual. The rights of and the wrongs suffered by the victims are therefore of primary interest. Take the case of Captain Dreyfus. He was accused and found guilty in 1894 of having passed secret French Army documents to the Germans. He was palpably innocent, but he was a natural suspect because he was a Jew. Even when his innocence was perfectly clear no court would clear him and the Army argued that the innocence of the individual was less important than the honor of the Army, which could therefore never admit that many of its officers had perjured themselves. The Army officers felt that their primary obligation was to the Army and to France as they saw it, not to the French republic, that is, to the political order that they were supposed to serve. Moreover, they managed to successfully persecute anyone who published evidence proving the innocence of Dreyfus, now on Devil's Island. They in effect ostracized the man because they thought it best for the state as a whole. Finally, to be sure, the government was forced to pardon him, and only in 1906 did an appeals court finally quash his sentence.

When war broke out in 1914 Dreyfus immediately rejoined the

Army and served with distinction. At no time did he ever cease to be anything but a superpatriotic, loyal French citizen. He merely wanted his honor as a loyal officer reestablished. It never seems to have occurred to him that he was living in a corrupt society and serving in a criminal officer corps. His sense of loyalty to the Army and to France was theirs in fact. Here is an example of loyalty sustaining an obligation he may not even have owed to a state that had rejected and betrayed him. Certainly here, loyalty overcame injustice.

It is an interesting case because the victim's sense of obligation was greater than that of the official authorities of the state. The point may be that he was not an exile from a systematically oppressive regime or an imposed one like those of Eastern Europe during the Cold War. Does that, as it were, render his loyalty to France and his enduring sense of obligation to its institutions justifiable or even meritorious?

One might suppose that at the very least Dreyfus might have led a political campaign against the way the French Army conducted itself or he could have emigrated to the USA. Dreyfus's obligations to the state clearly were terminated when it exiled him and betrayed him. He however defended only his own conduct, remained loyal to France and to its army, and thus sustained his sense of obligation. I think he was crazy, but many people admire him, because they think that loyalty to one's nation is the highest political virtue. I do not think he was just a victim identifying with the oppressor; he did look at himself as they did. Far from admitting that he was unfit to serve, he regarded himself as a model officer. He was one of them, and the victim of an error. At the least what this case demonstrates is the way in which loyalty can sustain obligation.

Dreyfus's case is not unique. No one was ever exiled more completely than the Americans of Japanese ancestry who were interned after Pearl Harbor. In 1943, after all that had been done to them, it became mandatory to declare themselves loyal or disloyal to the USA. That was because the War Relocations Authority wanted for various reasons to empty the camps as much as possible. Not least there was a manpower shortage and the military wanted to draft the young men, some of whom had fathers who had fought in Europe in the First World War. The exiles were asked to swear allegiance to the USA and to renounce any loyalty to Japan. Three-quarters of them chose to do so and others said they would have done so had it not been for the internment. It was in any event clear that among those who refused to swear there was a deep and justifiable sense of betrayal. Not they but their country had betrayed them. Why should you not act as an enemy alien if you are treated as one?

The parents of the young men were especially bitter at the demand that their sons now fight for the USA. For them, family values, always important among Japanese people, now seemed all that was left. The more Americanized the individuals were, the more likely they were to swear allegiance to the USA and also feel the most outraged by what they knew to be a violation of their rights.

As one of the internees put it,

> I felt that the Constitution had failed me. Actually, it wasn't the Con-
> stitution that failed me; the Supreme Court failed me, and the other
> people who were entrusted with the upholding of the Constitution
> failed me. . . . They failed because the will of the people wasn't behind
> upholding the Constitution.

One of the most important points in this awful story is a human one. Each one of these people had to make a personal choice involving a family and one's own future. For many, a return to Japan was unthinkable, so they really had no choice. In the event, a Japanese-American regiment fought with great distinction in Italy. Segregated, of course. Here there is both conflict between obligation and loyalty as well as a reconciliation between the two, but at the expense of the exiles. Recently the federal government has apologized to the internees, but the principles which made these official acts possible remain intact.

No such relatively easy denouement is possible in the case of radically unjust states. Willy Brandt returned to Germany after years of forced exile in Norway and said that he had kept faith with the real Germany, the true Germany. He cannot have meant the majority of his people, only their better possibilities, to which he remained loyal. He even returned to Germany to see his friends secretly. At no time did he lose faith in the German labor movement. But he certainly supported the Norwegians in the war against Germany. His obligations to Germany had evidently lapsed and been transferred. He acquired Norwegian citizenship and worked for the Norwegian government briefly after the war. From the first he emphasized and publicized the difference between criminal and other Germans. And ultimately he resumed his citizenship, becoming first mayor of Berlin and then chancellor of West Germany.

The German Jews, however, could retain no conceivable obligation to Germany even after the destruction of the Nazi state, and only a handful returned. They also had no grounds for loyalty, since their erstwhile fellow citizens had abandoned them with such alacrity. One can look at their condition in Lockean terms. Both contracts had been broken, the first between members of society as well as the second between citizens and the state. They were betrayed at both levels, excluded from civil no less than from political society. Personal ties of fidelity remained occasionally and so did nostalgia. "How shall I sing the Lord's song in a strange land?" sang an exile in the saddest of Old Testament Psalms. And for many of them that is what exile came down to. What I am trying to show is that the extent of the rejection determines whether there is, even after the elimination of any obligation, any possibility of retaining some loyalty to the native land. It makes all the difference to the exile and it is an issue that may also create problems for the host state to which the exiles are now obliged.

For enduring loyalty can often cause some real damage to new political obligations. If exiles retain ties of loyalty to the country that expelled them, they may be less than either loyal or obedient to the laws of the host state. Brandt only remained loyal to an idea of Germany and the Jews not even that, but often new political obligations are rendered murky by the volatility of loyalty. Diasporas can be unreliable, if they do not feel wholly alienated from the state that exiled them or from ideologies that were acquired there. Nevertheless, it is surprising how few American traitors were actually foreign born.

It might be argued that the problems of exiles are not so special but, rather, just like those of everyone else faced with having to decide whether to obey the law or not, and trying to assess the degree of evil in the government that has provoked the question in the first place. They have to ask themselves whether the government that betrayed them is a tyranny or whether just some of its policies are manifestly unjust, but capable of being altered. Clearly, Dreyfus and the Japanese Americans unlike Willy Brandt and the German Jews had to deal with a reasonably just state, not Hitler. How do their questions differ from those of a Southern black student in the 1960s in the USA? I think that there is a difference in the degree of exclusion between exiles and other victims of public injustice. Refugees who have been expelled beyond all hope of return have no political obligations at all to their former state. After such an expulsion there is no point in trying to reclaim one's rights as Dreyfus and the Japanese Americans did, and ultimately did successfully. That is, however, not the only consideration. Most exiles today simply have nowhere to go, whatever they might wish to do. The dreadful reality of our world is that no one wants to accept this huge exiled population. What they need is a place to go to, and these are increasingly hard to find. It is at least a tolerable solution for ethnic groups to emigrate en masse if they have a welcoming home country, such as the *pieds noirs* from North Africa who went to France or Jews who can go to Israel. But these are exceptions. Most people do not merely fear foreign exile; many of them will be exiles in pure limbo.

The dwellers in refugee camps can best be compared to America's African slaves. And as we all look on helplessly at the ever-growing numbers of human refuse heaps, we might perhaps listen to the voice of conscience. At the very least we might reexamine anew the claims that are made for and against the call of conscience in the face of group loyalty. That is why a look at the secular abolitionists may not be irrelevant. An injustice as great as slavery, especially in an otherwise reasonably just state, is bound to create moral outrage. And some of the Americans who were determined to end slavery found themselves in a very curious situation. Those among them who felt that the entire Constitution, not only specific laws, was a slave document could have no obligation to obey the laws at all. For some, religious loyalty was the only significant bond left. These were the majority of abolitionists who were members of radical Protestant congregations or abolitionist societies, most of which were religious as well. But what of the secular abolitionist, like Thoreau, for example? I should like to undertake a defense of his position in an essentially psychological way, by suggesting that he had little choice but to base himself in his conscience and nothing else, to make what one might call a "pure conscience" argument. I do not propose to examine its ultimate validity, but to see it in the context within which it emerges.

What we get here is personal isolation of the most extreme sort. Now Thoreau's argument for disobedience relies exclusively on his conscience in refusing to obey to pay his taxes. *No* government that rules over slaves is good enough to rule him, and while he is perfectly ready to leave the running of many insignificant public matters to the lawyers in state houses, the evil on his mind is not trivial. So he refuses to recognize his obligations. If he had a friend or a group who shared his cause we do not hear of it. He was not choosing between loyalty and laws. Not at all. He was asserting the unconditional primacy of conscience in the face of what he regarded as absolute evil. The moral "empire of me" was created because there was no other.

The situation of an American abolitionist was wholly different from that of European radical vintage 1848. It was more like the condition of the opponents of Nazism who remained in Germany cut off from their exiled friends by war, and utterly alone among their Nazified countrymen. Abolitionists lived not in the midst of ideologi-

cal struggles but in a moral vacuum and their agony was being implicated in an evil they abhorred. Every time they put on a shirt they
were abetting the slavery of the blacks who had picked the cotton.
But in no way could they identify with the slaves, be part of their
society, or become blacks.

A Thoreau had neither the camaraderie of the revolutionary, nor
a shared identity with the slaves. There was no "we." They were
alone to the point of self-exclusion. The "Inner Civil War" as it is
called could only be ended by the real war. They could not resort to
loyalty because they had no local support. It was to be sure a social
cause, but there was no community; the object was too remote. Although, unlike most abolitionists he was not a racist, as far as we
know, Thoreau certainly could not join the blacks. Nor could he be
expected to do so. He was protesting on their behalf, but abolitionism
did not require him to take the slightest interest in the actual life and
future of the enslaved population. There is often nothing *there* when
one protests against abstract and absolute evil, and it is exceptionally
isolating.

I want to consider this example of exclusion because I think that
the pure conscience argument has often been misunderstood, at least
as it appears in America. The general *fons et origo* of the case against
conscience as the sole ground for either disobedience or disloyalty
has been Hegel and I won't repeat all of his argument, but it comes
down to identifying conscience with a sort of moral egotism and shift-
iness. I would suggest that if we evaluate conscience claims in politics
in terms of their setting, we will recognize the voice of men and
women who have been so completely isolated by the injustice they
perceive around them that ties of loyalty and fidelity may be eroded
along with political obligation. It is this situation that has in our century been called "internal exile," and it is expressed in the pure conscience argument and justifies it. It is also a very rare occurrence. In
the USA it receives its relevance solely from a single, though searing,
experience of enduring injustice to one group in an otherwise constitutionally respectable polity. It was repeated in Europe in our century, under circumstances which Hegel did not foresee.

In spite of these considerations, loyalty to groups, to causes, to a
class, a caste, a party, or any association has long had a far better
press than the dissociated insubstantial conscience. None have done
better than ethnic solidarity and nationalism which inspire the most
intense political loyalty, especially in their most xenophobic aspects.
The approval of group-based loyalty and arguments for and against
political obligation based on such loyalty tends, however, to mute,

indeed to forget, that exclusion is an unavoidable and essential feature of such loyalty. This is the case even when exclusion is not a given group's primary purpose and hostility to outsiders is not encouraged. In the political world of the present, political loyalty is however often very exclusive, especially nationalism, which has done much to create the current refugee population and certainly ensures their and their children's continued exile. Who can these people be expected to trust, especially if they are dumped into states which refuse to grant citizenship to anyone who is not a member of their nation? Would they be bad citizens? The experience of Canada and the United States denies it. Diaspora groups in countries that permit naturalization are usually quite law abiding and as bound by obligation as the native in paying their taxes and following public health rules. Here I need only mention again Japanese Americans who are one of the least crime- or spy-ridden communities in the country.

Even if in open immigrant societies the lot of the refugee is at first a difficult one, their troubles do abate. We need not forget the endless efforts to shoehorn citizens into Anglo-Saxon conformity which began with the mass immigration of the 1880s from Eastern and Southern Europe and which have not entirely ended yet. But these hurdles are as nothing compared to those of permanent refugee groups, guest workers, camp dwellers bereft of every civic tie and hope, surviving as best they can in countries that will never grant citizenship to anyone but their own nationals. This is the consequence of making political obligation dependent on group membership and loyalty both national and ethnic. Religious sects once had such policies as well and in some countries this is still the case, but it is the national and ethnic loyalty that undermines legality and the principles of political obligation. By excluding people who would obey the law, but might speak a foreign language, the actual consequences of communal cohesion, so often praised as the only valid ground for either political resistance or obedience, reveals its primary and insuperable defect. It is the path of injustice. Great as the gratifications and privileges of membership may be and natural as their desperate cohesion in a world of endless migrations and civil wars is, the plight of the dispersed and excluded is unbearable.

This suggests that human rights may have much to do with the way these conflicts evolve. If citizenship in *some* country is, as Hannah Arendt argued, the one necessary human right of our century because all others depend on it, then offering citizenship to exiles may prove the most significant means of taming political loyalty. The evidence is clear that when political obligations are assumed they are not lightly shaken off, and when they are, it is usually because there is real and reasonably perceived injustice, as in the various cases of exclusion that I have recounted. In short it might be a good idea to discuss issues raised by legal and political obligation not as issues of individual autonomy and legal doctrine, but more politically in terms of the prevailing policies of states as they affect excluded groups.

I am not good at conclusions. The desire to arrive at them strikes me, frankly, as slightly childish. A need for an "and they lived happily ever after" ending does not seem to me to fit a type of discourse that is unending. However, in order to remain reasonably conventional, I would suggest that injustice not only cancels obligations and undermines loyalties, however resilient the latter may seem; it also engenders the conflicts between obligation and the affective ties that bind us. The hatred that injustice perceived and real, and most perceived injustice *is* real, creates stirs up most of the trouble. It is, I fear, vain to hope that the simple effort to establish just institutions can create a modus vivendi, let alone build a shared sense of political right, once these conflicts have emerged. Nevertheless, the less injustice there is, the less likely it is that refugees will populate the world and bring with them their terrible misery and mischief.

Editor's note: Judith Shklar gave this text as a lecture at the University of Wisconsin on March 23, 1992. It was work in preparation for the series of lectures that she had been slated to give in 1993 at Cambridge University. Thanks to Bernard Yack of the University of Wisconsin for making the text available and to Gerald Shklar for giving permission for its publication. It is only fitting that Dita be given a chance at a last word, one which she conspicuously refuses in the last paragraph.

CHAPTER FOUR

The Bonds
of Exile

Lecture 1: "Noble Exile"

The four lectures I propose to give are to deal with one topic, the political obligations and loyalties of exiles. An exile is any person who has been compelled involuntarily to leave a country in which he or she has been living as a permanent resident or citizen. Mostly exiles are forced to leave because they are threatened with death, imprisonment, or torture if they remain, but famine may have the same effect. No one becomes an exile willingly, although occasionally morally upright persons do force themselves to leave their homeland and so to exile themselves, because they would inevitably be implicated in criminal policies if they remained. It is the intensity of the public pressures that forces individuals to leave a country which they regard as their home that makes people exiles rather than just travelers.

What political duties can one ascribe to exiles? Am I not just being wayward in asking such a question? As we look at the masses of refugees all around us we might well think so. Must we not say of human beings so utterly deprived of their dignity that one cannot possibly impute any political or even moral duties to them? That was precisely what was once said about the evil of slavery: that it deprived human beings of the very possibility of making moral choices. And it is true that the condition of the helpless and hopeless inhabitants of the bulging refugee camps of our world is in this respect like the slaves' condition. However, not all exiles have historically been as abject as these men and women, though surely they too have their predecessors in the conquered populations of the past, who were

This unpublished essay was written in 1993.

slaughtered and enslaved en masse. Along with them, however, there have in every age also been notable individual exiles to whom one can impute both obligations and loyalties, because they have had a range of political choices available to them. They are typically political exiles, not ordinary criminals on the run. To be sure, the definition of crimes is politically very volatile, but murder, theft, racketeering, embezzlement, armed robbery, and rape are pretty universally treated as nonpolitical crimes, whereas treason, espionage, and subversion are characteristically political offenses. Political exiles are people charged with these and similar acts. At the very least they are accused of being a threat to the government and to the polity as a whole.

There has been rather little said lately by political theorists about exiles. They have been left to the historians and poets, and that is a pity. Perhaps their numbers and variety have discouraged philosophical inquiry. It is not easy to generalize about exiles, nor do they lend themselves to abstraction. Yet exile is a common experience and so searing that it should invite reflection. No experience is more fundamental, and not one has been used metaphorically more seriously. Let us not forget Adam and Eve and the many people, pagan and Christian, who have felt that all their life on earth was nothing but one long exile of the soul. In fact, most books that have the word *exile* in their title have nothing to do with expulsion from one's homeland. Even if one limits oneself, as I shall, to political exiles, there is much to be said that is not insignificant for political theory generally. Exiles can help us, I believe, to think imaginatively about one of the most traditional topics of political philosophy, political obligation. I have no intention of going over the old debates about why one should obey, or to reexamine the debate about how one should think about one's duty to obey the law. The question becomes historically interesting, as a rule, only when someone is caught in a clash between irreconcilable obligations, beginning with Antigone and until the present. The experiences of exiles can illuminate this sort of political conflict in a particularly concrete and extreme way. Exiles often must decide both whom to obey and in what ways, because they may well feel torn between their loyalties to their former homeland and their obligations to their current place of residence. They may also have political obligations, such as trying to restore the legal government, or at least their own party, from abroad. It is one of the anguishing aspects of exile that its victims cannot forget their former homes, nor can they wholly discard the bonds that tied them to it. Exiles cannot do what most people do, accept their political obligations and loyalties as simple habits. Displaced and uprooted, they must make decisions about what sort of lives they will now lead. As political agents they must at the very least think about these decisions and sort out their various and incompatible political duties and ties.

When the governments that force people to flee are tyrannical, or at least repressive and unjust, their victims certainly cease to have any obligations to the regime's laws. Hitler's only service to political theory is that no one argues for unconditional obedience to governments now. Among his disservices is that he hovers over every discussion of the topic. It is, however, not the case that exiles are always the victims of oppressive regimes. Political exile may be an integral part of the law of a reasonably just political order. What are the obligations and the loyalties of the exiles from such relatively unobjectionable regimes?

To answer that question we have to think of obligation in a far more public and less personal way than we usually do. Exile may be preferable to political trials. It may be better than a too paralyzing and disturbing struggle between factions and personal rivals. And it is surely a good way to control the possibility of civil war, because anything that prevents this supreme political evil is desirable.

Public considerations of this order not only render exile a palatable policy, but they also raise specific questions about the appropriate political conduct of people who have been exiled from their acceptably just countries. The victims of tyrannies may retain loyalties to their country, but surely no direct obligations to the government that so unjustly exiled them; but what if they were thrown out for good political reasons, though they committed no crime? If one accepts the idea of exile as a legitimate policy, one might have to apply only public, and not personal, standards to the exile's conduct as well. Here is a way of looking at political obligation that must expect exiles, like their foes, to think, not in terms of their personal moral convictions or their sense of justice, but only as public agents. And their conduct is measured in terms of its public bearings, not their personal rectitude. This is a strange way of thinking about obligation, and it emerges with particular clarity in the stories of the ancient exiles of Athens and republican Rome.

One would, as I mentioned, expect exiles generally to retain some feelings of loyalty to the country from which they were expelled. I deliberately distinguish loyalty and obligation, because I think that they have very different meanings, and that exiles bring out the contrast in a very telling way. By obligation I mean rule-governed conduct generally, and political obligation specifically refers to laws and lawlike demands made by public agencies. We are called to obey because it is right to do so according to natural law, natural reason, utility, and the historical mission of the modern state. The reasons for accepting or rejecting political obligations in liberal democracies are said to derive from consent, explicit or tacit, while the modern state that merely enforces the rule of law is legitimated by the security and fairness that it gives its citizens. The very word *legitimacy* reminds us of the law-bound character of political obligation. And whatever else tyrannies are and have been, they are always lawless regimes that we may resist.

I do not need to choose between the grounds for political obligation here; I merely want to underline their rational, rule-related character. We have a duty to comply with the rules of the political society in which we live, it is said, because it is rational to do so, even though the definition of rationality may be disputed. It is rational to follow or reject rules because it is prudent to do so when all consequences to oneself and others are considered. It is rational to obey or not because there is a universal moral law we recognize when we consider impartially and impersonally what duty and justice imply. It is rational to obey because we have in some sense promised to do so, and promises must be kept for reasons of coherence, or because that is what promising *means*, or because breaking promises is to lie, and lying is against the universal law. Possibly our fellow citizens have come to rely on our performance of implicit contracts. This is a fair sample of conventional rational, rule-immersed thinking. Natural law, utilitarianism, deontology: all agree there are rational rules to guide us. Obligation is a matter of rules which are based on rule-like principles, which clearly enable us to know what we should do.

What distinguishes loyalty from rule-guided obligation is that it is deeply affective and not primarily rational. It also may not be a chosen commitment. Membership in an ascriptive group to which one has been brought up to feel a deep loyalty since one's earliest infancy is scarcely a matter of choice. And when it comes to race, ethnicity, caste, and class, choice is not obvious. Whereas obligation is rule driven, loyalty is motivated by the entire personality of an agent. Political loyalty is evoked by nations, classes, castes, ethnic groups, and parties, and by the doctrines, causes, ideologies, or faiths that form and identify such associations. And no one in our horrible century can be unaware of the passion that is invested in such attachments. Whether it is chosen or not, loyalty is generated by a great deal more of our personality than calculation or moral reasoning. It is all of one that tends to be loyal. That may account for the endurance of some political loyalties. Loyalty also demands a great deal more from us than just not breaking the law. It requires positive demonstrations of commitment to, and of being at one with, the other members of the association with which we are identified.

What happens to the obligations and loyalties of political exiles? Let me begin with ancient Athens and republican Rome. We know virtually nothing about unimportant exiles in antiquity, but thanks to the historians, and especially Plutarch, we do have a great deal of information, and not only about what happened to the great men in exile; we also can figure out how their conduct was judged. How did exiles who had been political leaders of an ancient republic respond to the demands of both loyalty and obligation? How were they judged and what norms were applied to them? To the extent that they were not being punished but suffered the sting of defeat, they might be expected to seek revenge or conspire to be recalled, or they might loyally refrain from any action at all. They might express an obligation to bring a better form of government back to their city, or they might feel bound by the decisions of their fellow citizens. All of these courses of action were, in fact, pursued, but the theory of obligation that I want to illuminate does not depend on these choices but on a far more public and far less personal point of view. The great question is whether the exile does anything to promote civil war. There is one clear criterion for judging his conduct. To the extent that he can be said to have any obligations, it is to avoid civil war. This is not a common view, but it is one that both Thucydides and Aristotle defended and which still leaves traces in the stories of that great chronicler of noble exiles, Plutarch. It can be recognized clearly in his stories, because it has been joined by a very different, stoic ethos, which looked only to the personal fortitude that the exile displayed in mastering his misfortunes.

It is remarkable how many of the great men of antiquity were sent into exile. Most of Plutarch's subjects spent some time in exile, so it is not at all surprising that he wrote an essay on banishment, and that this was a favorite topic of stoic philosophy at that time. How were these notable exiles supposed to behave? What were their duties? How, if at all, did their obligations and loyalties affect them? One thing is constant: Their conduct was not a matter of indifference; it was much discussed by the historians and moralists from Herodotus to Plutarch, and even by commentators as late as the second century A.D., who fabricated a set of letters by Themistocles, which were not exposed as forgeries until the seventeenth century, when Bentley took a critical look at them.

That letters should be attributed to Themistocles is not surprising.

He was the most interesting and the most frequently discussed of the great classical exiles. Cicero still deeply identified with him as an exile. Themistocles was ostracized and then accused of treason in absentia. Whether he was actually tried is not clear, but he had every reason to remain out of Athens for the rest of his life. Ostracism was a peculiarly democratic practice. It was originally designed to remove potential tyrants and their cohorts from the city, but it eventually became a football in the factional and personal rivalries that agitated democratic Athens in the fifth century. In case anyone has forgotten, the assembly would decide every year whether to have an ostracism at all. If a majority was for it, the agora would presently be fenced off, and under the supervision of civil and religious authorities, the citizens would scratch the name of the man they wanted ostracized on a piece of pottery. There had to be a quorum of six thousand votes in all, and whoever got the most votes was exiled, for ten, then five years. He could be recalled by a vote of the assembly. There was nothing spontaneous about it. Rivals handed out pottery pieces with names on them to the citizens. Ostracism was said not to be a punishment for a specific crime, and in principle it was not a disgrace, but that is, it seems to me, a superficial judgment. Political defeat and the infighting that preceded it were bruising experiences, and the evicted loser was not likely to regard his fate calmly.

It has been said that envy and resentment were the driving forces behind ostracism. One citizen said that he voted to ostracize Themistocles' rival Aristides because he was fed up with hearing him called "the just." And Themistocles was apparently an inveterate boaster. The rivalry between him and Aristides was such that the latter said that either one of them would have to leave Athens or they would both be hurled to their death. In the event, Themistocles got Aristides ostracized. Not long after that it was his turn, in spite of his immense services to the city in the Persian war. Many Greek cities were perfectly ready to receive a man like Themistocles as an honored guest; he was no refugee. However, when a charge of treason was brought against him on the basis of Spartan intelligence by the pro-Spartan party in Athens, it became impossible for him to remain in Greece, and he eventually simply went over to offer his service to the king of Persia, to Athens's greatest enemy, against whom he had fought all his life.

Themistocles was not only the most remarkable of the exiled statesmen, he was also the most controversial. Herodotus had a poor opinion of his character and hinted darkly that he might have tried to ingratiate himself with the Persians all along, while Xenophon speaks only of his unusual political talents. The account that is theoretically significant is that of Thucydides, because he completely approved of Themistocles' conduct during his exile. After briefly mentioning Themistocles' enormous services to Athens, first in defeating the Persians and then in outwitting the Spartans and fortifying the city, Thucydides went into considerable detail about what happened to him after he was ostracized. Thucydides clearly was not very impressed by the accusation of treason. The Spartans claimed that Themistocles had been an accomplice of their king, Pausanias, who certainly was a traitor. Their story was naturally taken up by their allies in Athens who were also Themistocles' political opponents. The Spartans were particularly eager to see Themistocles stand trial. Themistocles knew what to expect, and thanks to his ingenuity, was able to offer his services to the Persians. He learned the language, dressed in the Persian manner, and was much favored by the king, whom he promised that he would conquer Hellas for him. He died of an illness before he could do so. Thucydides mentions, without comment, that some people thought that he had committed suicide because he was unable to keep his promise to the king.

Themistocles seems to have felt no lingering loyalty to Athens and certainly no sense of obligation. If he had he might have continued to meddle in its politics to stir up popular feeling on his own behalf, claiming that his return was in the best interest of the city, a not implausible notion given his talents. Not even the writers who disapproved of him, however, accused him of fomenting civil strife. And if, like Thucydides, one knows that civilization is on very thin ice and that nothing is more horrible than civil war, because murderous rage is always close to the political surface, then loyalty and obligation will seem far less significant than adaptability, moderation, and prudence. Themistocles had a strong sense of his own achievements, and Thucydides appreciated his qualities as a statesman no less. "Themistocles," he wrote, "was a man who showed unmistakable natural genius; in this respect he was quite exceptional, and beyond all others deserves our admiration . . . this man was supreme at doing the right thing at the right time." There is nothing like this sort of praise on any other page of *The Peloponnesian War*. Themistocles clearly was a phenomenally successful survivor, and one might simply say that as a man aware of his own greatness, he was a law unto himself. But that is not what Thucydides says about him. He says that the man was a political genius, perhaps the greatest to emerge in democratic Athens. He did well in Athens, and then he did well in Persia.

Significantly, Plutarch, who was rather less of an admirer, also noted that what "most redounded to his credit was that he put an end to all the civil wars of Greece, composed their differences, and persuaded them to lay aside all enmity during the war with the Persians." It was indeed Plutarch's view that their incessant internal and mutual petty wars had undone the Greek cities, so that Roman domination was no more than they deserved and was indeed what they needed. As for ostracism, he did not think much of it. The people, in exiling men like Themistocles, "by fixing this disgrace upon them, might vent some of their rancor." He was not alone in mentioning envy as a motive for the practice. Nor did Plutarch credit the story of Themistocles' involvement with Pausanias. There are, however, two very significant differences between his view of Themistocles and Thucydides' unequivocal admiration. Plutarch thought that Themistocles was greedy and had enriched himself at the expense of the Athenian treasury. Moreover, he was inclined to believe that Themistocles had committed suicide by drinking bull's blood in order to avoid having to keep his promise to the king of Persia. Plutarch offered two possible explanations for his suicide. Themistocles might have been afraid that the Athenian general Cimon might defeat him. Alternatively, there was a popular story that claimed that Themistocles was at the last moment overcome by loyalty to Hellas and unwilling to lead a Persian army against his own people. The tale also comes up in the forged letters, in which Themistocles, overcome by loyalty to Hellas, refuses to attack his erstwhile country. It is not really a probable notion. Themistocles was sixty-five years old by then, too old to lead a military expedition in any case.

I am not here concerned with the historical facts of the case or the speculations that it has attracted. I only want to illuminate the difference in the ways that exiles are judged in comparing Thucydides' and Plutarch's views of Themistocles. For Plutarch his loyalty was a big issue, and he approved of a heroic suicide, a noble gesture in Roman times and a suitable personal act for a great man. Plutarch generally professes a personalizing morality that is quite unlike Thucydides' and Aristotle's wholly political ethics. He is not indifferent to Themistocles' public achievements, but he cannot ignore his personal character in judging him, especially his loyalty and personal probity. Considering all that Themistocles had done for Athens, did it matter that, being poor, he helped himself to some of the public funds? Petty peculation does not incite civil war. On the contrary, a few greased palms can avoid much mischief.

Plutarch was also deeply impressed by the righteousness of Themistocles' rival, the just Aristides, who simply accepted his ostracism
obediently. But was it quite that simple? Aristides the "just," who
was ostracized at the instigation of his rival Themistocles, also seems
to have waited it out. He was recalled when Xerxes began to march
through Attica, because it was feared that as an exile he might collab-
orate with the enemy. The Athenian demos had at any rate a very
realistic appreciation of the probable loyalties of its exiled great men.
Aristides did not defect, in fact, and he even urged his followers to
join Themistocles. On his return, he also cooperated with his erstwhile enemy but stalled some of the latter's more amoral foreign and
defense policies. In order to meet his high sense of his obligations,
Aristides had no political friends and never showed any favoritism
to his personal friends. This particularly impressed Plutarch, since
this was the sort of aloofness that Roman stoicism particularly
stresses. But this ostentatious justice, which his fellow citizens had
resented, also did not impress Thucydides, who mentions this paragon only in passing. And although Plutarch goes on at length about
his poverty and civic devotion, his Aristides cannot boast of Themistocles' achievements. He simply was not a spectacular politician such
as Themistocles or Pericles. And he was of no particular psychological interest, unlike Themistocles, Coriolanus, and Alcibiades, even in
Plutarch's version, not to mention Shakespeare's. Thucydides mentions neither his services nor his ostracism.

No one ever claimed that Alcibiades had a flawless character, but
from the point of view of Xenophon and Thucydides, his refusal to
stir up civil strife in Athens itself did much to redeem him. Neither
Xenophon nor Thucydides was in the least bothered by his services
to Sparta, where, being as adaptable as Themistocles, he lived like a
Spartan, black soup and all, which cannot have been easy for him.
According to Thucydides, he no longer felt any loyalty to the actual
Athens, but he still longed to return to his home. This tension is
very typical of exiles, and Alcibiades talked of himself very self-
consciously as an exile. He offered his services to the Spartans because his old city was dead, and he was attacking it because it had
treated him unjustly. Nevertheless, he claimed that he loved it enough
to want to return, but he intended to do so with a Spartan army. He
was an exile because of the villainy of those who drove him out and
said that "the Athens I love is not the one that is wronging me now
. . . I am trying to recover a country that has never ceased to be mine."
Alcibiades was a man without a country, and what drew him back

was a memory, neither the present nor the future Athens. He had no real place in either, as he was to discover even after his brief recall. He was not as self-sufficient as Themistocles had been and was more prone to self-deception about his uncertain loyalties.

What seemed praiseworthy to Thucydides was not Alcibiades' self-serving and eccentric declaration of loyalty but his refusal to do anything at the cost of initiating a civil war. Thucydides mentioned this twice and it was also commended by Xenophon, who claimed that at least some people believed that Alcibiades would never do anything to bring on a civil war or violent change. Typically, however, it was his lingering loyalty to Athens that impressed Plutarch most, for Alcibiades had in the end not marched against his own people. Even when in overt imitation of Themistocles he went over to the Persians, he announced at once that he would not fight against his own people. Plutarch had attributed every human vice to Alcibiades, but his political stance as an exile counted heavily in his favor. He was in the end a better man than the austere Coriolanus, who was loyal only to his mother and whose arrogance also precipitated a popular uprising. In sum, an exile is now required to demonstrate his political virtue by not flirting with treason and by neither joining an enemy power nor conspiring to overthrow the regime of his city.

Judgment of exile politics generally depends to some degree on the reasons for the original expulsion. Alcibiades had in fact not been ostracized but had been charged in absentia with acts of impiety which neither Thucydides nor Plutarch, nor Aristophanes for that matter, took seriously. He was exiled for failing to show up at his trial. Nevertheless, his exile was not unlike an ostracism, since it was the result of the same kinds of factional and personal political animosities that had led to the ostracism of Aristides, Themistocles, and Cimon previously. Thucydides does not tell us whether he approved of ostracism as a policy, but he certainly was heartily in favor of the last of the ostracisms, that of Hyperbolus, whom he regarded as a scoundrel and a disgrace to Athens. Hyperbolus was evidently not exiled because he was a great man and potential tyrant. Plutarch thought that Alcibiades and Nicias had ganged up on him. Again looking at it wholly morally, he found ostracism a distasteful act, which at best was a way of avoiding greater injustices. It "was speciously used to be the mere depression and humiliation of excessive greatness and power; and was in fact a gentle relief and mitigation of envious feeling which was allowed to vent itself in infliction of no intolerable injury." In contrast, the most scientific and least moralis-

tic view is Aristotle's, and it is very close to that of Thucydides. Ostracism was not absolutely just, but it was prudent and could well serve
the public good.

In his *Constitution of Athens*, Aristotle offers us a simple historical
account of how and why ostracism was instituted in Athens, and how
it worked. But in the *Politics* he presents the most subtle of all analy-
ses of the whole difficulty the truly great man poses in any normal
political system. The discussion in the *Constitution* is not without
interest, because it distinguishes ostracism from other forms of exile,
for homicide, for example, or as part of the reign of terror by the
Thirty. And it brings out with great clarity why Athenian democracy
needed ostracism. But in the *Politics* he goes to the heart of the matter. If there is a man so superior to the rest of the citizens as to be
incommensurable with them, then he cannot be regarded as a member of the city. He would be like a god among men, and there could
be no law for him. No legislation would apply to him. Just as the
Argonauts were supposed to have left Heracles behind because he
exceeded all the other sailors, so democracies must practice ostracism
to maintain their laws. Otherwise they could not survive. Their self-
preservation is not to be confused with the practices of tyrannies and
oligarchies, which also cut down great men. For in its original intention, ostracism was a rational, just, and necessary means for the protection of a reasonable regime and for the good of the city. When it
became an instrument of factional infighting, it ceased to be just, as
it had originally been. In deviant regimes the exiling of preeminent
citizens is just in the sense that it is in keeping with the prevailing
values, but it is clearly not just in itself. The threat of greatness disap-
pears only in the best regime, where men would recognize true greatness and voluntarily accept the rule of a genuinely great man, thus
combining freedom with one-man rule. The idea of the perfect regime
is meant, however, to highlight the problems of actual cities, which
are far from perfect. Their chief problem is to avoid revolution and
civic violence, and to that end ostracism is both prudent and just. It
stabilizes cities, moderates factional conflict, and is as such beneficial
for the city as a whole. In a tyranny the exiling of distinguished men
serves only the personal interest of the ruler, but that is not the case
in less deviant regimes. Ostracism is, in short, as good as the political
system that it sustains.

Neither Thucydides nor Aristotle had any notion of a state or of
a legal system apart from the government in power at any given moment. Every regime has its own balance of power between the few
and the many. Each has its own ideology and notion of justice, and

this will determine who will be exiled. Ordinary cities cannot afford gods or beasts who fall outside the norm of human powers. In practice the priority of the city over the individual citizen certainly serves to justify exiling anyone, however superior he might personally be, if exiling him serves to maintain existing civic order. It is to be expected that oligarchs are not likely to be as loyal as the people. Their pursuit of personal preeminence makes them inherently uncooperative and insubordinate, and the mixture of an edgy people and insolent aristocrats is not a stable one. It is one that makes political exile a necessary policy if civil strife is to be avoided. And though he does not spell it out, Aristotle makes it abundantly clear that treason is an aristocratic crime. We know that it was punished severely.

In the *Politics,* Aristotle has almost nothing to say about punishment in general and about exile as a penalty for ordinary crimes in particular. Nothing sets him apart from Plato more evidently than this fastidiousness. In contrast, the death penalty and exile for polluting crimes hover over Plato's *Laws.* If one reads the *Laws* as a work of political science, as a detailed model of a truly traditional society, then the importance of pollution in determining penalties, especially exile, is perfectly coherent, especially if punishment is not a moral cure so much as a cleansing. Pollution has been of particular interest to contemporary scholars, not only because we are all so deeply and rightly conscious of the irrationality of all politics but because our own age has seen such a revolting revival of ideologies of pollution. I refer here to Nazi racial genetics and its variants in less extreme forms to explain why pollution seems so familiar to us. It is no great surprise, therefore, that Jean Pierre Vernant should have suggested that the ostracized citizens of Athens were, among other things, scapegoats, chosen to lift the miasma that might afflict the city as a whole. Politics might determine who was chosen, but not the full purpose of the exile. So the ostracized men were religious as well as political exiles, and their exile averted both political and religious dangers.

Plausible as this sounds to us, whom experience has taught to look for the deepest irrationalities, it must be said that there is little textual reason to accept this notion, though there is every reason to believe that the average Athenian was a lot more religious than the philosophers and historians. Why should we doubt that many citizens were genuinely convinced and disturbed by the charge of impiety brought against Socrates?

Socrates was in no danger of ostracism, but he refused exile twice, first as a punishment at his trial and then as a way to escape the death penalty. His refusal to leave was based on arguments of both obligation and loyalty to Athens, but he did not pretend that he was anything but an exception. Not only was he following a unique inner voice, he was committed first and foremost to preserving philosophy as an intellectual vocation and his own conduct as a heroic philosopher against any imputation of immorality. This does not mean that he did not acknowledge the inherently subversive character of his conduct as a gadfly. Thus, although Socrates fully accepted both his contractual obligation and his familial loyalty to Athens, he did not pretend to be an ordinary citizen. It was therefore possible for Roman stoics to picture him as a citizen of the world and a model of apolitical virtue. They convinced themselves that as a philosopher he was a spiritual exile, unburdened by political ties, which is not at all what Socrates actually said.

Stoicism was certainly important in the responses to exile, especially from Rome, of both Cicero and Plutarch. There is no explicit parallel in Roman life to the exile of Themistocles, but Camillus serves that purpose just as well. Camillus, who was as great a military hero as any Roman, alienated the people by ostentation and failure to distribute the booty properly among the soldiers. He also went into exile before being condemned for having misappropriated the spoils of war, but he just went abroad until he was called back to lead an army against the invading Gauls. Moreover, he did nothing at all until the legal procedures for such a recall were completed. He then saved the city and served it well until he died of old age. This paragon is meant to illustrate how a noble exile should behave. And it was what the Romans expected of each other. Tensions between the people and the patricians might be intense, but it was utterly unacceptable to join the enemies of the people. That accounts for the strictures that Plutarch and Cicero heaped upon Coriolanus.

Camillus had not been ostracized, because the Roman Republic did not practice it, but he was also exiled legally. Polybius approvingly mentions that a Roman accused of a capital crime who found out that he was sure to be condemned by all the tribes voting in the popular assembly had a right to go into permanent exile before the sentence was pronounced. Given that Polybius mentions this right as part of the way in which the democratic part of the Roman constitution contributed to the stability of the whole, one may assume that it was a way in which patricians could evade prosecution by the plebs. Gibbon speaks of the usage as a form of "civil death." But then he, like Cicero before him, looked at exile entirely from the point of view of the individual citizen who might be exposed to it, whereas Polybius, like his model Thucydides, was interested only in the inner stability of the Roman state, which accounted for its superiority to the faction-ridden Greek cities.

If Camillus lived up to his obligations by staying far from Rome in inactive exile, Coriolanus exhibited every form of conduct that a noble Roman was supposed to avoid. Although he was a great military hero, he squandered his popularity by a fanatical contempt for the people. Not only did he do everything to arouse the many, he also gathered a group of devoted young aristocrats around him. Clearly they were headed for civil violence. When Coriolanus was finally indicted for attempting usurpation and was to be tried by a popular court, he fled and went right over to Rome's sworn enemies, the Volscians. Politically no man deserved more blame, and Plutarch did not spare him. Injustice, imprudence, and fomenting civil war and treason, however, were not the sum of Coriolanus's political sins. He had wholly unacceptable loyalties. All aristocrats tend to be more loyal to their ancestral house and to their caste than to the city, but Coriolanus went beyond that. His father had died when he was young and he was utterly devoted to his mother, continuing to live in her house even after his marriage. When it became clear that the Volscians under his leadership would conquer Rome, Coriolanus was deaf to the appeals of Rome's leaders. But when his mother came to plead with him, he broke down and followed her wishes, at which point the Volscians killed him. What outraged Plutarch was the total reversal of personal and public loyalties. To betray one's city was bad enough, but to return to it in response to personal love, with no public concern, was revolting. Unjust, reckless, and unbalanced was the least he could say of Coriolanus. We might recall that many centuries later, Hobbes pointed to Coriolanus's devotion to his mother to illustrate the inscrutability of human motivation.

Plutarch set a very different standard for exiles than Thucydides had. He expected them to remain loyal to Rome. That also was Cicero's view. But by then exile had become a subject of philosophical reflection, not merely a political practice. Cicero is my last example, not least because he had time in his retirement to reflect upon exile. Cicero's exile followed a threat of impeachment for instigating illegal executions, and he left without a trial. But after he was gone he was outlawed, as was usual in such cases. He could settle in no city within five hundred miles of Rome, and so had to go to Greece. He suffered no hardship, but was utterly desolate, writing frantic letters, bemoaning his own mistakes and the treachery of many of his fellow citizens. When he was finally recalled, he gave a long speech to explain that he had in fact never been exiled at all. He said that exile as a punishment did not exist in Roman law, and that his impeachment and outlawing had both been grossly illegal and as such null and void. Indeed, he now claimed that he had left voluntarily in order to prevent civil strife in the city. It was again an exile's desperate act of denial. Cicero could not bear the thought of so extreme a political defeat. Rome was dead, the Republic gone, when he was forced to flee. Not he but Rome was gone. Alcibiades had said much the same thing about Athens. It absolved both of them of their obligations to the state that had exiled them but to which they longed to return. Cicero was in no position to commit treason, nor would he have done so. He held Coriolanus in contempt. He was, to be sure, unjustly exiled, a victim of the savage politics of the last years of the decaying Republic. Nevertheless, his actual conduct fell so short of the standards he had set himself that he earned Plutarch's contempt. Comparing him to Demosthenes, who had been exiled for taking bribes and was not as blameless as Cicero, Plutarch nevertheless thought that the Greek orator had behaved better in exile. He had gone up and down warning the Greeks against the Macedonians, in this way proving himself a better citizen than Themistocles and Alcibiades had been in similar fortune. That was not how Cicero saw himself. He would not die in exile like Themistocles, he wrote. Themistocles, in fact, lacked foresight, for he did not see how to avoid the hatred of the Spartans and of his fellow citizens. But a similar fate had befallen Scipio. It was Cicero's hope that Caesar would be exiled in time as well. As he looked back on his own exile, he remembered only that it had done much to restore his reputation and strengthen his moral fiber.

In his exile Cicero may in fact have temporarily ceased to be a Roman citizen, but he certainly denied this notion. It really did not matter, as he knew. His political career was over even when he returned to Rome, and so he turned to philosophy. As a philosopher he agreed with Plutarch that exile was an affliction that a wise man should be able to endure readily. This was why Plutarch found Cicero's letters from exile so deplorable. In some ways Cicero's avowed turn to an Epicurean notion that it does not matter where one leads a pleasant life rings hollow. It comes after a grim account of exile as no disgrace for a wise man, one who never courted popularity in any case. Like torture, childlessness, deafness, blindness, and poverty, exile is something a wise man can easily bear. This does not make as much sense as Cicero's more plausible claim that philosophers have always been travelers and that they can pursue wisdom anywhere, relieved of burdensome political duties. This essay is so self-deceiving that in its way it reveals more about the enduring wounds of exile than about the healing powers of philosophy.

Cicero was of course right to note that intellectuals are footloose. Plutarch was himself an itinerant lecturer, and his experience of exile was that of a voluntary emigrant, not of a persecuted politician. Plutarch therefore notes that although exile is an irreparable loss for some people, others rejoice in doing better in a new country. Themistocles is particularly singled out for praise for starting out all over again and doing so well in Persia, thus "losing none of his renown." Exile is no disgrace at all, and for intellectuals it has advantages. One can do mathematics anywhere in the world, and not being a citizen relieves one of all cumbersome political duties. Unjustly exiled people, like Cicero, will not be demeaned by banishment, for only fools think that such an exile is an ignominious thing. And then comes the punch line, and it is new. The soul is in eternal pilgrimage in any case. We are at the end of politics.

Curiously enough, Plutarch thought that he had learned his cosmopolitanism from Socrates. He cannot have read the *Apology* or the *Crito* very carefully, because all the arguments for why death should be chosen over exile can be found there. Cicero thought he should have committed suicide too, but he did not, and in any case it was a matter of tradition. The reasons for Socrates' choice were both personal and public. The personal indignity of exile, especially for a man of his age and vocation, is such as to make it impossible to be a noble exile. Decent people would shun him abroad, and he would have to flee to Thessaly, which sounds like a sort of Las Vegas. Not a way for a serious philosopher, a lover of truth, to spend his last years. But above all, both loyalty and obligation to Athens itself made exile impossible. Neither family nor friends could compete with the primacy of these. And there were two distinct arguments. One was contractual: he had made an implicit promise to obey the laws rather than save his life, and he owed the city all the loyalty one is expected to feel for one's parents. Both require obedience, but the considerations are different. There were, to be sure, conflicting loyalties here, to his own children and friends, but he made his choice and it was against exile.

All the other great men I have discussed chose exile over death. Do they stand condemned by Socrates, or was he so unique in his self-proclaimed ignorant wisdom as to be no model for other men? He was not a great statesman, after all. It is an open question. In any case, he rejected exile as a legal punishment and then as an illegal way of saving his life, and the same arguments, personal and public, would hold in either case. To leave Athens was to fail his country, and it clearly had a reality for him apart from the current regime. On the other side of the question stands Themistocles as Thucydides and Plutarch saw him and the problem of the great man in politics as Aristotle presented it. There is nothing disgraceful in being superior, and it does make the great man a law unto himself. He has every reason to rise above political defeat and the envy of lesser men and to put his talents to work wherever he can find an outlet for them. Intellectuals have, in fact, always acted on this assumption, even when they are not as spectacularly intelligent as Themistocles. In either case, one may have an obligation to obey the laws wherever one is and to be loyal to those who have benefited one personally, like the king of Persia or any other patron or benefactor. Gratitude is surely more like loyalty than obligation. We ought to feel it, as Socrates did for Athens. The Spartans were right not to trust Alcibiades. Unlike Themistocles, he did start all over again. So did Coriolanus. Alcibiades' heart had remained in Athens, and Coriolanus's loyalty was fastened upon his mother, not Rome or any other country.

This way of looking at exile is, of course, profoundly personal. Socrates, Cicero, and Plutarch, at least in his essay "On Banishment," look only at the individual exile, the great man ejected from his position and his city. How should he behave? seems the most relevant question. But is it? Could we not argue as Thucydides and Aristotle did, and even Plutarch occasionally, and consider only the public implications of exile? Is it prudent to exile great men? What is in the interest of the city as a whole and how is civil war to be averted? If the exile prevents internal strife, then it is for the best. And the way to judge the conduct of the exile is objective: does he or does he not stir up domestic trouble? Themistocles did not; neither did Aristides and Cimon. Alcibiades may or may not have done so, and Coriolanus had no other end in mind. Whatever their personal virtues, loyalties, and public obligations were, that is all that matters. From that point of view, loyalty becomes a rather questionable political virtue, if it be one at all.

PART TWO

Learning about Thought

CHAPTER FIVE

Squaring the Hermeneutic Circle

Professional trend watchers cannot have failed to notice the appearance of a novel interpretive social science, and much must already have been written to introduce this literature to the public. There is bound to be more, but it is not my intention here to contribute to that enterprise. I do not propose to analyze or explain the emergence or progress of this intellectual development, nor to predict its future course. This essay is concerned first with the implications of an image that invariably turns up in the writings of the new interpreters, "the hermeneutic circle." It will then go on to ask what, if anything, this notion contributes to our sociological understanding, and specifically what place it might have in a comprehensive theory of the "sciences of man," a phrase that most usually refers to anthropology, history, sociology, and political science in their less formal and mathematical aspects. I shall try to do this in the most simple and everyday language, because, in spite of appearances, the issues at stake do not call for, and have not evoked, the kind of precision that alone can justify a resort to a specialized vocabulary. At first sight, my qualifications for this undertaking must seem poor at best. I am not, after all, either a philosopher of science or a practicing social scientist. I do, however, have a fair amount of experience in interpreting the classics of political theory, and hermeneutics, whatever else it may mean, is first and foremost a way of reading scriptures.

Interpretation and Explanation

Hermes carried the messages of the gods, and hermeneutics is the art of reading them. The circle with a message, the hermeneutic circle,

This chapter is reprinted with permission from *Social Research* 53, no. 3 (Autumn 1986): 449–73.

was a Neo-Platonic image designed to intimate the relation of an infinite, eternal, and omnipresent God to his creation, and it makes its most significant appearance in the late Middle Ages, never to leave our imaginative literature thereafter. God is a sphere whose center is everywhere and whose circumference is nowhere. He is entirely in every part of this circle. Dante speaks of the poet's soul moving toward God, who is the center and circumference of all. The human soul is like trembling water in a round vessel. In keeping with Neo-Platonic cosmology, God is an overflowing source of energy of both love and knowledge who recreates himself in ever-diminishing reproductions. This is the great chain of being, which is formed by concentric circles in a descending order of microcosms, each a replica of the macrocosm. It is thus that the human soul is a miniature of the divine center.

This lovely vision has undergone a vast number of transformations, without ever quite losing its original character. Post-Cartesian psychology used the circle to represent the passions of the soul which from our center animates the body and maintains all the parts of the human organism in harmony. The poetry of the circle stretches all the way from the metaphysical poets of the seventeenth century to Rilke. And the most psychological of novelists have resorted to it. Flaubert thought of memory, especially at its most treacherous and illusory, as the center of the emotional circle. Henry James in turn spoke of our groping efforts to reach a shifting world of other people in its terms. These are but a few examples of the uses of the circle, and many more can be found in Georges Poulet's excellent *Les métamorphoses du cercle*.[1] It does not, however, answer the question of what the circle is meant to do in the sciences of man today. It was transferred to this new intellectual territory by way of Protestant theology, which was from the first under considerable pressure to find an interpretation of the Bible that was independent of tradition. Protestants therefore built a system of biblical interpretation in which the circle has an obvious place. Every part of the divine scripture is related to every other and to the whole, as in a circle, of which the author, God, may be found.

This is how the hermeneutic circle came to Germany and was eventually adapted by Schleiermacher in his theological writings. Human faith, rather than a traditional deity, stood at the center, and the project was to encompass every form of knowledge within a single whole in a system by reference to that center. Schleiermacher's biographer, Dilthey, picked up the phrase from him and even wrote an essay on the history of hermeneutics. The current popularity of the hermeneutic circle may be traced to Dilthey, whose name is in fact routinely invoked by interpretive social scientists. This practice is also due to his claim that the methods of the natural sciences and those of literary and social studies were inherently different. There is, however, no evidence that his works are much read, and Gadamer has shown very convincingly that Dilthey's writings really have no direct bearing on contemporary hermeneutics.[2]

That does, however, leave the meaning and function of the circle rather up in the air. One would expect a group of theorists who claim to have made the interpretation of symbols their main business to show some interest in their own imagery, but that is not the case. As far as an outsider can judge, the hermeneutic circle is meant to signify the activities of interpreters whether they offer an addition to or a replacement for other ways of understanding the history of mankind. Interpretation is said characteristically to be the study of wholes in terms of their constituent parts, which are already identified by their places within that whole. It is a movement back and forth. Why there must be a center to this operational field is not clear. Is there only an interpreter at the center of his spiderweb, or is there an organizing and illuminating principle apart from him there at the core to be discovered? Nor is the circumference of the whole defined. The hermeneutic circle makes sense only if there is a known closed whole, which can be understood in terms of its own parts and which has as its core God, who is its anchor and creator. Only the Bible really meets these conditions. It is the only possibly wholly self-sufficient text.

Given these obvious, indeed self-evident, confusions created by the image of the circle, why do interpretive social theorists cling to it, as if it were some sort of talisman? It is, at best, an identity badge worn to mark them off from "mainstream" social science, from an abhorrent "positivism," and from those who wish to adapt the methods of the natural sciences to the study of social phenomena and who do not believe that scientific inquiry constitutes an ethical disaster. The interpretivist response to the proposition that explanations in the social and natural sciences are at least similar ranges from claims that this is impossible or, worse, misguided, to a more moderate suggestion that it is insufficient. The impossibility argument rests on the peculiar assumption that unique events in the past cannot be explained in the same way as recurrent ones, and that in any case we are psychologically incapable of understanding anything beyond our own tradition. The accusation of mischief points to the failure or inability of the social sciences to rise above "brute fact" (they are always "brute," never "simple") and to deal with the "big questions," such as the malaise of "Western Man" and the predicaments of "Twentieth Century Man," marked by identity crises, despair, and cultural disintegration. The readers of "mainstream" political science, moreover, are being dangerously misled, to the point where it becomes impossible for them to understand their world or to react properly to its disruptive tendencies. A hermeneutic social understanding would, one must assume, replace and improve upon these defective current practices of social science.

This is not, to be sure, the only case for interpretive thinking. Far more persuasively, there are variations on Weber's theme of "understanding" and the belief that something more than explanations of social conduct is required for a full social science. We want to understand what the groups we are looking at make of their own activities, and to relate their views to our own and others' ways of thinking about the same subjects. The question here is, what is this extra step like? Emotional empathy has to be dismissed as too rare and too unreliable, but is its replacement, the analogy of reading a text, an improvement? In what respects, if any, is finding out about the natives' moral ideas by listening to their conversations and looking at their art or at their games and rituals like reading a book? The metaphor may save the circle, but at the cost of all verisimilitude. It is certainly not implausible to say that an anthropologist is writing the natives' story by matching what he finds out about their perceptions of their lives, and about their beliefs, against what he already knows of their history and institutions, and about these phenomena in general. It is he, however, who is the author, and it is he who walks the path back and forth between the knowledge he brings to the natives and what he gains from listening to them and their signals, as well as from translating their figurative language into his own. The two are brought together by him and he can, if he wishes, think of his narrative labors as pacing back and forth, but it is on a straight line, not a circle. There is no center, and above all there is no mystery in what he is up to.

There are indeed tremendous obstacles in figuring out what alien signs are meant to indicate; we have enough trouble understanding what is said to us by familiar people. To call every type of communication "reading" can only add to our confusion. It is by recognizing differences, and sorting out what we are told, that we can make sense of it. To treat critical reading of texts and rendering alien attitudes intelligible as similar operations is not likely to help us. There is, also, no reason to believe that making limited knowledge intelligible is a new form of comprehension. Historians have always done that. It ought indeed to be remembered that they have always concerned themselves with the "natives' " views.[3] It has been a familiar though difficult art known to all readers of Jakob Burckhardt's *Renaissance in Italy*. To be sure, such interpretations, whether more or less complete, are dependent on prior explanations, and are not prescribed as substitutes for it.

There are, as I said, those who would substitute interpretations for explanations. One way of doing this in historical studies is to simply assume that historians *must* be concerned with the recovery of a tradition (the "a" is important; there is only one), which is a legacy left to us by our forefathers.[4] We can as scholars, if we develop the proper habits and affinities, though to be sure each one in a different way, relate our contemporary conceptions to that tradition and be altered by it in the process. The purpose of this movement would be to strive for truth, presumably, but how is it to be found at the center of a circle? The tradition must be the rim, the historians the parts, and by an act of free faith they must have the hope for an irradiating truth at the core.

This version of the hermeneutic circle is explicitly modeled on Aristotle's *Ethics*, where we are especially warned not to expect more certainty than the subject can offer. The reader is expected to bring to philosophy the habits of ethical living in a society. Otherwise, he could neither understand nor profit from an account of the rational ends that customs ought to serve. The aim of ethics is the pursuit of science for the few, and a life of just and virtuous political activity, ruling and being ruled, for the rest of the male citizens. There is no effort to pin down exactly what a natural justice would be. Like the center of the circle it is to be sought and taught, as it is interpreted in varying circumstances. This means, among other things, that just as a citizen can live a happy life of virtue only in his own city, so the historian can have an affinity for only his own tradition.

The question is clearly what is meant by tradition here. Can Gadamer himself understand Aristotle? How is ethnography possible? How could Halévy get the English right? How can Bullock do Hitler? Is the tradition all that timeless and unsituated? If it is not a social tradition, what is it? If it is the tradition of an ongoing discipline, such as social history, then why is interpretation in a privileged position among all the other approaches to the study of society? And finally, why would anyone choose to enlist Aristotle in an argument against explanation in social science? What greater attention could anyone pay to effective causality, to the "why" of political formations, than the author of the *Politics*? Consider only the explanation for the brittleness of oligarchies, which certainly amounts to a law of political science.[5] It may well be that those who appeal to Aristotle in defense of a hermeneutical social science may be profoundly unfair to him. The art of taking apart wholes, such as cities, and then putting them together again, involved for him the most careful causal explanations, especially of the two most important members and their moral psychology. There are ample accounts of why democrats and oligarchs act as they normally do in the *Politics*.

Taylor and Ricoeur

The notion of history as the interpretation of a tradition or an ethos has at least one advantage. It tells us what a hermeneutical social study would, more or less, look like. It would limit itself, of necessity, to reading a single body of books that it would choose as constituting a tradition. These would through interpretation be made available to readers here and now. To write the history of past men and events, even with an insistence that each one is utterly unique, would be difficult from this hermeneutic stance, because without a thorough understanding of *why* the forefathers did what they did, the past which they have left for us to "read" cannot be interpreted. Only texts remain "open," always, of course, subject to our present needs and styles. Nevertheless, within its limits, one can see what is being proposed. That is more than can be said of Charles Taylor's effort to provide a hermeneutic alternative to "mainstream" American political science,[6] by which he seems to mean mostly the work of Robert Dahl.

Taylor's objection to political science is that, as long as it tries to model itself on the natural sciences, it will not be able to address itself to such burning issues as the identity crises of contemporary North Americans and Europeans and the endemic divisions that haunt pluralistic societies and make them seedbeds of despair. The absence of fundamental agreement does not trouble the political scientists as it ought. It is not something that can be explained or analyzed by their methods of observation and reliance on mere "brute" facts. What they should attend to is "intersubjective" meanings. No example of how one might discover an "intersubjective" meaning of political practices and beliefs is offered, but one can be sure that facts brutish or otherwise would not come into play.

For the "intersubjective" consciousness which waits to be revealed is not a shared, recognized, or openly common set of meanings. It has to be brought to light by the interpretive social scientist. The assumption is that there is "a substrate" beneath the overt practices and beliefs of those whom a political interpreter might choose to study. It may be a common tradition, religion, or language, but it is more than they can in their present conscious sense of their mutual differences understand. The task of social interpretation is to dispel this imputation of diversity and to show beyond any possible doubt that there is an "intersubjective" meaning that actually does in truth inform the practices of a society, even though none of its agents or social scientists seem to be aware of it. Indeed, it is because its members are blind to the meaning of their own political conduct and allegiances that fact-finders also miss it. People have not internalized the reality of the substrate, because they are caught in an atomizing ideology and misled by a political science that thinks that they mean what they say and do.

If this is reminiscent of the Marxist distinction between objective and subjective truths, and the menace of a "false consciousness," it ought to be remembered that Taylor does not use that vocabulary but the metaphors of the hermeneutic circle. He would have us move back and forth from the substrate to the particular meanings until the latter were seen as parts of a whole. At the center stands presumably the interpreter, in some way in touch with the whole from the first, and as such authoritative. This is not just a matter, for example, of relating the practices of voting in Massachusetts to the whole history of representative government and the ends it has historically meant to achieve. There is more to hermeneutics than that in Taylor's version. We are summoned to uncover the "intersubjective" meaning that voting has for us here and now by some form of consciousness-raising. If in consequence of this undertaking I find myself in disagreement with other interpreters, the difference can be settled by finding out which one of us understands the other and which one does not. How this is to be discovered, much less how the other can be expected to accept such a judgment, is not exactly clear. That there may be no substrate of meaning and that intellectual differences may be at many levels irreconcilable is a possibility not considered, but it would render this hermeneutical project impossible if it were allowed to become evident.

It is not merely that Taylor is confused in proposing that the hermeneutic circle should replace causal explanation in the social sciences, but that he also thinks of interpretation as a way of uncovering submerged mentalities. Consciousness-raising, in short, is to replace the mere effort to make sense of what we can describe. Common sense, the law, and, more recently, "speech act" analysis have never doubted that interpretation has a necessary part in many explanations. What an agent does and says cannot be understood apart from the context within which her conduct occurs. One need only imagine the many meanings of "There's a fire," said under varying circumstances, to realize that the meaning of what is said or done must first be interpreted as part of a "whole," of a scene, to make it possible to understand the intentions of those whose social acts we are observing and then explaining.

This is not, however, what Taylor has in mind at all when he claims that interpretation must replace causal explanation. He does not just want to tell a static story, or to devise tableaux. He means something far less simple or naturalistic. He means, in fact, to dredge up a possible, but not yet existing, state of communal consciousness. It will be recognized in the course of the interpretive labors of the author, for they are at the very center of his circle. That circle is the intersubjective substrate which he has invented and which it is said we should read like a text. It is there and we have to learn to decode its meanings, both for ourselves and for the various members of a society or civilization whose beliefs and practices we share, whether we know it or not. The hidden is to be made manifest, recovered as it were by the interpreter.

How good is the analogy between reading a poem and writing social history? According to Paul Ricoeur, the two are virtually identical, but there is perhaps less to his account than meets the eye.[7] To begin with, one has to accept what he means by reading. For while he appears to offer an analysis of reading in general, he is, in fact, presenting a recipe for how we should read, and does so without any argument in favor of his preferred practice. We are simply told that, first of all, a text, *any text,* is fixed, unalterable, and just obdurately there. In this it is wholly unlike a conversation, which moves in a shared environment. Second, the intentions of the author must be disregarded. They can have no significant bearing on the meaning of the text. The text is also not addressed to any specific audience, but is open to a universal range of readers. Most important of all, a text points only to its own content. It is about something, to be sure, but we cannot determine its implications by looking outside the text itself to either the author or to the context in which it was originally composed, or to subsequent interpretations. These "nonostensive references" are all irrelevant. Instead, we are summoned to feel free to make our own personal world out of the possible worlds presented by the text.

I do not believe that many people would choose to read *Paradise*

Lost in this way, and I know that this is not the way one goes about interpreting the great works of political philosophy. The intentions of the authors are not a matter of indifference to a Marxist, or a Straussian, or an analytical historian of ideas. All would, moreover, pay close attention to certain circumstances external to the composition of the book. Class conflict, or the need to hide certain ideas and to deal prudently with the elites of the time, or the author's place in the republic of letters of his time, are all candidates for interpretive attention. Nothing is more important than the references to specific events and to other authors in the text, since all of the author's references are privileged information and also what we know about him from his contemporaries. All references are seen in his as well as our terms. Finally, relating parts to each other, and then to some idea of the whole work, is not a matter of guessing as Ricoeur claims it is. There are severe, shared rules of common sense and of evidence, and the views of previous interpreters are also to be taken into account. In the end it is, of course, what it may mean to us that provides the motive and purpose for scholarship, but that is obvious and would give us no satisfaction unless we had rational grounds for believing that our reading was at least a plausible version of the author's intention. If we did not think him a greater man than his readers, we would not undertake the labors of interpretation in the first place. The idea of making every reader the true author of the text has a nice anarchic ring to it, but it does not correspond to the experiences of the common or the scholarly reader.

Let us assume, however, for the sake of argument, that Ricoeur's version of reading a text is credible. In what ways does it correspond to research in the social sciences? It must be noted that, although he begins by claiming that the resemblance is complete, he seems to end by withdrawing that proposal. At first it seems, however, that the resemblance between the two is very close. Social acts, the subject matter of social science, are like the sentences of a text: first, because they too are fixed and unalterable. They are essentially like "illocutions," that is, sentences that constitute actions in themselves, like promises or warnings. Once uttered, they are "there," completed givens. Second, social actions are also entirely divorced from the intentions of the agents who have performed them, as texts are independent of their authors' purposes. This is so because we cannot control or even foresee the effects of our actions or "the force" of our "illocutions." Once done, they acquire an existence all their own. The relative unpredictability of ultimate outcomes is here identified with the notion of social action as unrelated to the aims of the agent. The only illustration offered for this proposition is the notion that cultural superstructures are eventually independent of their origins in the substructure of the processes of material production. But how a speculative theory of social change can be regarded as an example of a social action is less than clear. Even more astonishing is the third claim that social acts must be understood apart from their contexts and general historical circumstances, just like texts. This view is particularly odd since every analysis of "illocutionary" acts stresses the conventions and contexts which govern their meaning.[8] For a historian, moreover, it is very difficult to imagine social actions that are seen as neither interactions among people nor as responses to past events and expectations of future ones. Isolated and changeless, they seem to be anything but human conduct. To justify his belief that social acts, like texts, are to be understood apart from any context, Ricoeur makes the bizarre assertion that really "important" social acts have a life apart from their time and place. Since no illustration is offered for this at all, one must assume that what is meant here is that "important" events are memorable and are invoked for a great variety of purposes long after they take place. Why that makes their original context insignificant and disposable for a historian is, to put it simply, incomprehensible. To complete the analogy, finally, we are told that social acts are also open to all interpreters. If that means that there is no difference between a trained historian or an anthropologist and any member of the public, the statement is just not true. Social science is the work of people with quite well-defined intellectual skills. They do not in this respect resemble the readers of novels. So much for the analogy between reading a text and recording social acts.

What are we to make of the claim that this way of looking at social action, divorced from circumstances and processes, will overcome the fissure between interpretation and explanation? When we read a text, we do encapsule sentences in a linguistic whole, so it must follow that social science encloses actions in a social whole. What, one asks, is the social whole in that case? How do we get back and forth between parts and wholes? As Ricoeur sees it, the whole can only be guessed at, and there are no rules for making right or wrong guesses. Happily it is not as random as one might think. There are ways of verifying whether the parts that are supposed to constitute the whole actually fit into it. If too many fail to fit, then the guess must be inadequate and another one attempted. This procedure is said to be a copy of those legal verifications in which extenuating circumstances are used to determine the exact legal character of an action. The object of such procedures in law is to settle the legal definition most applicable to an act, and it is at every step governed by known public rules. The causes of the action are part of its legal status, and there is very little guesswork about the whole that is called a legal system.

What this analogy does achieve, however, is to save the preeminence of the hermeneutic circle. It still stands fast as the movement between social acts and social wholes. The parts are rigid, the whole indeterminate, and sooner or later one can readily impose one's own vision of the whole, a world as it were, on them. It is at this point admitted that causal explanation can play no part at all in this circle. In the end Ricoeur allows that he is not even trying to deal with the problem that Weber presented and that he set out, in some manner, to solve. The one and only example of a social science that he suggests as corresponding to his demands is Lévi-Strauss's reading of myths. That will not do, however, as a model for the analogy of text and social science in general, since myths are texts to begin with. As a philosophy of social science, it must be said that this is either the hope that any act of the imagination involving wholes and parts can pass for social science, or a conventionalism so uncritical and mindless that it cannot perceive that societies are not simply out there as legal systems are when they are frozen to serve the purposes of a purely analytical jurisprudence. A social science without change and context is not imaginable, and Ricoeur's picture of decoding social action is at best a photograph of a pure idea. No history could conceivably be written on this plan, and in this case the hermeneutic circle seems to achieve nothing, not even as a reminder or as a symbol.

There is very little reason to suppose that either Taylor or Ricoeur has any serious understanding of the best works of social science. Readers of the literature that celebrates the hermeneutic circle might therefore be surprised to learn that interpretation is also regarded as an integral part of social understanding by "mainstream" social theorists. It is, to be sure, treated as an addition to, not as a rival of, explanation. Far from being self-celebrating, moreover, social theory can be deeply aware of the complexities and limits of social knowledge, and to a degree that facile analogies to decoding cannot even begin to grasp. Nor is most social theory reductionist as so many hermeneuticists believe. Their complaint is that it is somehow morally diminishing to interpret religious, political, or intellectual conduct in terms of psychological or economic-historical categories of understanding. There is actually nothing obviously demeaning about having a fundamental emotional and economic life, nor are production and personality inferior to politics and religion. If one is, however, inclined to think that reduction does occur in these cases, then why would one choose to think of one's fellow citizens as inert texts, fixed and given, even if there were to be any similarity between reading and studying their social conduct? It does not seem to me that even Taylor's intersubjective meanings are to be found by quite so free an act of interpretation, though it is clear that, no less than Ricoeur, he expects both the text and the reader-author to be altered by the turn around the hermeneutic circle. "Mainstream" social science, as he says, is not like that, but one is at a loss to know what Ricoeur imagines it to be.

To argue that interpretation is not circular, and that it does not replace explanation in the social sciences, does not however mean that it has no intellectual standing. Obviously, we do want to understand the beliefs and practices of the social agents whom we study, and this is certainly constitutive of what "mainstream" social science tries to achieve. Can one imagine, for example, a study of the legal profession which ignored the ideologies of bench and bar and did not relate them to the various political conflicts of the time? A serious history of any period would simply be incomplete if it did not elucidate the self-understanding of the various individuals and groups with which it dealt. Such an interpretive "fitting" would of necessity enhance the descriptions and explanations that would precede or accompany it. To see how that is to be achieved, however, requires a sympathetic approach to standard social science and an appreciation of the enormous part that causal explanation plays in social understanding. To really integrate interpretation into the methodology of the social sciences, in short, demands a far more careful account of what social scientists actually have tried to do than their hermeneutic critics at present offer.

Runciman

There are, in fact, far more adequate theories than theirs, and one cannot do much better than turn, for example, to W. G. Runciman's splendid *A Treatise on Social Theory,* vol. 1, *The Methodology of the Social Sciences.*[9] I propose to examine it at some length, not only because of its intrinsic merits, but also because it shows how irrelevant the hermeneutic anxiety about "brute" factualism is. It is a lucid work, written in simple English and amply illustrated by apposite examples drawn from the works of historians, anthropologists, and sociologists. The reader is treated with respect, since conflicting theories are presented fairly and accurately, so that one can judge for oneself. The stated purpose of the work is to provide a methodology which will demonstrate that explanations in the social and natural sciences follow the same rules. This may, however, not be the most illuminating aspect of the book, which presents a fairly complete phenomenology of the sociological understanding. What is so impressive here is Runciman's account of the three steps involved in coming to a full understanding of social phenomena. They are reportage, explanation, and description. These terms may be somewhat idiosyncratic. Reportage refers to what most people think of as description, and what Runciman calls description turns out to be what is usually meant by interpretation. Given the literature of hermeneutics, one can well understand why he would avoid that terminology, and in any case one knows what he is talking about. It is more interesting to note that his tripartite methodology bears a real resemblance to Hegel's scheme in the *Phenomenology*.

In the section on consciousness in the *Phenomenology*, Hegel tells the story of mankind's pursuit of certainty. It begins with the undeniable but mute certainty of sense experience, which has to alter because of the need to classify which speech imposes upon us. The mind is, therefore, driven on to description, to grasping the properties of the objects of observation. The limits of description are quickly reached because differentiation inherently demands answers to the question of why these differences arose and how they are constituted. To analyze natural phenomena and to explain change, the task of science, follows. Hegel called it understanding. It embraces both natural science and Kantian idealism with its recognition that causality is a category of the knowing mind. From there one must move on to the self-generated question, "Why are we what we are as knowing beings?" The answer to that takes us out of the pursuit of certainty into the quest for truth, which is the self-consciousness of a complete retrospective knowledge of the pattern of our entire cultural ascent.[10] This, of course, is a far more ambitious vision of philosophical knowledge than would be entertained by any theory of social science today. Runciman's phenomenology has only three successive steps, but within its smaller and far more defined sphere it is a study of the same kind, an account of the stages of social understanding.

The first step in sociological understanding, Runciman's reportage, may well be the most difficult. Strictly, it is to be an account of a chosen phenomenon without explaining or describing it. (I shall stick to Runciman's vocabulary to avoid confusion.) A strike is suggested as an example. First, it is clear that one must already know a great deal about social history, the labor force, the organization of production and ownership, to know what a strike is at all. Then there is the excessive flexibility of our vocabulary. An honest reporter must be very mindful of the impact of his statements and their implications within the context which will determine their bearing. It is not only that interpretations and evaluations can be slipped in all too easily, our normal vocabulary has too many words that refer to too many different historical phenomena. On Runciman's own showing, neither "ownership" nor "revolution" can, for instance, be used uncontroversially. That is so at least in part because they cover too much social territory. The second and far more intractable difficulty is that there are bound to be conflicting taxonomies. What class of events a strike belongs to may be settled, but not whether a given armed struggle was a civil war, a revolution, or an intra-elite coup. Here ideology is bound to rule, and it is not surprising that arguments about taxonomy are not easily resolved. Indeed, theories of classification themselves, such as Foucault's, are subjects of the most extreme disagreement. What, finally, counts as a relevant boundary for reporting a set of occurrences? When does a strike begin, when is it over? Until the next one? Or must an adequate report cover both historical developments and concurrent events (diachronic and synchronic reportage)? These are by no means all the difficulties of reportage that Runciman discusses, and I can think of more, but they suffice to give a sense of just how very inadequate even the best survey research often is. It does not have to be so in principle, but there is no denying that telling the story right is not the easiest thing. The mutual accusations of hidden evaluations and inaccuracy that rival observers may hurl at each other may be more readily disposed of than the absence of a stable standard for classification, definition, and the setting of boundaries. Since, moreover, both explanation and description depend upon the neutrality of reporting, as well as upon its completeness, it can be said that all the uncertainties of social sciences are built into it at this, the very first stage of our understanding. In this respect I may be slightly more pessimistic than Runciman, even though I have not gone beyond his own argument.

With the reporting done, the question "Why did they do it?" or "Why did the strike happen there and then?" presents itself at the very boundary of the story. How easy it is to avoid explanations in reporting is not clear. Intentions and motives do their duty here, the first being constitutive of the conduct that is being reported, while the second must provide a great part of the explanation. If, however, a neutral and accurate report has been completed, which is possible, then explaining is comparatively less difficult. It begins with "because" and then goes on to test that hypothesis by eliminating all the conceivable counterfactuals. This is the equivalent of testing by controlled experimentation. If the alternative causes have been shown to be based on inadequate evidence or to entail other consequences than the actual events, then the suggested explanation stands. This is as true of unique occurrences as it is of recurrent phenomena. The cause of Henry VIII's divorce from Catherine of Aragon was her inability to produce an heir. There is no argument about the fact that he did divorce her. It is a report that is as neutral as Clemenceau's celebrated remark about the historical fact that the Belgians did not invade Germany in 1914. One can, however, impute other motives to Henry to explain his conduct, but these would turn out to be untenable counterfactuals. When we come to a broad social phenomenon, not a once-only event like Henry's divorce, the pattern of explanation is the same. Why is there a rising rate of divorce in the United States? That it is so is not in dispute, again. The number of causes to explain the change will be very great, but it will still be a matter of eliminating counterfactuals, until only sufficient and necessary causes remain.

The trouble here is ignorance. In both cases social explanation is insuperably dependent upon psychology. Unless we really know what the motives of social agents are, we cannot get it perfectly right. That does not mean that psychology is all one has to know. It is group, not individual, conduct and change, that are at stake, but there is no answer to the question "Why?" without a scientifically adequate psychology. Nothing of that order is now available, as Runciman well knows. We do not even have an idea what such a psychology might look like. If we did, I daresay, he would be out there working on it and I also would not be writing this article. If reportage is flawed by partiality, explanation suffers from something worse: enormous ignorance. In principle, that is not unavoidable, but it would be unfair to readers to hold out a too-promising prospect.

Compared to this dispiriting state of affairs, the conflicts engendered by explanations seem trivial. They are either no greater than is to be expected among rival researchers engaged in a common enterprise, or they are expressions of moral dissent. The latter usually amounts to the charge that, because explanations do not urge a specific course of action upon the reader and avoid overt evaluation, they are wicked and insidiously misleading. They lull the reader into believing that whatever is explained must be thus and has to be passively accepted as the only possible state of society. By not being with a party of action one is covertly against it. There is no way of countering this conspiratorial and Manichaean view of sociology, and the accusation that this sort of "positivism" is a disease of our century will have to be endured by most social scientists. It is not particularly onerous, and one owes it to one's readers to believe that they can take care of their convictions themselves.

It might be said that I have presented a theory of explanation that would suit historians but not the other social sciences. There is in fact nothing here that would preclude a functionalist explanation, as long as it did not bracket the origins of a given social state completely. If the latter is plausibly presented there is nothing irrational with a naturalistic teleology that explains the parts of a social system in terms of equilibrium and disequilibrium. It does, however, come as close as a genuine explanation can come to an interpretation or, as Runciman would call it, a description. This is for him as for Clifford Geertz the art of looking at matters "from the native's point of view." What do all those involved in a strike think that their conduct means? What is the worldview, ideology, or belief system that each participant in this whole conflict brings to the scene, and how does it fit into what the social scientist knows about it? The decay of the labor movement in Ruritania, its old and corrupt leadership, the incompetence of management, the decline of markets for its out-of-date industries, and much else is known to her, and must be in place for a description to take place at all.

For it is at this point that it is important to emphasize that social science goes well beyond the common sense of a given place and time. We simply know a great deal more about the economics of inflation than did the Spaniards of the sixteenth century. A sociologist similarly knows more about strikes than do those who are involved in them or most other citizens. His knowledge would, however, be very incomplete without an understanding of the perceptions of the agents and the belief systems that inform them. Again, the difficulties are immense. One cannot ask all the questions in one's intellectual repertory. Selection and choices of emphasis are required, and it is easy to make errors of judgment in these. Runciman lists the major failures under two headings, misapprehension and mystification. The first comes from a refusal to listen carefully and is relatively easily eliminated. It is mystification that haunts us. We meet it as suppression, exaggeration, ethnocentricity, derogation, and hagiography. In all these cases an unstated evaluation poses as interpretation, and it is unfair to the subject no less than to the reader. It is the flaw of every hermeneutic circle because each one assumes some teleology or some external or hidden social purpose and slips it into the interpretive moment of understanding. There is no need for *any* circle here. The interpretation adds to and flows from the explanation.

If there is to be evaluation, it is discretionary. Runciman thinks that social scientists should declare whether the phenomena they have brought to full understanding are a "good thing" or not. This might, I suppose, lessen the temptation to slip in evaluations prematurely, but it is a chancy proposition. It is very likely to color at once every reader's response to a study if too much is made of evaluation. If it really is unavoidable, one might as well get it over with as briefly, as honestly, and as early as possible, but I think we should quit when we have completed our interpretation. Interpretations are not unlike medical diagnoses; they suggest, but do not compel therapies. In the social sciences, however, the division of intellectual labor is quite different, and I think that evaluation implies social action. That is to be left to the instructed reader, better only in being less ignorant than before.

Natural and Social Sciences

Even with the help of Runciman's remarkable book, I have obviously not dealt with a great many other problems inherent in the sciences of man or even their efforts to interpret their findings. The picture is grim enough, but there is one difficulty that I must still discuss at least briefly, since it agitates both "mainstream" social scientists and their hermeneutic critics, though scarcely in the same way. That is the vexed question of the similarity between the natural and the social sciences. One way not to go about answering that question is to say that there is no difference and then attempt to prove it by comparing the alleged inadequacies of the social sciences to those in some of the natural ones. The outcome of this unfortunate ploy is something like this. The social sciences offer generalizations that are uncertain, but then so does embryology. They cannot conduct controlled experiments, but then neither can astronomy or geology. Are there no predictions? Meteorology cannot succeed there either. Mechanics, finally, comes up with limited generalizations, as do the social sciences. And if social science cannot create a technology, that is true of many other sciences as well, which are nevertheless all bona fide natural sciences.[11] In short, the social sciences suffer from every weakness of all the natural sciences combined, when this score is added up. As a defense of their scientific validity, it is less than successful. Yet this is not a caricature. It is a very common form of argument in favor of identifying the natural and the social sciences. It does nothing to clarify the real character of sociological understanding, which may well be naturalistic but not share all the characteristics of the sciences of nature.

Since it does not really help social scientists to understand themselves, why bother with comparisons to the natural sciences? To be sure, the natural sciences enjoy more prestige, recruit the finest minds, generate cures and marvelous technologies, and ensure their own intellectual progress. This naturally is bound to give rise to a fair amount of envy, especially in a university setting. But that is not the real cause for concern on the part of social scientists. What bothers them is the certainty of scientific knowledge and the level of agreement among qualified researchers. This, far more than the difficulty of framing general laws or predicting future social events, has always seemed an unbridgeable difference. Even the recent recognition that the natural sciences are also subject to the vicissitudes of social historicity can give comfort only to the naive, because it does nothing to alter the intellectual gap between the two kinds of science here and now.

The question one might therefore ask is why is agreement so important? Why should it matter so much? Is disagreement such an intellectual weakness? Is it really a disaster that there are likely to be rival understandings of the same phenomena? It is not easy to imagine that reportage will reach unanimity in the social sciences. There is, to be sure, enough general acceptance of factual information to make a reliable body of historical writing possible. Norway did not invade Germany in 1940, we may recall with relief. Nevertheless, there will be plenty of differences in reportage, and since explanation is built on it there can be no reconciliation at that stage. It is, perhaps, the case that there is a common acceptance of what a good explanation should look like among all "mainstream" social scientists, but at the margins there are ideological doubts of some considerable depth. And these burst forth fully when we come to interpretation. That is why the hermeneutic circle seems so attractive, for it promises to achieve a community of understanding and a degree of agreement that other interpreters cannot possibly offer. An interpretation that seeks to uncover an intersubjective substrate or text of which the subjects of investigation are not aware is not only trying to get *them* to recognize their hidden unities of belief, it is first of all meant to reveal the necessary agreement among interpreters who are willing to enclose themselves within the hermeneutic circle and its ends. That, evidently, is not the aim of what Runciman calls describing, and it is a procedure that is not likely to yield agreement. Choosing the representative subjects for inquiry, and then interpreting their social, religious, and moral belief system, is too indeterminate to convince those who have made different choices. Who, moreover, cannot be accused of mystification by a hostile critic? Between an authoritative act of consciousness-raising and an interpretation that simply relates two areas of understanding, there can really be no compromise. The former aspires to change the readers until they cohere, which would be the cost of agreement in the sciences of man at present. Under these circumstances a rational social scientist might well learn to relax and to enjoy the rich diversity and uncertainty that mark his calling in general and interpretations especially.

Notes

1. Paris: Plon, 1961.
2. H. G. Gadamer, "The Problem of Historical Consciousness," in Paul Rabinow and William M. Sullivan, eds., *Interpretive Social Science* (Berkeley: University of California Press, 1979), pp. 103–106.
3. Clifford Geertz, "From the Native's Point of View," in Rabinow and Sullivan, *Interpretive Social Science,* pp. 225–241. This splendid reconstruction of the philosophical views of members of three different and very remote societies does honor to the author's skills as an ethnographer but has no discernible theoretical relation, in spite of his avowals, to textual hermeneutics.
4. Gadamer, "Problem of Historical Consciousness."
5. *Politics,* 1305b–1306b.
6. Charles Taylor, "Interpretation and the Sciences of Man," in Rabinow and Sullivan, *Interpretive Social Science,* pp. 25–71.
7. Paul Ricoeur, "The Model of the Text: Meaningful Action Considered as a Text," in Rabinow and Sullivan, *Interpretive Social Science,* pp. 73–101.
8. Quentin Skinner, " 'Social Meaning' and the Explanation of Social Action," in Peter Laslett and W. R. Runciman, eds., *Philosophy, Politics and Society,* Fourth Series (Oxford: Basil Blackwell, 1972), pp. 136–157.
9. Cambridge: Cambridge University Press, 1983.
10. Judith N. Shklar, *Freedom and Independence* (Cambridge: Cambridge University Press, 1976), pp. 14–30 and the literature cited there.
11. For example, Ernest Nagel, *The Structure of Science* (New York: Harcourt, Brace & World, 1961), pp. 447–502.

CHAPTER SIX

Politics and the Intellect

T he question "Can eighteenth-century values be defended?" is
often asked, especially during this bicentennial year. It cannot
be answered because it is a badly put question. There was no
single, self-consistent set of values in the eighteenth century, or indeed
in any other century. Europe's intellectual tradition is one of multiplicity and conflict and no useful end is served by ignoring the diversity of the past. Even that part of the eighteenth century that we call
"the Enlightenment" was a state of intellectual tension rather than
a sequence of simple propositions. Not even its central significance,
the emergence of the modern intellectuals as an identifiable social
group, can be registered in terms of uniform individual experiences
or responses. Indeed, the proper place of men of learning in society,
the exact political location of the republic of letters, the duties of the
educated and well-informed, in short, the right ethos for intellectuals,
was the subject of considerable controversy. And it is one that still
agitates us. We may therefore say with some confidence that the morals and mores of the eighteenth century need no defense today, since
we still share them. It is the purpose of this essay to show that we
may discover ourselves in the eighteenth century and that this is one
of the values that any part of our past has for us.

Before turning to the debate about the political obligations of intellectuals one must ask why the picture of a monolithic Enlightenment
remains so popular. For the notion of the uniformity of the "philosophes" depends on their having identical political and social aspirations. In spite of all the evidence to the contrary it is still assumed that

This chapter is reprinted with permission from *Studies in Eighteenth Century Culture* 7
(1978): 139–51.

the Enlightenment was "a movement among intellectuals to assert themselves as a social force and to introduce, or at least talk about, a new technique of social change."[1] But surely they did not say the same things. A sociological category, "intellectuals," tells us little about their thoughts. We remember that Diderot among others rejected Helvétius's over-confident "education can do everything." And Condorcet's vision of progress propelled by the twin engines of science and public education was indeed "as much a caricature of the Enlightenment as its testament."[2] Condorcet's rejection of the past, the need to forget in order to learn, the apparently unlimited hope for a future free from the errors of the ages was far from being the only mood of the age. It was shared by others, to be sure, as an essential aspect of the campaign against traditional religion. However, the very skepticism, eclecticism, and self-awareness that were needed for that struggle inspired doubt, pessimism, and self-criticism among some of the boldest prophets of the new age. It was a conflict within individual minds as much as between opponents. Sociological classifications should not blind us to such spiritual realities.

Sociological generalizing is not the only source of simplification. The two momentous revolutions that marked the final quarter of the century also tend to constrict our retrospective eyesight. We are too eager to reduce the "causes" of these events to manageable lists. The opinions and acts of the generation preceding these storms are seen as inexorable steps leading to a known finale. It will not do. We know how deeply the American revolutionaries differed from each other and from their fathers; the French were not different in this respect. It may be inconvenient for the historian, but Atlantic intellectuals were not a simple group. We cannot even follow de Tocqueville in ascribing the ambitions and opinions of the French men of letters to their complete lack of political experience. Jefferson shared most of their views and he was a very experienced public man.[3] Here the tendency to make a false uniformity is due to the demands imposed by a political theory. That also is deceptive.

Instead of a single-minded, power-and-reform-mad platoon of intellectuals, we in fact find an immense range of views about their own role. Condorcet's views are the ones usually identified with the age and are too well known to need reviewing. However we should recall that Montesquieu, Rousseau, and d'Alembert held quite different positions. These four constitute the best defined intellectual poles. In between these a very great number of degrees and combinations were possible, among them those chosen by John Adams and Jefferson.

Montesquieu argued that however great the merits of intellectual achievement were on their own account, they had no effect on a man's basic moral character. A despot is no less despotic because he is well read and patronizes scholars. On the contrary, learning not only fails to protect us against the temptations of power, it may even enhance them. Moreover, if the intellect has little moral force, it may, in the long run, also be insignificant socially. Men of letters may simply not be very significant on the great stage of history. It is a position of heroic moderation and surely as such, admirable. Most intellectuals tend to detest or worship their own caste; few will even consider the possibility of their own unimportance.

Oddly enough, Rousseau also did not grant the intellectuals a place of primary importance in the corruption of mankind; he rejected not only them, but all their works as well. At best they coated the pill of injustice. Perhaps the entertainment they offered prevented the worst degeneracies, but they could do no good. Moreover, they could do a lot of harm if they invaded relatively unspoiled places, like his native Geneva. Finally, there was d'Alembert's response to Rousseau's challenge. By separating the arts and sciences from those who practiced them he was able to cherish the former and reprove the latter for their moral defects, among which servility and vanity were the foremost. However, he did not despair. For if men of ideas were to stand outside the prevailing systems of power and prestige and adopt an ethic suitable only to their own, isolated vocation, they might yet serve as an inspiration to their fellow citizens and so, indirectly, be socially useful.

In the closing years of their lives and era John Adams and Jefferson also discussed the place of the educated man in the polity. Adams leaned more toward Montesquieu, Jefferson toward Condorcet. Yet both agreed that it was the new intellectual vigor and freedom that had made their century "the most honourable to Human Nature."[4] What gives their correspondence its particular interest in this debate is that they were not concerned with the moral hazards of the ancien régime, but with the services that educated men might render in a free, republican, and relatively egalitarian political order. Here again there was tension. For Adams spoke for the party of memory, remembering how power had depraved and been abused by the learned, no less than by the ignorant. Jefferson spoke for the party of hope, for those who looked to a new kind of public-spirited aristocrat, republican and decent as few had ever been before.

Let us, in honor of the bicentennial year, begin at the end. The great problem to which both Adams and Jefferson turned in their last years was how to prevent the rise of political oppression in an inevitably inegalitarian society. They were entirely at one about what was most to be dreaded, but they differed greatly in their responses to their common fears. Jefferson, in spite of his practical involvements, was intellectually indifferent to politics. It bored him. He had none of Adams's passionate desire to create a science of politics. When his friend sent him an important book, he replied candidly, "but it is on politics, a subject I never loved and now hate. I will not promise therefore to read it thoroughly."[5] History was to him often, as in the case of his obsession with the ancient Anglo-Saxons, a source of mythology. At other times it was reduced to anthropology. The natural sciences alone claimed his full attention, especially those that might prove economically or educationally useful. In fact Jefferson wanted education to replace politics. Primary education would create citizens capable of protecting themselves against usurpation and governing themselves directly at the small, local "ward" level. Here education would render ruling superfluous. Secondary education, more selective, would presumably supply America with its skilled working force, capable of creating and maintaining an intelligent, well-administered economy and, above all, serve as a selection ground for the universities. Higher education open only to the few most able would provide the nation with a "natural aristocracy," an elite distinguished solely by its intellectual talents. True merit, as demonstrated by the capacity to learn and advance intellectual and, especially, scientific disciplines, was to replace all other standards for distinguishing ranks in society.[6] It was simply assumed that intelligence and public virtue would always be joined among the well-educated. That this career open to natural talent would do nothing for equality did not trouble Jefferson, for that was not his aim. What such a system did ensure was change. It certainly would make sense for every generation to reject the political legacy of its predecessors, if scientific knowledge determined and measured all social values. As the former advanced, the latter would have to be adjusted.[7] In this way politics, the struggle of competing interests, the distribution of moral and tangible values, the relations between allies and enemies, all this becomes problem-solving by education and by the already educated. The expected certainty of knowledge replaces the turmoil of political passions.

In Europe this faith in perpetual, if not infinite, progress was largely supported by a Manichean view of history. Reason and superstition had fought an unequal war, until with the rise of science and the invention of printing, the tide of battle had turned and reason could now enjoy an irreversible victory. Such thoughts were far from alien to Adams and Jefferson also. It may well be that in America the concentration on scientific progress was peculiarly appropriate because the prevailing reality was the struggle between man and nature, rather than among men.[8] However, neither Adams nor Jefferson was blind to human hostility in general or to the part that organized religion played in it. It is in fact surprising to find Adams still so furious at religious dogmatism. Both looked upon Connecticut with contempt and dismay as if it were a veritable kingdom of darkness.[9] Adams, ever suspicious, sensed the resurgence of religious intolerance all about him.[10] These sons of the preceding century were, in fact, as anti-clerical as the disciples of Voltaire, and while both were theists, they spent far more time discussing the political crimes of religious zealots than the benevolence of God. It was as an antidote to organized religion that Adams, just as much as Jefferson, valued the progress in the arts and sciences that both had witnessed in their lifetime. It was one of the strongest intellectual bonds uniting them and it allows one to treat their correspondence as the joint product of a single mentality.

The difference between them was, nevertheless, very real. It went well beyond the obvious one that Adams noted between his own fear of "the few," of aristocracy, and Jefferson's of "the one," of monarchy. We have here a conflict of intellectual inclinations. Adams believed that no kind of aristocracy, whether defined by intellect, wealth, or birth, could be trusted with any degree of uncontrolled power. No one could be trusted to behave with self-control when the possibility of self-enrichment and aggrandizement arose. Jefferson was convinced that intellectual distinction was bound to express itself in public rectitude. Like many people of his age he assumed that when ignorance and superstition had been dispelled, their opposites, knowledge and enlightenment, would simply replace them to govern the new world. Adams was less sanguine. He was as suspicious of democratic egalitarianism as he was of aristocratic pretensions because all immoderate assertions worried him. Inequality was a political problem only because it invited imbalances in the distribution of power. Tyranny lurked everywhere, at least potentially.

It may well be that Adams saw everything through political lenses. He was certainly far more interested in political theory than Jefferson, as we saw, had ever been. History was Adams's source of political information and wisdom, and the very basis of his political science. Far from being a traditionalist, in the sense of revering the past with the piety due to one's ancestors, he looked back with the disenchanted eye of a social scientist. In this respect he was no less fact-minded than his friend who looked to nature. His whole disposition was to amass political examples so as to discover general political truths about recurrent political situations. Among these, mob attacks on the security of property and aristocratic oppression were the most threatening as well as the most common. What obstacles could be put in their path? Natural aristocracy he at once recognized as perfectly useless. Every sort of inequality may originate in natural superiority. Sooner or later it will translate itself into wealth, power, and prestige. If it be merely moral merit it cannot prevail against the real objects of ambition, good looks, wealth, and power. These give men reputation and these are the goals of ambition. All may be and are used to corrupt republics. In an electoral system an aristocrat is any man who controls more than a single vote. In his native Massachusetts education was diligently pursued, and as a result generations of Harvard men, from father to son, could beguile lesser men and govern. Since Adams was just as eager to promote learning as Jefferson was, he encouraged the latter in all his projects. To other correspondents he did not hide his contempt for the competitive quarrels among scholars that made academies scenes of battle and served only to retard the advance of knowledge.[11] Knowledge in fact did not lesson political inequality and indeed had no effect on morals at all.[12] Only careful institutional engineering, the careful balancing and separating of constitutionally established powers, would protect the republic against aristocratic corruption. As we know, that was not the actual course of political history. It was, rather, the theory and practice of Madison's organized political parties based on an extensive electorate that settled the relations between the few and the many. It was not a solution that would have appealed to the scientific or moral inclinations of either Adams or Jefferson, for this was no cure for factions but, in effect, a permanent dismissal of the idea of a principled and "true" public order. Jefferson's education and Adams's political science were designed to achieve a demonstrably right government, not a merely workable arrangement, however enduring. In that also they were in accord, even if one was of a hopeful and the other of a very wary disposition.

It has often been argued that Adams's undeniably grim view of human nature can be traced to his Puritan ancestors. That may be true, but perhaps no such explanation is necessary. A great many of Adams's contemporaries all over Europe, not only in Scotland, shared his attitudes to men and citizens. For all the differences in circumstances, style, in emphasis and character, they participated in

the intellectual tensions of their whole age and not only in those peculiar to their own country. Montesquieu's name is one of the few that
never appears on Adams's long litany of complaints against the *philosophes*. Nevertheless, he was also their most admired and influential
writer. How to organize political elites for commercial Europe, given
the decadence and incompetence of the hereditary nobility, was one
of the central issues raised in *The Spirit of the Laws*. That is the burden of its pages devoted to republics and to Great Britain. Montesquieu's response was not precise, but it pointed to the approach
Adams was to choose. Here there was no talk about "natural aristocracies," though much was said about religion and education. The
conclusion one would, in any case, draw from that work is that the
intellectuals of a society reflect rather than fashion prevailing regimes.
Moreover, Montesquieu had earlier drawn a far from flattering portrait of the modern "natural aristocrat."

In the *Persian Letters* Montesquieu offers his readers a hero who
is both an enlightened philosopher and a despot. Usbek, although he
is in fact a nobleman in Persia, prefers to be a "natural" aristocrat.
He despises the court and deliberately shakes off all his local ties to
seek knowledge and enlightenment abroad.[13] He is of course a good
deal less cosmopolitan when his personal interests are affected, for
his harem is left to the strict and cruel care of his eunuchs.[14] That
does not mean that his love of learning is insincere or superficial. It
may have begun as a mere pretense but it is now perfectly genuine,
and indeed Usbek *is* enlightened.[15] The perfectly detached outsider
can see French customs and follies with a penetration not possible
to others. His criticisms of the pettiness of every class of men, including the literati, of rituals and superstitions, of folly of every sort are
supremely intelligent. His analysis of the slave trade and the commercial consequences of imperialism and bigotry is brilliant in every
way.[16] Impartiality and a fine disinterestedness mark all his judgments
of others. And, naturally, he is a defender of the arts and sciences as
the greatest advantages of civilization. Without them we would revert
to barbarism. It is his gentler friend Rhédi who worries about the
tendency of knowledge to merely replace old evils with new.[17] In
short, Usbek is the very model of a *philosophe*. His detachment, however, does have characteristic failings. He cannot feel anything.[18] He
not only does not love his wives, he has no emotional life at all. When
he is tempted by fatalism, by a belief in Providence, he rejects it as
leading him to a loss of feeling, to insensibility. However the opposite
belief has the same effect. Why not commit suicide when life ceases
to please? Nature will not be affected and society is a mere contract

for mutual benefits. When one does not receive any, why not quit? Usbek does not, but it would seem that only curiosity keeps him alive—and his despotic rulership. For as every second letter reminds us, Usbek is an oriental despot of the most arbitrary sort. All his enlightenment, moreover, does not save him from the common illusion of despots, that his groaning subjects love him. He can talk abstractly about freedom and the strength of the weak, but he is unprepared for the despair, the rebellion, and the suicide of one of his wives. His views on justice, and law, are as sensible as his ideas on religion, but when his own traditional prerogatives are at stake he forgets all about them. He is simply no less selfish and no less a Persian than any other man is the creature of his passions and environment. To Montesquieu the lesson was clear. Enlightenment has all the virtues except those that count politically. Usbek's talents do not protect him against corruption.

When d'Alembert in his capacity as secretary to the Académie Française wrote Montesquieu's "Éloge" he mentioned only Usbek's enlightened views, which he insisted were the author's own.[19] And so they were. But d'Alembert on that occasion, which he meant to be a declaration of the *philosophes'* faith, ignored Usbek's other side. He had, however, been made painfully aware of it, and of much else, by Rousseau's assault on the arts and sciences and on their creators and consumers. Without being a simple democrat, Rousseau made the general welfare and civic virtue of the European peasantry his final standard of political right and wrong. That simply excluded the intellectuals. They could not be useful in a just society. Theirs was a function inextricably woven into the fabric of civilized corruption. We cannot do without them, but the good social order could dispense with them. Certainly they could do nothing to improve society morally. For if inequality is at the root of all our corruption, then indeed it is difficult to see how intellectual training or any aristocracy, however "natural," could be an instrument of social reform. Intellectual training and artistic creativity only emphasize differences in ability and in any case stimulate competitiveness among those who work to please and gain reputations. In a genuine republic the citizens receive a rigorously non-intellectual, patriotic training which integrates them into the public order. To be sure, inegalitarian societies need the arts and sciences to amuse the rich and idle and to weave garlands about the chains of political oppression. They are not the cause of inequality, but they are its servants and adornment. Finally, and this gave great offense, Rousseau did not see that the common people had more to gain from the *philosophes* than from the clergy. That was just another power struggle and he saw no reason why he or his clients should get involved in it.[20]

Without being in the least persuaded by these claims on behalf of a civic order, d'Alembert was shaken by Rousseau's arguments. Many of the charges appalled him. Even if savages were happier than civilized men, he replied, we cannot give up the arts and sciences now: "our vices would remain, and ignorance would merely be added to them."[21] Again, he did not for a moment doubt that in their attack on traditional religion the *philosophes* were serving the welfare of mankind as a whole. He was less sanguine, however, when he came to consider the conduct of his fellow intellectuals. He could not deny that they had, in their control over public opinion, become powerful, and that often they even boasted of it. In an imaginary dialogue he had Descartes declare that "sooner or later the men who think and write govern opinion, and opinion governs the world."[22] Under the impact of Rousseau's laments he now wondered whether this power was really being well used, and whether it did not, as all power does, corrupt. As he looked at the relations between the republic of letters and the court and the nobility his heart sank. When he considered the behavior of men of letters to each other he despaired. The republic of letters which should be a self-governing democracy was nothing but a Hobbesian state of nature. It took its standards from the polity instead of devising its own. There was a morality suitable for philosophers, just as there was one for men, citizens, legislators, and states, respectively. The aim of a philosopher should be to live happily apart from other men. In this respect one of the two cultures, that of the mathematicians, was far superior, for geometry is pursued wholly for its own delights. Talent in the arts might be a better title to distinction, and certainly a more durable one, than wealth or birth, but without austerity it was, just as Rousseau had said, only one competitive advantage among others. History, moreover, seemed to corroborate all these misgivings. In a finely reasoned history of royal policy and court culture, d'Alembert showed that in fact all along the king and the nobility had created, sustained, and dominated the world of the arts and letters. Reputations were still made in the ante-chambers of the great.[23] The response to this essay was, not surprisingly, cool. The "bragging of a young schoolboy" was a fair sample of opinion.[24]

D'Alembert's position was indeed a difficult one to maintain. Rousseau, by simply turning his back on civilization, had chosen an easier path. For d'Alembert, like Adams and their common master, Montesquieu, was utterly devoted to the life of learning and was an ardent promoter of every art and science. All worshiped knowledge.

D'Alembert's ideas about a suitable modern education were just as science- and utility-oriented as Jefferson's were to be.[25] Adams had no objections at all to his enterprising friend's designs for instruction and indeed congratulated him warmly. The great division within these men's own minds, and between them and their more daring friends, was whether intellectual distinction, however great, was politically beneficial. For all the answer was far from being a simple yes or no. Enlightened views were clearly socially better than clerical and traditional lore. However, it was paradoxically only by withdrawing from the society and the mores of the political world that the men of learning could hope to advance either knowledge or its beneficial influence. Whether social or natural, the sciences could not create a politically superior "natural aristocracy" without corruption, both their own and that of the polity. Their avenue must be indirect.

It is worth remembering that eighteenth-century intellectuals were a pre-technological elite. They could not yet claim to be economically indispensable to society. They thought of themselves rather as teachers and guides, as the rulers of opinions and so, indirectly, of the polity. They would do well just what the clergy had, in their view, done so badly. It is not surprising that someone should rise to reject such enormous pretensions, whether clerical or anti-clerical. Rousseau's mission was all but inevitable and his day was to come, even in America. If the Revolutionary generation owed him little, later ones were to be much in his debt. Adams could only misquote him; Jefferson's agrarianism had other sources, but soon Americans were to be swept along by Rousseau. The apparent simplicity of his scorn appeals to many well-educated people who in a revulsion of self-hatred turn upon the "intellectual elite." Their often petulant and pseudo-democratic zeal is untempered by Rousseau's tragic insight into the insuperable moral limitations of man in society. Nor should we identify d'Alembert's rigorous self-judgment with the facile laments, so common today, about the disruptive impact of intellectuals upon liberal societies. Those who now express these fears would prefer the academy to conform more perfectly to the morals and manners of the market place and the bureaucracies. Theirs is in no sense a genuine self-criticism, nor do they offer insights into the real moral paradoxes of intellectual life. They merely want the "natural" aristocracy to become more conventional. As Adams saw, that happens in any case, inevitably. The prestige values and personal aspirations of intellectuals remain very stable. They are also adaptable generally. The reports of the dangers that they are likely to pose to an established order may well be greatly exaggerated. Flattery, especially, goes a long way here. The real and tormenting problems are those that were already plain at the moment when the modern world, both social and intellectual, was born. When the watchmen at the gate of the new age warned the men of letters to retreat to what is now often sneered at as the "ivory tower," they were not telling them to forget their obligations to society, but rather to assume them in a more respectable way. We might also ask ourselves, as some of them did, whether we really matter all that much. It is, after all, an open question.

Notes

1. Charles Frankel, *The Faith of Reason* (New York: Columbia Univ. Press, 1948), p. 10.

2. Peter Gay, *The Enlightenment* (New York: Knopf, 1969), II, 122. Gay altogether offers a new and greatly improved account of the spirit of the age. See especially pp. 98–125.

3. Alexis de Tocqueville, *The Ancien Régime and the French Revolution,* trans. Stuart Gilbert (New York: Doubleday, Anchor, 1955), p. 13.

4. *The Adams-Jefferson Letters,* ed. Lester J. Cappon (New York: Simon and Schuster, 1971), p. 456.

5. Ibid., p. 259.

6. Ibid., pp. 387–92.

7. Letter to Samuel Kercheval, *The Portable Thomas Jefferson* (New York: Viking, 1975), pp. 559–61.

8. Daniel Boorstin, *The Lost World of Thomas Jefferson* (Boston: Beacon Press, 1960), *passim.*

9. *Letters,* pp. 510, 512.

10. Ibid., pp. 461–62, 607–8.

11. *The Political Writings of John Adams,* ed. George A. Peek, Jr. (Indianapolis: Bobbs-Merrill, 1954), pp. 184–85, 189–90, 198–99, 204–5.

12. Ibid., pp. 207–9.

13. *Lettres Persanes,* Lettre I. *Oeuvres Complètes de Montesquieu,* ed. André Masson (Paris: Nagel, 1950), I.

14. Ibid., II.

15. Ibid., VIII.

16. Ibid., CXVIII, CXXI.

17. Ibid., VI.

18. Ibid., LXXVI, CXIX.

19. *Oeuvres Complètes de d'Alembert* (Geneva: Slatkine, 1967), III, 442–43.

20. *Oeuvres Complètes* (Paris: Gallimard, 1959), III, 7, 21, 25, 49–50; I, 967–68.

21. D'Alembert, O.C., I, 82.

22. Ibid., IV, 474.

23. Ibid., I, 231–34; IV, 335–73.

24. Ronald Grimsley, *Jean d'Alembert* (Oxford: Oxford Univ. Press, 1963), p. 127.

25. D'Alembert, O.C., IV, 481–89.

CHAPTER SEVEN

Learning without
Knowing

It is not unimaginable that some day history will be considered obsolete. It will be said then that we know more than enough about the past, that history has reached its intellectual limits and that its possibilities have all been exhausted. If this should ever be seriously claimed, it will not be because the boundaries of history as a field of knowledge have finally been reached. Rather, it will be because of moral revulsion inspired by historical inquiries and literature. In principle, history cannot come to an end, but there might be no first-rate minds willing to study it.[1]

Historians can always find new subjects to consider. Obviously, the immediate past becomes a topic of historical concern tomorrow, often even before all the participants are dead. The opportunities for reinterpretation always remain open. No one needs to be reminded that every generation must reconsider its predecessors in the light of new experiences. The last word can never be said about history. There are at any time many good books on the same subject that in no way eliminate or diminish one another in the esteem of their public. Nevertheless, at various times since the first stirrings of the Enlightenment, historians have lived under the shadow of two self-accusations: uselessness and inaccuracy. And it would be these or similar charges rather than the inner logic of history that might reduce it again to its medieval insignificance. This is not a likely prospect but a reflection on the moral self-doubts that have characteristically placed limits on the possibilities of history as a form of knowledge.

"Learning without Knowing" is reprinted by permission of *Daedalus, Journal of the American Academy of Arts and Sciences,* from the issue entitled "Intellect and Imagination—The Limits and Presuppositions of Intellectual Inquiry," 109, no. 2 (Spring 1980): 53–72.

Some sciences are discarded because they are found to be false, like phrenology. Others simply accomplish their task, like certain kinds of logic. Occasionally, a science is superseded by a superior one or transformed, even if its name does not alter, like pathology. History is not likely to suffer this fate. Inner tensions generated by moral uneasiness and self-rejection may, however, yield a pervasive sense that the discipline is futile, inadequate in its practices, and limited or misleading in its results. Historians have frequently experienced these periods of intense self-doubt. That does not mean they are likely to do so in the immediate future. On the contrary, at the moment most historians are seriously committed to the progress of their collective endeavors, and interest in the subject among the general public appears to be unflagging. To reflect on the recurrent attacks of paralyzing skepticism that have from time to time haunted historians is not to predict its imminent reemergence. It is rather meant to illuminate the patterns of moral thought that induce scholars to perceive the confines of their disciplines and the limits of their knowledge. The ways in which historians have measured and judged the possibilities of history is a general study in the practical import of various kinds of skepticism; for, while skepticism is sometimes invigorating and may inspire new ventures in historical research, it may also lead to a deadening sense of the limits of history.

Historians have a professional obligation to bring a skeptical judgment to bear on the study of the past. The records that the men and women of the past have left are usually misleading and inadequate in the quantity and quality of information they convey. Jumping to conclusions is not a sport in which a self-respecting historian can indulge. To be aware of that does, however, expose one to the hazards of pyrrhonism. It is of course quite true, as philosophers have reminded us, that if we do not trust the evidence of the past, we cannot believe anything at all.[2] While that is correct as a general proposition, it does not touch the psychological impact of history. Indeed, the philosophy of history, whether epistemological or eschatological, has almost nothing to say to or about the working historian and his actual difficulties. "The cosmic periphery" never even comes close to the area where intellectual decisions are made and professional standards established. The skepticism of historians reflects neither philosophical illiteracy nor competence. And it does not matter to historians that many other sciences also suffer from similar uncertainties.[3] No one is truly comforted by the troubles of others. The difficulties of historians arise directly from their craft: historical evidence is simply unreliable. Anyone who has interrogated witnesses to an accident will know that the film *Rashomon* was not so wide off the mark. The historian must also distrust his own impartiality. Finally, new evidence and new interpretive skills combine to make history so unstable, that a lifetime's work can be suddenly destroyed. And the intractable philosophical difficulties—such as, what is evidence at all—do not go away simply because working historians do not encounter them day in, day out. To become a historian is to learn what is and what is not to be recognized as a credible account, but this education does not occur in a vacuum. Philosophy is an unsettling presence for history.

These may be risks that all scientists face, but they affect historians with peculiar intensity. Because history is ineluctably didactic, general doubt tends to be translated into a sense of social futility. Even those historians who do not aspire to influence the public politically hope to do more than flatter and entertain their readers. The most ambitious expect to encourage desired social change; the most modest mean to dispel illusions and myths that thrive on historical errors. Even those historians who write for their professional peers expect history cumulatively to have a broadening and sobering impact on the practical consciousness of the educated public. Historians are therefore always at least partly teachers. With a few notable exceptions, most have spent their entire adult lives in universities, so that teaching has generally been a part of their daily self-awareness. Whatever the extent of a historian's didactic intentions may be, their fulfillment depends on his credibility. It he comes to doubt the possibility of recreating the past accurately, he also loses his social purpose. Skepticism thus undoes the historian doubly. Under these discouraging circumstances the most able young people may well decide to choose another scholarly career. Fortunately, historians do persevere, because there is an elemental pleasure in recovering and shaping the records of the past into an explicable order. Moreover, in spite of their uncertainties, historians learn to establish and adhere to common standards of verification and communication. Theirs is not a world of arbitrariness, because they have created a common professional ethos and an institutional setting within which history is appreciated, judged, and taught. There is thus protection against doubt, but it often falters. Not only can doubt undermine history as teaching, but didactic failure can also inspire severe doubt. Why, one then asks, does history achieve so little improvement? Could it be because it is inadequate knowledge?

The question that bedevils historians and also expresses their deepest worries is, What is the use of history? It had already tormented the *philosophes,* and as J. H. Plumb has noted, "In many ways the historian of today is in the position of the historian of the Enlightenment. He cannot accept the interpretation of the past of his immediate ancestors or even of the mass of society in which he lives. . . . Many historians therefore have taken refuge in the meaninglessness of history."[4] Those who do not choose to take that easy path to melancholy have felt compelled to defend the utility of history. In this they also resemble their Enlightenment ancestors. One returns to the Enlightenment, then, because its uncertainties are alive again, and because self-interrogation leads one to reflect on the origins of one's present condition. It was in the eighteenth century that intellectuals emerged as a self-conscious social group obliged to define and justify their social place and functions. They had to prove to themselves, as much as to their public, that they not only aspired to serve humanity, but that their writings were in actuality useful. It was not clear that history could meet that test. Had it been perceived as ineffectual, it could not have served as a refuge for them. To be futile was for the *philosophe* the ultimate failure. That is how craft and social role came to be ill at ease with each other in the mind of the historian.

Why was history so often condemned in the eighteenth century as frivolous learning? First of all, it was second-hand information taken on trust. It enjoyed none of the certainty that mathematics could claim. The historian was not an autonomous intellect directly in touch with truth. The world of two cultures was already deeply entrenched, and the republic of science already seemed to threaten the self-confidence of the older society of men of letters. More important, the subject matter of history was unedifying. As Locke put it, "What were those conquerors but the great butchers of mankind?"[5] In both cases, history fails as education and as a state of mind. It is a faulty way of thinking about unworthy subjects. Its uncertainty and uselessness reinforced each other in the eyes of its detractors. According to d'Alembert, "the bitter critics" of history said we had nothing to learn from such a record of error, superstition, and brutality. History was entertainment for an uncritical audience. It wasted time that might be better spent on thinking about God, nature, or oneself. Antiquity might be worth remembering, but all that was worth knowing about it was already known, so there was no point in adding erudite minutiae. In his defense of history d'Alembert necessarily stressed its moral advantages, since that was the issue. History "consoles, instructs, and encourages us" if it is written intelligently. It is, to be sure, highly speculative, but conjectural knowledge reminds us of our limitations and teaches tolerance and forbearance. Like medicine, history is finally uncertain, but "our only hope for improvement."[6]

Voltaire, who was a practicing historian, unlike d'Alembert, could think of even less to say on behalf of the subject. The only use history has is "that it teaches us our duties and rights without appearing to do so"—a moral primer, in short. In principle, he was committed to writing a new history that would deal with culture, peoples, and the heroes of the intellect instead of kings and wars. In practice, he did nothing of the sort, but agonized over the pitfalls that face the honest historian. Unreliable records and partisan, self-serving, stupid, and improbable testimony are all he receives from the past. Having turned to history in order to discredit the Christian tradition, Voltaire was eventually crippled by a historical pyrrhonism that made it difficult for him to believe in learning much about the past. Caught between the allure of mathematical certainty and historical vagueness, he suffered the typical fate of historians who are incapable of trusting the evidence of the past enough to make an effort to put it into a new order.[7]

One obvious question raised by these doubts was whether so defective a subject should be taught to the young. *Émile* does not learn much about the past. What, after all, is history without war? Who needs scholars and intellectuals at all, for that matter? Unedifying, false, and useless, the history of the past was wholly inferior to the history of the human heart that Rousseau himself wrote. His skepticism was so complete, that introspection was his only foothold in reality. His history of the human heart was therefore, of necessity, his own story, but that was more instructive than the tales about knights and nobles. This was certainly a logical response to history in disgrace. As fable, it might be well suited to the human heart, but its facts were simply inconsequential.[8]

Not all forms of skepticism are as hostile to history as Voltaire's and Rousseau's. Different as these two were, both made a fetish of distrust. A calmer, more diffuse skepticism is quite likely to favor history. Gibbon's religion had been tepid, and so was his atheism. He was even surprised that his readers should be offended by his purely "human" account of the origin and spread of Christianity. His general skepticism, like Hume's, did not single out history for special doubts. Gibbon began with a general state of doubt but avoided historical pyrrhonism, because it would only lead him to the sort of skepticism that contradicts the experience of daily life and ends in madness. History as an exercise of common sense, of critical judgment and reliable erudition, was a hedge against the pathology of skepticism.[9] That is why Gibbon considered himself a historian long before he had ever written a line. There is a passage in his memoirs that has puzzled many historians. Before he found his final subject, Gibbon toyed with a variety of possible topics. Among others, he considered the history of Charles VII of France, the Crusade of Richard I, the life of Sir Walter Raleigh, and the history of Swiss liberty and that of Florence under the Medicis.[10] There is no discernible relationship between these subjects, and none is suggested. Gibbon was simply hunting around for something to which he could attach his mind. What was never in any doubt was that he had a historian's mind.

"Without engaging in a metaphysical or rather verbal dispute, I *know* by experience from my early youth, I aspired to the character of an historian."[11] Gibbon, like most of the great historians of the subsequent century, wrote history because he felt compelled to do so, without a doubt about his vocation and with a feeling of utter indifference toward all and any metaphysical obstacles. When he entered Parliament he noted that it was "a School of civil prudence, the first and most essential virtue of an historian."[12] His moral priorities were the exact reverse of Voltaire's and d'Alembert's. They expected history to instruct us in our social duties. Gibbon felt obliged to acquire political virtues in order to become a better historian. He never even raised the question about the possible uses of history. On the contrary, he simply admired the scholars whose patient labors the *philosophes* disdained, and found Voltaire's histories excessively tendentious.[13] History was its own civilized and civilizing reward; it was not meant to impart crude lessons about tyranny and superstition. Men obsessed with these aims were not in a position to write history for its own sake. The *philosophes* took it to be their duty to disabuse and mold public opinion. They were far from sure about their ability to do so and whether history could be a useful means to that end. When they did write history, it was inevitably very inferior to that of a genius who simply had a vocation to account for the *Decline and Fall of the Roman Empire,* and did so by remaining above the spectacle of human folly that he observed and recreated.

Even a brief look at the pronouncements of the great European historians of the post-Napoleonic era reveals attitudes as remote from Voltaire's as from ours. There is no moral or intellectual self-doubt. Yet, these were critical historians of the first order, and in no sense credulous men. Some, like Ranke, were genuinely religious; others were not.[14] All were deeply involved in the institutional life of their societies. The nation and the universities did not merely provide a setting within which historians worked. These scholars were actively involved in shaping and sustaining them. Ranke, Droysen, Mommsen, Michelet, Fustel de Coulanges, and Burckhardt were teachers in the most extensive and intense degree imaginable. They did not have to seek out a place in the polity or strive to replace some clerical body in ruling the empire of opinion. They had found an honorable estate for their calling.[15] Theodor Mommsen was certainly critical of the practices of the German universities, and deplored the superficialities of their offerings, but he did not doubt that a university degree was the only "patent of nobility" worth having, or that history was as demanding as it was a noble vocation in Germany.[16] When Droysen spoke of history as the study of "the self-consciousness of mankind," he was expressing a shared professional belief.[17] It also implied that history had replaced philosophy as the summit of knowledge.

Even some of the more repressive German governments recognized the dignity of history and were ready to support mandarin historical faculties that were not expected to return any political favors. It was to be their glory to maintain the culture of Europe generally and of their nation especially. Their task was to educate future scholars and a cultivated laity capable of continuing and promoting their literary and scientific inheritance. In the view of these mandarins, even the state existed to serve culture. They were intensely national in their loyalties, but it was a political allegiance that was more comprehensively cultural than governmental.[18] The honors that the king of Prussia bestowed on Ranke were certainly deserved, but they signified official respect not only for a great scholar, but also for history generally. The kings of Bavaria were no less generous in their patronage of historians.[19] By the middle of the nineteenth century the German universities and their historians enjoyed a degree of prestige that could not have been imagined fifty years earlier.[20] In France, the social respect for history and the cultural ideals supporting it were no less secure, in spite of the political difficulties suffered by individual historians. History as the epitome of mandarin culture was free from all the doubts that had assailed the *philosophes*.

The first two national reviews devoted to the profession spoke for all. The *Historische Zeitschrift* would be neither partisan in politics nor merely antiquarian. It would deal with the past as "a vital link to present-day life." That meant paying special attention to the modern era and to Germany. "For our science has, fortunately, attained such significance . . . that its existence and progress have become part of our national life." Somewhat later the *Revue historique* announced its prospective purposes in very similar terms: "France has always honored historical research. . . . the study of France's past . . . is today of national importance."[21]

The sense of national importance did not necessarily imply an excessive degree of aggressive nationalism.[22] It reflected the deepest intellectual experience and the facts of life as then perceived. National sentiment had given historians a new and enormously energizing sense of continuity, a sense that, as most historians knew, the French Revolution had also rendered emotionally precious. When Fustel de Coulanges spoke with disdain of the facile analogies that the Jacobins had drawn between the classical past and their own situation, he revealed both the source and character of history as a science.

> History is not an easy science, its subject is infinitely complex. . . . the chances for error are countless and no one can hope to escape them. If we are not discouraged . . . it is because we believe that the honest search for truth is always rewarding. If we accomplish nothing else but throw some light on hitherto neglected points or call attention to some obscure problems, we shall not have labored in vain, and we should have contributed our share to the progress of historical science and to the knowledge of human value.[23]

It was years before a professional British journal appeared, and it modestly announced itself as a forum for university scholars. The beginnings of historical scholarship in England had also been modest. The universities came to sponsor historical studies as a way of side-stepping the theological and sectarian wrangles that culminated in Newman's conversion.[24] There was no state sponsorship and no organized research. Scholarship was, moreover, from time to time threatened by wayward outsiders, such as the autodidactic Buckle and Carlyle. The first proclaimed that history would have to become a "science" or deserve to die, while the second would have it reject our "merely vulpine intellect" and restore us to "faith and action."[25] History was ill-served by these prescriptions, because they raised exaggerated hopes it was bound to disappoint. Academic history was, by continental standards, diffident. It is not surprising that Bury looked at the achievements of European scholarship with envy. In his inaugural address of 1902 he noted with admiration what "the coincidence of the scientific movement and resurgent nationality" had wrought. History had been a means to social unity, but "science had controlled while the national spirit had quickened" minds above ideological partiality. Nationality had broadened the intellect to encompass the development of peoples, not just of states. Bury saw a future for British historians in the study of the "Celtic civilization," the "ethnical problem," and the "part played by race . . . and the effects of race blending . . . and that mysterious pre-Aryan fore-world." Bury did not seem to feel challenged by other sciences, but he was afraid of democracy as a material and spiritual threat to historical work. As always, America was the metaphor for all that was feared at home. On the continent the success of history was due to its public character and role. In England it remained private, and in a "democratic state [statesmen] are hampered by the views of unenlightened taxpayers. The wealthy private benefactors . . . , especially in America, are deplorably short-sighted; they think too much of direct results and immediate returns." They would have to be shown that history "is not luxury . . . but a matter of inestimable concern to the nation and the world."[26] If one considers what Bury's historical and political intentions were, one shudders. Mandarin attitudes were not impeccable then and are not so now.

Bury was not intellectually unsure of himself in the way that Voltaire had been, but he had every reason to worry about his immediate social environment. Moreover, America was in this case not merely a reminder of the unwelcome advent of plutocratic democracy at home. Turner had a decade earlier made a far more abject defense of the utility of history to this unresponsive public. He did not doubt the spiritual worth of history, but its public value was a concern for him. One of his most admiring pupils remembered that Turner was actually fond of quoting Droysen's definition of history. He had as high a sense of his calling as any European historian, but he did not see himself as part of a mandarin culture. His burden of detachment was as heavy as theirs, even though, unlike them, he wrote a thoroughly democratic history of a democratic country. Like them, he had to make an effort to separate the man from the scholar.[27] But as an isolated, self-made mandarin he had to justify himself to a public that did not particularly respect history. Turner might rejoice in the knowledge that "even in young America Rome still lives," but his audience might well not care. To them, he had to speak of progress to be traced and of history as lessons in good citizenship for the pupils of public schools. It should inspire, as it had in Germany, a sense of public service. Finally, it would help Americans understand those European immigrants and their socialist ideas that were altering the country.[28]

Such were the humiliating claims that a learned and sensible man made on behalf of history as an intellectual discipline in a democratic society. So great a tension between personal and public views was bound to undermine the confidence of more sensitive historians. The fear of the cold indifference of the public was not altogether baseless, and found echoes in the minds of historians. For it was not just, as Bury seems to think, the vulgar who asked, "What is the use of history?" Historians also felt compelled to raise that devastating question. Those who were either not part of a stable university culture or who had no reason to look upon institutions of learning as the very heart of national life were most likely to doubt their own worth. They did so especially when they compared themselves to their colleagues in the natural sciences. Social dislocation and skepticism then acted upon each other in such a way as to turn doubt into despair. One need only read Henry Adams's account of his spiritual sufferings to understand the dynamics of intellectual self-contempt.

A comparison between Henry Adams and Jacob Burckhardt easily suggests itself, because they were so similar in their general outlook.[29] The differences may, however, be even more revealing. They shared a disdain for Grant's America, for what Burckhardt called "the arrogant belief in the moral superiority of the present," and a fear of the barbarians at the gate.[30] If anything, Burckhardt looked toward the future with more foreboding. The nightmare of a regimented egalitarian future did not make him a "pessimist," but a "malist," which was, in effect, an extreme apprehension.[31] But it never caused him to doubt his calling as a historian. Quite on the contrary, he felt an intense duty to save the past from the ravages of the future. "We shall study," he told his students, "the recurrent, constant, and typical as echoing in us." The revolutionary upheavals of the age had given historians a new will to remember and preserve. The time was the best possible for history, with no governmental or ecclesiastical censorship to obstruct scholarship.[32] In his middle years he was disappointed by his own work, but he blamed only himself for it. As a young man, proud of his work in Ranke's seminar, history had been "sheer poetry" for him, and his devotion did not waver.[33] Science posed no threat at all. "There is a friendship between science and history. . . . [both] are alone capable of a detached disinterested participation in the life of things." His skepticism was therefore only a scholarly necessity, not a consuming malaise. "False skepticism," by which he meant universal doubt, he thought a fashion that came and went. "True skepticism" is always welcome, however, because it is the only way to deal with flux, with "a world where beginnings and ends are unknown."[34] He was, finally, thoroughly at home in his native city and in its university. He refused to give public lectures in any city but Basle, where he thought it a gratifying civic obligation to address general audiences several times a year. Eventually he admitted to reducing all political questions to one: "Is it good for the University of Basle or not?"[35] In such a situation, it was not difficult to give one's life to what lasts, to the masterpieces of art, and to teach others to do so as well.

It is worth noting that what united history and science in Burckhardt's view was a common morality. Their utility or lack thereof did not concern him. Knowledge was for him not a product but a way of behaving, a specific type of self-restraint and an effort to efface the self, in order to promote a consciousness of the past that is quite simply loved, like poetry. It is not surprising that after the Second World War Burckhardt was revered as the very conscience of history, the best representative of its traditions, and, above all, as "the least deceived of nineteenth century historians."[36]

Burckhardt had a younger friend who reminded him of the uselessness and even dangers of history. Nietzsche's *Use and Abuse of History* was very much meant for Burckhardt's eyes. History was worthless as mere memory, political lessons, and as a detached science. It must serve "unhistorical" forces such as art or vitality. Creativity required new myths, not academic history.[37] Burckhardt politely ignored Nietzsche's onslaught. It was above his "poor head." He did justify his own teaching as an effort to help his students toward a "personal possession of the past," rather than to throttle them with information, but so personal a remark was an evasion.[38] Burckhardt knew that Nietzsche was not criticizing him—indeed, he knew he admired him extravagantly—but was attacking history as a science. Burckhardt did not even choose to reply. His entire life was, after all, a repudiation.

Henry Adams had no comparable resilience. He accepted his detachment as a burden. Circumstances and personal character combined to make him a "free-floating" observer, but it was not a situation he liked. He had no respect for himself, for his work as a historian and as a teacher, or for his readers. America had lost its values, and there was nothing he could do to raise its standards. Service at Harvard was the "most honorable in America," but Adams found it a useless occupation. He had not been trained for a profession, and had no desire to become a member of a scholarly society. History itself was "incoherent and immoral," and would have to be falsified to be taught to the young. It was, moreover, "a hundred years behind the experimental sciences" and without a theory of its own. It was neither as useful nor as certain as physics, chemistry, or economics. Nevertheless, Adams wrote many volumes of excellent history. When he considered his work, it disgusted him. No one wanted to read it; America had no use for the past, a point Burckhardt had noted also. However, Adams went on to agree with his countrymen. Why should anyone read a mere "antiquarian" who really was lost in the eighteenth century and who had "no use for history or method"? It was useless as education, as knowledge, and as character-building. However feebly, Adams therefore resorted to Nietzsche's advice and manufactured myths. Since cause and effect in history could not be known, the sequence of past events should be described in terms of "force and mass." Nice brutal words with a scientific ring to them, and if a need for order overwhelmed one, there were always the images of the virgin and the dynamo to satisfy a mind ignorant of science.[39]

When one abstracts what was purely idiosyncratic and personal from Adams's account of his wasted learning, there remains a quite typically disoriented historian. He had studied hard without achieving social power or intellectual certainty. His skepticism was as limited as Voltaire's. He did not doubt the truth of science, even though its findings upset him. It was history alone that was inadequate. "The historian," he wrote, "must not try to know what is truth, if he values his honesty; for if he cares for his truths, he is certain to falsify his facts."[40] From this he went on to doubt the possibility of education in a world in constant social flux. Yesterday's lesson is today's misinformation and practical obstacle. This world of becoming, so unlike that of the eighteenth century, could not be understood, controlled, or enjoyed. All was ignorance, save science, which only explained the flux. For Adams, this meant not only that he had failed to discover the right education for himself, but also that there was no way of learning the psychic skills needed to survive as an intellectual being. Those who seek knowledge about man must fail to profit from learning.

Henry Adams's difficulties were in fact more severe than those of the *philosophes*. Every form of skepticism is the denial of some specific form of certainty. The two are unthinkable without each other. From mathematics and religion the *philosophes* had inherited criteria of certainty that history could not meet. Their notion of utility was, however, comparatively modest. History had to destroy superstition and teach political common sense. The tests of credibility for Henry Adams were different. Could history yield laws on which reliable predictions could be made? Did its truths "work"? Were there technically applicable principles? History completely failed these tests. Moreover, standards of utility had been raised. To be useful, history must now do more than guide individuals; it must yield large measurable and tangible advantages, calculable as social wealth, for that had become the definition of utility. History did nothing to raise the standard of living or to promote the national interest abroad. For many, that was a death sentence pronounced on historical studies. Nevertheless, as one reads Adams, one recognizes that he willfully chose to leave Harvard and to adopt opinions that were designed to cast contempt on his own excellent work and that of other historians. He need not have been so self-destructive, and if he had reached a state of intellectual exhaustion, he had no one to blame but himself.

Henry Adams was not the last American historian to relive the predicament of the *philosophes* in this new and aggravated way. What came to be known as "relativism" worsened it for many scholars. The "true skepticism" of the historian, who recognizes the full extent of change within continuity and the distance that separates men in time, proved too much for some historians. In addition to being inaccurate and useless, history had to be written by men who were, like all their predecessors in history, part of their own time. Historians could not escape from their peers, their language, and their personal and public situation. It conditioned them, and they felt reduced. The fact that American history was now being pursued by a profession, socialized in universities and drawn from a broad geographic and social field, only seems to have enhanced the sense of being the spiritual prisoner of one's time and place.

Carl Becker was a perfect example of this mentality. History was, he fondly repeated after Voltaire, "a pack of tricks we play on the dead."[41] For a historian who was not also a poet, playwright, novelist, philosopher, businessman, and wit, that was surely a mortifying admission. Becker did not enjoy his modesty. Detachment was impossible, even "the cause of not espousing any cause" was due to the prevailing "climate of opinion."[42] Flawed records from the past, the necessity of selection, and the weaving of these remnants into a coherent account, all removed the final work from the realm of reliable knowledge. Historians make myths, and these should at least be useful. Becker did not even believe that this wayward effort could succeed. For him, the very character of historical knowledge was self-destructive and psychologically intolerable. He therefore took Rousseau's and Adams's path and rejected history both as education and as knowledge. Yet, he was very far from being a general skeptic.[43]

As in the case of Beard, Becker's skepticism was fueled by deep political emotions. At the end of a long debunking essay on historical facts, he suddenly, without even a transitional passage, moved from history's unreliability to its social inconsequence. The cause of this collapse of confidence was not primarily due to his adherence to a crude pragmatism. It came out of a devastating comparison between history and the natural sciences, now uneasy partners in American universities. History had failed even as a university subject, and no less so than as a social power. It was useless, because in a democracy, education meant no more than a distribution of information. Its universities were "institutions partly commercial and partly penal."[44] Teaching could not, in short, redeem history. Above all, the influence on public policy of one hundred years of historical research had been slight, especially when compared to the natural sciences, which inspired Becker's vision of utility and certainty. Inevitably, they also structured his skepticism and, with it, his desperate sense of futility. Both were expressions of a sense of inferiority vis-à-vis the natural sciences and an obviously overwhelming disillusionment. "A hundred years of scientific research has transformed the conditions of life. . . . It was scientific research that made the war of 1914, which historical research did nothing to prevent, a world war. . . . because of scientific research it became a systematic massed butchery such as no one had dreamed of or supposed possible."[45] The influence of history on social life had been "negligible," because it was incapable of preventing the self-destruction of the European world. It is very easy to perceive the flaws in the argument, but that does not lessen its interest. Becker identified usefulness with political power. He gratuitously assumed that all historians shared his political expectations and ends, and he was aghast at their ineffectuality. It was thus the situation of the intellectual classes and their failure to save the world that troubled him and made him lash out at "history."

Becker was not a particularly distinguished historian, but he still haunts the minds of historians, "an eccentric phenomenon" that continues to call for "special treatment," in the words of J. H. Hexter.[46] In his day he was widely respected by his peers and spoke for a substantial number among them. His very mediocrity makes him significant as a type. That he was not alone is equally clear. What Becker and Beard were saying in an American context was very much like Karl Mannheim's sociology of knowledge that emerged in Weimar Germany. In the midst of the ruins of mandarin culture he did not repine, but sneered at the pretensions of his predecessors. It had all been "ideology." Mannheim's proposition was simplicity itself. Every point of view is the expression of the social situation of those who pronounce it. Science was in fact excluded from this determination, because only a suprasocial observer can know the truth about the social causation that gave rise to ideologies and utopias. Moreover, eventually Mannheim came to insist that there was a pool of detached intellectuals who were rational, thanks to their disconnection from society. These paragons would therefore have both the interest and ability to be the planners of a future democracy.[47] This caricature of *philosophe* ambitions differed from Becker's view only in its estimate of the kind of control science would exercise over society. Historians would remain the passive voices of their social groups, "relative" to their time and place. This disheartened Becker, but not Mannheim, who was sure of his own rationality as an observer of the relativity of others, and who saw himself as the prophet of a new political class. He found in social science a replacement for the old mandarinism. Becker had to leave the world to what he took to be the destructive powers of science. He left it all in the hands of men who could neither know nor learn, because he had no mandarin resources at all, not even those of Turner, his teacher. Since no one was listening to history, Becker came to wonder whether it was really worth any attention. That is how the question of "What is the use?" arose, which, if it is asked under these spiritual circumstances, has to be answered negatively. Mannheim did not identify his own science with the irrationality he saw all around him and that he tried to explain. Becker was, however, defeated by unreason, because he thought he shared it.

In Becker's own eyes, it was not democracy that was disturbing his equilibrium. History was inherently too feeble to impose itself credibly on political man, as the comparison with the sciences revealed only too clearly. It was not merely the obstacles posed by democracy that Burckhardt, Adams, and Bury had seen. The whole European order had actually collapsed before his eyes, proving the moral weakness of all universities and all their historians. The war between history and democracy was in fact over. If history had any use at all, it was to serve Mr. Everyman, from whom professional historians did not differ. Because they were slightly better informed, they could help Mr. Everyman brush off a few errors and myths, but they were no more impartial, and commanded no greater intellectual resources, than he. This was a democratic mind in full revolt against the pretensions of mandarinism. To be a man of his place and time meant, for Becker, to adopt the mores of this peculiar figment of an uncommon imagination: Mr. Everyman. Becker was to suffer a final shock when he discovered that some Everymen were Nazis, and that there were historians who, sharing their climate of opinion, were also ready to offer their services to them. Always ready to accept new blows, he thought his brand of "relativism" had contributed to this disaster.[48] It is, in fact, difficult to see how a democratic modesty, perhaps a trifle spineless, could have contributed to the rigidly domineering fanaticism of the Third Reich.

In any event, the Second World War cured American historians of Becker's malady. Happy to distinguish themselves and their institutions from Europe, encouraged by grateful refugee scholars, they dwelt on the uniqueness of America and of its history. Mandarinism, the care and preservation of a culture by scholars who were impartial and aloof from political struggles, turned out to be a state of mind that was quite congenial to American historians and teachers celebrating a democratic culture.[49] For mandarinism is not simply the expression of a nineteenth century European situation. It can arise in a variety of settings. For most historians, this is the best state of mind to bring to bear on their refractory material. In using a neutral vocabulary, in keeping within a collegial framework, and in choosing topics professionally recognized as important they will be able to muster the evidence without undue distortion.[50] To be part of a republic of letters and adopt mandarin attitudes is the best choice for a historian who wants to preserve his self-confidence and avoid Becker's syndrome.

In spite of their eventual reconciliation, the quarrel between history and democracy had not, however, been without substance. Democratic theory, as has often been noted, does have decidedly unhistorical features. They are easily discernible in Paine and Jefferson. No generation owes anything to its predecessors, because the earth "belongs in usufruct to the living."[51] When one speaks of "the consent of the governed" and of majorities in general, one means those living "here and now," not their predecessors or their successors. It is the ultimate argument against tradition and also against foresight, as Madison replied. Men who do not care about the past will care as little about posterity.[52] Progress might automatically take care of the generations to come. The reverence needed for social cohesion, which Madison also mentioned, was wholly neglected. In the event the logic of democracy has not prevailed; few democrats have been as explicit about it as Jefferson had been. If democracy means a people's self-appreciation, it should provide a large audience for popular national histories, as indeed it has. Nevertheless, science, which deals with the "here and now," however much scientists depend on their predecessors and look to the future, never faced a comparable conflict with democracy. The historian who has no pure will to preserve the past, as Becker apparently did not, will regard this primacy of the "here and now" as a sentence of death upon history. The internalization of one aspect of democratic theory proved fatal for Becker and his kind. The sense of the past could withstand it in other historians, both American and European, though Otto Hintze, Ranke's last heir, must remain the most extraordinary example of the intellectual will to survive honorably.[53]

That democratization can be integrated into a mandarin mentality need not be doubted, even though it can be a very difficult exercise. When historians become aware of a new and less class-and-caste divided public, and believe that they ought to become more democratic in their whole character, they may well face a real crisis of confidence, unlike Bury, who simply turned his back on that new world. After the Second World War a sudden rush of self-doubt spread among English historians. No one suffered anything comparable to Becker's difficulties, and mandarin habits of mind were adapted to new views and circumstances. Nevertheless, democratization was not a simple experience, and it opened new avenues of thought that affected, not the fringes of the profession, but some of its most established members. The basic question asked over and over again was whether there could be history without a directing moral purpose and sense of the future.[54] In a very real sense, the debate on either side of this issue was about whom historians should educate and how they should go about it. That history is meant to educate an identifiable public had always been understood, but the public had altered, and historians wondered what their place now was. With that, the uses of history were again in doubt. Most English historians have been university teachers, but not all took that part of their work as seriously as Burckhardt did. Many had followed Voltaire in looking for a far more general influence, because the subject matter of history was overwhelmingly political, and universities trained public men. Hitler's war and the memories of the decade preceding it gave these concerns a new direction. Historians not only turned to contemporary history and ceased to eschew moral judgment, but many were also convinced that they had a special duty to give democratic society a sense of its future direction and purpose.

Democratization *is* transforming, and it demands both changes in the content of what is taught and in what is to be learned by historians. Since history is for and about everyone, and is, in fact, more or less taught to all schoolchildren, no democratic historian can remain indifferent to the needs of this enormous audience. That was a great perplexity for English historians. It does make a difference whether one teaches the future rulers of an empire or an undifferentiated middle class, an oligarchy or the people. Plumb, for one, welcomed a more extensive public, because he was persuaded that democracy offers the best setting for the disinterested pursuit of historical learning. Until now, the past was exploited to serve some oligarchy or other. That sort of past is now dead. In its place, history as the science of social change can now at last reach its intellectual maturity. This would also have a direct educational value. History might yet serve the multitude by taming "the education in techniques" that prevails so generally.[55] Above all, it might teach people to acquire those flexible attitudes necessary to live and prosper in a world in flux. It is history for the future, but it is not directly didactic in a crude sense. It is a well-meaning manifesto, but it is the work of a newcomer to the intellectual world of democracy. Plumb invests history with the hopes that John Dewey had for an education in the natural sciences. The relation between school curriculum and character has proved to be more complicated than he imagined, and the fact is that Henry Adams was right. We do not know what sort of education can prepare young people for an uncertain future.

Given this difficulty, one might simply try to make the middle classes of a democracy happier. R. W. Southern thinks that when historians teach the citizens of a modest state, such as Great Britain, they cannot just teach politics and law, but must expand their subject matter. More significantly, he thinks that one should teach history as a form of "enlightened enjoyment rather than as a rigid discipline." To that end, he recommends intellectual history as the ideal teaching subject. "The study of the environment can never lose its interest, but all this is preparatory to the study of the thoughts and visions, moods and emotions and devotions of articulate people. These are the valuable deposits of the past."[56] The guardianship of this legacy and its dissemination for the personal development of students is, in fact, the ultimate purpose of academic history. The moral stamina of the historian depends on recognizing and accepting that, for without it he will surely suffer the kind of disorienting skepticism that upset Voltaire and completely disintegrated Adams, Becker, and other victims of a rudderless intelligence.

That cultural history—the history of the creators of philosophy, literature of every kind, science, and the arts—ought in any case to be a primary concern of historians is not a new suggestion. Collingwood's *The Idea of History* is best taken as a defense of this history of states of mind. His argument is really quite simple. If history is about human consciousness, and if its end is human self-knowledge, then it is the study of minds. Every record that is examined is the expression of some thinking being. What historians look for is the mental world into which it fits. This reconstruction requires much imagination, empathy, and more than a touch of the novelist's art. It is not like science.[57] Collingwood did not think that the mental world of the inarticulate should be recreated, which was probably mere snobbery. For teaching purposes, however, its restoration *is* really less significant than expanding the spiritual faculties of young people by making them rethink those "valuable deposits" left by the great men of the past. Cultural history is also the most suitable way of providing an essential common education in a fragmented world of knowledge, and of preventing a pluralistic academic world from becoming a Hobbesian anarchy—or state. It can discipline this scholarly society as well as give students a shared mnemonic system. William James once noted that "you can give humanistic value to almost anything by teaching it historically."[58] You can also make it more interesting. It is an impractical project only if one thinks that the educated young individual gains nothing from possessing his past, sharing the language of its recreation with his fellows, and that the gift of "enlightened enjoyment" is beyond him. The chief difficulty is that it does call for a return to an older idea of usefulness as personal pleasure rather than as measurable social wealth.

If the history of ideas can reconcile historians to democracy as a subject of both teaching and learning, so can its very opposite: quantitative history. Nothing has done more to make peace between mandarin historians and democracy in America and France. Nothing has done more to quell skepticism among working historians. The democratization of values has in fact created a wholly new style of history. It devotes its attention to ordinary inarticulate people who leave few traces. It is of necessity statistical, since it deals with large groups of human beings and their usual concerns. Death, birth, food, migration, family life, conditions of labor, and disease are its obvious subjects. Quantification is only secondarily the instrument of accurate history. It is first of all and primarily the servant of the people. Originally, it was thought that such history would have to pay no attention to politics, the game of the elites. This is the history of the patients, not of the agents, of power, but a new sociological political history of the structures of power is not rejected, and even great men cannot entirely be excluded.[59] The history of political movements is, especially in America, far from alien to democratic thinking. It is, in fact, not so much quantification as expansion that is the trademark of democratic history. It includes groups never considered before: peasants in Europe, immigrants and blacks in America, and women and children everywhere. This all-embracing concern has its disadvantages. It is, paradoxically, highly undemocratic in one respect: readers do not like it. There is no public for quantitative and minutely sociological history. The closer history moves to the social sciences, the less popular it must be. The second disadvantage is specialization. It may enhance some skills, but it not only narrows the minds of young historians, it also poses a real threat to the quality of their work. Writing for a minuscule and intellectually highly homogeneous special audience can reduce criticism to details. It induces an atrophy of intellectual ambition. Nevertheless, democratization has given a "here-and-nowness" to history that has wiped away historical skepticism and its attendant despairs.

The plotting of long-range secular trends and mathematicization have not only given history a natural science–like appearance; they have reassured historians that theirs is a respectable endeavor. Productivity curves, price changes, demographic change, and the like that reflect "the typical and representative" are truly scientific, according to LeRoy Ladurie. Events and persons, the subject of the old history, are "merely anecdotal." His is not a view of science as effective technique, which was so fatal to Becker and his generation. This is a science that constructs "dynamic models" that may properly assess the relationships between diverse social phenomena over long periods of time. Unscientific history, which might appeal to nonprofessional audiences, belongs to the "cultural supermarket."[60] The intellectual barriers created by graphs and tables clearly have fortified the status of history. That is how quantification managed to create a democratic history that is not merely compatible with mandarin attitudes, but supports them. There is, moreover, no concern for usefulness at all. Indeed, one of the founders of this *real* history of Everyman, of the invisible many, Marc Bloch, opened his justly celebrated essay *The Historian's Craft* with the question, "What is the use of history?" but did not bother to answer it. He quickly turned to the opportunities and technical refinements of historical scholarship. Moreover, he saw his task in a highly traditional way, in spite of the great changes he had himself introduced, because he saw these changes as expansions of the manner and matter of history, as an improvement, not as a rejection. For Bloch, human consciousness was still the subject matter of history. "The interrelations, confusions, and infections of human consciousness are for history reality itself." That was, to be sure, exactly what Droysen had said a century earlier. Bloch was, moreover, not trying to educate France as a whole, much less Everyman. He knew that a historical tradition flowed through him from his teachers to his pupils in an unbroken, though highly critical, argumentative, and changing line of communication.[61] He spoke of his craft, not of his social role, and he found his usefulness in the former. This sense of intellectual continuity still prevails. His heirs rejoice in the democratization and expansion of historical subject matter that he began. Intellectually, there is now a tradition of historical writing that shuns the particular and stresses the general. Once it was very new, but now Bloch's successors look back to him as he did to his teachers. No crisis of usefulness occurred, and there was no collapse of mandarin consciousness.[62]

In their self-assurance, no less than in their awareness of the institutional requirements of their work, these new historians are very much like the most traditional English historians who see no need to reconsider either their craft or their role. In these respects they share the conservative common sense of G. R. Elton, who, in most respects, is a strictly political historian, differing from Bloch and his heirs quite significantly in his work. For Elton, university education does not alter to suit a changed clientele, or society. The educative value of history is that it gives a certain solidity to the understanding, though it can also corrupt. For undergraduates, its chief value is that it extends the intellectual imagination by showing them how very different things can be from what they are here and now.[63] The practicing historian ought not to concern himself with the usefulness of history at all; it will only lead him to fiddle with the evidence.[64] A concern for usefulness is proper only for the tasks of education, which are an integral part, socially and psychologically, of a historian's professional life, not a tax extracted from him by society. Even so great a historian as Maitland was crippled, in Elton's view, by having no research students and no serious institutional support.[65]

Such views are perfectly suitable for an excellent historian who will surely train others like himself. Nevertheless, democratization and wars of our century were not trivial changes, and intellectual readjustment was unavoidable. A tradition is only as good as its ability to claim the allegiance of thinking men and women. An enlightened mandarin ought to ask why so many historians cannot accept his state of mind. One reason is that history can be taken as a refuge from the present, as the best path to the present, or as a link to the future. In the last case, especially if he has ideological loyalties, the historian will have every reason to make history politically effective here and now. An ardent democrat such as E. H. Carr accepts it as his obvious duty to give democratic society a sense of its future direction and moral purpose. Progress is certain, and historians must be, and in fact are, "consciously concerned to make contributions to the shaping of society in a particular mould." The historian has a special task: to help the majority of mankind to a "historical consciousness" and a positive sense of the inevitability of progress. Unlike Becker, Carr is buoyed by Mannheim's doctrine of the ideological sources of all knowledge, because he regards it as an invitation to join the conflict of opinions. Why seek a detachment and a certainty that must forever escape historians? He does not, moreover, compare himself unfavorably to the scientist in this respect, though his reasons for not doing so depend on a facile use of the notion of "indeterminacy" in physics.[66] The historian need be no more unsure of his facts than the physicist, and he has, in addition, a very special didactic social mandate.

Carr is, of course, quite right in recognizing that detachment is a pedagogic ideal, a striving for personal integrity by teachers in relation to their immediate and remote students. Max Weber had surely explained that years ago in *Science as a Vocation*. It is an aspiration that is never perfectly achieved, moreover, as most teachers know. Carr is, however, mistaken in thinking that impartiality is not also a purely scholarly goal. It used to be thought that it was easier for scientists to attain it than men of letters. That is an idea that is not as firmly held as it once was, not, however, because of the complexities of quantum physics, but because the social interactions among scientists and their place in the polity are known now to affect their work also. That does not mean that the pursuit of scientific knowledge is an uncontrolled personal impulse. It remains a highly disciplined activity in which personal inclination is checked by professional standards, tried and proved, and knowledge is steadily acquired, even if it lacks some of the security it once enjoyed. No historian should expect to enjoy either the kind of technological effect, public recognition, intellectual self-assurance, or new information that biologists achieve now. Carr is unrealistic in believing that he need no longer feel remote from scientists in these matters, and that he is somehow joining them by rejecting the ethos of personal detachment as neither possible nor particularly worthwhile. His is, however, surely a plausible reaction for anyone who is so certain of his ability to promote the welfare of mankind through writing a specific kind of history. Nevertheless, he may expose himself to all the ravages of Becker's skepticism if he resigns himself to the malleability of facts.

There is something deeply self-defeating even in Carr's happy "relativism," because his credibility also depends on his accuracy. A less resolute mythmaker may not be able to convince even himself that a history made to suit the occasion is acceptable. To trade off accuracy for usefulness seems worthwhile when one thinks that the alternative is an unattainable certainty sought at the cost of social irresponsibility. It may seem less appealing when the likelihood of intellectual demoralization is also taken into account, for only a very high level of ideological faith can render such an exchange tolerable. It has, of course, been argued that the mandarin stance is bound to support an established order and that it is therefore in its effects highly political. That does not reduce the difference between detachment in the interest of accuracy and a deliberate bending of the facts in one direction or the other. The mandarins may never reach their aims, because of the limits of available evidence and their personal inadequacies, but they can be judged according to their avowed standards. If taxed with the indirect political implications of their position, they can only say that these positions fall outside their work as historians, even though as citizens they may have concerns that oblige them to live at least two, if not three, moral lives, which is difficult, but not impossible. The historians who write history to promote a given social end directly make a far less straightforward decision even though it may seem easier to have only a single life. For the primarily useful historians also make a claim to accuracy. Otherwise they would not be believed and would cease to be effective. In doing so, however, they involuntarily validate the mandarin ethos—which they reject. They will not fall victims to skepticism as readily as the complex mandarins. Radical historians tend to scorn "positivism" and "objectivity," and argue about whether they should create a radical tradition or promote the coming revolution in their histories; but the spirit of doubt does not afflict their labors.[67] They do, however, live on the brink of dishonesty.

The demand for usefulness is always a threat to the equilibrium of the mandarin historians, who will be seized by skepticism when they are asked to account for themselves in terms that the craft of history cannot meet. That is the point at which the limits of history may be reached. Then it might be chosen as learning or abandoned as a moral and scientific failure. The past and an interest in it will, however, not disappear now that it has become a pervasive part of the cultivated consciousness. We no longer have the option of remaining ignorant of history, and, knowing that, historians will continue to work at their craft in a more or less mandarin manner. They need not think of themselves as victims of time and circumstances. The setting within which they can work best is strengthened or enfeebled by what they do. It is not a lot into which they have been fitted by some external force. They have created a discipline that demands some skepticism and much discrimination, a fair amount of self-restraint, and an ability to endure inner conflicts. These are acquired attitudes adopted in order to learn and teach history. The awareness of these and other limitations is simply inherent in history, not a fate imposed upon the historian. The uses of history are not those of science, which may be socially painful, but historians are not mere boarders in the university or outsiders in the world of learning generally. The psychological perils of didactic uncertainty and of unsteady knowing are real enough, but one does not need to be superhuman to accept them. Mandarins join the republic of letters knowing its imperfections. They will benefit from those who reject it by being reminded that the history of the wretched of the earth always remains to be written and that intellectual standards have to be reaffirmed rationally. If historians cannot believe in their own worth enough to do so, history will have reached its limits, and there will be an end to learning.

Notes

1. I use the word history for both the subjects historians study and the works they write.

2. See, for example, A. C. Danto, *Analytical Philosophy of History* (Cambridge, England: Cambridge University Press, 1965), pp. 63–87; Isaiah Berlin, "The Concept of Scientific History," in *Concepts and Categories*, Henry Hardy (ed.) (London: Hogarth Press, 1978), pp. 103–42.

3. Bernard Bailyn, "The Problems of the Working Historian," pp. 92–101; Lee Benson and Leonard Krieger, pp. 32–41 and 136–42; Ernest Nagel, "Relativism and Some Problems of Working Historians," pp. 76–91, all in *Philosophy and History*, Sidney Hook (ed.) (New York: New York University Press, 1963).

4. J. H. Plumb, *The Death of the Past* (Boston: Houghton Mifflin, 1970), pp. 138–9. See also his essay "The Historian's Dilemma" in *Crisis in the Humanities*, J. H. Plumb (ed.) (Baltimore: Penguin Books, 1964), pp. 24–44. I am much indebted to the latter.

5. John Locke, *Some Thoughts concerning Education, Works* (London: 1823), IV, § 116, pp. 182–4.

6. Jean le Rond d'Alembert, "Reflexions sur l'histoire," *Oeuvres Completes* (Geneva: Slatkine, 1967), pp. 1–10.

7. Voltaire, "Histoire," *Dictionaire Philosophique, Oeuvres Completes,* Louis Moland (ed.) (Paris: Garnier, 1877–1885), XIX, pp. 346–70; J. H. Brumfitt, *Voltaire Historian* (Oxford: Oxford University Press, 1958), passim.

8. Jean-Jacques Rousseau, *Émile, Oeuvres Completes* (Paris: Gallimard, 1959), IV, pp. 526–35, *Discours sur les sciences et les arts*, III, pp. 6–30.

9. Robert Shackleton, "The Impact of French Literature on Gibbon," *Daeda-*

lus, Summer 1976: 37–48. See Hume, *Enquiry concerning Human Understanding* (La Salle, Ill.: Open Court, 1945), S. XII, Part II.

10. Edward Gibbon, *Memoirs of My Life,* Georges Bonnard (ed.) (New York: Funk and Wagnalls, 1966), pp. 157–9, 120–3.

11. Ibid., p. 119.

12. Ibid., p. 156.

13. Jean Starobinski, "From the Decline of Erudition to the Decline of Nations," *Daedalus,* Summer 1976: 189–207.

14. Franklin L. Ford, "Ranke: Setting the Story Straight," *Proceedings of the Massachusetts Historical Society,* 87 (1975): 57–75.

15. Felix Gilbert, "The Professionalization of History in the Nineteenth Century," in *History,* John Higham (ed.) (Englewood Cliffs, N.J.: Prentice-Hall, 1965), pp. 320–39.

16. Theodor Mommsen, "Rectorial Address," in *The Varieties of History,* Fritz Stern (ed.) (New York: Meridian Books, 1956), pp. 191–6.

17. Johann Droysen, "Art and Method," Stern, *Varieties of History,* pp. 137–44.

18. Fritz R. Ringer, *The Decline of the German Mandarins* (Cambridge, Mass.: Harvard University Press, 1969), passim.

19. Theodore Schieder, "Die Deutsche Geschichtswissenschaft im Spiegel der Historischen Zeitschrift," *Historische Zeitschrift,* 189 (1959): 1–104.

20. Josef Engel, "Die Deutsche Universitäten und die Geschichtswissenschaft," *Historische Zeitschrift,* 189 (1959): 334, 350.

21. Stern, *Varieties of History,* pp. 172, 174.

22. Ford, "Ranke."

23. Fustel de Coulanges, "Introduction to the *History of the Political Institutions of Ancient France,*" Stern, *Varieties of History,* p. 190.

24. R. W. Southern, *The Shape and Substance of Academic History* (Oxford: Clarendon Press, 1961), pp. 7–8.

25. Thomas Buckle, "History of Civilization in England," in Stern, *Varieties of History,* pp. 122–8; Thomas Carlyle, "On Heroes and Hero-Worship," Ibid., pp. 106–7.

26. J. B. Bury, "The Science of History," Ibid., pp. 209–23.

27. Carl Becker, *Everyman His Own Historian* (Chicago: Quadrangle Books, 1935), pp. 204–9.

28. Jackson Turner, "The Significance of History," Stern, *Varieties of History,* pp. 198–208.

29. See, for example, James H. Nichols, "Introduction," Jacob Burckhardt, *Force and Freedom* (New York: Meridian Books, 1955), p. 5.

30. Burckhardt, *Force and Freedom,* pp. 77, 133, 264–5.

31. Jacob Burckhardt, *Judgement on History and Historians,* Henry Zohn (tr.) (Boston: Beacon Press, 1958), pp. 221–30; *The Letters of Jacob Burckhardt,* Alexander Dru (tr.) (London: Routledge & Kegan Paul, 1955), pp. 170–1.

32. Burckhardt, *Force and Freedom,* pp. 74, 82–83.

33. Burckhardt, *Letters,* pp. 68–69, 70, 75.

34. Burckhardt, *Force and Freedom,* pp. 91, 78.

35. Burckhardt, *Letters,* pp. 132, 171–2.

36. C. V. Wedgwood, *Truth and Opinion* (New York: Macmillan, 1960), p. 52.

37. F. Nietzsche, *The Use and Abuse of History,* Adrian Collins (tr.) (New York: Liberal Arts Press, 1949), pp. 5–12, 52–53, 69–70.

38. Burckhardt, *Letters,* pp. 158–9.

39. Henry Adams, *The Education of Henry Adams* (New York: Modern Library, 1931), pp. 329, 294–6, 301, 306, 302 and 315, 379–90.

40. Ibid., pp. 496, 457.

41. Carl Becker, *Detachment and the Writing of History: Essays and Letters* (Ithaca, N.Y.: Cornell University Press, 1958), p. 27; *Everyman His Own Historian,* p. 169.

42. Ibid., p. 26; *The Heavenly City of the Eighteenth Century Philosophers* (New Haven, Conn.: Yale University Press, 1932), pp. 1–31. The *philosophes* were "credulous and skeptical," because Becker's own values and attitudes were really very close to those of the *philosophes.* That is why he was so angered by their failure to reach his unhappy conclusions about progress and posterity.

43. Robert Skotheim, *American Intellectual History and Historians* (Princeton, N.J.: Princeton University Press, 1966), pp. 109–23.

44. Becker, "Learning and Teaching," *Detachment,* p. 120.

45. Becker, "What Are Historical Facts," Ibid., pp. 63–104.

46. J. H. Hexter, *On Historians* (Cambridge, Mass.: Harvard University Press, 1979), p. 18, and John Higham, *Writing American History* (Bloomington, Ind.: Indiana University Press, 1970), pp. 54–56.

47. Karl Mannheim, *Ideology and Utopia,* Louis Wirth and Edward Shils (trs.) (New York: Harvest Books, 1936); *Man and Society in an Age of Reconstruction* (London: Kegan Paul, 1940), passim.

48. Becker, *Everyman His Own Historian,* pp. 233–55; Hexter, *On Historians,* pp. 37–40.

49. Higham, *Writing American History,* pp. 44–45, 158.

50. Bailyn, loc. cit.

51. "Letter to James Madison, September 6, 1789," *The Portable Jefferson,* Merrill D. Peterson (ed.) (New York: Viking Press, 1975), pp. 444–51.

52. "Letter to Jefferson, February 4, 1790," in *The Mind of the Founder,* Marvin Meyers (ed.) (Indianapolis: Bobbs-Merrill, 1973), pp. 230–4.

53. See, for example, "Troeltsch and the Problems of Historicism," *The Historical Essays of Otto Hintze,* Felix Gilbert (ed.) (New York: Oxford University Press, 1957), pp. 368–421.

54. See, for example, E. H. Carr, *What Is History* (New York: Knopf, 1962), p. 176; Plumb, *The Death of the Past,* pp. 139–45.

55. Plumb, Ibid., pp. 17, 57.

56. Southern, *Shape and Substance,* pp. 26, 23.

57. R. G. Collingwood, *The Idea of History* (New York: Galaxy Books, 1957), pp. 205–334.

58. Quoted in Jacques Barzun, "Cultural History: A Synthesis," Stern, *Varieties of History,* p. 392.

59. Jacques Le Goff, "Is Politics Still the Backbone of History?" *Daedalus,* Winter 1971: 12.

60. Emmanuel Le Roy Ladurie, *The Territory of the Historian,* B. and S. Reynolds (trs.) (Chicago: University of Chicago Press, 1979), pp. 15, 26, 111.

61. Marc Bloch, *The Historian's Craft,* Peter Putnam (tr.) (New York: Knopf, 1953), pp. 151, 3–4.

62. Le Roy Ladurie, *Territory of the Historian,* pp. 17–24.

63. G. R. Elton, *The Practice of History* (Sydney: Sydney University Press, 1967), pp. 39–50, 146–54.

64. See also Oscar Handlin, *Truth in History* (Cambridge, Mass.: Harvard University Press, 1979), p. 103.

65. G. R. Elton, "Maitland and His Work," *The Cambridge Mind,* Eric Homberger (ed.) (Boston: Beacon Press, 1970), pp. 77–79.

66. Carr, *What Is History,* pp. 190, 199, 22–23, 83–94, 107–9.

67. See Edward Saveth, "A Decade of American Historiography," in *The Reinterpretation of American History and Culture,* William H. Cartwright and Richard L. Watson (eds.) (Washington, D.C.: National Council for the Social Studies, 1973), pp. 17–36.

CHAPTER EIGHT

Subversive Genealogies

Genealogies are rarely accurate. Their most usual purpose is, after all, to discover eminent ancestors, and a sense of veracity is not likely to inhibit such an enterprise. Social pretensions are too important to let the truth interfere with them. The Homeric heroes who boasted of divine ancestors to secure "sanction for aristocratic privilege," were neither the first nor the last noblemen to embellish their family trees. Indeed Homer's thoroughly aristocratic gods were no less prone to display their pedigrees.[1] However, if divine ancestors are the ultimate source of honor, it ineluctably follows that vulgar and disreputable ones are an intolerable disgrace. The traditional vocabulary of insult reveals nothing more clearly. To abuse a man's relatives and ancestors is the surest way of impugning his dignity and of assaulting his social position. That is why genealogies can serve as readily to destroy as to enhance claims to social supremacy.

Political theorists have often noted the rebellious possibilities of genealogies. For the search for origins need not be limited to families. Inquiries into the beginnings of regimes may lead to a god who engendered a royal house, but they can, and often do, uncover fratricides and worse. Such diverse thinkers as Hobbes and Burke entirely shared Kant's opinion that "The origin of the supreme authority is . . . not open to scrutiny by the people who are subject to it, that is the subjects should not be overly curious about its origins as though the right of obedience due it were open to doubt . . . these are pointless questions that threaten the state with danger if they are asked with too

"Subversive Genealogies" is reprinted by permission of *Daedalus, Journal of the American Academy of Arts and Sciences,* from the issue entitled "Myth, Symbol, and Culture," 101, no. 1 (Winter 1972): 129–54.

much sophistication."[2] In short, the search for origins will be subversive, especially if pursued by men of subtle intelligence.

If Hobbes was right in his belief that "there is scarcely a commonwealth in the world, whose beginnings can in conscience be justified," it is clear that curiosity about the origins of public authority is inevitably dangerous, as is all history, certainly the "most effectual seeds of death of any state."[3] It must always be rebellious in intent. That may well be an exaggeration. Ancestor worship is a reverent reversion to origins. It is because origins can glorify that they can also defame. To recognize the destructive possibilities of genealogy one must also appreciate the pride in noble ancestors, as Hesiod certainly did.[4] But the fears of the philosophers are, in any case, justified. Since Hesiod's day the myth of origins has been a typical form of questioning and condemning the established order, divine and human, ethical and political. The myth of creation that Hesiod devised out of the depth of resentment has been a model for writers of similar inspiration. His imitators in antiquity were legion, and in the modern age both Rousseau and Nietzsche, to name the most notable, used creation myths to express their unlimited contempt for their world. The enduring hold of this myth on the politically disaffected imagination is itself interesting. It may even illuminate our understanding of how political imagery is transmitted from age to age, how it continues to mold the memory of each literate generation, and how we are brought to political self-awareness by myths.

Although it is always called a creation myth, Hesiod's *Theogony* only describes the family tree of the gods. Birth, either parthenogenetic or by copulation, accounts for the divine population. The gods and the cosmos itself are self-evolving and not the products of a creative act or series of such acts, such as occur in the Book of Genesis.[5] Chaos (Void) simply "came to be" and then Earth and Eros appeared.[6] All subsequent deities are procreated in one way or another by these and their offspring. Moreover, the *Theogony* is less concerned with etiology, that is the "causes" of natural phenomena and forces, than with the organization of powers and of functions among the gods. Older, more nature-oriented myths were also myths of order and evaluation, but only incidentally.[7] In Hesiod the political order among the gods is the central theme and the offices of rulership are clearly dissociated from the cosmic order.[8] He was already far removed from nature worship in any form, nor were his myths recorded as part of an established order of ritual practices. He was a self-consciously original poet who wrote to instruct and entertain.[9] Hesiod was justifiably proud of his spiritual independence. To him, and to him alone, the Muses, who so often lied, had chosen to speak the truth.

Hesiod's awareness of his own powers of insight served to intensify his dissatisfaction with his actual condition as a mere "shepherd of the wilderness."[10] His other poem, *Works and Days,* is an exhaustive inventory of complaints against the state of mankind in general and his own situation especially. Known throughout antiquity as "the helot's poet," Hesiod speaks in the unmistakable tones of men who have every reason to resent their condition. The harsh natural world, the inherent inner hardness of men in general, and the specific burdens of the wretched and powerless peasantry combined to make bitterness his great poetic theme. The injustice and suffering that marked his own life led him to reflect upon the origins of the powers that rule over mankind, just as cosmic violence in turn recalls the ills of daily life. His is a song of universal dissatisfaction. Social and political evil permeates the world of the deities, and men reflect that world as they suffer from it and contribute to its already abundant store of miseries.

The *Theogony* is not merely the natural genealogy of the gods. The genesis of the social order among them does not follow a natural family tree. No father rules by natural right here. Generational strife, not ancestral piety, lies at the roots of the political regime of the cosmos. Earth created Heaven (Uranus) to breed with her, but he proved a cruel parent. Afraid of his own progeny, he imprisoned some of them within their mother, Earth. "Heaven rejoiced in his evil-doing," but Earth "groaned within" and plotted with her children against their father, who had done these "shameful things."[11] Her youngest child, wily Cronus, acts against his hated "lusty sire" and cuts off Heaven's genitals. Thereafter Heaven called his presumptuous brood the Titans, "the strainers."[12] As was just, given the enormity of the crime, retribution was sure to follow. Perhaps as an explanation Hesiod tells of the birth of "hateful Doom," "black Fate and Death," "Blame and painful Woe," and of the Destinies, right after his account of the Titan's crime against Heaven. "Murky Night" gives birth to them "though she lay with none." Death and Nemesis affect only mortal men, but the others, especially the avenging destinies, certainly act upon the gods also.[13]

Heaven is avenged when Cronus's son Zeus, "father of gods and men," rises against his own father. Now Zeus is clearly not the actual father of gods and men; he is so only metaphorically, as the founder of Olympian society. He is not particularly creative, in spite of his numerous progeny. Most of the moral and natural "gods" have already been "born" by the time he appears. It is Earth who is really creative. Zeus establishes a civil order, but he does not bring its members into being. Even in his rise to power Mother Earth is his guide. It is she who takes the initiative in his early struggles, just as she led Cronus on. In introducing Zeus at once as a "father" Hesiod makes us aware again of his second, political, myth of origins, the one that deals with the creation of the Olympian order.

Cronus swallowed each of his children as they came forth from the womb of his spouse Rhea, so that none of them "should hold the kingly office amongst the deathless gods."[14] However, he was not able to escape his fate. Rhea conspired with her parents, Heaven and Earth, to save Zeus. Cronus is forced to vomit up his children and Zeus, who had grown up under Earth's protection, also sets free the other sons of Heaven whom Cronus had enchained. The results of this liberation were not, however, altogether satisfactory. For ten years there was perpetual war between the Titans who occupied Othrys and the sons of Cronus on Olympus. Finally Zeus assumed leadership of the Olympians, and with the aid of some particularly monstrous deities, and after a violent struggle, the Titans were conquered, subdued, and isolated. Prompted by Earth, the victorious gods asked "far-seeing Olympian Zeus to reign and to rule over them."[15] He begins his rule by dividing "dignities among them." Rewarding one's allies clearly is a mark of foresight in a ruler.

Heaven evidently was avenged and Cronus met the destiny that must overcome anyone who violates his father. However, Zeus's conduct is no less unfilial. His triumph in the struggle for "honors" over the Titans, and his imprisonment of his own father, Cronus, must surely be avenged. They are not. Zeus avoids Cronus's fate by a shrewd stratagem. Following the advice of Heaven and Earth, he swallows his first wife, Metis, the wise. This was the best way to avoid any challenge to his royal authority. Metis's daughter by Zeus, Pallas Athene, is born after her mother had been swallowed, so she sprang directly from Zeus's head. Without a mother, such as Earth or Rhea, she would never be able to conspire against her father. Subsequent mates appeared to pose no threat, perhaps because of their immense number. Zeus remains secure in his power thanks to his superior intelligence and the help of Heaven and Earth. Thereafter his supremacy is never questioned. Nevertheless nothing is more evident than that his rule is based on acts of violence and on outrages. His power is defined by the very fact that he evades the just retribution that sooner or later meets other rebellious sons, just as he manages to avoid the normal hostility of his children.

Zeus is an artificial father, a creator in his own right. He is the political progenitor of the new civil order among the gods and men. It is a political order that is based on his omnipotence and omniscience. At no point is it suggested that Zeus's character alters in time, or that he redeems himself in any way. He is a god to be feared and to be obeyed. Toward mankind his conduct is, moreover, ambiguous at best.[16] If he enforces retributive justice among men, there are a mass of evils in the world that express his undeviating hostility toward them. Hesiod's genealogy of the gods accounts admirably for the obvious—that we live in a world of pervasive suffering, moral and physical. Zeus "holds the aegis" and we know what he is and does and how he came to rule.

Some readers of Hesiod have wondered why he felt it necessary to explain Zeus's supremacy, since Homer had, after all, already made clear how perfectly established that dominion was.[17] Homer was certainly not much interested in the prehistory of Olympus. It is only mentioned twice in the *Iliad* and then it is of no particular significance. Poseidon grumbles that Zeus, who is his brother, should not dominate him. However, Zeus is the older of the two, and Poseidon gives in, as is apparently only right. Homer's heroes simply have no interest in investigating the genealogy of Zeus's reign, since, in fact, their own claims to prestige are based on descent from divine ancestors. They are all related to the gods. Only their mortality makes them different from the Olympians. Zeus, as befits his unique position, remains aloof from the great struggle that embroils the heroes and gods, but in Achilles he has at least a partial counterpart among the heroes. Nor is Zeus willfully cruel. He is even moved to express pity for the tragic lot of mortal beings. The princes of the world have no reason to question the character of the Olympians, who so faithfully mirror their own ways. Hesiod, however, had ample cause to fear and resent princes who oppress peasants, and the gods who were their models and who had fashioned the iron race. He had therefore an obvious incentive to investigate their origins. If Homer's gods are amoral, happy warriors, the heroes did not mind. Hesiod, however, looked for justice and did not find it among the rulers of men and of gods.

The politics of the gods are typically palace politics, with the confusion of personal passions and general purposes, pervasive sexuality, and endless intrigues. Procopius and the Duc de Saint-Simon had their precursor in Hesiod. Court history, such as this, is not mere scandal-mongering. It expresses a profound sense of moral dissonance. The restraints that are imposed upon the ruled are seen to have no effect upon the rulers, because no one can force the latter to behave. It is not that the kings of the world are subject to an ethos different from the common morality because of the demands of politics. That might readily be justified by the necessities of their office. The outraged "secret histories" of princes and their courts measure only the distance between those who must be industrious, just, and monogamous and those who are not thus constrained. The distrust that these historians often arouse is less due to their readers' innocence, or to a belief that the scandals are exaggerated, than to the recognition that this is not the whole of politics, not even at court.

The extent of Hesiod's bitterness can be seen even better in his second creation myth, which deals specifically with the origins of mankind. As the *Theogony* presents a picture of palace politics, of the intrigues and quarrels of the mighty, so *Work and Days* shows us what all this means for the lower orders, especially for the humblest, the peasantry. At no time are men anything but the playthings of the gods. That much is already made evident in the *Theogony*. There we hear of Hecate and Calliope, who take an interest in men. The first protects nurslings, but for the rest distributes her favors quite arbitrarily among competitors in war and sport. The second gives eloquence to "wise princes" which helps them politically. Some men evidently receive favors from the gods which accounts for inequality in fortune and talents. However, the lot of mankind in general is not really improved by these intercessions as the story of Prometheus makes clear. Prometheus encourages men to eat the meat of a sacrificial animal that he has cleverly disguised to fool Zeus. It is prudent, of course, not to waste the meat, but Zeus cannot be deceived. Prometheus's gift of fire to men is another sign that he is indeed "kindly." But men must pay a heavy penalty for his favors. For Zeus not only punishes the presumptuous Titan, but also his hapless protégés. "In his heart he thought mischief against mortal men which also was to be fulfilled."[18] He "made an evil thing for men as the price of fire"—woman, who is nothing but trouble to men. No one can deceive Zeus.[19] It is simply not possible to go beyond the will of Zeus. Mankind's misery is the corollary of Zeus's omnipotence. In *Work and Days* this lesson is driven home relentlessly. The story of Prometheus is here embellished. It is told to explain why "the gods keep hidden from men the means of life."[20] Zeus now not only devises plagues for men, but "laughed aloud" as he does so.[21] Moreover, he does not merely send woman this time, but Pandora with her fatal jar, as a sheer, hopeless snare for his victims. Foolish Epimetheus forgets Prometheus's instructions and delivers her, as prudence is always defeated by folly and regret is the normal form of understanding. The contents of Pandora's jar are scattered among men—sorrow, disease, and misery. Only hope does not escape, because Zeus prevents it from leaving the jar. Even hope is denied men. "So there is no way to escape the will of Zeus."[22]

Prometheus's daring is not the only possible explanation for the origins of suffering. Hesiod offered an alternative: the tale of the Five Ages. In the age of Cronus the gods made a race of golden men whom they loved. These men were perfectly happy and they died as if overcome by sleep. Even now they hover about mankind as its guardians. They were succeeded by another, less successful creation of the gods, men of silver, who were simpletons. The reign of Cronus is now over and we are in the era of Zeus. He is angered by these foolish creatures, who fail to honor the blessed gods, and he puts them away. Zeus now makes all the subsequent generations, and they are terrible. First a hard of heart, fearful race of bronze is fashioned. These destroy each other. Then Zeus produces a superior, more noble and righteous race of bronze among whom are the heroes who fought at Troy. When they pass away they go to the "island of the blessed," where they live happily under the kindly rule of Cronus, now released from his bonds. The division of the men of bronze into two separate generations has puzzled many readers. Some have suggested an undue reverence for Homer's heroes. Perhaps Nietzsche was right in suggesting that Hesiod wanted to bring out both sides of heroic man, his frightfulness and his nobility of character.[23] In any case, the heroes do not endure, and are followed by Zeus's final creation, the men of iron. This is the age of history to which we all belong. Now men "never rest from labor and sorrow." There is no justice, no decency, no shame, no righteousness, and no help against evil. Such is the work of omnipotent Zeus, "the father." It is worth noting that Cronus is the creator of happy men and the guardian of the island of the blessed, while Zeus, the successful usurper, makes and rules over a deformed humanity.

At the end of the myth of the Five Ages Hesiod inserted a little fable that underlines the parallel between the order on Olympus and that which prevails on earth. One day a hawk dug his talons into the little neck of a nightingale and said, "Miserable thing, why do you cry out? One far stronger than you now holds you fast and you must go wherever I take you . . . He is a fool who tries to withstand the stronger, for he does not get mastery and suffers pain, besides his shame." This fable is addressed to "princes who themselves understand" and it is followed by a warning to his wayward brother, Perses, to "listen to right." "For violence is bad for a poor man."[24]

Clearly, the princes of the world can afford to act like hawks and so does Zeus. If men act unjustly Zeus punishes them sooner or later. To that extent he is a god of justice. Before him the hawklike princes must also tremble, just as peasants are helpless. That is the sole element of positive worth in Zeus's conduct toward men. It does not, however, modify his original and enduring malignity and ill-will. Zeus's omnipotence is what really matters. That inspires overwhelming terror, and its only value is that this fear is the only restraint effective among iron men. Moreover, there are many ills from Pandora's jar beside injustice, such as disease and work. The whole world that Zeus made for man is like Hesiod's own native village "bad in winter, sultry in summer, and good at no time."[25] Avoid the anger of the gods, protect yourself against them by sacrifices and magical devices, and work incessantly and ritualistically as a substitute for hope. Such is Hesiod's final advice to us. It is the counsel of an angry and resigned man.

Creation myths have generally been treated as primitive man's science. If their political character has been noticed at all, it is usually as mirrors of historical events. The Babylonian creation myth has been described as a cosmic state, a reflection of the political experiences of that people.[26] Again, the transition from Homer's relatively easygoing deities to Hesiod's harsh ones is attributed to the anxieties generated in Greek society as it became more patriarchal and authoritarian.[27] That is, however, only one way of interpreting political literature. The political implications of these myths may well lie in the sentiments they directly express. They may just mean exactly what they say. The Greek moralists from Xenophanes onward, who chastised Homer and Hesiod for attributing immoral and wicked conduct to the gods, evidently took their authors at their word.[28] So did Plato, who deeply disapproved of both. In the *Republic* he insisted that Hesiod's tales about Heaven and Cronus ought not to be repeated at all, or at least told only to the wise, who, presumably, would not believe them.[29] Their effect on the moral life of the less than wise was altogether clear to Plato. Foolish Euthyphro argued that since Cronus and Zeus punished their fathers, he, Euthyphro, should also neglect his filial duties and initiate criminal proceedings against his parent for a minor and justifiable act of violence.[30] Euthyphro was merely obnoxious and stupid, but lack of respect for one's parents was for Plato also one of the vices peculiar to democracy.[31] It was the mark of moral anarchy. There was therefore little doubt in his mind that Hesiod had an unsettling impact upon the self-assertive young.

Among more recent readers of Hesiod only one has shared Plato's sense of the moral disorder presented by the *Theogony*. Norman O. Brown has quite aptly compared its Zeus with Machiavelli's Romulus.[32] Zeus is also the founder of a civil society who shrinks from no crime to establish a secure political order and to ensure his own power. His justification is to be found in success, in the stability and might of his polity and of his own rule. There is, however, an important difference in the two portraits. Going to the foundations to expose the fratricide at the origin of even the greatest of republics was, for Machiavelli, a revolutionary enterprise. It showed others how it could be done and what rewards they might expect from successful imitation. It was meant explicitly to encourage conspirators and aspiring princes to forget any remaining scruples and to act as others, like Romulus, had in the past.[33] Machiavelli may have had a vision of political greatness that involved more than success acquired by all and any means, even the most vicious, but if he could not wholly admire the butcher, he certainly was not inclined to deprecate his final success in winning power.[34] The myth of foundations, or rather, the countermyth of Machiavelli, has revolution and the repetition of the creative blood bath as its object.[35] Hesiod's myth had no such designs. His response to a Zeus who was a Machiavellian prince was one of overt obedience and covert rejection more subtle than that of hawklike princes. To tell the truth is subversive in a way that violence and injustice are not. The latter may be offenses against Zeus's rule, as are excesses and failure to honor the gods. However, these punishable crimes are insignificant in comparison with Hesiod's philosophic indictment. If his is in no sense a defiant stand, it is only ostensibly an obedient one. It is surely remote from the abject submission to the God of Abraham or Job.

In the Old Testament man himself is the origin of evil. There is something inside Eve that responds to the serpent, so that it is not possible to blame that animal for the fall of man entirely. Above all, evil is not primordial, coextensive with the generation of the divine being. The God of the Old Testament is the creator of everything except evil. Man is wholly responsible for his own unhappiness. He cannot look to God, as Hesiod does, and see human evil as a mere mirroring of a cosmic pattern. Human violence is almost justified by Olympian violence. There is no occasion or possibility for a fall in this scheme. The Adamic myth, in stark contrast, is wholly anthropological. A human ancestor, a being just like us, originates evil. There is a perpetual tension, therefore, between the complete perfection of God and the radical wickedness of man. In the Christian tradition this tension crystallized in the notion of original sin. However, even without this later elaboration, the Adamic myth offers a totally different view of the origins of good and evil. A God so wholly outside the natural order, so wholly other as to be without any human features, can only receive humble obedience. And that is the response of Abraham and eventually of Job. Man cannot judge God or even comment intelligently upon his ways. Zeus neither invites, nor receives, such submission. These two creation myths, the biblical and the Hesiodic, offer archetypal alternatives upon which subsequent speculation could and did build.[36]

The thinking that followed the Hesiodic pattern was essentially philosophic, critical, and in search of understanding rather than of moral rules. However, we may, nevertheless, speak of it as religious in the cultural sense of that term. It is a kind of religiosity peculiar to many members of a known group, the modern European men of letters and learning. The need for myths is most likely to arise for them, as for other men, when they are faced with extreme moral perplexity, when they reach the limits of their analytical capacities and powers of endurance. In the face of intellectual despair and intolerable moral tension, men tend to turn to what is called religion. The myth does not "solve" intractable ethical paradoxes, but it is the only available vehicle of expression for an overwhelming sense of such paradox.[37] It has been said that religion makes pain sufferable. That is surely true, but there are various ways of achieving that end, given the variety of religious possibilities and cultures and the various degrees of intellectual intensity among these. Hesiod's myth is only one way of coping among many. But it is an exceptionally intellectual way, a model of and for philosophy. By opening an avenue to the truth that lies at the very foundation of all experience, it appeals to minds not only in revolt against the structure of actuality, but also unable to rest with any obvious solution to its most tormenting paradoxes. The Book of Genesis is not adequate to these demands. The creation myth which solves nothing but illuminates everything answers the needs of those who seek a method for expressing anger and doubt, rather than means to assuage them. Ritual will sooner or later come to the aid of those who want remedies, who want "to do something." Philosophy is not for them. It elucidates, but does not remove intellectual distress. It is a way of living with it.

In the modern age the rejection of the notion of original sin created a host of such painful puzzles. If men were inherently good and destined for happiness, why was their historical existence so uniformly miserable? The question of the origins of universal human suffering, and the need to affix the blame anew, became tormenting again. No philosopher felt it more intensely than did Jean-Jacques Rousseau. He spoke at least twice of his life's work as a tracing of "the genealogy" of the human vices. And at the root of all vices he found inequality. It was for him the source and essence of evil.[38] With this in mind it is not difficult to recognize his *Discourse on the Origins of Inequality* as a new creation myth and one that follows the Hesiodic pattern very closely.[39]

Like Hesiod, Rousseau was "the helot's poet." He also spoke for the peasants, and like the old poet he found them wronged and oppressed. In an age when inequality was almost universally accepted as necessary and just, Rousseau felt as isolated as Hesiod. If not the Muses, nature had told him the truth, and only to him. All other writers lied.[40] It does not, therefore, matter whether Rousseau had ever read Hesiod, had become familiar with his creation myth in one of its many Latin imitations, or had just resorted to the same model of exposition, because it corresponded to his own style of thought. Determined to expose the evils of actual society, Rousseau proceeded to look for its origins and to show that inequality was the ancestor of all other human vices. If he did not speak of his genealogy as a myth openly, he at least did take great care to explain that he was not writing history of any sort, either sacred or profane.[41] He had little respect for historians in any case. As for the ethnologists of his age, some of whom he did admire, he disposed of them by lamenting the unreliability of the information provided by travelers and the undeveloped state of the science of comparative anatomy. This device permitted him to construct his genealogy without directly contradicting the ethnologists in such a way as to seem ignorant of their science.[42]

To dispose of the myth of Adam and of the belief in original sin, which had for so many centuries served to justify social inequality as part of the necessary order restraining and disciplining fallen mankind, Rousseau began by simply brushing aside "supernatural information" and the sort of "facts" supplied by Moses.[43] His most serious readers were in any case not likely to worry about his religious conformity; they also were looking for an alternative to the Book of Genesis. The Bible was, however, not the only book with which Rousseau had to contend. Hobbes's *Leviathan,* with its version of the origins of society, designed to support the whole structure of political inequality, had also to be overcome. To this end neither revelation, history, nor ethnology would do. Moreover, psychology was a serious obstacle as well, not least because Rousseau's own social psychology was not altogether remote from Hobbes's. The new creation myth had therefore to be not only prehistorical but also prepsychological. That is typical of modern creation myths in general because the paradox of a being made for happiness who can never reach his end requires some image of man with a psychic structure unlike his actual self-contradictory and self-destructive character. Cosmic protest is now protest against man's ontological status, as the one and only animal wholly at odds with himself and totally unadapted to his environment.[44] Ill-made and badly placed, man is doomed to be what he is, and that, surely, is enough reason for outrage.

To go behind Hobbes and anthropology one had to set aside scientific books and their kind of facts. They have no bearing on the question at hand.[45] To conceive of original man, as he was, is not directly possible, since he may never have existed. Rousseau was quite candid. The notion of a state of nature is required solely to "judge our present condition."[46] As in any creation myth, one must go to "the real foundations of human society" to see original man, to recognize his real needs and duties in order to condemn the present.[47] The "veritable origins" are not the object pursued by science, but by that art that learns directly from nature to praise our first ancestors, to criticize our contemporaries, and to terrify future generations.[48]

What does nature tell us about our admirable first ancestor? He was, apparently, a pure clod. Original man was strong, healthy, and suffered from nothing, not even death. Like Hesiod's man of gold, he dies without being aware of it. For even disease is the result of inequality. It makes some men starve, while others suffer from the effects of gluttony.[49] Original man differs from beasts only in his ability to make choices rather than to follow instinct compulsively. Man can avoid starvation by changing his diet, animals cannot. Moreover, he can perfect himself through this faculty of choice. He has potentialities which can be awakened and which can alter him. Man originally is, in short, chaos, void, but he can be activated. Without language, imagination (foresight—Prometheus) or memory (hindsight—Epimetheus) he lacks even fire.[50] Sex is casual and momentary. Whatever natural, genetic inequalities of strength, intelligence, or age exist are insignificant, since in the absence of any social relationships, they do not manifest themselves. The law of the strongest simply can have no place here. Original man is neither Hobbes's "robust child" nor Adam. He is a total stranger to virtue and vice.[51]

Originally man is, moreover, passive. Some external force must act upon him, like the Eros of Hesiod's myth, to dislodge him from his lazy inactivity. Rousseau did not, to be sure, resort to divine personifications of natural phenomena. However, his environmentalist

psychology fulfills the same mythical function. What are the environmentalist's "external forces" that impinge upon man to mold him if
not depersonalized gods? In either case man's victimhood, his helplessness in the face of uncontrollable powers, is manifest. Unlike
Adam, original man is expelled from his Eden not through any fault
of his own or of his mate. That is not the pattern Rousseau's creation
myth followed.[52] Original man is compelled by some alien force to
leave his mindless state. A "fortuitous combination of several strange
causes," accidents which need never have occurred, somehow dena-
ture him.[53] Vulgar readers need not concern themselves with their
exact nature. Certainly history is silent. Rousseau, in short, is being
frank about his inventions. They are necessary to link man, the tabula
rasa, to man, as he is known to us. That is a matter of moral arithme-
tic, the addition of stages of moral change that bring man to the final
departure from nature: the establishment of the division of labor and
of property.[54]

The end of harmony between natural man and the natural environment is due to hostile, sinister "accidents" in the natural order. Moreover, man's own nature includes all those potentialities which develop to render him miserable. Clearly nature is not unambiguously
"good," however frequently Rousseau may insist upon its perfection.
The old Hesiodic nature gods, the Titans, were, as we saw, well disposed toward man. Cronus and Prometheus, respectively, created the
golden race and gave man fire. Hecate takes some interest in our do-
ings. The terrible war between the Titans and the Olympians which
shakes the earth violently ends in a divine regime far less favorable
to mortal men. Like the gods, Rousseau's nature seems to come in
two generations. The first, as it operates *within* man, as his original
natural state, and as a cooperative environment, seems wholly favorable to him. The succeeding nature is not. It is violent in thrusting
man out of this satisfactory situation. It is positively malignant in the
form of that innate capacity for perfectibility which now becomes
man's chief inner driving force. Both as environment and as man's
psychic structure nature is, in fact, both good and evil. The two, in
short, are inherent aspects of the cosmos from the first, though this
becomes evident only gradually. In any case, man suffers no fall. He
is rather betrayed by the regulative forces of a world into which he,
unlike the other beasts, does not fit properly. Man may be one of
nature's mistakes, but he is not a sinner. There is no fall of man. To
be sure, nature is not the real villain at the root of Rousseau's genealogy of evil. Society is the evil ancestor. Nevertheless nature, human

and nonhuman, far from protecting man against his doom, actively propels him toward it, as did the gods in the classical past.

The first steps out of nature are due to accidents of nature. Men move to new areas, which require more adaptation. Learning begins. Such accidents as lightning or volcanoes teach men about fire. The intellectual powers required to make measurements and comparisons are awakened.[55] Men begin to recognize their kinship to each other and to enter into temporary common enterprises, such as hunting.[56] All this may take centuries. The first real revolution does not occur until the relations between the sexes undergo a fundamental change. Like Hesiod, Rousseau did not think sexual love an unmixed blessing. Moreover, it is the root of domesticity. Huts and family life follow.[57] With that the march out of nature proceeds steadily and unalterably. Work and dependencies—human chains, in short—are forged. New "accidents" contribute to changing the entire face of things.[58] The fourth age, succeeding those of nature, fire, and family huts, is the last happy one. In fact it is the best of times. It is the age of villages, the age of gold. It has its faults; men are cruel, and vanity and public opinion begin to dominate them. It is also marred by the birth of inequality. Nevertheless, good and evil are in balance and men are now as well off as they possibly can be. It does not last. Again a "sinister accident" interferes and the fifth age, the age of grain and iron, dawns.[59] This is the world of history, the classical age of iron man, "the perfection of the individual and the decrepitude of the species are at hand." All latent powers are now active in each "member" of the race, which is now rushing to collective misery.

Not gold and silver, but iron and grain are the ruin of mankind. For with these come the division of labor, the application of naturally unequal talents in work and its results, wealth and poverty.[60] This is Hesiod's fifth age, that of men of iron doomed to labor and injustice. The strong and able now dominate the weak and incompetent.[61] The master needs a slave and the slave a patron, each depends on the other.[62] The final addition to this pattern is the establishment of property and of civil society. They do not alter men fundamentally in the way earlier changes did. They only ensure that they will never leave the iron age. It is like the reign of Zeus, the rule of justice. It transforms inequality and all its pains into recognized obligations. The rich, in order to escape the Hobbesian state of nature, which the division of labor and property create, impose a fraudulent contract upon the poor. The poor are tricked into accepting an order which protects the property of the rich and which seems to offer the dispossessed an escape from arbitrariness.[63] The origins of law and government have now, at last, been revealed. At their foundations are fraud and force. Not fratricide, but the manipulation of the dull and weak by the strong, secures thrones. If a Lycurgus had created states, they would certainly be different. However, that is not what actually occurs.[64] Nor do benevolent gods preside over their birth. The gods are mere inventions which the powerful use to legitimize their rule and to frighten their subjects.[65]

The conditions that give rise to political authority justify it. The vices that tend to it ensure its continuation and deterioration. That is why it will never be destroyed.[66] Genealogy is a one-way street. It is irreversible. The child cannot be the father of its parents. That is why the Hesiodic creation myth is the perfect form for expressing a specific sort of pessimism. It is the myth that expresses the outrage of those who know all the evils of the world and recognize their necessity. It permits defiance and rejection, without arousing the slightest hope or impulse to action. As Hesiod implores his brother to behave justly, so Rousseau, far from believing that any return to nature was possible, called for an acceptance of justice. He did so knowing perfectly well that justice and equality are incompatible. Not even the worst regime ignores justice entirely, he argued. All reward merit and punish crime to some degree. However, a system of rewards and punishments, even when perfectly fair in its practices, ensures inequality. Distributive justice is merely the consistent administration of inequality. It remains wholly opposed to the equality of nature which knows no differences of merit.[67] Society means drawing distinctions between men, even if these need not be, though they always are, based on wealth.[68]

If Hesiod and Rousseau spoke for the peasant, their sympathies extended to mankind as a whole. Rousseau did not think the rich were really happy. We are all losers. That is why he felt pity to be so valuable a sentiment. However, one may despise the weak and scorn pity and still cling to the creation myth. Nietzsche had a far narrower range of sympathies than Hesiod or Rousseau. In fact, he scorned Hesiod as a crude poet and hated Rousseau as the incarnation of every pseudo-Christian, democratic degeneracy.[69] Yet, he also resorted to the creation myth in structuring his indictment of European culture. He certainly knew exactly what he was doing. An incomparable reader of Greek tragedies, he saw it as his life's mission to remind his impoverished historical-critical age of all that had been lost when tragic pessimism and myth had been expunged from European culture.[70] In his youth he had entertained some hope these might be revived, but that did not last.[71] What remained was his uncompromising hatred for the biblical-priestly spirit. He had known from the first that Adam and Prometheus were hostile opponents. Prometheus's story recognizes the painful and irrevocable contradiction between man and god in a way that confers dignity on sacrilege, and justifies human evil, while Adam's fall expresses a feebleness, a sense of evil as mere weakness and disgrace.[72]

What can be only inferred from Rousseau's genealogy is explicit in Nietzsche's; both shared a contempt for history, sacred and profane, as a self-justifying form of knowledge. Neither had any use for historical facts. That the author of *The Use and Abuse of History* should ever have attempted a historical account of European moral development is unthinkable. And, indeed, he did not. He wrote *The Genealogy of Morals*, not a history of values, and he wrote it with the same daring and abusive intent that inspired Hesiod and Rousseau. Even if the evils he exposed were not generally the same ones, he was at one with them in suspecting that the origins of justice were marked by hidden irregularities.

Nietzsche's *Genealogy* is meant to trace down to its remotest ancestor the present moral outlook of Europe. It is no mere mnemonic exercise, but an effort to expose the ultimate progenitors of the morality that has now revealed its final aim and nature: nihilism, the longing for nothingness. The rot sets in, as in Hesiod's myth, with the end of the heroic age, with the passing of the men of bronze, who, Nietzsche admitted, were both terrible and violent, and yet noble. They combined the character of both of Hesiod's bronze races. The men of iron are for Nietzsche the men of the age of the slave spirit triumphant. After two thousand years their exhaustion is evident, as Hesiod also foresaw, when he predicted that eventually the men of iron would be born senile. For Nietzsche's story of Prometheus is, also, never quite over and done with. Noble figures—most recently, Napoleon—do appear from time to time, but they have no enduring effect upon the overwhelming power of the priest-led slaves, who dominate Europe with only rare and brief interruptions.[73] Indeed, the metaphors that Nietzsche applied to some of the manifestations of slave morality are more reminiscent of the Babylonian creation myth *Enuma elish* than of Hesiod. A watery, passive chaos rather than divine malice seems recurrently to threaten the world of order and culture. English psychologists, whom he regarded as the chief purveyors of vulgarity, are characterized as frogs creeping around in "the swamps" and in a "mud volcano."[74] This fear of watery chaos goes well beyond Hesiod's sense that nothing in nature is ever destroyed, not even Heaven's dismembered genitals. Tiamat the primordial, passive female water deity who is overcome and must be kept down in the Babylonian myth is hauntingly revived in Nietzsche's fear of the passive, massive drift toward spiritual nothingness, and the end of all creative action. It is, however, only one of his themes. The major battle is not between the active and the passive forces of culture and nature, respectively, but between the far from passive, crafty priest class and the noble heroes.[75] The victory of the shrewd priest over the simple-minded hero is complete and total—as Zeus's over the Titans.

At the beginning of morality, as we know it, there is war, a conflict between two irreconcilable wills to power, the priestly and the noble. The priest triumphs, since like Zeus he is far more intelligent than his victim. He is certainly no slave himself. On the contrary, he is an aristocrat and formidable as such. Even if he is sick and morbid with his obsessions about the "clean" and "unclean," he alone has made man "an interesting animal," for he has made the human soul "evil." He is the inventor, the creator, the father of "evil," in fact.[76] Without him history would have been dull.[77] As dull, one would guess, as Hesiod's ages of golden and silver men were. The noble hero may be healthy and spontaneous, rather than ill and reactive, but he is not clever.[78] All epics end badly for the heroes. Who can forget the mournful sight that meets Odysseus in Hades? Culture cannot be the creation of these lovely heroic animals, and it is culture that permanently organizes the masses. In its final decay, Nietzsche saw priestly culture as an exhaustion. "We are weary of man."[79] This is not a historical decline. It is an uncovering. The heroes are pure prehistory, the Titans in whom we must believe if we are to see the meanness of actuality. There has not, since pre-Socratic Greece, been anything but priestly culture. Europe had never been adequate, and the heroes are necessary for the creation myth as a contrast, to show that this society and its justice have their origin in an abusive act, in the elimination of something infinitely valuable. It begins with destruction because its course and end must be seen as wholly ruinous manifestations. The heroes serve the same purpose as the happy ages of Hesiod and as Rousseau's original man. They exist solely to be destroyed, and so to show that the evil of the end is present at the beginning.

The second section of Nietzsche's *Genealogy of Morals* seems, at first, quite remote from this "archeology." In prehistory noble men were happy and fulfilled, while the peasants were pillaged and mistreated, as Nietzsche admitted. It ended when priests led these natural inferiors in a triumphant war against their natural masters. Such was the beginning of history, that is of Europe's slave culture. Now this theme seems to be abandoned as Nietzsche turns to the real scene of battle: within the human soul. The metaphoric personifications, or quasi-gods, are dropped. The psychic struggle is now directly revealed, without overt mythmaking. Priests and heroes drop their names, roles, and disguises. It is man's own will that is now at work. Fate is, after all, character. Rousseau had known that also. It is man's endowment, not all those "accidents," that really create "evil" and suffering. And as for Rousseau, it is memory and imagination which undo man. Mnemosyne is for Nietzsche also united with Epimetheus, regret. The evils they bring upon mankind are indeed so immense that one is surprised that Hesiod reversed the one and only ascribed idiocy to the latter. But he still believed in truth, as Nietzsche did not. Memory is now our illness and torment.[80] It is part of that will to power which drives men, not from without, but from within. That does not make it any less compelling. The will to control the future, to understand and dominate the world, the will to society, all prohibit forgetfulness. Man must be made "calculable" if he is to master the world and himself. He must make himself into a promise-making, accountable, predictable social being and all this requires the creation of memory, a profoundly painful, self-denying process. It is cruelty self-inflicted.[81] Like Rousseau, Nietzsche speaks of untold eons that must have passed to reveal this "perfectibility" so.[82] Yet both knew that this self-destruction is ever-present.

The psychic origin of justice according to Nietzsche's genealogy is cruelty. The first promise is one that allows the injured party to get his own back by exercising his cruelty upon his injurer—for the sheer pleasure of it.[83] Justice is nothing but licensed cruelty. Reflecting on the Greek gods, Nietzsche saw that they enjoyed spitefulness for its own sake. Their justice is an occasion for seeing men suffer. The pity that tragedy was said to arouse derived its "sweetness" from the cruelty of the spectacle.[84] Zeus uses Prometheus's disobedience as an occasion for enjoying the sight of the humbled Titan. "Without cruelty there is no festival."[85] Hesiod had made no bones about that either. Zeus laughs as he inflicts every misery upon his victims. The gods, Nietzsche recalled, certainly enjoyed the Trojan war. It was a play produced for their delight.[86] That, at least, gave suffering some intelligible purpose. It was not wholly pointless, since the gods at least derived some pleasure from it. Suffering is made comprehensible. One knows how it came about, why these things happen. That is not, however, a justification; quite the contrary. Unlike history, "genealogy" refers to both the past and the present simultaneously. It deals with the past that is wholly present in the offspring. That is why the prehistory of justice, its primordial cruelty, is not just a thing of the past, but something "which is present in all ages and may always reappear."[87] It is not an etiology, just an analysis, and one that does not use explanations as excuses.

The exchange of cruelties is the justice appropriate to noble equals. It cannot prevail between unequals. What is now called justice is a quite different type of cruelty. It is resentment, the anger of those who cannot fight back.[88] As long as the distinction between strong and weak was clear, punishment was a fate, not revenge or retribution, but just the sense that something had gone awry. Punishment had no rational sense, served no useful ends. It was merely an infliction.[89] Only when the strong were subdued in a civic order and Zeus's justice was internalized in the self-mutilating form of "bad conscience" was punishment rationalized. Law creates the idea of punishment as deserved, as something the guilty ought to suffer.[90] Now the nobles no longer enjoy the cruel privileges of the gods. Cooped up in cities with their erstwhile inferiors, they also must now be dominated by universal deities, such as Zeus, the juristic monopolist. Their ultimate point of degradation is reached when that "maximum god," the Christian God, god of the guilty, finally achieves supremacy.[91] The ascetic ideal is now triumphant within us, and that is not surprising. Because its great invention, guilt, renders pain not merely intelligible, but valid. Suffering is now approved by the sufferer. History is justified. The Adamic myth that destroys the animal in man offers him considerable intellectual compensation. He has his guilt now. The priest in each of us, our bad conscience, has given us a consistent morality. Fraudulence was not what upset Nietzsche as he looked into this scheme. It was the self-destructiveness of cruelty turned inward that seemed so outrageous. For the immense intellectual advance of bringing cause and effect to bear upon the experience of suffering, the myth of pain as the consequence of sin, is a systematic repression of vitality.

The priest in the long run proves no physician to his sickly flock. At best guilt is a pain killer, a hypnotic device. When sin becomes unbearable, religion can hold out only the promise of nothingness, a mere absence of experience.[92] At best men learn to love their pain, a sort of sick voluptuousness. Nevertheless, Nietzsche held on to one hope; even the will to nothingness is still a will, a sign of life.[93] That is not very encouraging. It is not a vision of a cycle, or of a return to heroism. Nietzsche may have believed in some sort of future, but his genealogy of moral oppression gives no grounds for more positive expectations. His healthy noble animals are not only mythical beings, they are also born losers, like the Titans. They have no purpose other than to expose their destroyers, the originators of European morality, and especially of their justice.

If Nietzsche seemed to admire Hesiod's shamelessly cruel Zeus, it is only because he so greatly appreciated the tragic pessimism with which the Greek poets responded to Zeus. He recognized that Zeus was already the precursor of the biblical deity. Nietzsche found in the cruel god, and in the spirit he evoked, the contrast which he needed to reveal the indignity and sheer neurotic sickness of the Adamic myth. For him biblical religion played precisely the same part that Zeus played in Hesiod's myth. The victory of either one suffices to ensure man's humiliation. Whether it be the subjugation of the nobles by priest-led slaves and the repression of vitality by the calculating resentment in ourselves, or the defeat of the Titans by shrewd Zeus and the creation of a defective humanity, the result is the same fatality.

There are differences to be sure. For Nietzsche it was not suffering as such that mattered, but how men bore it. That is the great difference between his aristocratic stance and that of the two peasant-philosophers. To Nietzsche the contrast between the noble and the priest was one between heroism and cowering guilt, between facing fate and blaming oneself. The progeny of the two reveal it also. Art is at least an acceptance of nobility, while philosophy is the expression of priestly guile. The struggle between Homer and Plato, poetry and philosophy, is only a battle in the war between creativity and asceticism.[94] Why truth? It also is an assertion of the will to power by the priestly intelligence. That it ends by exhausting religion and even itself does not hide the fact that philosophy also is a member of the priestly family. Philosophy and science are not alternatives to religion; they are merely new expressions of the same ascetic principle.[95] Truth is only another priestly narcotic to evade the meaninglessness of nature. With that Nietzsche recognized the paradox of his own efforts. For his genealogy is also a pursuit of truth. Just as Rousseau acknowledged his own degeneracy, Nietzsche knew himself to be in the grip of an intellectuality he derided. Both saw the inescapability of the inheritance whose origins they had so mercilessly exposed. There is a profound self-hatred in this creation myth and in the subversive intent that it fulfills. To be a member of a race of iron is a doom from which no amount of understanding can deliver one. Truth is here no consolation. Adamic guilt is not the only form of self-humiliation.

Indeed the immense energy that the Adamic myth releases derives in no small degree from its belief that guilt can be expiated and fallen man redeemed. Hope is not locked up in a Pandora's jar for biblical mankind. The most Hesiod can say about the age of iron man is that he wished he had been born before or after it, since things could not possibly be worse. That does not imply a cyclical or any other view of history. It does not say that anything must follow the historically known world. The genealogy of the gods that the daughters of Mnemosyne reveal is one in which past and present are joined. It is an account of the past as an integral part of the present. Genealogy deals with the ever-present, indestructible actualities. So also Rousseau and Nietzsche found monotonous repetition, not really a cycle. Especially at the psychological level there is perpetual recurrence. For Rousseau natural man is reborn in each child who must go through the same stages of imperfect denaturation. The Nietzschean struggle between asceticism and vitality is a timeless one. This theme of psychic repetition is also evident in Freud's anthropological writings. The guilt experienced by the first generation of sons who cannibalistically disposed of the father-ruler of the primeval horde is relived, and in identical form, by all future generations.

It is indeed not surprising to find a late restatement of the Hesiodic creation myth in Freud.[96] He undertook his anthropological investigation with the intent of exposing the roots of that "collective obsessional neurosis," religion, above all biblical belief. *Totem and Taboo,* and especially *Moses and Monotheism,* which he had the good sense to call his "Moses-novel," were inspired by a profound hatred of religion.[97] Like his Enlightenment predecessors, Freud stood before the paradox of men driven by the pleasure principle to seek a happiness that must inevitably escape them.[98] The contribution of religion to this misery of mankind was particularly revolting to him. In one utopian outburst he considered the possibility of dispelling this damaging illusion. Mostly he entertained no such expectation. Quite on the contrary, he was convinced, on Lamarkian grounds, that the guilt feelings that give rise to religion were inherited and not acquired through learning. Religious beliefs and the characteristics and rituals of religious groups were, therefore, just as unalterable as any part of man's genetic structure. It was not a matter of tradition, of ignorance, or of oppression. Moreover, the primal act, the murder of the father, was not a recurrent fantasy. It was an actual event.[99] He quite literally meant the Faustian assertion, "In the beginning was the deed," that closes *Totem and Taboo.*[100] The Jews had killed the foreign, despotic Moses and had ever since been hereditary victims of his religion and of their guilt. Like Hesiod, he had very ambiguous feelings toward this Hebrew Zeus. If he was a god-obsessed tyrant, he was also a great man and the Jews owed him all their best characteristics— pride, intellectuality, and ethical vigor.[101] Nevertheless, they, and Christendom also, could thank him for a religion which had made them far more profoundly ignorant and unhappy than they would have been without it. Moreover, these fathers, Moses among them, were oppressors and their murder is as inevitable as Cronus's and Zeus's crimes. As in the original creation myth, it is not this or that act alone that matters, but the sequence of deeds as a whole. The evil father destroyed by evil sons does not disappear, and the myth of oppression, murder, guilt is ritually repeated over and over again. In Freud's, as in Nietzsche's myth, guilt and self-punishment directly contribute to making historical life a miserable, iron one. Asceticism, justice, and half-repressed violence make man's history what we know it to be. What renders Freud's a true creation myth is its genealogical character. There actually were acts of patricide, and from these are born, in successive order, blood-stained sons who inherit all the debilities of their murderous ancestors. Nor is this analogous to original sin. As in Hesiod, man is cursed rather than guilty. For Freud guilt itself and its illusions are the curse and a hereditary one. He drew a family tree of the belief system which had made men suffer. As in Hesiod, it is man's helplessness in the face of the misery imposed by his culture that evoked a subversive genealogy, and one that, quite consistently with all of Freud's thinking, demonstrated the indestructible presence of the past.

Since the main use of the creation myth in the modern age has been polemical, one may well ask whether it has been effective. Surely it has been and still is. Reductionism remains the most powerful of all methods of polemical abuse. To destroy the prestige of a convention, nothing will do as well as to show that it *really* is not what it appears and pretends to be. If its beginnings were sordid, surely its essence cannot be worthy. To unmask is to display an ambiguous parentage at best. Since we accept the origins, that is the motives, of actions as their moral definition, it makes sense to show up these less than admirable beginnings.[102] If the motives of conduct are its roots, then reductive criticism, a tracing back to the psychic or social origins of overtly moral behavior, can be shattering. As people continue to derive their sense of their own worth to some degree from that of their families, it is likely that they will be vulnerable to attacks on their pedigrees, whether moral or social. By analogy, the origins of their personal habits, character, and beliefs will also remain sensitive to such scrutiny.[103] The art of reductive unmasking today has come to depend on a sociological and psychological vocabulary, rather than that of traditional morality. Its resemblance to subversive genealogy is, however, clear. In pragmatic terms, surely, the creation myth has proved its value as a combative weapon in repeated and unabated practice.

If tracing a man's character to its psychic roots, or a social institution to its founders, could, and still does, effectively destroy their claims to honor, then the creation myth is certainly a most enduring archetype of polemical discourse. That is, however, not all that can be said about its archetypical character. It is not merely a form of intellectual warfare. In its most comprehensive character it is an evocative reconstruction of an abiding state of mind which arises out of the sense of the terrible distance between what we work for in history and what we always get. Such states of mind are not directly observable phenomena. They must be expressed in metaphorical language to be recognized and shared by others. Without going into the vexed question of what myths always are and how they *must* function in societies, one can take it that Hesiod wrote myths to "express unobservable realities in terms of observable phenomena," and that his successors have done the same thing in order to convey, in elaborate forms, their felt discord with their surroundings.[104] These myths deal not with "things encountered" but very much with things "remembered and considered."[105] They are meant to make evident and clear what is often merely felt. Actuality is to be revealed, shown, and shown up by a review of its origins that does not delineate the causes, but the awful character of this aging world. This is neither pseudo-history nor pseudo-etiology nor primitive science. It is neither the rival nor the precursor of more rigorous forms of thought. It is psychological evocation, an appeal, with the aid of very familiar memories, to others to accept a picture of social man as a permanently displaced person.

Creation myths appeal to the memory. They are mnemonic devices. Hesiod relied on familiar tales no less than on common experiences, and so did his successors. Within any culture there is at any time a wealth of mythical memory upon which the philosophical fable can draw to structure its message for its audience. From Mother Goose to beloved childhood stories to television commercials we have all acquired a less than half-remembered store of mythical building blocks. Among the highly educated there is, moreover, a literary

memory which certainly includes the great myths of classical antiquity. The modern writer of creation myths evokes these memories in
us to make us understand his particular reconstruction. That is also
why their reformulations continue to interest us and to speak to us
so immediately. One does not tire of Rousseau or of Nietzsche because they awaken literary and mythical memories in us which we
can attach to their suggestions. We possess the "associative clusters,"
so that the new telling of the old myth is sufficiently familiar to be
understood.[106] Yet it is also novel enough in its images and metaphors
to make us rethink it. Hegel was surely right when he noted that the
memory *re*-members, that it is a faculty that integrates thought. It
acts to make us entirely conscious of ideas, states of mind, intellectual
possibilities that rested in disordered and unstructured form in the
recesses of our minds. When we are made to recollect them philosophically, these ideas are liberated and re-formed.[107]

The actual experiences which give these myths their emotional
power are often as obvious as they are general. The sense of inferiority and its anger are common enough. Gods and men, fathers and
sons, strong and weak, astute and dull, the many and the one, the
rich and the poor; there are endless possible occasions familiar to all
to render the subject matter of creation myths instantly stimulating.
Rousseau may have exaggerated in seeing inequality as the defining
character of all association. There is more to politics than inferiority
and superiority, and the powerlessness of the weak. It is not an insignificant aspect of all known social history either. The harshness of
justice in a dismal age, the defeat of the creator by the shrewd manip-
ulator, the misery of self-generating guilt, all speak of and to remembered experiences of defeat. The creation myth addresses itself to
these recurrent failures. They do not always afflict the least intelligent
men. For them the creation myth is an archetype that acts as a model
of their own experiences and as one for their own efforts at making
sense of their yet unformulated ideas. They might use it to tell their
own version of the myth, or they can rest content with following its
many known forms. The latter is not a wholly passive rereading of
completed texts. Interpretive latitude is, after all, very great in recon-
structing the political literature of the past. Today, indeed, the study
of the history of that literature, and of its critical remaking, has taken
the place of the art of articulating present experience through older
myths. However, though criticism is not able to produce new metaphors or images, it is not entirely unlike the more imaginative retell-
ings of the past. For that also was a matter of recreation, even though

far less inhibited by the sense of history and the limits of the given than is the art of interpretation. Yet both are at one in this: by appealing to our memory they stir our imagination and, above all, our will to understanding. Both bring down the barriers between past and present, and free the individual from the confines of personal and contemporary knowledge by opening to view intellectual possibilities that could not have been imagined in solitude or found among the merely living.

Notes

1. M. I. Finley, *The World of Odysseus* (New York: Meridian Books, 1959), pp. 142–144. For pedigrees among Olympians, see H. P. Nilsson, *A History of Greek Religion*, trans. F. J. Fielden (Oxford: Clarendon Press, 1925), p. 148.

2. *The Metaphysical Elements of Justice*, trans. John Ladd (Indianapolis: Bobbs-Merrill, 1965), p. 84.

3. *Leviathan*, ed. Michael Oakeshott (Oxford: Blackwell, 1946), p. 463. For Burke's views, see *A Vindication of Natural Society*, in *Works* (Boston: Little, Brown, 1869), I, 9–10.

4. Hesiod's *Catalogues of Women* is a genealogy listing those women who by mating with a god founded noble families.

5. W. K. C. Guthrie, *In the Beginning* (Ithaca: Cornell University Press, 1957), pp. 27–28, 63–69, and *History of Greek Philosophy* (Cambridge, Eng.: University Press, 1967), I, 142; Werner Jaeger, *The Theology of the Early Greek Philosophers* (Oxford: Clarendon Press, 1947), p. 16.

6. *Theogony* in *Hesiod*, trans. Hugh G. Evelyn-White (Cambridge, Mass.: Harvard University Press, 1936), p. 87.

7. Thorkild Jacobsen in Henri Frankfort and others, *Before Philosophy* (Harmondsworth: Penguin Books, 1949), pp. 139–140, 162–165.

8. J-P. Vernant, *Mythe et pensée chez les grecs*, 2d ed. (Paris: Maspero, 1969), pp. 291–292. It is a point that Hegel particularly noted. See especially *Lectures on the Philosophy of Religion*, trans. E. B. Speirs and J. B. Sanderson (New York: Humanities Press, 1968), II, 229–239.

9. Frankfort and others, *Before Philosophy*, p. 250; W. K. C. Guthrie, *The Greeks and Their Gods* (Boston: Beacon Press, 1954), pp. 51–53; Werner Jaeger, *Paideia* (New York: Oxford University Press, 1939–1944), I, 54–73; Rzach, "Hesiodos," Pauly-Wissowa, *Real-Encyclopädie* (1912), XV, 1167–1240; Bruno Snell, *The Discovery of the Mind*, trans. T. G. Rosenmeyer (Cambridge, Mass.: Harvard University Press, 1953), pp. 138, 304; Friedrich Solmsen, *Hesiod and Aeschylus* (Ithaca: Cornell University Press, 1949), passim; M. L. West, ed., *Theogony* (Oxford: Clarendon Press, 1966), 1–39.

10. *Theogony*, p. 81.

11. *Ibid.*, p. 91.

12. *Ibid.*, p. 95.

13. *Ibid.*, pp. 95–96.

14. *Ibid.*, p. 113.

15. *Ibid.*, p. 143.

16. Kurt von Fritz, "Das Hesiodische in den Werken Hesiods," in Kurt von

Fritz and others, *Hésiode et son influence* (Geneva: Fondation Hardt, 1962), pp. 3–47.

17. For example, M. H. James on "Mythology of Ancient Greece," in S. N. Kramer, ed., *Mythologies of the Ancient World* (Garden City, N.Y.: Doubleday, 1961), pp. 265–266. See Cedric Whitman, *Homer and the Heroic Tradition* (New York: Norton, 1965), pp. 241–248. Also Guthrie, *The Greeks and Their Gods,* p. 298; Nietzsche, *On the Genealogy of Morals,* trans. and ed. Walter Kaufmann (New York: Vintage Books, 1967), I, § 11.

18. *Theogony,* p. 119.

19. *Ibid.,* p. 121.

20. *Work and Days,* in *Hesiod,* p. 5.

21. *Ibid.,* p. 7.

22. *Ibid.,* p. 9.

23. Vernant, *Mythe,* pp. 20–22; Whitman, *Homer,* p. 43; Nietzsche, *Genealogy.*

24. *Work and Days,* p. 19.

25. *Ibid.*

26. Jacobsen, in Frankfort and others, *Before Philosophy,* pp. 139–140, 162–165.

27. E. R. Dodds, *The Greeks and the Irrational* (Boston: Beacon Press, 1957), pp. 44–46.

28. Xenophanes in Kathleen Freeman, trans. and ed., *Ancilla to the Pre-Socratic Philosophers* (Oxford: Blackwell, 1948), p. 22.

29. *Republic,* 377b–379a.

30. *Euthyphro,* 6.

31. *Republic,* 562e–563a.

32. Norman O. Brown, "Introduction" to his translation of Hesiod's *Theogony* (New York: Liberal Arts Press, 1953), pp. 21–22.

33. Niccolo Machiavelli, *The Prince,* VII; *Discourses on the First Ten Books of Livy,* I, ix, xxvi; II, xiii; III, vi.

34. *The Prince,* VIII, vi; *Discourses,* I, x.

35. See Hannah Arendt, *Between Past and Future* (New York: Viking Press, 1961), pp. 136–139.

36. Paul Ricoeur, *The Symbolism of Evil,* trans. Emerson Buchanan (New York: Harper and Row, 1967), pp. 206–278.

37. These remarks are an application of the ideas of Clifford Geertz to a very specific cultural group, the literati of Europe, which as such has "historically transmitted patterns of meaning" no less than the groups he discusses. See his remarkable monograph "Religion as a Cultural System," in Michael Banton, ed., *Anthropological Approaches to the Study of Religion* (London: Tavistock Publications, 1968), pp. 1–46.

38. *Oeuvres Complètes* (Paris: Gallimard, 1959—), Bibliothèque de la Pléiade, III, 49–50; IV, 936.

39. I cannot agree with the suggestion that the fairy tale of the Sleeping Beauty underlies Rousseau's theories, because I think it is a misreading of his texts to impute hopes of a bright future to him. In the work under discussion here he certainly makes his dread of the coming ages perfectly clear. The Sleeping Beauty joke occurs in Northrop Frye's otherwise admirable *Anatomy of Criticism* (Princeton: Princeton University Press, 1957), p. 354.

40. *Discours sur l'origine et les fondements de l'inégalité parmis les hommes,* in C. E. Vaughan, ed., *The Political Writings of Jean-Jacques Rousseau* (Oxford: Blackwell, 1962), p. 142.

41. *Ibid.,* p. 151.

42. *Ibid.,* p. 142.

43. *Ibid.,* pp. 141, 196.

44. For the most explicit statement of this see *Emile, Oeuvres,* IV, 305, 814.

45. *Discours,* pp. 138, 141.

46. *Ibid.,* p. 136.

47. *Ibid.,* pp. 136, 138–139.

48. *Ibid.,* pp. 140, 142.

49. *Ibid.,* pp. 145, 151.

50. *Ibid.,* pp. 152–153.

51. *Ibid.,* pp. 159–160.

52. The notion that Rousseau is following the biblical archetype of the fall has often been put forward, most recently by Jean Starobinski in his "Introduction" to the *Discours, Oeuvres Complètes,* III, lvii. It is, I think, wrong.

53. *Discours,* p. 168.

54. *Ibid.,* p. 169.

55. *Ibid.,* pp. 170–171.

56. *Ibid.,* pp. 171–172.

57. *Ibid.,* pp. 172–173.

58. *Ibid.,* p. 173.

59. *Ibid.,* pp. 174–175.

60. *Ibid.,* p. 176. Rousseau did have a direct precursor, Dicaearchus, a follower of Aristotle, who also saw agriculture and metallurgy as man's undoing. Guthrie, *In the Beginning,* pp. 74–76.

61. *Discours,* pp. 177–178.

62. *Ibid.,* p. 179.

63. *Ibid.,* p. 181.

64. *Ibid.,* p. 183.

65. *Ibid.,* p. 189.

66. *Ibid.,* pp. 193–194.

67. *Ibid.,* pp. 219–220.

68. *Ibid.,* pp. 191–192.

69. This opinion of Hesiod is an early one and appears in Nietzsche's lecture notes prepared for his course when he was still actively engaged in teaching, *Gesammelte Werke* (Munich: Musarion Verlag, 1922), V, 97–103. Unflattering remarks about Rousseau occur frequently in most of Nietzsche's works. A fair sample can be found in *The Twilight of the Idols,* trans. R. J. Hollingdale (Harmondsworth: Penguin Books, 1968), § 48. Here and throughout I cite sections rather than pages in Nietzsche's works. I have relied throughout on Walter Kaufmann's remarkable translations and my paraphrases follow them no less than the direct quotes. I use the paragraphs because these make it easier to follow the original German if anyone should choose to do so, and because Kaufmann does so. Additional outpourings against Rousseau are to be found in *The Will to Power,* especially §§ 94, 98–100.

70. *Birth of Tragedy,* trans. and ed. Walter Kaufmann (New York: Vintage Books, 1967), § 23.

71. "Attempt at a Self-Criticism," in *Birth of Tragedy*, § 6.

72. *Birth of Tragedy*, § 9.

73. Nietzsche, *Genealogy*, I, § 16.

74. *Ibid.*, I, §§ 1, 4.

75. *Ibid.*, I, § 6.

76. *Ibid.*, I, § 6.

77. *Ibid.*, I, § 7.

78. *Ibid.*, I, § 10.

79. *Ibid.*, I, §§ 3, 11.

80. *Ibid.*, II, § 3.

81. *Ibid.*, II, §§ 2, 3, 4.

82. *Ibid.*, II, § 1.

83. *Ibid.*, II, § 5.

84. *Ibid.*, II, § 7; also *Beyond Good and Evil*, trans. Walter Kaufmann (New York: Vintage Books, 1966), § 229.

85. *Genealogy*, II, § 6.

86. *Ibid.*, II, § 7.

87. *Ibid.*, II, § 9.

88. *Ibid.*, II, § 11.

89. *Ibid.*, II, §§ 14, 15, 23.

90. *Ibid.*, II, § 16; III, § 9.

91. *Ibid.*, II, § 20.

92. *Ibid.*, II, § 21; III, §§ 15, 17.

93. *Ibid.*, II, § 24; III, § 28.

94. *Ibid.*, III, § 25.

95. *Ibid.*, III, §§ 24, 25, 27.

96. Robin Fox, "Totem and Taboo Reconsidered," *The Structural Study of Myth and Totemism*, ed. Edmund Leach (London: Tavistock Publications, 1967), pp. 161–176.

97. Ernest Jones, *The Life and Works of Sigmund Freud* (New York: Basic Books, 1953–1957), II, 350–360; III, 349–374; Paul Roazen, *Freud: Political and Social Thought* (New York: Knopf, 1968), pp. 125–192.

98. *Civilization and Its Discontents* (London: Hogarth, 1946), pp. 26–28, 39–40.

99. *Moses and Monotheism* (New York: Vintage Books, 1967), pp. 102–114, 126–130, 167–175.

100. *Totem and Taboo* (New York: Vintage Books, 1946), p. 207.

101. *Moses*, pp. 109, 135–147, 158.

102. Nietzsche was, I believe, the first to observe that the search for moral motives was derived from the aristocratic concern with pedigrees. See *Beyond Good and Evil*, § 32.

103. That Freud was not above using psychoanalytic technique to destroy a public reputation can be seen—whatever the degree of his collaboration—in his and William C. Bullitt's *Thomas Woodrow Wilson* (Boston: Houghton Mifflin, 1967).

104. This definition, though it is evidently used very differently here, is drawn from E. R. Leach, "Genesis as Myth," in John Middleton, ed., *Myth and Cosmos* (New York: Natural History Press, 1967), p. 1.

105. Again for purposes quite different from those of their originator I have

taken these phrases from Susanne K. Langer, *Philosophy in a New Key,* 3d ed. (Cambridge, Mass.: Harvard University Press, 1969), pp. 144–145.

106. Frye, *Anatomy of Criticism,* p. 102, and "The Road to Excess," in Northrop Frye and others, *Myth and Symbol* (Lincoln, Neb.: University of Nebraska Press, 1963), pp. 7–8.

107. *The Phenomenology of Mind,* trans. J. B. Baillie, 2d ed. (London: Macmillan, 1949), pp. 789–808. It is evident that this essay has throughout been informed by ideas drawn from that work and especially its closing pages. As such it could be called an effort, however insignificant, of applied Hegelian phenomenology.

CHAPTER NINE

The Political Theory of Utopia: From Melancholy to Nostalgia

W
hat does the plaintive question, "why are there no utopias today?" mean? Does it merely express the nostalgia of those who were young and socialist in the thirties? Is it just that they resent the lack of sympathy among younger people? Do some of the latter, perhaps, long to re-experience the alleged political excitements of the romanticized thirties, but find that they cannot do so? For it is pre-eminently a question about states of mind and intellectual attitudes, not about social movements. And it says something about the historical obtuseness of those who ask, "why no good radicals?" that they do not usually consider the obvious concomitant of their question, "why no Nazism, no fascism, no imperialism and no bourbonism?" If the absence of utopian feeling mattered only to that relatively small number of intellectuals who are distressed by their inability to dream as they once did, then it might concern a social psychologist, but it would scarcely interest the historian.

There is, however, more to the question than the temporary malaise of a few relics of the inter-war period. The questions "after socialism, what?" and "can we go on without utopias?" were already being asked before 1930, specifically by Karl Mannheim. Here, an entire theory of history and of the historical function of utopian thought was involved.[1] Mannheim's now celebrated proposition was that all the political thought of the past could be divided into two classes, the utopian and the ideological. The former was the "orientation" of those aspiring classes that aimed at the complete or partial

"The Political Theory of Utopia: From Melacholy to Nostalgia" is reprinted by permission of *Daedalus, Journal of the American Academy of Arts and Sciences,* from the issue entitled "Utopia," 94, no. 2 (Spring 1965): 367–81.

overthrow of the social structure prevailing at the time. Ideology, on the other hand, was the typical outlook of the dominant classes, intent upon preserving the established order. It is, of course, more than questionable whether the vast variety of Europe's intellectual past can be squeezed into this Manichean straitjacket. And, in fact, it was a perfectly deliberate falsification of history on Mannheim's part. As he blandly admitted, the historian's concern with actual differences, contrasts, and nuances was a mere nuisance to one who sought to uncover the "real," though hidden, patterns beneath the actual men and events of the past. As seen through the spectacles of the "sociology of knowledge," history *had* to show successive waves of revolutionary fervor as the chief constant feature of European intellectual and social life. This meant, among other things, that so marginal a figure as the "chiliastic" Thomas Müntzer had to be pushed to the very front ranks of intellectual luminaries. He was the first in a series that included such first-class thinkers as Condorcet and Marx. Karl Kautsky had indeed allowed Sir Thomas More to share with Müntzer the honor of being the first socialist, but he saw More rather as a unique intellectual prophet of the socialist future than as a mere class manifestation.[2] Mannheim, however, rejected Sir Thomas More summarily as a figure of no sociological significance in the "real" history of utopian thought. This entirely Marxian view of the past as dominated by incidents of revolutionary conduct and its reflected thought is of considerable importance, because it is what makes the contemporary absence of such zeal appear so entirely new, unique, and catastrophic and thus gives the question, "why no utopias?" its tense historical urgency. Certainly it had that effect upon Mannheim. If "art, culture and philosophy are nothing but the expression of the central utopia of the age, as shaped by contemporary social and political forces," then indeed the disappearance of utopia might well mean the end of civilization. And since Mannheim assumed that the classless society was at hand, and that no challenging, utopia-inspiring classes would again appear, the new "matter-of-factness" seemed threatening and ominous indeed. The disappearance of "reality-transcending doctrines" brings about "a static state of affairs in which man himself becomes no more than a thing" and in relinquishing utopia men lose the will to shape history and so the ability to understand it. What, above all, is to become of the heirs of Müntzer, Condorcet, and Marx, of the intellectual elite who, until now, have been the producers of utopias? Mannheim's response, natural under the circumstances, was to provide a blueprint of a future society to be run by an intellectual elite trained in the sociology of knowledge, capable of both transforming and controlling history in the interests of freedom, democracy, and rationality.[3]

Since the social role and ideas of the intellectuals are the central concern of the sociology of knowledge, and since Mannheim, unlike Marx, seemed to believe that this elite was of supreme importance in shaping the pattern of history, it is not at all surprising that their notions of utopia should have differed so much. While Mannheim accepted Marxian ideas about ideology, utopia was for him the intellectuals' vehicle of self-expression and it was they, not the voiceless classes, who ultimately shaped the ages. Yet Marx's and Engels's views on utopian thought were historically far more sound in at least one respect. The classical utopia, the critical utopia inspired by universal, rational morality and ideals of justice, the Spartan and ascetic utopia, was already dead after the French Revolution. Doomed to impracticability, since the material conditions necessary for its realization had not been prevalent, the classical utopia could be admired even though it had lost its intellectual function with the rise of "scientific socialism." This judgment, according to Marx and Engels, was also applicable to such socialist precursors as Owen, Fourier, and Saint-Simon. Their successors, and indeed all non-Marxist socialists, were, however, utopians in a very different sense. For these rivals *were* in a position to understand the true course and future of bourgeois society and to act accordingly. *They* had the benefit of Marx's theories of surplus value and of dialectical materialism. They could recognize both his "scientific" truths and the necessity for revolutionary activity. Instead they produced "duodecimo editions of the New Jerusalem," preached the brotherhood of man to the bourgeoisie, and ignored the Eleventh Thesis against Feuerbach.[4] Here, "utopian" clearly becomes a mere term of opprobrium for un-Marxian, "unscientific" socialists. One wishes that Marx and Engels might have chosen another epithet. Certainly many useless verbal wrangles over the "true" meaning of the adjective "utopian" might have been avoided. What remains relevant in their views, however, is the serious importance they attached to the classical utopia and their recognition that it was a thing of the past because socialism had replaced it in their own age. To this, one must add that it was not only Marxian socialism, but all forms of socialism and, indeed, all the social belief systems (especially social Darwinism) which prevailed in the nineteenth century, that joined in this task. Moreover, all of these, in spite of Mannheim's idiosyncratic vocabulary, are now called ideologies. In short, it was ideology that undid utopia after the French Revolution.

To understand why the classical utopia declined, not yesterday, but almost two hundred years ago, demands a more detailed analysis of its character than either Marx, Engels, or Mannheim offered. It also requires a return to that historical way of looking at the past which they despised, because it does not try to uncover "real" patterns, nor to establish laws. Instead of concentrating on paradigmatic, even if obscure, figures which fit a preconceived scheme, it looks at the acknowledged masters of utopian literature: at Sir Thomas More and his successors. Paradoxically, this utopia is a form of political literature that cannot possibly be fitted into either one of Mannheim's categories, for it is in no sense either revolutionary and future directed or designed to support the ruling classes. All the utopian writers who followed More's model were critical in two ways. In one way or another all were critical of some specific social institutions of their own time and place. But far more importantly, utopia was a way of rejecting that notion of "original sin" which regarded natural human virtue and reason as feeble and fatally impaired faculties. Whatever else the classical utopias might say or fail to say, all were attacks on the radical theory of original sin. Utopia is always a picture and a measure of the moral heights man could attain using only his natural powers, "purely by the natural light." As one writer put it, utopia is meant "to confound those who, calling themselves Christians, live worse than animals, although they are specially favored with grace, while pagans, relying on the light of nature manifest more virtue than the Reformed Church claims to uphold."[5] No one doubts the intensity of Sir Thomas More's Christian faith, but the fact remains that his Utopians are not Christians, "define virtue as living according to nature," pursue joy and pleasure and are all the better for it—which is, of course, the main point.[6]

The utopian rejection of original sin was, however, in *no sense* a declaration of historical hopefulness—quite the contrary. Utopia was, as Sir Thomas More put it, something "I wish rather than expect to see followed."[7] It is a vision not of the probable but of the "not-impossible." It was not concerned with the historically likely at all. Utopia is nowhere, not only geographically, but historically as well. It exists neither in the past nor in the future. Indeed, its esthetic and intellectual tension arises precisely from the melancholy contrast between what might be and what will be. And all utopian writers heightened this tension by describing in minute detail the institutions and daily lives of the citizens of utopia while their realization is scarcely mentioned. "Utopus" simply appears one day and creates utopia. This is very much in keeping with the Platonic metaphysics which inspired More and his imitators as late as Fénelon. For them, utopia was a model, an ideal pattern that invited contemplation and judgment but did not entail any other activity. It is a perfection that the mind's eye recognizes as true and which is described as such, and so serves as a standard of moral judgment. As Miss Arendt has said, "in (Platonic contemplation) the beholding of the model, which . . . no longer is to guide any doing, is prolonged and enjoyed for its own sake."[8] As such it is an expression of the craftsman's desire for perfection and permanence. That is why utopia, the moralist's artifact, is of necessity a changeless harmonious whole, in which a shared recognition of truth unites all the citizens. Truth is single and only error is multiple. In utopia, there cannot, by definition, be any room for eccentricity. It is also profoundly radical, as Plato was; for all historical actuality is here brought to judgment before the bar of trans-historical values and is found utterly wanting.

If history can be said to play any part at all in the classical utopia, it does so only in the form of an anguished recollection of antiquity, of the polis and of the Roman Republic of virtuous memory. This is a marked feature also of utopias not indebted to Platonic metaphysics, even those of libertine inspiration. The institutional arrangements of Plato's *Laws,* Plutarch's *Lycurgus,* and Roman history also served as powerful inspirations to the utopian imagination. Thus, to the melancholy contrast between the possible and the probable was added the sad confrontation between a crude and dissolute Europe and the virtue and unity of classical antiquity. It is this, far more than the prevalence of Platonic guardians, perfected and effective education, and rationalist asceticism, ubiquitous as these are, that marks utopia as an intellectualist fantasy. Until relatively recently nothing separated the educated classes from all others more definitely than the possession of laboriously gained classical learning. It might be more correct to say classicism possessed them. They identified themselves more deeply and genuinely with the dead of Athens and Rome than with their own despised and uncouth contemporaries. And inasmuch as utopia was built on classical lines it expressed the values and concerns of the intellectuals. It was to them, not to unlettered lords or peasants, that it was addressed. As such, it was the work of a socially isolated sensibility, again not a hope-inspiring condition. But it survived even the literary and scientific victory of the Moderns over the Ancients. Nothing seemed to shake the long-absorbed sense of the moral and political superiority of classical man. That is why wistful Spartan utopias were still being written in the second half of the eighteenth century.

Of course, the political utopia, with its rational city-planning, eugenics, education, and institutions, is by no means the only vision of a perfect life. The golden age of popular imagination has always been known, its main joy being food—and lots of it—without any work. Its refined poetic counterpart, the age of innocence, in which men are good without conscious virtue, has an equally long history. The state of innocence can exist, moreover, side by side with a philosophic utopia and illuminate the significance of the latter. Plato's Age of Kronos and Fénelon's Boetica, in which wisdom is spontaneous, are set beside rational, Spartan-style models.[9] The state of innocence is what moral reason must consciously recreate to give form and coherence to what all men can feel and imagine as a part, however remote, of their natural endowment. Both utopias, in different ways, try to represent a timeless "ought" that never "is."

Among the utopias that do not owe anything to classical antiquity at least one deserves mention here: the utopia of pure condemnation. Of this genre Swift is the unchallenged master, with Diderot as a worthy heir. The king of Brobdingnag, the city of giants, of supermen, that is, notes, after he hears Gulliver's account of European civilization, that its natives must be "the most pernicious Race of little odious Vermin that Nature ever suffered to crawl upon the Surface of the Earth." A comparison of his utopian supra-human kingdom with those of Europe could yield no other conclusion. Gulliver, then, tastes the delights of a non-human society of horses, an experience which leaves him, like his author, with an insurmountable loathing for his fellow-Yahoos. Here, utopia serves only to condemn not merely Europe, whether ancient or modern, but the human louse as such. To the extent that Diderot's account of Tahiti slaps only at European civilization, it can be said to be more gentle. However, after observing the superiority of primitive life, his European travelers return home wiser in recognizing the horrors of their religion, customs, and institutions, but in no way capable or hopeful of doing anything about them. The aim, as in Swift, is to expose absurdity and squalor simply for the sake of bringing them into full view.

This all too brief review of classical utopia should suffice to show how little "activism" or revolutionary optimism or future-directed hope there is in this literature. It is neither ideology nor utopia in Mannheim's sense, but then neither is most of the great critical political literature before the end of the eighteenth century. Machiavelli, Bodin, Hobbes, Rousseau: were they "reactionary ideologues" because they were not "revolutionary utopists"? Significantly, it is only during the course of the English Civil War that action-minded utopists appear. However, even the two most notable among them,

Harrington and Hartlib, were concerned with constitutional and educational reform, respectively, rather than with full-scale utopias. Nevertheless, for once imminent realization was envisaged. As for poor Winstanley and his little band of Diggers, they have merely been forced to play the English Müntzer in Marxian historiography in search of precursors and paradigms. These were all voices in the wilderness, part of a unique revolutionary situation. It is only as partial exceptions to the rule that they are really illuminating. They seem only to show how unrevolutionary the general course of utopian thought and political thinking was before the age inaugurated by the French Revolution. The end of utopian literature did not mark the end of hope; on the contrary, it coincided with the birth of historical optimism.

Utopia was not the only casualty of the revolution in political thought. Plutarchian great-man historiography and purely critical political philosophy were never the same again either. Nor was it solely a matter of the new theory of historical progress. As Condorcet, one of the first and most astute of its authors, observed, the real novelties of the future were democracy and science, and they demanded entirely new ways of looking at politics. If a democratic society was to understand itself it would need a new history: "the history of man," of all the inconspicuous and voiceless little people who constitute humanity and who have now replaced the star actors on the historical stage. The various historical systems of the nineteenth century, with their "laws"—whether progressive, evolutionist, dialectical, positivist, or not—were all, in spite of their endless deficiencies, efforts to cope with this new history. To write the history of the inarticulate majority, of those groups in society which do not stand out and therefore must be discovered, was a task so new and so difficult that it is scarcely surprising that it should not have succeeded. After all, contemporary sociology is, in a wiser and sadder mood, still plodding laboriously to accomplish it. As for science, Condorcet recognized not only that technology, that is, accumulated and applied knowledge, would transform material and social life, but also that science was not just an acquisition, but an entirely new outlook. With its openmindedness and experimentalism it had to replace older modes of thought which were incompatible with it. As such it was not only the vehicle of progress, but also the sole way in which the new society-in-change could be understood and guided. Scientific thought was inherently a call to action. The new world, as Condorcet saw it, would be so unlike the old that its experiences could be grasped, expressed, and formed only by those who adopted the openness of scientific attitudes.[10] It was this that his systematizing successors, the victims of classical habits of thought, did not appreciate in the slightest. Whatever one may think of Condorcet's own historiography with its simple challenge-and-response ladder of improvement, he, at least, had the great merit of understanding why classical history and critical political theory had to be replaced by more democratic, dynamic, and activist social ideas.

Given the revolutionary changes of nineteenth-century Europe, the preoccupations of the classical utopists were no longer relevant. Original sin and the critical model were not vital interests. Marx, in spite of his protestations, was not the only one to take over the critical functions of the old utopists and to expand them into a relentlessly future-directed activism. All his rivals were just as intent upon action as he was. It was merely that some of them thought, as Saint-Simon had, that philosophers would exercise the most significant and effective authority by ruling over public opinion, rather than by participating directly in political action. Thus "the philosopher places himself at the summit of thought. From there he views the world as it has been and as it must become. *He is not only an observer. He is an actor.* [Italics added.] He is an actor of the first rank in the moral world because it is his opinions on what the world must become which regulate human society."[11] This bit of intellectualist megalomania could be illustrated by endless quotations not only from socialist sources, but also from liberal writings and from the distressed conservative deprecators of both.

The activism of the age was, moreover, not a random one. The future was all plotted out, and beckoning. "The Golden Age lies before us and not behind us, and is not far away."[12] The inevitable had only to be hastened on. Certainly there was no point in contemplating the classical past. However, the impact of the polis was not quite gone. Especially in socialist thought, even if not so openly as in Jacobin rhetoric, the ancient republic was still an inspiration. The ideal of its unity, of its homogeneous order, colored all their visions of the future. Certainly Marx was no stranger to the nostalgia for that cohesive city or its medieval communal counterpart. It was the liberal Benjamin Constant who noted that efforts to impose the political values of classical antiquity upon the totally dissimilar modern world could lead only to forms of despotism, which, far from being classical, would be entirely new.[13] John Stuart Mill, following him, found this notion, "that all perfection consists in unity," to be precisely the most repellent aspect of Comte's philosophy.[14] Indeed, the engineered community, whose perfect order springs not from a rational perception of truth, but from a pursuit of social unity as a material necessity, provides neither ancient nor modern liberty. The imagery is revealing. Cabet delighted in the vision of factory workers who displayed "so much order and discipline that they looked like an army."[15] Bellamy's "industrial army" speaks for itself.

The form of such works as Cabet's *Voyage to Icaria* and Bellamy's *Looking Backward* should not lead one to think that these pictures of perfected societies are in any sense utopias. Precisely because they affect the external format of the classical utopia they demonstrate most effectively the enormous differences between the old and new ways of thought. The nineteenth-century imaginary society is not "nowhere" historically. It is a future society. And, it too is a summons to action. The purpose of Cabet's expedition to set up Icaria in America was not simply to establish a small island of perfection; it was to be a nucleus from which a world of Icarias would eventually spring. No sooner had Bellamy's work appeared than Bellamy societies, often (and not surprisingly) sponsored by retired army officers, appeared to promote his ideas. Theodore Hertzka's *Freeland* led to similar organized efforts, as its author had hoped it would. He declared frankly that the imaginary society was merely a device to popularize social ideas which he regarded as practical and scientifically sound. This, in itself, suffices to account for the literary feebleness of virtually all nineteenth-century quasi-utopias. There was nothing in them that could not have been better presented in a political manifesto or in a systematic treatise. They were all vulgarizations and were devised solely to reach the largest possible audience. The form of the classical utopia was inseparable from its content. Both were part of a single conception. The social aspirations of the nineteenth century found their literary form in the realistic novel, not in the crude and unstylish fiction of social theorists turned amateur romancers. Even the "utopias" based on scientific, rather than social, predictions were either childish or tedious. Either their fancies displayed no insight into the real potentialities of technology or, if they were well-informed, they were rendered obsolete by the actual developments of technology. Not even the last and most talented of latter-day contrivers of imaginary societies, H. G. Wells, could save the genre. He at least saw that his utopia had nothing in common with the classical works of that name. Now the perfect model is in the future, that is, it has a time and a place and is, indeed, already immanent in the present. It must be world-wide, devoted to science, to progress, to change, and it must allow for individuality. Only the intellectual ruling class of "samurai" is left to remind one of the classical past.[16] As a liberal socialist, Wells was, no doubt, especially aware of the need to root out the remnants of that illiberal, self-absorbed, and closed social order which classicism had left as its least worthy gift to the democratic imagination. However, the novel of the happy future did not prosper in Wells's or in any other hands. For it was simply superfluous. Its message could be presented in many more suitable ways. Certainly it was in no way a continuation of the classical utopian tradition.

It has of late been suggested that the radicalism of the last century was a form of "messianism," of "millennialism," or of a transplanted eschatological consciousness. Psychologically this may be quite true in the sense that for many of the people who participated in radical movements social ideologies fed religious longings that traditional religions could not satisfy. These people may even have been responding to the same urges as the members of the medieval revolutionary millennialist sects. In this sense one may well regard radical ideology as a surrogate for unconventional religiosity. It should, however, not be forgotten that millennialism always involves an element of eternal salvation.[17] And this was entirely absent in the message of even those social prophets who called for new religions as a means of bringing social discipline to Europe. For them it was only a matter of social policy, not of supraterrestrial truth. Marxism and social Darwinism, moreover, did not even involve this degree of "new" religiosity. Whatever they did for the fanaticized consciousness that eagerly responded to them, the intellectual structure of radical doctrines was not a prophetic heresy either in form or in intent. It represented an entirely new chapter in European thought. As Condorcet had clearly seen, it was a matter of new responses to a new social world; and the aspirations, methods of argument, and categories of thought of these historical systems were correspondingly unique, however primordial the human yearnings that they could satisfy might be. One ought not to forget the rational element, the effort of intellectual understanding that is perfectly evident in the writings of Saint-Simon, Marx, Comte, and all the rest. The various political revolutions after 1789 gave more than a semblance of reality to a vision of social history as a perpetual combat between the forces of progress and of conservatism. Conservative and liberal social observers no less than socialists took that view of historical dynamics. Even John Stuart Mill, who recognized that the categories of order and progress were inadequate concepts for a deeper analysis of politics, could see the past as a sequence of struggles between freedom and repression.[18] The theory of class war was by no means the only one that, in a projection of nineteenth-century experience into the past, saw the history of Europe as a series of duels. Some saw it as progress, some as doom, but all perceived the same pattern. Looking back, of course, the century before the First World War appears infinitely more complicated than that, and so do the eras preceding it. However, if it is quite understandable why one should be sensitive to pluralistic social complexities today, it is also not difficult to see why dualistic patterns tended to dominate the historical imagination of the nineteenth century. Nor is it totally irrational that the experience of these rapid changes, so unlike those of the past, should lead men to entertain great expectations of the future. Neither the view of history as a dualistic combat of impersonal social forces nor the confident belief in a better future which would at last bring rest to mankind was a "millennial" fancy, nor was either really akin to the chiliastic religious visions that inspired the apocalyptic sects. If they were not utopias, neither were they New Jerusalem. The desire to stress similarities, to find continuities everywhere, is not always helpful, especially in the history of ideas, where the drawing of distinctions is apt to lead one more nearly to the truth.

The reason that ideology has been represented so often as a type of religiosity is, of course, a response to the terrifying fervor expressed by the members of modern mass-movements. It is the emotional element in Nazism, communism, and other revolutionary movements all over the world that is so reminiscent of many of the old popular heresies. The dynamism of mass parties, however, is really at stake here, not the actual systems of ideas which were produced in such great quantity by nineteenth-century Europe. Ideology, however, when it refers to those systems of ideas which were capable of replacing all the inherited forms of social thought, utopia among them, was clearly more significant intellectually than the brutish "isms" that animate both the leaders and the led of these movements. The latter should not be confused with either ideology, or utopia, or even with the religious extravagances of other ages. Nor is the question, "why no utopias?" really concerned with the organization of mass-parties. Indeed, even in Mannheim's theory, utopia and ideology refer to highly developed modes of thought and not to quasi-instinctive mental reactions. If, unlike Mannheim, one does not identify utopia with the charted mission of the intellectual class, one can recognize that "the end of utopia" involves not sociological, but philosophical, issues. It is the concern of political theory—of the high culture of social thought. What is really at stake is the realization that the disintegration of nineteenth-century ideology has not made it possible simply

to return to classical-critical theory, of which utopia was a part. The
post-ideological state of mind is not a classical one, any more than
an ex-Christian is a pagan. On the contrary, the end of the great
ideological systems may well also mark the exhaustion of the last
echo of classicism in political theory, even if, occasionally, a nostalgic
appreciation for the integral classicism of the more distant past can
still be heard.

The occasional contemporary efforts to construct pictures of perfect communities illustrate the point. They are compromises between
the old utopia and the newer historical consciousness. Thus, for example, Martin Buber and Paul Goodman argue only for the historical
non-impossibility of their plans, not for their inevitability. *Kvuzas*,
or perfectly planned cities, are feasible, and certainly their admirers
hope for their realization.[19] These are still calls to action, but modest
ones. Their scope, moreover, is limited, and their very essence is a
revival of that dream of the polis, of the "authentic" small community that truly absorbs and directs the lives of its inhabitants. These
relatively mild and moderate proposals, and the more general concern with *real* community life, do show, among other things, the lingering power of classical values. Here the longing for utopia and nostalgia for antiquity are inseparable. And indeed the question, "why
is there no utopia?" expresses not only an urge to return to antiquity,
but also, and far more importantly, a sense of frustration at our inability to think as creatively as the ancients apparently did.

Classicism, in one form or another, was, as we have seen, an integral part not only of utopia, but also of most political thinking.
Hobbes and Bentham in their firm rejection of the conventional classical model were intellectually far more radical than the later ideologists. For in spite of occasional liberal protests, socialist doctrines
were by no means the only ones that contrived to perpetuate classical
notions throughout the nineteenth century. Long after Platonic metaphysics and the critical-contemplative mode of thought had been
abandoned, classical imagery and values retained their hold on the
political imagination, and classical methods of description and argument continued to mold the expression of political ideas in a social
context in which classicism had ceased to be relevant. In this respect,
all the ideologies served to retard political thinking. Their decline
now has left political theory without any clear orientation and so
with a sense of uneasiness. It is not that political theory is dead, as
has often been claimed, but that so much of it consists of an incanta-
tion of clichés which seem to have no relation to social experiences
whose character is more sensed than expressed. Could it be that clas-

sicism, not only as a set of political values and memories, but as a legacy of words, conceptions, and images, acts as a chain upon our imagination? Is it not, perhaps, that language, mental habits, and categories of thought organically related to a social world completely unlike our own are entirely unsuitable for expressing our experiences? May this not be the cause of our inability to articulate what we feel and see, and to bring order into what we know? Certainly a vocabulary and notions dependent upon Greek and Latin can no longer be adequate to discuss our social life-situation. Nor will the continual addition of implausible neologisms composed of more Greek and Latin words help, for they do not affect the structure of thinking. The malaise induced by this state of affairs is responsible for much of the ill-tempered and ill-informed hostility of many humanists toward the natural sciences which do not share these inherited difficulties. It also accounts for many ill-considered efforts to "imitate" science by the metaphorical or analogical use of words drawn from biology or physics. Nor is analytical philosophy of much use, for it does not address itself to concerns which are more nearly felt than spoken and which involve not so much what can be said as the difficulty of saying anything at all. To be sure, nostalgia is the least adequate response of all to these discomforts. And that is just what the question, "why is there no utopia?" does express in this context.

With these considerations, the question, "why is there no utopia today?" has, hopefully, been reduced to its proper proportions, which are not very great. To the extent that it depends on an erroneous and dated view of the European past, it is simply irrelevant. As a psychological problem its interest is great, but of a clinical nature. Lastly, it is only one item in the far more complex range of questions that concern the possibilities of contemporary political philosophy. Here, however, it does at least have genuine significance, even though it does not ask for an answer. For it is more a comment upon an intellectual situation than a real query. That is why a journey, however quick, through the utopian and ideological past seemed a fitting response, since it might show what the question implies, even if it does not offer any solutions.

Notes

1. Karl Mannheim, *Ideology and Utopia*, tr. by Louis Wirth and Edward Shils (New York: Harvest Books, n.d.), pp. 193, 195–197, 205, 222, 255–257, 263, et passim.

2. Karl Kautsky, *Thomas More and His Utopia*, tr. by H. J. Stenning (New York: Russell, 1959), pp. 1–3, 171.

3. Karl Mannheim, *Freedom, Power and Democratic Planning* (New York: Oxford University Press, 1950).

4. Lewis S. Feuer, ed., *Marx and Engels: Basic Writings* (New York: Anchor Books, 1959), pp. 37–39, 70, 81, 90, 245.

5. Gabriel de Foigny, *Terra Australis Incognita*, in Glenn Negley and J. Max Patrick, *The Quest for Utopia. An Anthology of Imaginary Societies* (New York: Schuman, 1952), p. 402.

6. Sir Thomas More, *Utopia*, tr. and ed. by H. V. S. Ogden (New York: Appleton-Century-Crofts, 1949), pp. 48–49.

7. *Ibid.*, p. 83.

8. Hannah Arendt, *The Human Condition* (Chicago: University of Chicago Press, 1958), p. 303.

9. H. C. Baldry, *Ancient Utopias* (Southampton: University of Southampton, 1956); Fénelon, *The Adventures of Telemachus*, in Negley and Patrick, *op. cit.*, pp. 424–437.

10. A.-N. de Condorcet, *Sketch for the Historical Picture of the Progress of the Human Mind*, tr. by June Barraclough (London: Weidenfeld and Nicolson, 1955), pp. 163–164, 168–170, 184–202.

11. Quoted in Frank E. Manuel, *The New World of Henri de Saint-Simon* (Cambridge: Harvard University Press, 1956), p. 151.

12. Edward Bellamy, quoted in Negley and Patrick, *op. cit.*, p. 80.

13. *Oeuvres* (Paris: Bibliothèque de la Pléiade, 1957), pp. 1044–1058.

14. J. S. Mill, *The Positive Philosophy of Auguste Comte* (New York: H. Holt and Co., 1873), p. 128.

15. Etienne Cabet, *Voyage to Icaria*, in M. L. Berneri, *Journey Through Utopia* (London: Routledge & Kegan Paul, 1950), p. 234.

16. H. G. Wells, *A Modern Utopia*, in Negley and Patrick, *op. cit.*, pp. 228–250.

17. On this important point, see Sylvia L. Thrupp, "Introduction," in *Millennial Dreams in Action, Comparative Studies in Society and History* (The Hague: Mouton, 1962), p. 11.

18. J. S. Mill, *Representative Government*, in *Utilitarianism* (London: Everyman's Library, 1944), pp. 186–192, in contrast to the dialectical argument of *On Liberty*.

19. Martin Buber, *Paths in Utopia*, tr. by R. F. C. Hull (London: Routledge & Kegan Paul, 1949), pp. 127–148; Paul Goodman, *Utopian Essays and Critical Proposals* (New York: Vintage Books, 1964), pp. 3–22, 110–118; and Paul and Percival Goodman, *Communitas* (New York: Vintage Books, 1960), passim.

CHAPTER TEN

What Is the Use
of Utopia?

Before one can even begin to answer the question I have asked one would have to offer some definition of "utopia," and that has become very difficult and controversial. The reasons for these protracted disagreements would take too long to explain, but I must at least draw some sort of map to help us get around the vast territory now called utopia. There is one solution that seems obvious but is not really helpful. Why not limit the term to the one and only true utopia, Sir Thomas More's immortal work? He started with a pun, for his state was both *eutopia*, the happy city, and *utopia*, the one that was nowhere. The difficulty is that though one has to begin with Sir Thomas More, one cannot simply stop with him, because his subject ran away from him. There is an absolutely staggering number of works that have been written since then and still are being written, all of which are meant to offer the same combination of a happy state and nowhere. They have a perfectly good claim to be utopias. Calling them imitations does not solve the problem of how to put some sort of order into the mass of material.

The utopian literature is not only large; it is also very diverse, reflecting the historical and political circumstances and personal aspirations of the various authors. In addition there are the many practical projects that have flourished since the nineteenth century and that are meant not only to be happy but somewhere, in fact, to be put in place here and now. These communal enterprises are also usually referred to as utopias, even though they are quite visible. They deserve the name because they were based on visions that closely resem-

This undated essay has not been previously published.

bled the old utopias. Finally, the inherent significance of utopian thinking as such became a subject for heated debate and still is. Let me just mention that in the United States alone there are now two journals devoted to utopia and alternative societies, respectively. The monographs just keep piling up, and there seems to be no end in sight.

The chief source of the confusion is not to be found merely in this profusion and the variety of literary materials. It is due, I believe, above all to the abusive use of the word "utopian" to label projects that are regarded as both undesirable and impossible. This labeling began very early. I came across it in the tracts written by American Tories in the early 1770s, and I am sure that they were by no means the first. All these complaints against the government, Tory writers foresaw, were clearly contemplating independence from Great Britain, which was to be dreaded and which was in any case "utopian," meaning not feasible and dangerous. I mention this particular example because independence turned out to be eminently feasible and, from our point of view, it was a very good thing too. The usage, however, has survived, and "utopia" and "utopian" have come to mean mostly a project that is not just a fantasy but also one that will end in ruin.

Disaster does not, in fact, always follow radical enterprises, but they do stimulate conflict. The rather acrimonious debates about the meaning and worth of utopia have thus often been driven by ideological conflicts, which were born in the age of the two great revolutions, the American and the French. But even more deeply it is a matter of hope. By now "utopia" stands for political hope. Should we permit ourselves to consider a better world or should we abandon hope and grimly accept things as they are? Less gloomily, should we strive for transformation or settle for cautious amelioration of the conditions under which we live? These are the issues that have since the Second World War acted as the emotional undertow of the question: "What's the use of utopia?"

What to do? Where to begin? People have always dreamed of a life of effortless abundance, peace, and well-being. The age of gold, the state of nature, the Garden of Eden: these are dreams that are as old as mankind itself. But not every image of a happiness that is remote from actual misery is a utopia. What sets Sir Thomas More's idea of happy lands apart from all others is that it is political, "of the Best State of Public Weal," and also philosophical. More had his predecessors, one of whom he acknowledged, Plato, and we know that there were other authors who wrote plans, now lost to us, for perfect cities. Nevertheless, after 1516, when More's *Utopia* was first published, his city became the archetype on which subsequent writers relied until the eighteenth century.

The chief difference among these classical or humanist imaginary cities is that some rely on the rational control of passion to achieve harmony, while others, notably Lord Bacon's *New Atlantis,* look to science and the accumulation of useful knowledge to reach the same result. The end of utopia is not just happiness. It is the happiness that is created by social concord and true knowledge. This is politically planned happiness that only the abolition of conflict among individuals and groups can produce. Such peace is, moreover, possible only because utopia is an expression of a perceived universal truth. For truth is one, and only error is multiple. Each utopian author adds his own touches. Some are keen on architecture and city planning. Others have astrological ambitions. Many are vegetarians. Some look to new, others to quite conventional, laws and institutions. All pay a great deal of attention to the education of the young, though not with an equal degree of psychological insight. The point is above all the elimination of erroneous and destructive beliefs.

One thing is common to all: the city as a whole is happy, because personal enmities and social factions and all the causes of individual and group hostility have been eliminated. The second shared feature is a sense of expansive human possibilities. Here nothing stirred the adventurous imagination more directly than the discovery of America. All those islands that one suddenly finds in the middle of the ocean are so many Americas, and their populations are imaginary Amerindians, even if they do not in any respect resemble the Native American population. Whether they turn up as noble savages, humane cannibals, or wise people of classical dimensions, they are derived from the actual hopes and tall tales that the great discoverers brought back from America. But most of all it was the very fact of the discovery of what they took to be a new world that made utopia a plausible intellectual enterprise. Raphael Hythloday, the narrator of More's *Utopia,* is a navigator and a discoverer, and so are many of his successors.

It is not, however, just that it was the first of its kind and that it turned out to be a boilerplate for so many other utopias, that makes Sir Thomas More's *Utopia* interesting. Both its contents and its intentions are remarkable and puzzling. That it is critical of Tudor England is not in doubt, but then the world is always awry, and it is not clear what lesson More meant to teach. First of all, this saint of the Church offers us a perfect and happy society that is not Christian.

Its people are rational deists, but they tolerate Christian visitors and people of all faiths because belief cannot be forced. (In his time as Chancellor, More was, however, a notable persecutor.) In addition, although the utopians forbid suicide, the terminally ill are encouraged to commit it. Death is not to be feared. The government is local and notably democratic with a lot of electoral activity. There is plenty of personal freedom, but education is communal and designed to create virtually identical citizens. Reason is one and moral, and rational uniformity is the necessary outcome of a true education and virtuous living. Economic activity is limited and controlled. People work only a six-hour day, and there is no poverty and little inequality. Idleness is forbidden, and the utopians enjoy nothing so much as cultivating their minds. This is the happiness of dignity rather than of plenty.

In some respects this is a very old, medieval form of social criticism. The "virtuous pagan" is held up as a reproach to Christian rulers, telling them that if a governor can be so just without being a Christian, how can Christian rulers be so bad, so inferior? But More is, I think, doing more. He is separating politics and religion in a very radical way. By limiting himself to the empire of reason, he is able to show just how much misery bad laws inflict and how much happiness reasonable and humane ones can yield. That is why he called upon Plato as his inspiration. He did not copy the institutions of either the *Republic* or the *Laws,* but in the first he found the idea of public happiness created by uncorrupted rationality and in the second the importance of specific and generally understood laws for achieving true social harmony. Along the way he was able to have his say about conduct that was neither rational nor Christian, especially greed, the oppression of the poor, and random violence.

What did he expect to accomplish? *Utopia* was written in Latin originally and addressed to the educated humanistic elite of Europe, people like his friend Erasmus, a very small group. Nor did he expect to affect political conduct. As he said in closing, he might "rather wish than hope" for utopian institutions to be established in "our cities." Like Plato's *Republic, Utopia* may have had no other design than to establish what reason is and then to measure the awful distance between what we are and what rational creatures might be. Its influence, if any, would be intellectual and indirect, not practical or immediate. As a story *Utopia* is surely meant to entertain, and it does, but it also conveys a humanist philosophical message. More's numerous imitators often had quite different philosophical and religious intentions, but instructive entertainment, food for reflection, is what they offered. That is why it may not be exactly right to speak of them as useful, at least not any more useful than philosophy and literature generally are. Classical utopias also can raise the human spirit in complex ways, here and now, but not as designs for the future.

I think that More's last and most significant heir was Jean-Jacques Rousseau, but not because his most famous work, *The Social Contract,* is, as is often said, an eighteenth-century democratic utopia. On the contrary, I want to dwell on him because he shows something latent in the classical utopia: its intense and radical critical spirit and its pessimism about actual states of government when compared to a utopian society. The differences between More and Rousseau are certainly striking, but they are united in two important respects: both used imaginary societies to expose the faults of the actual world, and neither one expected to change or improve it. Yet compared to Rousseau, More was positive. *Utopia* is meant to instruct, to educate, perhaps to make the ruling class more reflective. Moreover, original sin plays no part in More's island. It puts no limit on human improvement in *Utopia.* Rousseau does not expect to improve his readers morally. He is bent upon nothing but exposing the irremediable and intolerable evils of modern Europe. And then he went beyond political rage to reveal the hopelessness of the human condition, caught as we are between the inevitability of association and the psychological degradation that we are bound to inflict upon one another. It is a terrible story, and utopia finds its use here as a way of demonstrating the impossibility of a happiness that we can imagine and long for but cannot ever attain. This is a psychological fatality that is just as limiting and even more irreparable than natural sin. The task of politics ought to be to mitigate the pain, but it is unlikely to succeed.

All of Rousseau's utopias are therefore either remote or fleeting. There are at least three of them. First there is the pure state of nature, then the happy village, and finally Sparta. In the state of nature, human beings are pure clods, creatures of the senses, untroubled by memory or imagination. Solitary and wholly self-centered, they are interested only in their own well-being. Sexual encounters are casual, and mothers abandon their hardy young when they are a mere two years old. Disease is unknown. This is the purest happiness of which we are capable. Our psychological deformation begins as soon as we enter into lasting relationships, and it amounts to a transformation. We acquire a new social self created by the internalization of the demands others make upon us and the expectations they have of us. From the day we become half of a couple, nature and society are locked in a battle for our soul, and as neither one wholly wins, we are self-divided and miserable as well as competitive and immoral.

Inequality and domination follow step-by-step. For we are born with unequal talents, which do not matter in nature but determine our social success. In any case society is a system of enforced standards that some people meet and others do not. Some do well; others do not.

Along the way to the abyss of inequality and oppression that modern Europe, and especially Paris, had reached, Rousseau marked two reasonably satisfying possibilities, utopian models, in fact. The first of these is a utopia of rural happiness. Rousseau said that he had seen it in Switzerland, but that it had already been destroyed. Here families are self-sufficient and meet only rarely. There is private property and domestic education but little change and no occasion for conflict. Habits are simple, and needs and aspirations are in equilibrium. This is the best we can ever hope for, but we always destroy it, because inequality invariably sets in, and with it comes the injustice in which we in fact all live.

Since we cannot maintain a balance between nature and society, the best alternative is to stamp out natural impulses altogether and do as the Spartans did. Here the individual is socialized so completely that he does not even have a name: he is a citizen first and a person quite secondarily. This is the utopia of controlled passions, of discipline, patriotism, equality, and justice. These citizens may not be happy, but they are neither neurotic nor immoral. They have a full civic life, and their erotic energies have been completely redirected to public objects. This, Rousseau claimed, was a real republic. Like the reasonable classical utopia, it was not impossible, just totally unlikely. For like its rural counterpart, the civic utopia can flicker briefly at best. It also must perish, because everything we try must go under sooner or later. Even the saintly heroine of his novel commits suicide. Ultimately particular selves have an indestructible urge to prefer themselves and to seek a personal happiness and inequality. With inequality all the rest follows: luxury, excess, public vanity, wealth and poverty, and, in the end, despotic government.

Sparta is antimodernity, and it is as critical utopias go both psychologically and politically very effective. The very fact that many people find it repellent makes its point. We are just not fit to be citizens. The philosophical truths that Rousseau meant to convey can be found clearly enough in the *Social Contract*. It is too overtly hypothetical and procedural to qualify as a utopia, particularly compared to Rousseau's imaginary communities. *Social Contract* is meant to investigate the possibility of making duty and interest compatible. It is in the end not clear whether it is feasible to make them compatible, but if it should be, it would require transformative politics. The message is, I think, that once we understand what the requirements of rational justice are, we will also recognize that the internalization of its rules is beyond us. It is certainly impossible in modern Europe.

We know that many of the radical readers of the French Revolution found much in Rousseau to inspire them. A seething sense of injustice, a belief in the moral superiority of the people over its rulers, and a contempt for aristocratic culture were Rousseau's not inconsiderable legacies to the revolutionary generation. But whatever passions he may have lit in that dawn, he was, I believe, the philosopher of Europe's decadence, not of its hopes for the future. One need only read those writers among his contemporaries who believed in historical progress to see how remote he was from their confident visions; and, indeed, while they often admired his works, as Condorcet did, they rejected him as irrelevant and wrongheaded.

Before I come to the utopias of the nineteenth century, I want to pause for a moment to take a final look at the classical utopia. It had literary and philosophical merits that later utopia fiction never achieved. It is not until we come to the dystopias of the present that the imaginary society, now seen as a nightmare, regains some of its original literary verve. They too are protests, like the classical utopia novels. Novels such as Orwell's *Nineteen Eighty-Four* are rooted deeply in the immediate social and emotional experiences of their authors. They express genuinely lived experience, as did the classical utopia of More and Rousseau, now even more direct and harsh. Horror is much closer to history than is public happiness, but in both cases we are shaken to lament rather than to act. These are works of the political imagination that can and do awaken and warn and sometimes desolate us, but they do not prescribe or tell us what to do. Like all good books, they are more than just useful.

Because of its essentially reflective character, the classical utopia as a serious intellectual artifact comes to an end with the American and French Revolutions. Add to them the effects of modern scientific activity, and the realm of the possible is not just enlarged. It called out for realization. The utopia of the nineteenth century is a blueprint for a planned new society. And a good many of these societies were tried out in America, especially in the two decades before the Civil War. The ideas were mostly European in origin, but given plenty of cheap land and a free government, utopian experiments were more easily set up in the United States than elsewhere. I cannot possibly describe all of these social experiments but can only look at the most notable ones. They were genuine utopias in that they were meant to be perfectly happy and rational miniature societies that would act as beacons to the rest of America and then to the world. Their example would prove irresistible, and they would gradually transform this country and eventually Europe.

These communities were utopian not only in the derisive sense that Marx and Engels applied to them. The latter particularly excoriated these "utopian socialists" because they hoped to overcome class tensions peacefully and rejected "scientific socialism," meaning Marx's theory of history. The socialist communities of America were utopian in the simple sense of striving for perfect social harmony. They were also more political and ambitious than most of the communes that sprang up in recent decades, which are really alternative families. The utopian communities of the last century, in contrast, were set up not only for the benefit of their members but to promote, ultimately, the social transformation of mankind.

Of the wholly secular utopian communities, three were especially significant intellectually: Robert Owen's *New Harmony,* the many *Phalansteries* inspired by the writings of Charles Fourier, and Etienne Cabet's *Icaria.* There were of course many others, some with a religious component, but these three stand out as having broad political ambitions. All failed utterly and completely, and, I think, also entirely uselessly. Their practical futility does not, however, diminish their very real historical and psychological interest for us.

Robert Owen was by any standards a remarkable man. He began as a lowly clerk in an English factory and at nineteen was the manager in charge of it. By the time he began his experiment in America, he was a very rich man. His factory in New Lanarck took full advantage of technological developments in spinning, but it was also run on humane, though very paternalistic, lines. Workers had their own plots of land; hours and conditions of work were far superior to any others; and there were nurseries and other schools for the children of the workforce. Productivity soared. What drove Owen was a loathing for an economic system that treated workers as a commodity and was subject to constant business cycles, thanks to underconsumption created by low wages. He hated an unregulated economy, wretched working conditions, cities, and parliamentary government. Most of all he detested religion. On the positive side, he was an ardent believer in environmental psychology and education. In principle human beings could become perfect under the right social conditioning.

In England there was no way to put these ideas fully to work. So in 1825 Owen bought a huge tract of land from a religious sect in Indiana and invited converts to his ideas to put them into practice.

The greatest emphasis was to be on the education of the young, but economic arrangements were also important. It was to be a mixture of barter and scrip put away for the future: basically a cooperative retailing scheme and a central depository that provided equally for all. It was an egalitarian socialist community, and as long as Owen was there, it all went well. When he left, democratic self-government failed. The members squabbled, as one might expect, since they were a mixed lot of experienced farmers, intellectuals, and vagrant misfits. At the heart of the trouble was the contradiction of Owen's own role. In principle he was a democrat who had planned a self-governing community. In fact the community depended on his presence, and his members longed for his authority. He was by all accounts a mesmerizing person, and as Rousseau had foreseen, transformative politics require such leaders.

The free American social environment, which made New Harmony possible, also worked against it. The members could and did quit when they felt like it. The remainder were often the sort of people who could not make a go of the community under any circumstances. They were not his disciplined English workers who had no better place to go. As soon as disharmony set in, the whole purpose of the experiment was defeated. To set an example, to convert the world, the people of New Harmony had to be perfect or at least immensely superior to the rest of mankind. It was not enough for them to just survive. They had isolated themselves from the rest of society to be visible to all, to advertise the emergence of a new man. To fail in any respect was therefore to fail completely. It could not be patched up, so Owen dissolved it in 1828, having spent most of his fortune on it. He went on to become a founder of the English trade union and cooperative movements.

The utopian plans of Charles Fourier were minutely detailed because, unlike Owen, he did little in life except scribble away. There was one brief effort to set up a phalanx, as his communities were called in France, but it fizzled immediately. In America, however, there were more than forty phalanxes, the most notable of which was Brook Farm in Massachusetts. The main and deeply anti-Christian goal of Fourier's scheme was the satisfaction of all natural passions. There was to be a minimum of guaranteed sex and plenty of food for all. This was greatly muted in America. Indeed, Fourierism was touted as "practical Christianity" here by the journalist Albert Brisbane, who brought Fourier's ideas to America and who promoted them so successfully. Unlike the other utopias, this one was not fully egalitarian, but it was happy. Economically each phalanx was to be a joint stock company, and benefits were proportional to investment. What really made this a happy society was that work was to be made pleasurable: jobs were assigned according to the principle of "attraction." Each person did what he enjoyed doing. No one worked alone but always in small groups, and these competed with each other for efficiency, with prestige, not money, as the reward. People could change jobs as they altered and might do more than one kind of work at any time if they felt like it. A high level of personal comfort was assured to all. At the center of each phalanx was to be a specially designed community center where all ate the professionally prepared food. The children were to be brought up by people who really liked caring for children. This freed women from domestic work and gave them a chance, as the community gave to men, to do work that suited them personally. Management was to be elected from among "experts." It was never quite clear how these were to be identified.

In the actual American phalanxes, equality was the rule, and there was no effort to locate or elect experts. The phalanxes consequently tended to fail because of inefficient management. They went broke, and they suffered an unusual number of fires. The real trouble, it seems to me, was that the sort of people who would do well in a Fourierist phalanx would do well in American life anyhow, and would therefore be unlikely to join one.

As models for the eventual transformation of a society of hardship and painful work into one of ease and pleasurable production, Fourier's enterprises went nowhere. Nevertheless, planned pleasure is a notion that had a commercial future, though not as a way of reordering the modern world. Worker management of the workplace has also had its impact. The expectations, however, had been phenomenal. The Brook Farm members, when they turned from religion to Fourier's social science, really expected to make the "universal bond" stronger than the individual, to socialize America beyond the personal family, and to regenerate it. Brook Farm proved a disappointing experience, but its members were not crushed. Most of them were soon involved in a more serious cause: abolition.

Finally, a word about Cabet's Icaria. He had great hopes for all of mankind, but he wanted to hurry things along by demonstrating that the republican ethos of the Jacobins could prevail. Scientific progress and social education would yield a society of equality and fraternity. Regimentation was complete. Unlike Fourier, Cabet meant sex to be limited to rigid monogamy, but work was meant to be pleasant and not too onerous. Governance was to be democratic, but education and general drill were to be so uniform that in Icaria there would be almost no differences among individuals. Everyone was to get up, eat, go to work, and quit at exactly the same time. The reason that a few little Icarias survived even after the Civil War is that they split and split until the remaining ones consisted of only a few families. One died of prosperity. The community's land in California turned out to be very valuable. The members sold it at once, divided the profits, and gave up communal living.

I suppose that I should not ignore Noyes's Oneida entirely. It was based on a religious and even Messianic doctrine, but free love and high levels of cooperative living and ownership were among its great attractions. John Humphrey Noyes, who founded it, was in his way a genius. He invented one of the most refined techniques of modern thought control: "public criticism." Everyone's character was subject to peer review followed by public confession. A loss of ego and dependence on Noyes was the intended result. Oneida also went in for eugenics, a subject we no longer want to think about. Because Noyes was a very clever inventor, the community was always rich. Eventually the communities simply became too wealthy, as Oneida silver plating became immensely profitable. They just took their shares and ran.

I think these people had thought of themselves as a liberated prophetic community but not in a political sense. Oneida does remind us that the desire for sexual freedom played a considerable part in any of these utopias. The hostility that this aroused among the neighboring population was phenomenal.

All in all, over eighty thousand people tried to achieve "the redemption of collective men" in the years before the Civil War. There were obviously many people in the United States who longed for a more regulated and predictable life, and for direct personal authority. Others, like Brisbane, thought that poverty and class hostility, such as existed in Europe, could be avoided in the United States by adopting versions of Fourier's communal order. And it was not class resentment that destroyed the phalanxes, nor was investment a problem. Poor management and low productivity were the deadly difficulties.

Finally there was in all these utopias a built-in tension between educational and economic aims. One has to show a return for labor and investment quickly, and education takes a very long time. Utopia was undertaken by people who lacked the education needed for it and who may not even have been ready to act as adequate teachers of the young. So the communes failed long before they could raise the one crop they were really supposed to yield, a new humanity. The number of educational reforms that were suggested is staggering, and they are an enduring legacy. Some of these schemes were grounded in the belief that human nature only had to be rescued from a corrupt society; others assumed that general progress was preparing mankind for an education that would allow them to fulfill all human possibilities. Hence the sad ending of both utopian enterprises: one to liberate eros, the other to render labor fulfilling in a planned harmonious environment.

In the last two decades before the First World War, there was a deluge of utopian novels. To say that they are unreadable is a very charitable comment. They are dull and uninteresting beyond belief, uninspired mixtures of social and technological reform in fictional guise. Edward Bellamy's *Looking Backward* is far from being the worst of the socialist ones. They are all efforts to freeze in fictional form the various ideologies of the age, but they were expressed far more intelligently in tracts and treatises. The imagined means of getting to the promised land involved wars, revolutions, eugenics, mind control, technologically driven transformations, and other processes that do not particularly appeal to a reader today. The awfulness of the prescriptions is nothing, however, compared to the literary dreariness of these works. Only Samuel Butler, William Morris, and H. G. Wells can be read with some degree of pleasure. Certainly B. F. Skinner's essays give us a much clearer and more readable account of his belief in the psychological possibilities of altering human behavior by means of negative and positive external incentives than does *Walden Two*, which is a very boring and often confusing tale. All these books must be left to the cultural historian, for whom they do provide a treasure trove of insight into the age. To me it seems that the outstanding feature of this literature is a megalomanic political imagination.

Clearly the one thing that the utopian communities, as well as these dreadful novels, had in excess was hope. Now hope has not been the prevailing inspiration of social thought and action in Europe and the United States since 1945. Why should hope flourish, after all? We now know what we are capable of, potentially and actually. What reasons have we for moral or political confidence? In many ways the emergence of fascism, Nazism, communism, and the successive wars, hot and cold, seemed to vindicate all the naysayers of the world. One casualty of this by no means unreasonable state of mind may have been the ability to think creatively about politics at all. When I began my professional career I thought so. I proved to my own satisfaction that with the end of utopia, by which I meant the end of hope for a better future, we had run out of political ideas as well. To my surprise, a lot of people agreed with me and I did quite well out of pessimism. I now realize that in many ways I was wrong, because the end of utopia and transformative political ideas are still subjects of serious debate, which makes it worth asking: "What is the use of utopia?" Moreover, political theory, as it turned out, did not depend entirely on the survival of future-oriented ideologies.

To explain where I now think we are, I must say a few words about the history of political science generally. All political science, at whatever level of abstraction, requires models: some are merely heuristic, some are normative, and some are prophetic. Utopia is usually the latter sort of model, but there is also a normative model that tries to demonstrate the positive potentialities of existing forms of government. This essentially reformist model is the real challenge to the transformative utopia at present, as indeed it has been for quite some time, actually since classical antiquity. It began with Aristotle, who in the *Politics* undertook a devastating demolition of the utopias of his day, and most especially Plato's versions. Yet the last two books of the *Politics* look suspiciously like just another utopian plan, not so very different from the others. Aristotle did not think so. Even though he recognized that his aristocratic educative regime was something to be wished for rather than expected, he drew a clear line between utopia and an account of the best form of government. It is a subtle but a very real distinction that runs right through the history of political science. John Stuart Mill, so very different a thinker, still thought it necessary to offer a defense of the best form of government, though he also was unconvinced by utopian projects. His belief in progress did not terminate in paradise.

Aristotle's case against the utopians was, in brief, that their schemes were impossible, that their moral psychology was deeply flawed, that ultimately they would produce injustice, and finally, that it was an intellectual mistake to plan everything so precisely, as if there would be no need for alterations. Like many readers, I think that the criticisms of Plato are unfair in many respects, but this only underlines Aristotle's contempt for the utopian imagination. Throughout the following sections, he does not lift his eyes beyond those positive elements in the better of the actual, existing regimes that make for their survival, and in the case of the mixed constitution, for a high level of justice. Nevertheless, the last two books do offer an account of the best form of government as a necessary part of a full political science because it acts as a yardstick, a way of classifying and judging polities. And as he says over and over again, his best regime is perfectly possible, even if highly improbable. As we know, it turns out to be an educative aristocracy in which all work is done by slaves, so that the master citizens can enjoy the leisure for civic and personal self-development. Not perhaps everyone's idea of the best possible society, but given the right conditions, which Aristotle specifies, not a fantasy. And he takes care to remind us that he is not going into excessive detail. The purpose is to allow one to measure the level of perfection that some cities had reached or might attain if they could behave intelligently. It does not transcend the moral capacities of the best Greek males, and that is why it must disappoint the readers of Plato's *Republic*.

In many respects John Stuart Mill's *Representative Government* is very similar. Mill too thought that given the right place and population, he could point to the best form of government, in this case representative government. The purpose of depicting the best state is again less to urge people to change than to set standards. Does a government provide both order and progress, and to what degree? Both order and progress stand for specific human virtues, justice and prudence as well as energy and inventiveness, in short, improvement. What makes representative government superior to the rule of a single great legislator or an educated elite is that in such regimes the citizenry is reduced to passivity. Communism especially was in Mill's view an elitist utopia. The virtues of originality, energy, and independence would be forfeited. These are not the Aristotelian virtues, but that is not the point. What I want to stress is that the idea of a best form of government as a norm is not only not utopian but perfectly compatible with a very critical view of utopian theory. Models of good government are, in fact, an integral part of a complete political science. They are for that very reason acutely offensive to some radicals.

Political theory survived the decline of the great ideologies of the nineteenth century, not by returning to utopian models but by a revival of normative thought. To be sure, those ambitious visions, in which vast impersonal forces drove mankind into the future, are gone. The historical theories that underwrote the various forms of socialism, anarchism, social Darwinism, dramatic conservatism, and even liberalism have lost their attraction. The sense of destiny that the literate elites used to create national and international publics has lost all of its luster, the most spectacular casualty being Marxism. And it did seem for a while that we had nothing more to say, as I had once thought. I should have remembered that political thinking before the age of revolutions was not driven by history and that it might well overcome its phase of cosmic excess, as indeed it has.

In fact, the best political theory of the Anglophone world has been neither historicist nor utopian but either skeptical, as in the case of Michael Oakeshott and Isaiah Berlin, or devoted to setting up normative models of the just state. Here I refer, naturally, to John Rawls's justly famous *Theory of Justice*. In Germany, a similar, though less original, work, setting out the formal conditions for the best form of government, has lately been presented by Jürgen Habermas in his theory of communicative action. In both cases we have models to judge actuality, to bring the existing states of Western Europe and the United States before the bar of their own professed values of political freedom, justice, and equality, and to find them wanting. These are not fictions but formal and critical models immanent in constitutional democracy, embedded in it but not realized. They are pictures not quite of a good state but of the conditions that a such a state would have to meet.

The implication of these formal models of a just order are reformist in effect, and as such they cannot satisfy all expectations, especially among certain former Marxists. Unreconciled as ever to the welfare state, to representative democracy, to bourgeois society, the former Marxists have nevertheless absorbed the implications of the East European debacle more completely than anyone else. Critical theory, as it calls itself, lives in an extreme state of rejection. It is especially hostile to mere "normative" political theory, such as Rawls's and Habermas's. The complaint is that these philosophers have betrayed utopia. They have extinguished hope. They have abandoned transformative politics. Neither fraternity, nor solidarity, nor the creation of a new man plays any part in normative models. They do not offer a total critique of the actual, nor do they strive to "transcend," that is, to rise above and to transform the consumer society and the welfare state. They do not shake up the present enough by forcing us to envision a wholly new world order.

Gone is the proletariat; revolutionary violence does not beckon, and Marx's predictions are not taken seriously. His and Engels's rejection of utopianism is also to be circumvented. Critical theory posits a "concrete utopia" left in the debris of Marx. It remains possible, even in our time and age, to hope for a good and wholly different society, not because there is anything at present that indicates it, but because it is necessary to believe it, if we are ever to look beyond an unacceptable actuality. This argument has been made by the more radical members of the Frankfurt School and most ably by Seyla Benhabib. In a nutshell, it is her argument that unless we seriously con-

struct a model of an alternative society, unless we go beyond normative models, we will never develop the political will to transform
society. Justice and freedom are not enough. We must have fraternity.

One might ask at the end of the twentieth century why anyone
would yearn for transformative politics, but if one does, then utopia
remains very useful, perhaps indispensable. If, however, we do not
identify hope with transformation, then it is neither necessary, useful,
nor particularly stimulating. Neither the literary utopia nor the
planned imaginary societies that drove so many brave souls into the
wilderness seem to me to have much importance for political theory.
I can say nothing about other novels set in fantasylands, as I am not
a literary critic. For political theory, utopia has lost its uses except
in one significant respect. It remains a subject for heated controversy.

In closing, however, I must say something in mitigation of what
may seem a rather unkind view of contemporary utopianism. I do
not wish to join the rather large chorus that sees a great danger in
utopian thought. Since the French Revolution there have been doom-
sayers who see Jacobinism and the guillotine at the end of every
theory of progress and every utopian journey. Any reform is immediately branded as utopian, bound to fail, and dangerous in the extreme. Every political improvement is bound to end in despotic rule.
The idea of progress, or the hope for steady social and intellectual
improvement through political reform, or the quest for justice and
fairness, all are futile at best, tyrannical at worst. They threaten what
is left of our meager civilization and decadent culture. This particular
way of ending utopia, through fear of hope and of change, really
does make positive political thought impossible. It permits only the
repetition of lamentations and forecasts of decline. Here utopia is put
to bad use, as an idea to scare and threaten and to defame one's
opponents. There may be little use for utopia now, but that is not a
good reason for abusing it. We may well be able to get on without
utopia but not without the political energy required to think both
critically and positively about the state we are in and how to improve
it. And even if utopia is not useful, we ought to hope that the inspiration for so imaginative and fascinating a form of literature might revive to enlighten us again.

PART THREE

Learning about Thinkers

CHAPTER ELEVEN

Poetry and the Political Imagination in Pope's *An Essay on Man*

The simplest way of dealing with the political messages of Pope's *Essay on Man* would be to go over the whole poem line by line, because in one way or another it is always about power, or to be quite exact, about the abuse of power. To select passages and themes that are more distinctly political than others would not, therefore, be particularly helpful, or even feasible. I have instead tried to sort out the kinds of political ideas that come up and to arrange them to illuminate what I take to be Pope's overwhelming revulsion at our inhumanity to the animals around us, and indeed at our callousness generally. This rage is itself an expression of the political imagination, which is merely the proposition that the man-made order could always be different than it actually is and has been in the past. That is, of course, not compatible with the overt point of the poem, that "whatever is, is Right." But the contrapuntal tension between the stated and the immanent texts of the poem may well constitute its intellectual character as a whole.[1]

The most obvious place to begin is a fact: the poem is dedicated to and inspired by a politician, Lord Bolingbroke. Although he had long been out of power and would in fact never again return to office, he and his circle remained as attached to their program as in 1714 and were just as opposed to Walpole's party. In this Tory coterie there was, moreover, a man far more important to Pope and to us than Bolingbroke, Jonathan Swift. In the decade before he began to write the *Essay*, Pope and he had regularly exchanged letters about their respective political attitudes. Swift continued to care deeply

This undated essay has not been previously published.

about the old Tory principles. He had been and remained opposed
to the popish succession, he reminded Pope, because the "peace of
the state" depended on a royal line that had "much weight in the
opinions of the people." A revolution was justified if its consequences
were less pernicious than the grievances which brought it about,
which made the accession of the Prince of Orange acceptable. He
had, Swift went on, "a mortal antipathy to standing armies," always
a threat to freedom, and he "adored" the wisdom of "that Gothic
Institution" the annual parliament. The landed interests were "the
best judges of what is for the advantage of the kingdom," while the
"moneyed" interest was responsible for disasters such as the South
Sea Bubble. The thing to be most feared was excessive power in the
hands of the king and the spirit of faction.[2] In brief, Swift hated Robert Walpole's political system. Pope replied to this outburst that he
simply could not get very excited about these issues. As a Roman
Catholic he was excluded from politics, and he described himself as
an Erasmian, uninterested in sectarian conflicts of any kind. "I am
not," he told Swift, "violent or sower to any party."[3] Pope in fact
did not mind dining in the great Whig houses. There were, finally,
temperamental differences. Swift all but reproached him for hating
vice and folly without letting them affect his temper.[4] That suffices
to account for the absence of Bolingbroke's ideology from the *Essay*
and indeed explains its most famous couplet:[5]

> For forms of government let fools contest;
> Whatever's best administer'd is best. (III, 303–304)

By "best administered" Pope did not mean most efficient, as has often
been thought, but whatever produces the greatest social harmony under given conditions. What it does is to take him right out of the
constitutional and institutional politics which so preoccupied Bolingbroke and Swift. If a man's life is right, it doesn't really matter what
his political beliefs are, which is an evasive compliment to Bolingbroke.

Nevertheless, Pope does go on to ask why there is a political order
at all, but these sections about the origins and definition of politics
do seem very confusing and vague. We get a picture of a golden age
of patriarchal felicity when "Great Nature spoke, observant Man
obey'd" (III, 199), but it is not clear why or how we left it. Neither
the Stoic nor the Hobbesian exit is offered, presumably because these
are meant to underwrite quite specific political practices and institutions. What we have here is a state of nature which serves no political

purpose at all. Pope asks without answering, "Who first taught souls
enclav'd, and realms undone . . . T'invert the world and counter-work
its Cause?" (III, 241, 244). There is no reply, and for a justification of
God's ways to political man this is a total intellectual collapse. All
he says is that somehow "She," and I *do* emphasize that "She" here
includes tyranny and superstition, overwhelmed us and directed our
self-love to obey tyrants and their "ambition, lucre, lust" (III, 270).
Eventually general fear serves to join us "Forc'd into virtue thus by
self-defence" (III, 279), and we are aided by a system of laws such
as our "poet or patriot Search" (III, 285). Though how far this Solon-
like figure succeeds in helping us find "the private in the public good"
(III, 282) is not said. Indeed it is not ever made particularly clear that
it is worthwhile to be a patriot and "search." The final section of the
Fourth Epistle is meant to persuade Bolingbroke that had he succeeded in politics, he would only have been miserable, and that true
happiness could be found only in rural retreats far from the public
stage. Not only was public activity unrewarding, it was really quite
likely to be disgusting in itself. First of all, eminence does not give
us any joy. "Some are and must be greater than the rest / More rich,
more wise; but who infers from hence / That such are happier shocks
all common sense" (IV, 50–52). For happiness comes only from
"Health, Peace and Competence" (IV, 80). This, as it happens, is the
nonsense that bothered Dr. Johnson so much, because the rich and
smart are usually happier than those who are not, but let us leave
that for now. More interesting is the insignificance of political virtue
in the great scheme of things in which both Caesar and Titus, tyrant
and wise ruler, are necessary (IV, 146). The conditions of political
success are in any case degrading, its values meaningless, and the effort futile. What, after all, are official distinctions? "Stuck o'er with
titles and hung round with strings, / That thou may'st be by kings,
or whores of kings" (IV, 205–206). Noble blood is nothing. "What
can ennoble sots, or slaves or cowards? Alas, not all the blood of all
the Howards" (IV, 215–216). Fame after death is useless to us, since
we cannot hear it, and there is no advantage "in Parts superior" (IV,
254). For wisdom teaches us only how little we know and to see the
faults of others, but it will do nothing to save our "sinking land" (IV,
265). Politics is strewn with perfidy and betrayals as politicians rise
like Venice from "dirt and sea-weed" (IV, 292). As Machiavelli knew,
there are no clean hands except in private life. Nevertheless, love
yourself and then love "Must rise from Individual to the Whole" (IV,
362). The whole in this case must mean the whole great chain of
creation, not just one's country. No wonder that Bolingbroke was

displeased with this aspect of the *Essay*. He complained that it did not justify "the unequal distribution of Providence" here on earth but just left it all to the justice of the life hereafter. God's ways to man in politics have to be defended in terms of our life here and now.[6]

I suspect Pope's far from successful efforts to wave politics away were meant for Swift, in order to dispel what Bolingbroke called Swift's "black corrosive Vapours."[7] When *Gulliver* came out, Pope had apparently protested, and Swift replied with a biting letter. He was indeed, he said, a misanthrope, though not in the manner of Timon. "I have ever hated all nations, professions, communities . . . my love is all for individuals." And "I hate that animal called man, but love John or Peter." To this Pope answered feebly that he agreed with only part of it, that friendship was the basis of patriotism. That, Swift replied, was not what he had in mind at all. He was not a patriot; what moved him was "rage and resentment and the mortifying sight of slavery, folly and baseness about me." That is why he was interested in politics and why he and Bolingbroke remained "a little subject to schemes."[8] In the *Essay* Pope is trying not merely to talk his two friends out of their "schemes" but out of any concern for public affairs whatever. For to think about politics is to invite either degradation or raging misanthropy. The question, as one looks at the *Essay,* is whether Pope himself escaped from that blight or whether he in fact came to share Swift's revulsions, though not his madness.

Although Bolingbroke's politics evoked no response, he did suggest, or at least share, some very significant beliefs with Pope. The first of these was natural religion, the faith that "looks thro' Nature, up to Nature's God" (IV, 332). More significantly, Bolingbroke was convinced that we and the animals are far more alike than traditional Christianity and Cartesian science allowed. The first dismissed animals because they had no immortal souls, the latter because they were mere machines. Bolingbroke and Pope did not think that animals had been created solely for our convenience, nor that they were mindless machines. They did not argue as Montaigne had that animals were superior to mankind in *every* moral respect, but Pope's chain of being closes the gap between them and us. The great chain of being in the eighteenth century generally had ceased to be a ladder of mystic ascent to union with the divine. It had become an account of God's creation and a vision of the order of nature. Nature is a whole and the trees, animals, and we are all one rung of the ladder, and this imposes a whole new set of obligations upon us. We are called to treat the earth and everything in it as our fellow beings, not cruelly, but kindly. And this demand is bound to give rise to a sense of horror at man's usual behavior to nature, which again makes "whatever is, is Right" particularly hard to believe. The ladder, moreover, becomes deeply ambiguous from a political point of view. For higher may not be better, just more powerful. As Dr. Johnson noted, Pope's chain, with its rung of extraterrestrial "Superior beings" (II, 31) above us, whose puppets we are and who do to us what we do to animals, does little to improve the cosmic picture. Was Pope, he asked, really unaware of the suffering of the sick and the poor? In what ways do these superior beings supposedly enjoying our wretchedness make our misery any less afflicting? And finally, given Pope's insistence on our ignorance and metaphysical ineptitude, can we know anything about any links in the chain or the existence of such a chain at all? It is hard not to agree with Dr. Johnson, but I doubt that Pope was really as complacent as Johnson thought him. These superior beings can only remind us of Nietzsche's suggestion that the horrors of the Greek drama, no less than those of history, were meant to entertain the gods, since there can be no festival without cruel sport for them, or for us.

From the first, Pope, like Montaigne, looks at mankind from the animals' vantage point, which is, to say the least, not reassuring. It presents us with a vision of viciousness within nature and not merely the melancholy cycle of birth and destruction of nature of which Lucretius sang. It is the victims' vision. Here we are shown purposive cruelty: man's propensity to inflict pain upon other sentient creatures. We know that Pope hated hunting, but that only hints at the extent of his aversion. To show just how much of it there is in the *Essay,* one has to go through all the lines mentioning animals, and the effect is extremely oppressive. It is in fact an unconditional indictment of man's ways to nature, and it is so severe that it can only put God's arrangements in doubt. We begin with mankind's appalling history of irrationality in regard to dumb animals. The "dull ox" "is now a victim and now Aegypt's God" (I, 63–64). The poor beast is "This hour a slave, the next a deity" (I, 68), and treated accordingly. This state of affairs is our own as well. We are just as ignorant as the ox of the reasons why we become or make slaves, or why at times we think of ourselves as gods. We too are oxen in the hands of our suprahuman rulers. What is at stake for the cattle and us is the arbitrariness of ruling powers as such. The same implication follows from the comparison of men and sheep, and again it is the animal that is the material witness. "The lamb thy riot dooms to bleed today / Had he thy reason, would he skip and play?" (I, 81–82). Our brutality is clear, and it is not mitigated by our own helplessness, our jumping and playing when we should be remembering the hour of our death. For God sees "a hero perish or a sparrow fall" (I, 88)—the reference is, I imagine, to Hamlet—with exactly the same cruel indifference with which we cause lambs "to bleed." We may cry for ourselves, but we are not worth a tear. For how can you pity those who "Destroy all creatures for thy sport or gust" (I, 117)? In this we act as all superiors do to their inferiors. The chain does not justify political hierarchy. Far from it.

The excuses men offer for the extermination of animals are all false. Pride says that all nature, "herb, flower, grapes, roses, the juice nectareous and the balmy dew" are all there solely to please us (I, 136). "Thy foot-stool earth" (I, 140) is there for men to trample on. Why is this false pride? If there is a great chain we might well accept Renaissance depictions, such as that of Sir Thomas Elyot, which put men not only above the animals, but sees the lower creations as being there wholly for human purposes and pleasures. This becomes a delusion and false pride only when the gap between man and animal is closed by an inclusive and comprehensive nature, which embraces us all. Indeed so close is our proximity to the beasts that we often try to have their strength and fur, that is, we envy them. Nor can we claim that our reason forms a very great barrier between them and us. Since we are members of the natural world, it is as true of us as of them that, "But *All* subsist by elemental strife / And passions are the elements of life" (I, 169–170). The elements of life, the motives for action, are quite the same. Passion rules animals and men, and "man's imperial race" is in no preferred position in that respect. "Imperial" had strong implications. Pope reminds us of the "poor Indian" who has "no Christian thirst for Gold" (I, 99, 108), and again we recall all the victims. "Imperial" covers all our false pride and also our failures of sympathy. The animals may be separate from us but "for ever near," and to think that they were created for us is insane. "Vile Worm!—oh Madness, Pride, Impiety!" (I, 258). Indeed, pigs may grovel, but only man is vile. Our "imperial" pretense has indeed put us below the rest of animal creation politically—as we often are aesthetically. For many animals are far more beautiful than we are—moles, lynx, lions, hounds, birds, spiders, bees, pigs, elephants, all have something to be said for them. Only we are "vile." That is a fair judgment of a destructively "imperial" being that neither understands nor shares the world with other living creatures merely because the latter are weaker. That then is the implication of Pope's particular chain of being and of Bolingbroke's conviction that the world was not made for us alone but for us and all the other living beings. Nature is our book, not our empire, but we prefer to despoil rather than to read it.

The meaning of pride as the greatest of human evils now also acquires a new meaning. It is not the rejection of God that had made it the primary and all-inclusive "head" of the Seven Deadly Sins. In keeping with natural religion, the rejection of nature and our place in it now defines pride. It is so also in *Gulliver*, when the hero says of the Yahoos, "when I behold a lump of deformity and disease, both in body and mind smitten with *pride*, it immediately breaks all measures of my patience, neither shall I be ever able to comprehend how such an animal and such a vice could tally together." Perhaps Pope found it easier to be patient than Gulliver or Swift, but man as a "vile" worm is not remote from their view of the species.

When we get off the chain of being and look at politics directly in the Third Epistle, animal life returns. Indeed, men's relations to each other turn out to be, in Pope's imagery, a veritable zoo. The book begins benignly enough. Everything in nature runs according to general laws; God does not act in specific instances. He is a legislator, not an enforcement officer, and preachers are to remember that in their sermons. No one should blame God for specific occurrences. From such an opening one expects to move on to a scientific approach to nature, but that is not what follows. Instead we return to the right and wrong division of powers between ourselves and the animals. A proper view of the general laws of nature would impress upon us that we are meant to live in a condition of mutual support, not of domination. The vegetables prove how each organism has a part in the divine division of labor. "See dying vegetables life sustain" (III, 15), while the "all preserving Soul . . . Made Beast in Aid of Man, and Man of Beast" (I, 22, 24). But that may be illusory, for at this point we are shown that the goose we stuff thinks that we are there to "pamper" it, but we after all know better, and in fact we do very little for the beasts. We eat "fawns" and enjoy the song of the lark and linnet. "The bounding steed you pompously bestride" serves us, but what do we do for it? (I, 35). We give animals pastures, share our "floods," but it is in the end all for our table and pride. In fact we do very little for the welfare of the whole. Even if nature does check us to contribute something to the animals, in the end we must say, "Grant that the pow'rful still the weals controul / Be then the Wit and Tyrant of the whole" (III, 49–50). This is as far as justification of our exploitation of nature goes—it is the exercise of greater power, not of mutual service at all. For consolation Pope resorts as usual to the equality of death; in the end, both animals and men come to the same end.

This rather lame conclusion does not, however, end the matter. A second line of thought suggests that in spite of our depredations, the animals have an advantage over us, because they can live very well by simply following their instinctual urges. They never left the state of nature at all, while we in a self-destructive moment threw away our instinctual heritage and the ease of natural impulse. By choosing culture we entered upon a far less satisfactory history than that of the animals. The beasts have remained sanely self-ruling, while we need "Popes and Councils" to direct us (III, 84). "(The) nations of the field and wood" (III, 94), the spider spinning its web, the stork exploring, "Columbus-like," God has given them their skills and bliss (III, 105). They love themselves and their kind, their family life is easy and untroubled. When we were their fellow residents in the shade of nature we copied the animals. And we did not eat meat. That indeed had been a view of the state of nature put forward by Plutarch already, and it makes meat eating and cruelty, rather than sex, the real fall of man. For in the state of nature we and the beast lived in perfect amity with each other. "Man walked with beast, joint tenant of the shade; / The same his table, and the same his bed; / No murder cloth'd him and no murder fed" (III, 152–154). That was before we were proud, and that was when we were at one with the beast and we were not carnivorous. Moreover, we were prepared to learn from the animals and to copy their ways. They taught us then how to find food, the bees showed us how to build, the mole to plow, and the worms how to weave. Not only did they teach us how to survive, but also how to live sociably. "The Ants' republic and the realm of Bees" (III, 184) were what nature told us to imitate, and as long as we did, we were very well off indeed. Now, however, we are "Of half that live the butcher and the tomb / Who, foe of Nature, hears the general groan, / Murders their species, and betrays his own" (III, 162–164). We now see that Pope's state of nature is not politically random, after all. It does not introduce civil society, but the abattoir, not man the citizen but man as butcher and warrior. The message of retreat also acquires a more specific meaning. In retreat, faith and hope will sustain us as we contemplate nature, the great chain of being, and at its apex, nature's God. The chain is revealed less as an explanation of our condition than as an aesthetic object and as such possibly healing. It is the vision of harmony and it may transform us as we behold its perfection, so that we become less violent and more charitable.

Pope's passive contemplation of nature was not, however, the only possible path to man's rejoining the animals in a single natural world. It was not even the only approach to nature, once one had decided that the ways of providence were beyond our understanding and "The proper study of Mankind is Man" (II, 2). One of the conclusions of that self-study is that we are limited to uncertain and merely probable knowledge, but that does not commit us to a passive contemplation of nature and a mere adaptation to its harmony. There have, in fact, been two roads open since the eighteenth century put us into our place. One is to describe and preserve the balance of nature by a repentant and resigned retreat, not to real nature but to the garden, to what is taken as an imitation of nature's beauty and so an aesthetic equivalent, though not an actual moral return to the original balance. The second is to assert our few unique qualities and find a new place *within* nature. Curiosity and reason are peculiar to us, and science, the knowledge of nature, allows us to reestablish a legitimate superiority that is in no sense destructive over the natural world of which we are indeed only a part. For us to know is to fulfill our natural function in the greater scheme of things. This was what the "great Mr. Locke" proposed, and in this the Enlightenment in France was to follow him. Self-knowledge was no less primary for Locke, nor was he any less determined than Pope to replace a proud metaphysic with a modest psychology. But a being that can know itself must be capable of both moral and intellectual self-direction, of independence and, within its own known limits, capable of understanding the world around it in a way that none of the animals can. For though Locke objected as strongly as anyone to cruelty to animals, he took men to have powers of learning and calculation that gave them a peculiar intellectual place in nature.

Now Pope certainly knew his Locke, and at times he was quite capable of admiring Locke's great hero, his "incomparable Mr. Newton," but not in the *Essay on Man*. Here he turns his back upon man as an intellectual, researching animal. "Know then thyself, presume not God to scan" (II, 1) means know your hole for you are a worm. In the eyes of those superior beings who look down upon us from a perch closer to God, Newton looks like "An Ape" (II, 34). It is a very shocking line, but it should not surprise any reader of *Gulliver*. Science does not restore our dignity there either. In his third voyage Gulliver visits several scientific academies, and they are all useless, ridiculous, offensive to common sense, and in the end destructive. It is entirely in keeping with Swift's misanthropic hero's experience there to say, as Pope does in Epistle II, we reason "but to err" (II, 10). "Sole judge of Truth, in endless Error hurl'd" (II, 17). We can always try science, but all we will discover is that we are fools. "Trace Science, then, with Modesty thy guide; / First strip of all her equipage of Pride" (III, 43–44). When you have properly humbled science, you will find that it is useless at best and at worst contributes to vice.

Pope treats psychology like the rest of science, skirting close to Locke but then running away from him. Reason is not a creative but a calculating and comparing faculty that can direct the passions but cannot alter them. It disciplines self-love by organizing it. But passion and virtue are directed at pleasure and at avoiding pain, and here "Reason the card, but Passion is the gale" (II, 108). All this sounds like straightforward Lockean psychology. The senses inform the passions, which are then guided by reason. But we do not go on to an account of learning or of a psychological development. Pope veers off to a moral lesson that does not have to emerge from hedonism at all. Pope's novel claim is quite different. Just as we are born with the germs of the disease of which we will eventually die, so also are we all programmed to grow toward our special madness. "So cast and mingled with this very frame The Mind's disease, its Ruling Passion came" (II, 138). Our imagination inflames it "Nature its Mother, Habit is its nurse / Wit, Spirit, Faculties but make it worse" (II, 145–146). This is in fact a very peculiar version of the idea of the "ruling passion." Students of character from Theophrastus to La Bruyère had attributed an overwhelming fault only to some peculiarly flawed individuals, and only in order to reveal the danger of falling prey to any of the great social vices, such as hypocrisy, flattery, avarice, arrogance, and many more. None of them suggested that we were all subject to a single "ruling passion." On the contrary, it was an abnormal excess which could show us how awful these vices were and how they could mar a whole personality. What is so unusual in Pope is his assertion that we are *all* doomed to be possessed by one ruling passion and that it threatens each one of us with madness. Moreover, science and intelligence only make us more insane. That "all our Knowledge is ourselves to know" now makes very good sense. We must monitor the two diseases: our knowledge of the germs of our own death and our obsessive "ruling passion," so that we can somehow remain sane.

At least nature is kind to us. It has given us counterpassions that help us turn some of our vices into virtues. "What crops of wit and honesty appear / From spleen, from obstinacy, hate or fear!" (II, 185–186). "Thus Nature gives us (let it check our pride) / The virtue nearest to our vice ally'd" (II, 195–196). Ambition, for example, can make a tyrant or a good ruler. That is Pope's example, and it means that only the consequences, whether psychological or social, of madness differ. This is not, however, a position Pope could wholly accept, so he lashes out at anyone who might suspect him of having blurred the difference between vice and virtue. In fact, he goes on to say that we can all tell one from the other. A simple appeal to universal opinion suffices, which is not plausible, but it gets him back to his real point, to our confused condition. "The rogue and fool by fits is fair and wise" (II, 233); we are ever inconstant. Virtue is thus left hanging, and so is happiness, which is said to be the same thing. In fact our happiness is mostly delusive, a socially induced madness. "The learn'd is happy nature to explore / The rich is happy in the plenty given / The poor contents him with the care of Heav'n / See the blind beggar dance, the cripple sing, / The sot a hero; lunatic a king" (II, 265–268). No wonder Johnson thought this outrageous, untrue, and deeply vulgar. It is especially so if we assume, as Johnson did, that it is not a sneer at our madness but a consolation. And Johnson may be right; it may well be a bromide, since it does end "Man's a fool, yet God is wise." Still, mockery is a better explanation of the second half of Epistle II. If we are programmed to seek happiness and can find it only in fits of pride and madness, and when to pride we must add an incapacity for disinterested knowledge or love, then it is not consoling to say "God is wise" and "whatever is, is Right." On the contrary, it can only enhance one's fatalism and misanthropy. I do not wish to contradict Dr. Johnson, and indeed he was on solid ground. When their dear friend Gay died, Pope wrote Swift to tell him of their loss and ended his letter with that awful "whatever is, is Right," apparently to calm Swift down.[9] But given that he knew how desperate Swift's mood was, and that in the *Essay* he has us all hanging on the precipice of madness all the time, there may be some grasping at sanity in this sinister view.

"Take Nature's path and mad Opinion leave" (IV, 29) is not the advice of a complacent man. The faith in an orderly though ever-hidden cosmic order may in fact have been a necessary contrast and construct for Pope to reveal the madness of mankind run amok in nature and of all visible relations as imperial impositions of power devoid of purpose, sense, or compassion. Alternatively, of course, Dr.

Johnson may be right about Pope's intentions, in which case the poet's political imagination outran his purpose, and he did not, to put it bluntly, know what he was saying. More plausibly he was saying, as we all do, more than one thing at a time. One was about what he thought it would be best for himself and all of us to believe, and the other about what he experienced as his actual situation. The days of theodicies were in fact over, and with them not only God's ways to man but man's ways to all other sentient beings, from Indians to geese, became questionable. No one felt that more than Pope. By trying to reunite poetically what had obviously come apart, the traditional chain of being and the new humaneness, he only revealed the moral outrage that made such an effort seem both urgent and impossible. There are many passages in *An Essay on Man* which celebrate the harmony of the whole, its beauty and its balance, but neither Pope nor we are reconciled to our actual lives by this appeal to aesthetic sensibilities. Pope could not disguise his own anger at the sight of the suffering of the innocents, and there was no theodicy, just or beautiful, that could console him or us for our political failure.

Notes

1. The ideas for this paper came to me as I read Keith Thomas's absolutely indispensable *Man and the Natural World* (Allen Lane, London, 1983). My debt to it is so pervasive that I cannot usefully cite any one of its sections. For Pope's political world I found the following useful: Isaac Kramnick, *Bolingbroke and His Circle* (Cambridge: Harvard University Press, 1968) and Howard Erskine-Hall, *The Social Milieu of Alexander Pope* (New Haven: Yale University Press, 1975). I obviously learned much from Maynard Mack's *The Garden and the City* (Toronto: University of Toronto Press, 1969) about some of the traditional sources of Pope's attitudes to both retreat and political disaffection. Douglas H. White, *Pope and the Context of Controversy* (Chicago: University of Chicago Press, 1970) confirmed my views on Pope's untypical use of the idea of "ruling passions." The most interesting article of all, and one that like Mack's work stressed the imperatives of poetry, seemed to me J. M. Cameron, "Doctrinal to an Age," in Maynard Mack, ed., *Essential Articles for the Study of Alexander Pope* (Hamden, Connecticut: Archon Books, 1964), 329–345.

For Dr. Johnson's opposition to all forms of "cosmic Toryism" and the Great Chain of Being especially, I have relied on Basil Willey, *The Eighteenth Century Background* (Boston: Beacon Press, 1961), 43–56; and *Life of Pope, The Works of Samuel Johnson* (New Cambridge Edition, Cambridge, Massachusetts, n.d.), vol. 5, 185–337, vol. 6, 1–8; *Nature and Origin of Evil: Review of a Free Enquiry, ibid.*, vol. 7, 217–255.

2. Swift to Pope, 10 January 1720–21, *The Correspondence of Alexander Pope*, ed. George Sherburn (Oxford: Clarendon Press, 1956).

3. Pope to Swift, August 1723, *ibid.*, 183–186, and 28 November 1729, *ibid.*, vol. 3, 79–81.

4. Swift to Pope, 7 June 1728, *ibid.,* vol. 2, 497–498, and 3 September 1735, vol. 3, 491–493.

5. All references to Pope's *An Essay on Man* are to the Twickenham Edition of the *Poems of Alexander Pope* (London: Methuen, 1950).

6. Bolingbroke to Swift, 2 August 1731, *Correspondence,* vol. 3, 210–215.

7. Bolingbroke to Pope, 18 February 1723–24, *ibid.,* vol. 2, 218–222.

8. Swift to Pope, 25 September 1725, *ibid.,* vol. 2, 324–327; Pope to Swift, 15 October 1725, *ibid.,* 331–334; Swift to Pope, 1 June 1728, *ibid.,* 497–498.

9. Pope to Swift, 2 April 1733, *ibid.,* vol. 3, 365.

CHAPTER TWELVE

Ideology Hunting:
The Case of James Harrington

I t is well known that each age writes history anew to serve its own
purposes and that the history of political ideas is no exception
to this rule. The precise nature of these changes in perspective,
however, bears investigation. For not only can their study help us to
understand the past; it may also lead us to a better understanding of
our own intellectual situation. In this quest the political theories of
the seventeenth century and particularly of the English Civil War are
especially rewarding. It was in those memorable years that all the
major issues of modern political theory were first stated, and with
the most perfect clarity. As we have come to reject the optimism of
the eighteenth century, and the crude positivism of the nineteenth,
we tend more and more to return to our origins in search of a new
start. This involves a good deal of reinterpretation, as the intensity
with which the writings of Hobbes and Locke, for instance, are being
reexamined in England and America testifies. These philosophical
giants have, however, by the force of their ideas been able to limit
the scope of interpretive license. A provocative minor writer, such as
Harrington, may for this reason be more revealing. The present study
is therefore not only an effort to explain more soundly Harrington's
own ideas, but also to treat him as an illustration of the mutations
that the art of interpreting political ideas has undergone, and, perhaps
to make some suggestions about the problems of writing intellectual
history in general.

To begin with, Harrington is a seventeenth century figure of some
considerable intrinsic interest. Not only was he the only avowed

This chapter is reprinted with permission from the *American Political Science Review* 53
(1959): 662–92.

Machiavellian of the time but the controversies in which he was engaged, particularly with Hobbes, are of enduring importance as they touch upon the nature of both power and law. Beyond that is the question how he came to appear to later writers in such a great variety of roles. Why has he served each interpreter so differently?

What is at stake here is the intrusion of ideology upon historical analysis. And ideology must be understood in three distinct senses. First of all, there are simply the political convictions and preoccupations of later thinkers who read them into Harrington. Secondly, there was ideology, not as a mere matter of political preferences, but in its historicist, all-explaining form. Here the metaphors of historical explanation become personified entities, and catch-words like "feudal," "bourgeois," and "revolution" dominate the stage entirely, while individual thinkers and events are used solely to prove the reality and necessity of these abstractions. Few writers have been exploited for this purpose more thoroughly than Harrington. Nor has this been entirely accidental. As one whose own main concern was with revolutions he was sure to become a center of interest for those ideologists whose thought is both the product of, and a continuous reflection upon, social conflict. It is this circumstance that makes Harrington such an excellent case-study for those who wish to examine the play of ideology upon history. And to the extent that political thinking is now not so exclusively preoccupied with the dynamics of social war, it can define itself by critically reviewing this aspect of the history of political theory. Lastly, there is ideology in the more neutral sense, as a term in sociological discourse. At the level of abstraction at which social wholes are investigated, individuals and their ideas are treated as functions, if not as direct effects, of these wholes. The unique and individual, the level of biography, tends to be ignored, or even to be modified, in order to illuminate the logic of an entire situation. That this is liable to lead to distortion in writings on the history of ideas is obvious; and in this respect, too, Harrington has been a victim. The following pages will, then, deal with two levels of inquiry, one into Harrington directly, and another into Harrington as a problem in the history of the interpretation of political ideas.

I. Harrington in the Wilderness

Almost every account of Harrington begins with the lament that he is known to the world only as a republican theorist who composed a dreary utopia, and whose one distinction was to have declared that forms of government depend upon the distribution of property. Actually he is no longer quite so obscure a figure. If it was his misfortune to have been sandwiched in between Hobbes and Locke, the damage is being repaired.[1] The resurrection of the man whom Maitland called "the greatest of our Commonwealthmen" is all but complete.[2] And while this belated rise to fame has not always been to his advantage, it has thrown a good deal of light not only on him and his age; it has also done much to illuminate the character of much later political thinking.

Harrington's years in the wilderness were long and real enough. Only in America was he treated with much respect, a fact which, as we shall see, tell us something about the differences between English and American political thinking. But if he influenced Americans and so their institutions, this purely American Harrington was an utter bore. At worst he was made into a grab-bag of republican platitudes; at best, a prophet of written constitutions and an ingenious inventor of electoral devices.[3] In England, his logical successors, the Benthamites, did not look to history, and certainly not to the sad events of the Commonwealth, to support their plans for constitutional and electoral reform. Grote seems to have made some notes on Harrington, but utopias, however practical, did not appeal to the utilitarians. Indeed, so long as English liberalism traced its traditions only to 1688, or rested on utility without benefit of history, there was little point in thinking about Harrington. He is after all not self-sufficient, as Milton and Hobbes are; and anyone who preferred to forget the Civil War was bound to ignore those who are interesting mainly because of the part they played in those tumultuous years. After the Tories had their say on the Great Rebellion, it was politely ignored until the latter part of the nineteenth century when interest in revolutions revived spectacularly. They are not likely to be forgotten now. Nevertheless, even the few occasions on which Harrington was mentioned earlier are not without interest, if only to show the remarkable changes to which historical reputations are subject.

In his own time Harrington was generally rejected by all except a few personal friends and followers, as either an absurd dreamer or an atheist or both.[4] In the eighteenth century the second charge was no longer raised. It was not likely to arouse the indignation of that pair of "intelligent Tories," Montesquieu and Hume. Montesquieu dismissed Harrington as a utopian and scolded him for having exaggerated, and consequently false, ideas about liberty.[5] Since Harrington did in fact reject the traditional "liberties" that Montesquieu wanted to revive, this judgment is not surprising. Hume's admiration is rather more puzzling, for he thought of the Civil War as a case of popular madness. And indeed his praise of Harrington was qualified. Only after carefully noting the futility of all "imaginary common-wealths" and the inherent advantages of *any* established government, did he permit himself to indulge in the trivial pastime of following Harrington. Moreover, even though he accepted many of *Oceana*'s institutions, he noted that civil liberty was not well protected in it, and that it was impossible to enforce legal limits upon property hold-ing. Harrington had insisted that no conflicts of interest were to exist in his republic, and Hume, even in his airiest speculations, could not imagine such a state of affairs. What is even more interesting is that Hume recognized two distinct phases in Harrington's thought. There was the republican dreamer, whom he rather patronizingly enjoyed, and also the theorist who had made property interests the sole basis of government. This Hume rejected, as historically untrue and psy-chologically unconvincing. Opinions and habits, as all conservative historians know, matter just as much as interest in attaching men to their rulers. Indeed, if property alone were a legitimate basis for power, the Commons alone must rule, a prospect Hume did not favor.[6]

With this, the lines of interpretation were set. Harrington was ei-ther a political romancer, or a tough-minded defender of the place of property in government. In practice this meant that radicals, Whigs, and Tories could all ignore him. He does not even turn up in Godwin's history of the Civil War. Occasionally he was named, no more.[7] Only Burke, who was neither quite Tory nor quite Whig, felt at all inclined to deal with him. As a constitution maker Harrington was, of course, all that was most distasteful to Burke. For Burke was not, like Hume, a skeptical and self-confident conservative, who could take such matters lightly. Even before 1789, in presenting his American policy, Burke took pains to show that he was not Harring-ton, not a dreamer, but the defender of a political tradition.[8] In his more embittered later years, he went farther and compared Harring-ton to Sieyès, and to those "thorough-bred metaphysicians" whose "hardness of heart" allowed them to indulge in "analytical experi-ments" with no regard to the consequences.[9] The comparison was apt, since Harrington's scheme was certainly known to Sieyès, whose constitutional draft showed traces of *Oceana*. There were also differ-ences that Burke was in no mood to dwell on. For Harrington, radical republican though he was in his dreams of an equal commonwealth with "no contradiction," was also no eighteenth century philosopher. Neither the rights of man nor the theory of progress haunt the pages of *Oceana*.[10] That is why even Burke could appreciate some aspects of Harrington's doctrine, for he had seen something that Hume had not known: what happens when property and interest do not play their part in government. He was a bit unfair in saying that this was a condition that "the learned and ingenious" Harrington "could not imagine." In fact, Harrington had no need to *imagine* it, having lived through a military dictatorship; and his entire theory rested on the belief that the rule of force was the only alternative to the rule of interest.[11] A government by violence, and against nature, Harrington called it. What Burke added to this was a sense of the "dreadful energy," the dynamism, of the ideological state.[12] He was not the last to observe it.

II. The Disguises of the Nineteenth Century

For the better part of the nineteenth century we hear no more of Harrington, and very little about the Civil War. It is not true that Marx made historians aware of revolutions; the revolutions accomplished that by themselves. He was not even alone in regarding the Reformation, the Civil War, and the French Revolution as one continuous revolution, rather than separate events. De Maistre and Saint-Simon, before him, and Acton after, for rather different reasons, saw it so too. In England, it was the "Whigs," as is now well known, who restored the English Revolution to respectability. However, they were slow in coming to it. Macaulay, after all, begins with James II, and it was not until Gardiner's monumental work on the "Puritan" revolution, the one in which the whole nation rose in defense of its liberties, that the Civil War was really made sufficiently moral, and unlike the French Revolution, to appeal to the Whigs.[13]

There were of course remnants of the old Tory view. One of them was Isaac Disraeli, who not only defended the Stuarts, but also devoted an essay to Harrington. His picture adds little to Burke's. We have the same old "phantast" who guessed wrong in thinking the Restoration impossible, but who, at least, was a "gentleman" with "no vulgar notions of a levelling democracy."[14] And so, too, it was no Whig, Carlyle, who resuscitated Cromwell. However, as an increasingly conservative liberalism wanted a tradition, as historicism infected it, as it wanted radicalism but not class conflict, so the new Civil War, and Harrington with it, re-emerged.

A Whig Harrington. Not that Harrington inspired any great interest in anyone. Acton did pay some attention to him, and the same conflict between radical impulses and the fear of the radical danger to liberty is reflected here as in the rest of his writings. So Acton preferred Harrington to Cromwell because he had realized the need for a redistribution of property if the Commonwealth was to succeed, while "a timorous conservatism" and "legal scruples" prevented the Protector from going all the way.[15] Again he praised Harrington as one of that "little band of true theorists" in which he included Locke, Rousseau, Jefferson, Hamilton, Mill, and Sieyès, the last being especially praised.[16] In short, here all that Burke detested was being glorified. Yet Acton had many harsh things to say about Rousseau and the French revolutionaries when he came to consider the democratic danger. It is, in any case, difficult to guess what "the little band" had in common, except that all contributed to constitutionalism, of which Acton approved. However, the democratic taint that Acton came to recognize in some of the "little band," he never detected in Harrington. Far from it, he attributed to him the glory of having discovered a "separate science of society" based on the notion that "the sphere of religion, morality, economy and knowledge" was "organically distinct from the State."[17]

How Acton got this idea, it is hard to imagine. There is not a hint of the liberal antinomy of state and society in Harrington. If government, to be stable, must be adjusted to the "fundamental" distribution of property, there is no suggestion that government cannot, or ought not to, interfere with "society." *Oceana* has an agrarian law; a national, if tolerating, church; and there is a compulsory scheme of education and military service for all citizens. And everyone with £100 per year can vote. That is what "ancient prudence" and Machiavelli had taught Harrington. Yet Acton had no illusions about Plato's, Aristotle's, or Machiavelli's liberalism. Perhaps he had not read *Oceana,* but more likely, seeing it only in the light of the Civil War, he could recognize only a chapter in the history of English freedom. Harrington, to become a Whig ancestor, had to be ruthlessly liberalized.

This last guess finds at least some support in the fact that another contemporary of Acton's and Gardiner's completed the deradicalization of the now completely "Whig" Harrington. Lecky admired Harrington even more than Milton and Jeremy Taylor, because he had defended religious toleration not on grounds of faith, but on a comprehensive demand for civil freedom.[18] So far radicalism was all to the good, but Harrington was a true Englishman too "who had realized that government is an organism, not a mechanism, . . . that it must grow naturally out of the conditions of society and cannot be imposed by theorists."[19] This too was the burden of Maitland's early essay in praise of the distinctively English idea of liberty, in which Harrington is pictured as anything but a utopian. On the contrary he was an "inductive historian" who knew the limits of the possible.[20] One wonders what on earth Montesquieu and Burke had ever found amiss. What had happened to the old constitution maker, who had referred to his labors as "political architecture" and called for "invention" in politics? What indeed had happened to the Commonwealth? Nothing much, except that the Whigs by an heroic act of retrospective idealization had made it Victorian, and above all, English, in the sense of "non-French."[21] However, if the liberals drew Harrington into the nineteenth century struggle of ideologies, they did not keep him, or the Revolution. Both presently had to be shared with the Marxists. Harrington had in any case never occupied a great place in the liberal Pantheon. After all, it was not he who had written *Areopagitica.* In fact, he did not really quite fit. On the other hand, he turned out to be just what Marxist historians were looking for.

A Dialectical Harrington. That Marxists should concentrate on revolutions is hardly surprising—that *was* politics. And the Civil War as a part of the "bourgeois revolution" was bound to come in for its share of analysis.[22] Harrington, moreover, had more to contribute to the "bourgeois" than to the "Puritan" revolution. Indeed, as historicism turned to economism in general, Marxists were not alone in noticing how remarkably modern it was of him to have discovered "the principle that the economic elements in a State will determine its government."[23] Now this is fair enough: Harrington too prided himself on the discovery of the principle of "the balance," the idea that those who have the greatest share of property must rule. That power follows property was undeniably his belief. However, it was left to Eduard Bernstein to discover that this simple formula made him a precursor of historical materialism. There was of course Harrington's use of the word "superstructure" to describe political institutions to justify this suggestion, but there was more. Harrington, Bernstein felt, had accurately diagnosed the class relationships prevailing in seventeenth century England. Far from being mistaken about the impossibility of a restored monarchy, he had really foreseen that absolutism was impossible, and that the bourgeoisie must rule, as, in fact, it did after 1688. In short, Harrington had discovered the "bourgeois revolution," not just "the balance."[24] Since Bernstein offered his interpretation there has been a flood of imitative writings on the English Revolution, and in all of them Harrington turns up as a most remarkable fellow, with a stunning resemblance to Marx. He "was the greatest of a group of writers who penetrated behind the political facade." And he was able to do this because in a more limited way he was witnessing the same events that Marx was to face in 1848.[25] Not only is Harrington said to have seen that "political domination was directly and inevitably the function of economic power," he also had a theory of social development, a view of "history as a social process." In short, he was not only an economic determinist, but a dialectical historian. His errors were slight indeed. Only the fact that he was an aristocrat prevented him from being fully class-conscious, from recognizing the proletariat. That too is what led him to believe that the end of the dialectical process had already come, and that a harmonious constitutional order was possible. However, subtract the old constitutional "phantast" and you get an historical materialist.[26] From another point of view, it might be said that what Bernstein's *epigoni* have done is to separate the "real" from the "accidental" Harrington, and to describe him in terms drawn from a new vocabulary. That is exactly what was done to the Revolution as a whole, after all.

A Marx for the Gentry. One historian of the "bourgeois revolution," however, cannot possibly be so waved aside. For R. H. Tawney has surely done more than anyone else to make that revolution intelligible and he alone has given us a subtle and fascinating portrait of Harrington in the context of his age. He does not doubt that the decline of the nobility and the rise of capitalism were at the root of the Civil War, but at least we are told exactly who was rising and who was falling. According to Tawney's calculations there emerged along with urban capitalists a class of rural ones, the gentry, who by benefitting from Tudor policies and by improving their estates, came to be part of the new bourgeois order that rose to challenge the Establishment.[27]

If this is still the old bourgeois revolution it has at least been ruralized and we have been liberated from 1789, 1848, and 1917. For "Tawney's country" is seventeenth century England, his evidence is seventeenth century evidence, and the writers whom he quotes are seventeenth century writers. Moreover, if the gentry had their Marx it was at least not a nineteenth century Marx, but Harrington. To be sure, it is not everyone's Harrington. The old constitutional dreamer is quite gone. His specific political proposals are dismissed as trivial, but if he did have too much faith in "the magic of institutions," he was still no "English Sieyès." On the contrary, he was one of the first "to depict their conception of the society of the future as a necessary deduction from the facts of social history." *Oceana* is thus "partly social history, partly a program based on it." What matters is the former. For with Harrington we get for the first time a recognition of "the operation of impersonal, constant, and, it might be, measurable forces" in history. He was, indeed, the first English thinker to find the causes of the political upheaval in antecedent social change. The only fault that Tawney can find in this prodigy is the weakness of all "one key" explanations and the failure to grasp "the dynamic power of religious conviction."[28] It is, of course, the very charge he has for years brought against doctrinaire Marxism. What remains is impressive enough, and it has found many supporters.[29] It is a persuasive picture because due weight is given to Harrington's limitations, his preoccupation with peace and order, and his debts to earlier writers. However, it does not stand up. Poor Harrington simply cannot be made to bear the burdens of a twentieth century social historian.

There is much in Harrington to make Tawney's portrait a recognizable likeness. Harrington *did* see the English Revolution as part of a general European upheaval of which the Dutch Revolts, the Fronde, and the Thirty Years War in Germany were parts. He also took this to be the expression of the instability of the "Gothick Ballance" in its death pangs, that is, the end of the feudal system. Nor is there any doubt that he felt that Tudor policy, by repressing the nobility and enriching the "people," had made the war inevitable.[30] In his way he was an economic determinist. There was no question in his mind about the sequence of cause and effect. The distribution of property is "fundamental"; it is the "efficient cause" of the political "superstructure."[31] And if he believed that an even distribution of property could be maintained forever by a republican government, he admitted that it had never been attempted in the past.[32] So far Tawney's Harrington seems perfectly sound. The trouble begins when we ask: what did Harrington mean by property? Why was it "fundamental"? How did he describe the changes preceding the Civil War? What did he mean by the "Gothick Ballance"? And how closely did he really look at his own age?

To begin with, Harrington had no idea whatsoever of what we today call economic life. He never spoke of "rents, sales or profits," only of property. Changes in ownership of property, not economic development, were his sole concern.[33] Now the political consequences of the amounts of property held by either a few or many persons were indeed a matter of "necessity," but it was not "historical necessity," not the logic of an historical situation at all. The necessity that Harrington had in mind was the universal need to eat.[34] From this it follows that anyone who has the means to feed men, controls them. It also means that he has the power to maintain soldiers who depend on him. That is why property is power. For an "Army is a belly" whether it be a royal army, the retinue of a nobleman, or a citizen militia.[35] Moreover, Harrington was convinced that property will always be used to support armed men because no one is secure in his possessions unless they can be defended. The "matter of governments is . . . estate," that is, the defense of possessions.[36] If "industry secures possession," it is not *property* unless others recognize it as such, and respect the claim.[37]

There are two ways of enforcing claims to property, by violence or by due process of law. Now Harrington argued that the latter is possible only when possessions and military power are so evenly divided that no one can hope to encroach successfully upon anyone else. This is the economic basis of the *rule* of law. It will be an *effective* rule, moreover, because, once a common interest exists in maintaining the proprietary status quo, it can be defended by the pooled strength of a citizen militia, fed at the common trough. The alternative is competition for property, the use of private armies, and the enforcement of claims by arms. This is the economic basis of the rule of men. For property is secure possession and only might can accomplish that. If the people own the balance of property they can rule effectively through law based on common interest and common military power. If a monarch or an oligarchy has the balance, they will rule, but there will be no law, for there will be no shared interest and only conflicting claims and armies. All rule is based on the ability to maintain arms; the choice is between private or public armies, competing or harmonized interests, law or violence, war or peace. There are really two very closely linked arguments here. The first deals with, "what is law?" the second with, "when is the *rule* of law possible?" Neither is a question about the economic structure of society as such. That military power should play so large a part in it is not surprising. Harrington had lived through a civil war and had seen the rise of the New Model; nor was Machiavelli his idol in vain.

III. Harrington's Argument

To understand the development of Harrington's argument one must remember both what he was trying to prove, and whom he was trying to refute. Harrington was no relativist. He thought a republic not only a suitable form of government for England in 1656, but the absolutely and eternally best.[38] And he wanted to show that it was not only a possibility but a necessity, because there were no viable alternatives. Of these there were two that had to be demolished, the ancient constitution and Hobbes's *Leviathan*.[39] The latter was for Harrington far more important, not because it was a likely prospect, but because he fully understood its intellectual strength. *Oceana* is essentially a struggle between Machiavellian "ancient prudence" and Hobbes.

Anti-Goths. However, he did not ignore the traditionalists' views either. To them he had to prove that the traditional order could not, and never did, provide either the rule of law or, indeed, any sort of political stability. With Hobbes, Harrington insisted that anarchy was the inevitable result of divided sovereignty. Now the argument of constitutional theorists from Fortescue to the seventeenth century had been that the legal defense of "one's own," including property, social status or "liberties," and the power to rule the kingdom, were separate. Charles I on the scaffold still defended a form of this old doctrine when he proclaimed that the subjects' "liberty and freedom consists in having government in those laws by which their life and goods may be best their own. . . . It is not their having a share in the government; that is nothing pertaining to them." It was essentially a re-echoing of the Senecan phrase that epitomized the traditional idea of the constitution: "*ad reges enim potestas omnium; ad singulos, proprietas.*"[40] This is what Harrington called the "Gothick Ballance" and his whole point was to show that it had never worked because it was inherently unstable. The division of *gubernatio* and *jurisdictio*, the child of "modern prudence," had never produced a rule of law. It was, rather, a perpetual state of civil war. The nobility could not rule without a king, as they were perpetually competing with each other. Since feudalism in Norman England began as a system of military tenures they had always the means to defend and extend "their own" by arms. The king needed the military services of the nobility as they needed his political offices, but as they trenched upon his dominion, so he was a threat to theirs. Neither one could get on with or without the other. Both lived off the people. Happily the Tudor kings by statutes of alienation and by expropriating the clergy had enriched the people and destroyed the nobility. However, by depriving itself of the social and military support of the nobles the monarchy itself became impossible, for it was not a Turkish absolutism in which the king owned the balance of property.[41] In England the people now held the balance and it only remained for Englishmen to face the facts and set up political institutions compatible with this new order.

There is much that is ingenious in this account, but is it good modern social history? There is neither a notion of economics nor of class-conflict in all this. Nor did Harrington ever claim to have said anything new. He merely repeated the accounts given by Bacon, Raleigh, Selden, and Henry Wotton.[42] Not one of them spoke of the "rise of the gentry," but all described the conflict that our textbooks have long spoken of as the end of feudalism and the rise of absolutism. Harrington's only contribution to this history was to see the rise of the people as the consequence of Tudor policy and to explain the origins of the Civil War by that fact. The conflict itself had been one between absolutist legal institutions and a new economic-military balance of power. His originality was in the correlation of feudal history with the Polybian theory of constitutions. Had Tawney not insisted on treating Harrington's constitutional preoccupations as trivial, he would not have so distorted his ideas.

Anti-Hobbes. Against the traditionalists Harrington had to show only what conditions were necessary for the rule of law. He did not have to justify the inseparability of law and property, since their constitutional theory, too, rested on it. To refute Hobbes, however, he had to find a new answer to the question, "what is law?" And it is here that his theory of "interest" really comes to play its part.[43] Harrington's attitude toward Hobbes was extremely complex. He very much admired Hobbes's nonpolitical writings, and even *Leviathan* he knew to be among the best of the modern age. Above all, both men shared an ardent desire, not surprising in a period of revolution, for peace and order at almost any price. Both not only stood apart from the war of religious opinions, but also wanted to find some way out of it. A demonstrable politics, a certain, self-evident set of rules capable of convincing any sane person, seemed the only answer to both.[44] The trouble was that Hobbes had come up with a monarchical, and Harrington with a republican, solution to their common problem. It was impossible for Harrington to use the conventional religious and traditionalist attacks against Hobbes. These applied to him no less than to Hobbes.[45] Nor was it possible simply to assert his republican faith. Demonstrable proof of some sort had to be offered in answer to *Leviathan*. That was the true function of his theory of "interest."

In his direct references to Hobbes, anywhere in his writings, Harrington was often disingenuous, picturing their conflict as one between demonstration "by geometry" and "by nature" or historical example, as between logic and experience.[46] To be sure, Hobbes did argue for sovereignty as a logical necessity and rejected historical arguments as uncertain and merely prudential.[47] However, logic was not his only instrument, and certainly not the one most relevant to Harrington. It was Hobbes's psychology that presented the real obstacle to Harrington's republican rule of law. According to Harrington, Hobbes had simply stopped short the argument about legitimacy, or the valid sources of law, by saying that it was the will of the sovereign. To this Harrington replied that not only was the logic of consent an unhistorical argument, but that will must be supported by power, and arms by fodder, that is, by property. Effective law is made, in short, not just by will, but by the interest that moves this will and gives it substance, and interest is, for Harrington, property interest.

To say that Hobbes had not investigated the nature of power is, however, far from true. With horrified fascination he saw it everywhere. For him, however, it was not a quantity, like Harrington's interest, but a human disposition, an overriding urge. Power drove men in all they did and dominated all their relations. Science gave power, reputation gave power, riches gave power, authority gave power; that is why men desired them.[48] The one thing, however, that Hobbes never did, unlike Machiavelli and Harrington, was to admire or praise power. He hated it as he was obsessed by it. But the acuteness of his insight into the psychology of power relationships *did* make Machiavelli look like a "boy who had newly read his Livy."[49]

Now it has often been noticed that Harrington avoided all talk about human nature. His reputation as a sociologist and realist depends on it. Nevertheless, the absence of moral concern, though unusual in the seventeenth century, is not in itself any great proof of science. Partly it sprang, of course, from his desire to escape from the ideological deadlock; but he not only wanted to avoid moral and religious issues, he was determined to de-psychologize politics. It was his way of evading Hobbes, without answering him. Hobbes had made sovereignty and law expressions of the needs created by the rage for power. Harrington simply refused to ask himself why men need rules and rulers. He did not offer an alternative to Hobbes, he just described the institutional setting within which sovereignty and law could operate. So where Hobbes had insisted that authority, like all sources of legitimacy, was a form of power, Harrington replied that it was nothing of the sort, it came from "the goods of the mind."[50] To which Hobbes might have answered that the ability to convince people is also power. It would not have mattered; for Harrington has nothing more to say about authority. For, being a mental attribute, it has no place in his theory of legitimacy. Legitimacy is based solely on interest, on the balance of property. Effective law can only be made by those who possess the balance of property and stability depends on law expressing their interests. It follows that the only legitimate government, the only government that *should* rule, is that which must in fact rule—that is, the government of the dominant "interest." An intelligent government will acquire authority, but its legitimacy rests on the interests that it represents.[51] Against Hobbes's psychological account of the origins of law Harrington simply pitted an institutional one. It is an argument which, in rather less subtle form, still rages among political theorists.

Interest and Human Nature. There were other reasons for avoiding psychology. Not only must it not be allowed to interfere with the "interest" theory of law on which the legitimacy and necessity of the republic were based; it must also be kept out of history. The "autonomy of politics" for Harrington meant that once the stable rule of common interest was established, "political architecture" and institutional "invention" could build a perfect and eternal republic.[52] There was no need to worry about convictions, dispositions, and passions. This not only set him apart, as an historian, from Hobbes, but also from Machiavelli. In both cases psychological considerations, which from the republican point of view were unfortunate, had to be eliminated. For if the republic was an historical necessity and could be made to last for all time, it was important that no inconvenient psychological factors be allowed to disturb the clear course of history. Tawney is perfectly right in attributing to Harrington a sense for the "impersonal forces."

The trouble is that this came not from any historical sense, but from its total absence. One need only compare his account of the origins of the Civil War to Hobbes's. To Hobbes it was a war of ideologies. The doctrines of fanatical preachers, the seditious universities, and the fantasies of those who, like Harrington, had derived exaggerated notions about Greek and Roman liberty from their youthful readings of classical authors, these were the causes of the disaster.[53] Hobbes was as sure as any post-Gardiner historian that it was a war of minorities. The people had merely followed prospects of pay and plunder. As for "social factors," Hobbes noted the city merchants' disinclination to pay taxes, and the hopes of improvident gentleman who were out to make their fortune in war; but these were minor points for him.[54] Ideas and the passions they produced were at the heart of the war. Now Harrington, having friends on both sides, was not, like Hobbes, inclined to deal out praise and blame. It was not the characters of the king or of the rebels that had caused the war, it was the nature of the situation.[55]

However, Harrington never gave the barest account of what that situation really was. He never described the interests at work. He is even less sociological than Hobbes, not to speak of Baxter. After repeating his predecessors' accounts of Tudor policy he tells us in one paragraph that the balance of property and power had shifted to the people and the Commons. Elizabeth had been able to charm them into acquiescence. The Stuarts, prompted by false counsellors, had ignored their demands, and, presumably lacking charm, were bound to fall.[56] That is all he knew, that is all he had observed. Yet these were the crucial years during which the gentry is said to have been transformed. But Harrington had no interest in these events as such. He had read of republican institutions; he wanted them in England. His war was a very simple one between the monarchy and the people, a political war of institutions. There is no mention of the social or economic trends of his own age. He tells us nothing of the life of the towns, nor did he notice that the actual trend was toward the consolidation of estates. All that he saw was a repetition of those classical conflicts that Machiavelli had explained to him. However, he did not even follow Machiavelli when it came to psychology. He was not only ready to accept the latter's dictum that good laws make good men, he went further. Men can be bad and the commonwealth can still be perfect, because stability depends on "interests and orders," not on morality.[57] Not for him Machiavelli's cycle of corruption, or the flight of virtue from one place to another. It was not a decline in virtue, but changes in the balance of property, that brought republics down. Luxury was the habit of the nobility, it was their self-interest. When they ruled, so did their ways; but the cause of the change was not moral, it was institutional.[58] Had they protected themselves with a sound agrarian law the republic would have lasted as eternally as *Oceana*.

There is little left of Tawney's objective social historian; of the seventeenth century Marx nothing remains at all. There is only a very ingenious defender of classical republicanism, an institutional historian who applied a modified version of Polybius to the history of England.

IV. A Harrington for the Present

Since J. H. Hexter has exposed "the storm over the gentry" to the general public, there is no need to go into the details of this academic war here.[59] All that has to be said is that Tawney, Trevor-Roper, and their respective followers, armed with conflicting sets of statistics, are re-fighting the Civil War. Facing the "rising gentry" is now a very different species of gentlemen.[60] Trevor-Roper's gentry are far from prosperous. Stagnant economically, politically disgruntled, they are shopping for ideologies, first Roman Catholicism, then Puritanism, and in their last hour Harrington's republicanism. Since economic success was based not on estate management, but on trade or court favor, and as the latter was a limited source of supply, there was a permanent group of "outs," grumbling and plotting in rural discomfort. Their policies were nothing if not regressive. If they thought at all, it was negatively: away with the court, the common law, the established church, the city, the bureaucracy; away especially with a peaceful foreign policy, so that gentlemen might again enrich themselves by naval piracy as they had under Elizabeth.

The Gentry Fanatic. Of this unattractive group, Trevor-Roper tells us, Cromwell was the incarnation, and Harrington the ideologue— still the Marx of the gentry here, but a very different gentry and a very different Marx. The science of society has been replaced by disastrous prophecy. Instead of giving his clients an accurate view of their prospects Harrington gave them a dream-picture of what they wished to be. Like later ideologists he said "is" where "I hope" should have been. The statement, "the gentry have the land," Trevor-Roper notes, is analogous to Hitler's saying, "England *is* defeated," in 1940. At worst Harrington was an intellectualizing subversive, at best a "coffee-house politician" prating about his anarchic gentry-republic in his dream-parliament, the Rota Club.

It is an immensely persuasive picture. As Hexter says, we've seen these types before, and he mentions the Raubritter and Lord Eldon's entourage. But why stop there? Surely we have seen all this in our own day. As we have emerged from the twin myths of the eternal "right" and "left" and of the creativity of revolutionary movements, we have come to a new view of the nature of fanaticism and the forces that feed it.[61] And who knows more about the most ghoulish manifestations of nihilism than the author of *The Last Days of Hitler?*[62] The fact is that the picture of a group of socially displaced malcontents, animated by a pure wish to destroy the "system," corresponds far more to our own experience than that of a sturdy, solid group of consciously "rising" men, engaging in radical politics so as to assert the claims of their class against an order in which they are, after all, getting on. To which it might, of course, be very justly answered, that we have not been living through the "bourgeois revolution." The impression remains that psychologically Trevor-Roper wins hands down. It has simply become difficult to envision a class-revolution of any kind. The work of nihilistic discontent, on the other hand, is not unfamiliar.

Harrington on Gentry and People. The question here is, how does his new reputation fit Harrington, whatever the "ups" and "downs" of the gentry may have been? There is only too much in *Oceana* that justifies Trevor-Roper's view. Not only did he share many of the pseudo-policies that Trevor-Roper associates with his miserable gentry, but he *was* in the habit of saying "is" for reasons other than the demands of veracity. For instance, he did not say that the court was a bad thing, for which there was no place in a republic. Describing England in general he said, "men of Country-Lives have been still entrusted with the greatest affairs, and the people have constantly had an aversion from the ways of the Court."[63] No fawning courtiers in England, where only self-respecting country squires rule. That he saw the whole people, as such, rising in the Rebellion, and not specific groups, is itself an ideological symptom, fatal to Tawney's objective observer, but only too compatible with Trevor-Roper's myth-maker. It was in fact his closest friend Neville, not Harrington himself, who said that the "balance is in the gentry"; but to have said "the people" instead was probably worse.[64]

But it is in the structure of government of *Oceana*, and in its policies, that Trevor-Roper's case finds its greatest support. Although it is an active state it has no taxes and no bureaucracy; administration is local, even if the traditional division of England has been replaced by a more symmetrical one.[65] The "owner at his plow" is the genius of this society. The city is to be curbed, since ancient history "proves" that where city-life has had "the stronger influence" in a republic it led to turbulence.[66] The clergy and the lawyers, the natural deceivers of the people, are to be banished from political life. Indeed, one of the advantages of ending primogeniture was that it would end the flow of younger sons into these professions.[67] There was to be a national church, but its doctrines were never explained; it was not Anglican at any rate. Above all there is Harrington's jingoism and imperialism. One would never guess that the historian of the "bourgeois revolution" was a rip-roaring England-firster, whom Froude quite correctly regarded as the prophet of British imperialism.[68] Not only did Harrington repeat Cromwell's cant about a great Protestant war of liberation, but he added the Machiavellian argument that a "commonwealth for encrease" was superior to one for mere "preservation." And as usual he provided plenty of historical "proof" that such a commonwealth was bound to win.[69]

It is, however, in his attitude to the people and in his vision of a reconstructed gentry that Harrington most resembles the professional revolutionary. The "course of England" into a commonwealth is "certain" and "natural," but the people if left to themselves will be led by lawyers and clergy right back to monarchy, even though that could not succeed. Far from having the "unshatterable faith in the political virtues of his fellow country-men" that Tawney ascribes to him, he deeply distrusted their political intelligence unless supported by gentry leadership.[70] Only the gentry could provide both the military and the political leadership that England needed. Indeed "history showed" that only gentlemen, like Moses, Solon, or Cromwell had ever established a commonwealth.[71] In spite of Machiavelli's advice that a popular republic should begin by killing off its nobility, Harrington insisted that a gentry "not overbalancing the people" was "the very life and soul" of a commonwealth.[72]

There is indeed some reason to doubt Harrington's devotion to democracy. An agrarian law could settle the distribution of property forever, but nothing on earth would alter the natural division of men into freemen and servants, such as "live on their own" and such as do not. The latter have no place in political life and are even to be excluded from the army, like the Roman "proletaries," lest freemen be ruled by their servants.[73] A German author has even come up with the fanciful suggestion that this "socialist-aristocratic" order was an unconscious emanation of an "urgermanische Gesittung," an obscure longing for the long-lost organic, Germanic, peasant society led by its God-sent leaders.[74] One need not go to such lengths to see that *Oceana* is a rural gentry-paradise. Even if Harrington piously insisted on a nobility of merit, and not of privilege, he constantly identified the former with the existing gentry or "noblesse" as he put it, explicitly rejecting the division between nobility and gentry.[75] Here indeed is a "pseudo-realistic utopia," a mixture of prophecy, historical speculation, and exhortation that might well appeal to people like Trevor-Roper's rebellious hay-seeds.[76]

Nevertheless it is a false picture. Whatever may have been happening to the gentry, Harrington was not their Marx, and not their Lenin—neither a discoverer of the springs of history, nor a maker of ideology. All that Trevor-Roper has done is to turn Tawney's Harrington on his head, along with the "rising-gentry" and the entire "bourgeois revolution." It is a procedure that does little to explain him.

His Relation to Commonwealth Ideology. No one has ever denied that Harrington was a Commonwealthman, and that being eclectic

he shared some of the ideas of the Levellers and some of the Independents.[77] A written constitution was not his invention, neither were
frequent elections, nor religious toleration nor hostility to the legal
caste, to monarchy and to courtiers. The first question is whether
Harrington, in fact, provided the Cromwellian gentry with their oper-
ative political ideas. The second question is what light, if any, the
ideology of the gentry can cast upon the character of Harrington's
thought. For Trevor-Roper's Harrington depends not only upon a
positive answer to the first question. It also assumes that this function
of Harrington's thought, the role it played in gentry politics, corresponds exactly to Harrington's intentions. The present argument is
that both these propositions are false. The first is a simple mistake
in fact, the second a common, but extremely obvious, error in the
art of historical interpretation. One need only recall how often Rousseau has been treated as if the Jacobins had *written,* rather than
quoted, the *Social Contract,* to see, at once, what has happened to
Harrington. In both cases the intellectual biography of a man has
been distorted in the course of a far more general and complex argument about the "nature" and "causes" of a revolution. If Tawney is,
perhaps, mistaken in his view of Harrington's purposes and methods,
he at least has given us the portrait of a man, even if a rather impres-
sionistic one. The same can hardly be said of Trevor-Roper's Harrington. What we get here is not a picture of a thinker, but a personification, an artificial assemblage of the various roles that his ideas *may*
have played in gentry politics. This montage of their potential functions is then passed off as a genuine picture of Harrington's ideas.
There is, of course, nothing objectionable in describing the social
functions of ideas, that is, the study of ideology proper. It is an essential aspect of social history. After all, social psychology treats the
person as the sum of the "masks" he wears, the totality of the roles
he plays in the "orders" of society, whether political, economic, military, kinship or religious.[78] There is no reason why ideas should not
be treated in their social context, in terms of the part they play in the
activities of groups, especially of groups engaged in a violent conflict.

However, just as an individual may be regarded as more than a
social type, so there is more to the study of ideas than the identification of ideological processes. In analyzing an individual writer one
looks for more than just another social specimen. And when it is said
that an author ought to be studied in terms of his social experiences,
it is worth remembering that these are specifically *his,* and that his
personal situation and intellectual antecedents and concerns are not
to be ignored.[79] As a part of social history ideas are impersonal func-

tions of group-life; as the subject of the history of ideas they are the expressions of individual thinkers who communicate directly and personally with their predecessors, contemporaries, and us. There is no conflict between these two ways of looking at the past. One asks different questions and one gets different answers. Only the intellectual imperialist, out to conquer the realm of "real" history that lies behind men and events, will confuse them.

It is the habit of personifying events, ages, nations, classes and other groups, indeed history itself, that has led to the depersonalizing of individuals.[80] For it is now these abstract categories that have motives and intentions that must be uncovered and evaluated as one judges the behavior of individuals. Ideas are now rationalizations, deceptions practiced semi-consciously by groups, and the omniscient historian must expose them and grade them as "ideology," "utopia," or "false consciousness," depending on their relation to the true standard—the course of "real" history.[81] This has been the method of neo-Tories no less than of Marxists. According to the latter the "virtue" of the seventeenth century bourgeoisie was to have been "progressive," that is, in line with the demands of history. Their error was to have thought that they were a "universal" class, realizing general moral and religious values, not just their own aspirations; and this disguise must be pulled aside. Thus too the sin of Trevor-Roper's gentry is not that they were nasty, but that they attempted the impossible by vainly trying to interfere with the set course of England's historical development; and because they could not succeed their ideology was a mere cover for their impotence, "false consciousness." The terms of historical classification now become those of moral obloquy. Puritanism is "really" only the "veil of the bourgeoisie" or the "false consciousness" of the declining gentry. Hobbes's philosophy was "really" only "bourgeois ideology"; Harrington's, that of an array of distempered "mere" gentry. The revolution was "really" caused by the rising classes, or it was "really" caused by declining groups.

As has been well observed—and by a Marxist too—to describe Puritanism as the ideology of the declining gentry does little to explain the spiritual life of Milton or Vane.[82] To classify it as the rationalization of bourgeois aspirations does no better.[83] Nor does this distributing of identification disks throw much light upon Hobbes and Harrington. The only extenuating circumstance that excuses this rage for revealing the intimate secrets of groups and classes, and of history itself, is the political prudery of the Whigs, which was designed to bring out the worst in anyone. For to have said that the Civil

War was "really" about "faith and freedom," not a "social war" but "a war of ideas," was to invite abuse.[84] Whatever else wars may be, they are social events in which organized groups of men fight each other. Nor is slaughter improved when it is "motivated" by convictions and ideas. Ideological wars are no more edifying than other wars. In analyzing wars, or any identifiable social situation, we are, moreover, not looking for "real" causes, the "deep motives." Generalized concepts like "revolutions" or "classes" or "parties" do not have simple motives, open or hidden, that can be used to explain their character or general behavior. They are not individuals, after all. They are abstract concepts that we established so as to bring some order into our accounts of the past.[85] We can dissect them, identify the various strands that go into a chosen situation, and see how these modify and affect each other. Among these objectivized tendencies ideology, or "the symbol sphere," is surely an important one, no less so than the other "orders" of society. If this sort of analysis is the task of the social historian—and anyone who writes anything beyond the purest narrative history is just that—then there is no need to insist on metaphors, and on emotionally charged ones at that. It is indeed regrettable, as Stone has observed, that the Cold War has come to disturb the Civil War.[86] Perhaps it will console him to remember that something of that sort has always occurred when the question of the "real" causes of the Revolution was raised. Nothing less than partisanship could ever have induced so many learned men to ask so futile a question.

What Happened to Him. It remains to disentangle Harrington from the fortunes of the gentry and the "real" causes of the Great Rebellion. To begin with, Trevor-Roper accepts Tawney's view that Harrington described the "rise of the gentry," and in a way that was different from the earlier accounts of the decline of the nobility by Bacon, Raleigh, and Selden.[87] This, as we have seen, was not the case. If he appealed to the gentry this was not the reason for his popularity. However, the gentry did not in fact accept Harrington's ideas, and at no time did *Oceana* become the intellectual weapon, the verbal gunpowder, of the Independents. If they and Cromwell were the political leaders of the mere gentry, as Trevor-Roper claims, then Harrington never became their prophet. Even in the mad last year of the Commonwealth, Neville could muster only eight or ten supporters for Harrington's scheme in Parliament. Aubrey gives us one reason for its unpopularity, the overly democratic notion of rotation in office.[88] Burnet tells us of an even deeper reason, Harrington's paganism.[89] Moreover, if Trevor-Roper were not so anxious to destroy

Tawney's unreal Harrington, he might well have asked himself who, in fact, did write Cromwell's propaganda, who answered his critics and rationalized his policies? It was not Harrington; it was Milton. The dying gasp of Independent ideology is the *Ready and Easy Way*. Here is the disillusion with "the people," the call for the rule of the best, the best being the last Commonwealthmen. Here too is the religious fervor, the true note of seventeenth century ideological combat. It is here that the Commonwealth is held up as the will of God, as toleration had earlier been defended as the way to help men to God. As for Cromwell's radical Republican opponents, they talked of rights, consent, the "will of the nation," and "the cause we fought for." Whether the gentry was coming up or going down, these were the terms in which they, and the majority of their contemporaries, talked. It was not Harrington's manner any more than it was Hobbes's. That is why no one cared for them.[90] Cromwell tried to silence Harrington; the judges of Charles II persecuted him. Hobbes was exiled during the Commonwealth and kept quiet under Charles II. Neither produced ideology, the kind of ideas that could have played a part in the actual struggle. So much for history.

The facts known about Harrington's life can help us to see why he should have been so ineffectual. Tawney has suggested that Harrington may have seen the rise of the gentry in the fortunes of his own family, and Blitzer has shown that, in fact, many Harringtons had been climbing up the social ladder in a fairly spectacular way. Trevor-Roper has shown that some of them were slipping.[91] These circumstances, interesting in themselves, tell us nothing about Harrington. We do not know how much he knew or cared about the progress of his near and distant relations. Nor is their social status all that is relevant to a picture of his background. Many Harringtons had been scholars, travellers, and courtiers of note.[92] There is no reason to suppose that Harrington thought of himself as a "mere" gentleman or that he was under any inner compulsion to provide a pie-in-the-sky opiate for such men. If he aligned himself with any one of his family's traditions, it was that of the urbane, travelled gentleman-scholar. He had friends at court and in Parliament. According to all accounts he was a republican before the Civil War and remained one to the end. He loved Charles I and he admired Cromwell, or at least had illusions about him. But the origin of his views is not in his direct political activities, of which he, in fact, had none. His forum, the Rota, if it was a dream-parliament, was no more so than any debating society; and if it met in a coffee-house, the members were not such as one associates with the political cafés of modern Left-Banks.

Tawney is surely right in recalling that several members of the future Royal Academy were to be found there, as well as solid men like Pepys.[93]

Harrington got his notions from his beloved classics, not from any specific social experience. We may as well take Hobbes's word for the impact that the classics had upon the intellectual youth of his age. And Harrington was nothing if not an intellectual. He was precocious as a child and spent his early manhood in study and travel. Far from participating in the Civil War, he at once fled to his study; a true scholar, in short.[94] He had no wish to enter public life, because he preferred his books, and he boasted about the superiority of the intellectual to the man of affairs in season and out. No public figure had ever written a sensible word on politics, only "private gentlemen" could.[95] And before his judges he could think of no better defense than that if Aristotle and Machiavelli had been allowed to write freely under their respective rulers, then he too should be granted that privilege.[96] One can see with whom he identified himself. Socially detached, he cared only for his ideas, and for those of his great predecessors. If he addressed the gentry it was to call them to their duties, not to flatter them, "who understand so little what it is to be Lords of the Earth that they have not been able to keep their lands."[97] If *Oceana* was dedicated to Cromwell, he continued, on the strength of his classical examples, to call for a single, creative, but not ruling, legislator after Cromwell was dead.[98] Olphaus Megaletor, the great legislator of *Oceana,* does not resemble Cromwell, or any other contemporary; he is just a reincarnation of the Moses-Lycurgus-Solon-Romulus figure. As for the dedication, it is a puzzle, comparable to Machiavelli's dedication of *The Prince.*[99] Hobbes was surely right in insisting that realism was not the fruit of classical learning. And we have already seen how little there is to substantiate Harrington's reputation as a close observer of the English constitutional crisis. While he was abroad, for all his talk about the value of travel and historical knowledge for politicians, he was equally inattentive. His picture of Venice bears no resemblance to that republic in the seventeenth century, but it corresponds exactly to Contarini's popular myth.[100] Harrington was, in short, fatally addicted to his books, especially to Plato's *Laws,* Aristotle's *Politics,* Polybius, and, above all, to Machiavelli. *Oceana* was written to show the superiority of these "masters of ancient prudence" to those of "modern prudence," especially Hobbes and the defenders of the medieval tradition. If *Oceana* resembles Cromwell's *Instrument* and copies his military system, this was due to their common desire for stability. However, both knew perfectly well that their political values were not only different, but basically irreconcilable, as Puritanism and paganism were bound to be.

Harrington's Religious Views. It is possible that the gentry might have turned, as Trevor-Roper says, from Roman Catholicism to Puritanism in their search for a suitable ideology, though it is difficult to believe, since one of the few remaining certainties about the Great Rebellion is that Catholics and Puritans were never on the same side.[101] It is, however, totally improbable that they could at any time have moved from these to a pagan ideology. Nor is there any evidence that they did. They did not, and could not see themselves reflected in Harrington's Machiavellian paradise. And Harrington took to it precisely because he felt that peace and tranquillity depended on de-ideologizing politics, on ending the religious wrangles that raged about him with increasing heat. "Religion was not the thing at first contested, but God brought it to that issue," Cromwell noted.[102] Harrington's main aim was to get God out of politics. If he quoted the Old Testament it was as history. When he spoke of Christianity it was only to show that it was in no way incompatible with "ancient prudence." The rule of the Saints was an illegitimate oligarchy, in his eyes. Since they did not represent the balance, their rule was unstable and so unjust, and not at all godly.[103]

He also detested the asceticism of the Puritans. Like most admirers of the ancient republics, he wanted public games and entertainments.[104] As for his beloved Venice, it was not, as Filmer noted, a Christian place.[105] Nor was Harrington opposed only to Laud's church or to the Presbyterians. He was anti-clerical in the Continental manner, and indeed was fond of quoting French and Italian sayings about the political follies of the clergy.[106] Unlike Machiavelli he did not dwell on the political superiority of pagan religions to Christianity.[107] It was the sort of psychological reflection his optimistic mind eschewed. Moreover, the situation was different. Machiavelli saw only two alternatives, the Church or paganism. Harrington was faced with the problem of a multitude of sects. That his answer to it was fantastic is perfectly clear. Only as atypical a man as Harrington could have proposed toleration together with a national church and have suggested that the universities rationally settle all doctrinal disputes. What lies behind this fancy is a complete lack of religious sense. That is why Cromwell and Baxter condemned him. For his justification of this arrangement was that it did not matter what Christians believed as long as there was public order and an organ "representing the public conscience."[108] In this Montesquieu would have quite approved of him, for he too thought it was "necessary to the society that it should have something fixed; and it is religion that has this stability."[109] Thus Harrington, for all his tolerance, insisted on the exclusion of Jews and idolaters from *Oceana,* not because of their personal beliefs, but because they would not mix and become part of the public or share the national conscience. His specific suggestion was to send the Jews to Ireland where their industry would fill an evident gap in the national character of the local population.[110] It is not the content of faith that matters, but only its political and social consequences. Like Machiavelli, Bodin, and Montesquieu, Harrington was a *politique d'abord* man.

Survivalism. What else could "ancient prudence" have told him? What else could have drawn him to it? All knew stability, peace, order, and civic unity to be the highest of all social and political aims. Liberty, justice, and equality—these were all mere means to that supreme aim.[111] That is what Harrington said he had learned from them, and that is why he admired them so extravagantly. His dependence in every detail on Plato's *Laws* has often been shown.[112] Polybius was his master in the theory of mixed government.[113] In Aristotle, who was already "full of" the balance, he found the same doctrine.[114] If one is to see Harrington in the context of a tradition of political thought, one might well call it the "survivalist" tradition.[115] It includes all those for whom the fifth book of Aristotle's *Politics,* abstracted from all the rest of his thought, serves as the fountain of political wisdom, for whom the preservation of the political order is the first task of politics. Amoral, and a-ideological, it rests on the assumption that government cannot make men good, but that it can keep them from violent action. The strict adherence to the letter of the law is demanded not as just, but as the one means of stopping violence and resentment among the governed; mixed-government, as the way to prevent acts of hostility from rulers. That, in fact, *is* justice. The end of government is at the most civic harmony; at the very least it is to prevent clashes of interest and conviction from becoming violent. Such was the theory of Marsiglio of Padua, of Machiavelli in the *Discourses,* of Spinoza, of Harrington, and in its most sophisticated form, of Montesquieu. It is a philosophy that is sure to appeal to those who have seen enough of civil war and ideological wrangling to last them forever.

V. Harrington and American Political Science

After observing the complexity of the attitudes which Harrington has evoked among his English readers, it is with relief that one turns to the simple welcome he received in America. For if Harrington's ideas ever played any part in political life, it was in America. Indeed they came close to being the ideology of the American Whigs, especially Adams and Webster. If his agrarian law, his militarism, his imperialism, and such devices as his Plutarchian legislator clearly had no place in American thinking, the American Harrington did bear a very recognizable resemblance to the original.[116] Certainly it was a more genuine likeness than any we have seen since Hume's essays. For only in America could he be accepted as a whole, as both a social realist and as a constitution-maker. There was no need here to separate these two aspects of his thought and to ignore, disparage, or distort one in order to accept the second. The "interest" theory of legitimacy was no longer incompatible with "political architecture"; rather they supported each other. For constitution writing was now no less respectable than a due regard for the place of property in government. Thus it was possible for Adams to recall that during the Second Continental Congress he had been a second Sieyès, and to quote the very passage in which Burke had identified the latter with Harrington. But Adams was quick to add that even in those palmy days he had never suggested an "unbalanced" constitution.[117] In short, he had been a second Harrington from the first. There was not the slightest chance that he should confuse a seventeenth century republican with an eighteenth century revolutionary. On the contrary, Harrington provided him with all the necessary arguments against the latter. At last Harrington had found a niche in the world of politics.

Harrington and the American Whigs. Harrington's American success is no surprise. The Great Rebellion did not need refighting. Most Americans were born Roundheads. Adams was proud to be unfashionable in England, with his taste for seventeenth century republican authors. And then *Oceana* was much more like America than England. It was after all a society in which considerable differences in wealth and conviction did not have to lead to violent conflict. It was an agrarian community, the very condition that Adams was happy to observe in America.[118] And it was, as Adams insisted a republic must be, based on popular consent. After all, anyone with £100 a year was entitled to participate in politics.

It has not been proven that, except in the case of Massachusetts where Adams himself introduced Harrington, he exercised a direct influence upon the various state constitutions. Rather it was a matter of drawing on a common stock of seventeenth century republican ideas which later writers had already developed.[119] In any case, in this respect Harrington was not particularly original. Survivalist constitutionalism in general continued to have a career in America. Where the balancing of interests rather than the morality of consent, and mixed and stable government rather than individual rights were stressed, as in *The Federalist,* there the direct heirs of Harrington, rather than those of Locke, were at work.[120] Not that even Adams saw any real conflict between these two. The usual thing was to talk of Sidney, Harrington, and Locke in one breath as the three patron saints of republicanism.[121] This could be done quite easily by de-radicalizing both Locke and Harrington. The individualism of Locke was toned down and Harrington's demand for a harmony of interest was overlooked—probably because both had been realized to a sufficient degree not to be real challenges. To Adams the balancing of interests achieved by his bicameralism seemed just like Harrington's. Did not both believe in natural aristocracy?[122] Only Harrington's Senate represented not the *interests* of this aristocracy, but rather the brains of a nation with one common interest. Its function, like that of the great legislator, was "invention," not the defense of local or group interests.[123] Indeed Harrington believed in political leadership, in politics as an art, in a way that was unfamiliar to the Whigs. A due attention to "energy in the executive" did not amount to politics as perpetual contrivance, not to mention again the constitution-creating single legislator, that civilized Machiavellian *Prince.*[124] Mixed government for Harrington was a matter of talent and functional utility, not of balancing powers. *Oceana* was a model of civic solidarity to which no reality, not even America, could aspire.

Politics as Engineering. Constitutional engineering has been respectable in America. Its academic offshoot today is the study of "comparative" government in which incommensurables are placed side by side in order that the essence of constitutional and political truth may reveal itself.[125] It is the art of writing static history, both ancient and contemporary, in which Harrington and Adams excelled. Harrington juggled his ancient republics around to prove that they alone were capable of achieving stability, and that the failure to adopt agrarian legislation was alone responsible for their eventual decline. Adams followed the same procedure in order to prove to Turgot and Condorcet that mixed government alone was stable, that wherever power had been located in one center the republican order had died.[126] To be sure, for all his agreement with the Machiavellian principle that good laws make good men, Adams spent far more time than Harrington did in contemplating the infirmities of human nature. However, since the old Adam was an historic constant, and only the balance of interest was variable, he could proceed on Harringtonian principles.[127] He openly rejected Montesquieu's relativism as Harrington had denied Machiavelli's.[128] And so Adams and later Webster could congratulate themselves in sober tones upon the fact that in America the aims of *Oceana* had been all but achieved because their ancestors had divided the land equally and their contemporaries or fathers had adopted a sensible constitution.[129]

If this is a watered-down Harrington, he is at least more genuinely himself than Acton's liberal, Lecky's organicist, or Burke's split personality. Both his mechanical materialism and his political fancies were given their due. For the latter were no longer quite so absurd. What was and remains so is the notion that politics is like engineering, an exact technique to be learned from the models of the past—or by "analytical models" built by contemporary political scientists. It is this that makes Oakeshott's caricature of the "political rationalist" so uncomfortably convincing. It is Harrington, far more than the often dour Machiavelli, who is the real prototype of this mentality. "A perfectionist in detail," addicted to the "politics of creation," professing the morality of "the self-made man and the self-made society," for whom politics is always a matter of solving technical "problems."[130] To which it might be said that the politics of "the felt need" do not exclude creation, and that when traditions fail or die, it is better to invent than to lament, provided one does it with a sense for the situation. Harrington lacked the latter utterly. However, when the situation found *him,* he could provide not just a combative ideology, but a reasoned view of the bases of constitutional government. What more than justifies the critics of politics as engineering is the extent to which Harrington and his latter-day equivalents have misunderstood the prudential and historical nature of practical political thinking.

Politics as Science. A mania for regarding Harringtonian "political architecture" as a science begins early. Harrington fancied himself a second Harvey, and Adams compared his "law" of the balance to Newton's physics.[131] Harrington's latest American admirers have gone even beyond that. Now it is not too much to claim that Harrington felt an enthusiasm for science. However, enthusiasm for science is not the same thing as science itself. And Harrington, for all his fervor, showed not the remotest understanding of, or even interest in, the scientific work of his age. For all his admiration for Harvey, he only knew that the latter had discovered the circulation of the blood, "out of nature." Yet Harvey's work had been published twenty-eight years before *Oceana* appeared, and his reputation was so great that by 1656 nearly every literate person had heard of him.

In all his travels in Italy and Holland, Harrington seems to have heard of no other great man or work of science. Just as he copied his social history from books, so his "passion" for science did not go beyond an acquaintance with a celebrated name and with a few new-fangled terms from the vocabulary of mechanics.[132]

However, if his knowledge of the natural sciences of his own age was scant, his resemblance to the twentieth century political scientist seems only too evident. His insensitivity to intangibles, and to qualitative considerations, which came out in his argument with Hobbes, find their culmination in his pretensions to "science." However, what was only a part of Harrington's work is now taken for the whole. We are told that he "was trying to reduce political life to a form that would admit of quantitative expression, of measurement on a common scale" and to deal only with "the measurable element among . . . phenomena."[133] That is said to explain his interest in property and electoral devices, where something, presumably pounds and votes, could be counted. In short, Harrington was not just, as his English admirers feel, a modern historian, but an American political scientist. For he was determined "to formulate a comprehensive and coherent science of politics" by applying to politics the techniques that had proven so fruitful in the natural sciences. His passion for detail did not express a lively imagination, but a sense of the concrete and a "desire to avoid oversimplification and abstraction."[134] Since "concrete" in Harrington's case can hardly mean a sense of the possible, it must be identified with the measurable.

Happily there is no reason to suppose that Harrington was trying to "reduce" politics to twentieth century academic ideology. What he did was to use Harvey's name to prop up his argument that the "facts" of history proved his law of "the balance" and that a political system built on such a basis must inevitably succeed. He also fancied that his detailed model of a political order was "political anatomy" since he was providing the commonwealth with its bones and arteries. In this he assured himself he was emulating Harvey.[135] What it amounted to was argument by analogy and feeble analogy at that. For it never occurred to Harrington that Harvey had not built the human body nor "invented" the blood stream.[136] Essentially he was no more "scientific" than John of Salisbury in his famous comparison of the levels of the social hierarchy to the members of the human body. Nor was he at all able to distinguish between the laws of history and those of mechanics or between a "demonstration out of nature" and historical examples. Such distinctions would only have undermined his case against Hobbes. However, once the function of Harrington's "institutionalism" is understood, there is nothing to suggest that he was at all inclined to identify the concrete with the measurable. He never speaks of measurement nor did he limit himself to measurable political phenomena any more than had Plato in the *Laws,* in which numbers also play their part—if not exactly a scientific one. And no one has yet suggested that Plato was a precursor of contemporary "behavioral science."

This is not the place to discuss the value of statistical information, of the study of voting behavior, of constructing equilibrium models or of plotting legislative and judicial decisions on graphs. For the present it suffices to note that Harrington contributed nothing but the habit of reasoning by dubious analogy to this form of political thinking. For he did not limit himself to the measurable. If any affinity exists between him and those who reduce politics to mathematics, it is on the level of ideology. In both cases there is an image of a political world so bland and so harmonious that nothing need be said or done but to record and count decisions about indifferent issues, and one that seems so calm and stable that everything appears calculable and predictable. In both cases it is a matter of hope rather than of science.

VI. Conclusion

It is as a theory of political history, and especially of constitutional history, that Harrington and the whole survivalist tradition may still play a part in our thinking. And, in fact, with the decline of academic Marxism a return to this older tradition has taken place. Since it never entirely died out in America, it is perhaps not surprising that it was to find one of its earliest restatements here. Whatever may have been the failings of Charles Beard as an historian of the Constitution in general, and of the Whigs in particular, he was, paradoxically, an avowed disciple of their historical theory.[137] And when in later years, thanks to the experience of war and fascism, he revised his economic interpretation of history, he came as close to Harrington as anyone could in the present age. The economic man, he argued, was always in competition with the political and military man, and economic interest could dominate political life only when the latter two were in abeyance.[138] In his view of economics as "interest" and in posing the alternatives of a state based on force or on interest, he showed himself a true Harringtonian. To have underestimated the importance of military force was, in his eyes, the great fault of Marx, and he pointed to Tirpitz's naval policy and to fascism to show the independent dynamic of military and political forces.[139] Nevertheless, he insisted that politics without economics was "astrology," since, to survive, any state must pay due regard to its economic foundations.[140] Since he, like Harrington, had not the slightest understanding of ideological forces, he could not envision a government that might choose to destroy a nation.

Many others, having lived through the entire history of Nazism and having had to cope with Soviet politics, too, followed Beard in finding Marxian categories inadequate. Power has been reinstated as an independent factor in history, along with ideology. With this has come a return to the conception of political classes.[141] Once it was really accepted that political power shapes economic life here and now, not vice versa, and the often terrifying consequences of this circumstance were realized, the days of grandiose historical expectations were over.[142] And with a decline in ideological fervor a new appreciation for limited government and the values of peace and order emerged. It is this rebirth of survivalism that justifies this extensive discussion of Harrington, who was one of its most honest defenders.

Harrington cannot solve our "problems" for us; that is not, in any case, the task of political theory, past or present. It has not, moreover, been the aim of this paper to give a systematic account of his ideas. Anyone who wishes to know exactly what Harrington said must read him. It is, indeed, the mere cataloguing of "who said what" that has brought the study of the history of ideas to its present low repute. The purpose, however inadequately achieved, here has been to look at contemporary thinking by examining a part of its inheritance and its ways of dealing with it.

Notes

I should like to acknowledge my debt to Charles Blitzer's Harvard Ph.D. thesis, "The Political Philosophy of James Harrington," published as *An Immortal Commonwealth: The Political Thought of James Harrington* (New Haven, 1960).

1. For this source of Harrington's troubles see R. Polin, "Economique et Politique au XVIIe Siècle: L'Oceana de James Harrington," *Revue Français de Science Politique,* Vol. 2 (1952), pp. 24–41.

2. F. W. Maitland, *Collected Papers* (Cambridge, 1911), p. 21.

3. The most Americanized view of Harrington is that presented in the only book-length study as yet published on him, H. F. Russell Smith, *James Harrington and His Oceana* (Cambridge, 1914). On the strength of this portrait he has been dismissed as inconsequential by both J. W. Gough, "Harrington and Contemporary Thought," *Political Science Quarterly,* Vol. 45 (1930), pp. 395–404, and

by A. E. Levett, "James Harrington," *Social and Political Ideas of the Sixteenth and Seventeenth Centuries,* ed. F. J. C. Hearnshaw (New York, 1949), pp. 174–203.

4. Smith, *op. cit.,* pp. 113–121.

5. *The Spirit of the Laws,* Vol. II, Bk. xxix, s. 19 and Vol. I, Bk. xi, s. 6.

6. "Idea of a Perfect Commonwealth" and "Of the First Principles of Government," *Hume: Theory of Politics,* ed. F. W. Watkins (Edinburgh, 1951), pp. 227–230 and 149–152.

7. G. P. Gooch in *English Democratic Ideas in the Seventeenth Century* (Cambridge, 1954), pp. 250–251, lists the rare notices given Harrington. None shows any real interest in him. Thus Coleridge named him among others as a great political writer, but no substitute for the Scriptures. *Stateman's Manual, Works,* Vol. I (New York, 1884), p. 129.

8. *Works,* Vol. II (Boston, 1884), p. 154.

9. *Ibid.,* Vol. V, pp. 216–217.

10. *Oceana,* ed. S. B. Liljegren (Lund, 1924), pp. 135 and 185–186. There is some controversy about the actual importance of Harrington's influence on revolutionary France. That Commonwealth ideas in general were known has been shown, but beyond specific similarities in constitutional devices, which often were not original with Harrington, there is little evidence of a deep or direct intellectual influence. This is well brought out by R. Koebner, "Oceana," *Englische Studien,* 68, 1933–1934, pp. 377–396. See, however, Gooch, *op. cit.,* pp. 312–313; S. B. Liljegren ed. and introd., *A French Draft, Constitution of 1792 Modelled on James Harrington's 'Oceana'* (Lund, 1932), pp. 3–79; D. Trevor, "Some Sources of the Constitutional Theory of the Abbé Sieyès," *Politica,* Vol. 1 (1934–35), pp. 325–342 and 443–469.

11. *Works,* ed. John Toland (London, 1771), pp. 362, 465, 482, 483, 488. All future references are to this edition, except for *Oceana.*

12. *Works,* Vol. V, pp. 376–377 and 381.

13. R. G. Usher, *The Historical Method of S. R. Gardiner* (St. Louis, 1915), pp. 41–54, 76–94 and 123–143.

14. *Amenities of Literature* (New York, 1864), Vol. I, pp. 370–389.

15. *Lectures on Modern History* (London, 1912), pp. 204–205.

16. *Historical Essays and Studies* (London, 1907), p. 492.

17. *Ibid.,* p. 380.

18. W. E. H. Lecky, *History of the Rise and Influence of Rationalism in Europe* (New York, 1866), Vol. II, p. 80.

19. *Ibid.,* Vol. II, pp. 145–146.

20. Maitland, *op. cit.,* p. 22.

21. See especially G. M. Trevelyan, *England under the Stuarts* (London, 1922), pp. 195–196, for the clearest statement about the unique character of the English Revolution.

22. C. Hill, "The English Civil War Interpreted by Marx and Engels," *Science and Society,* Vol. 12 (1948), pp. 130–156; L. Krieger, "Marx and Engels as Historians," *Journal of the History of Ideas,* Vol. 14 (1953), pp. 381–403.

23. J. Bonar, *Philosophy and Political Economy* (London, 1922), p. 895; Smith, *op. cit.,* pp. 23–24 and 28.

24. E. Bernstein, *Sozialismus und Demokratie in der grossen englischen Revolution* (Stuttgart, 1919), pp. 259–267.

25. M. James, *Social Problems and Policy during the Puritan Revolution* (London, 1930), p. 304, and "Contemporary Materialist Interpretations of Society in the English Revolution," in *The English Revolution*, ed. C. Hill (London, 1949), pp. 83 and 86.

26. D. W. Petegorsky, *Left-Wing Democracy in the English Civil War* (London, 1940), p. 234; P. Zagorin, *A History of Political Thought in the English Revolution* (London, 1954), pp. 133 and 144–145.

27. "The Rise of the Gentry," *Economic History Review*, Vol. 11 (1941), pp. 6 and 18.

28. *Ibid.*, pp. 36–37; "Harrington's Interpretation of His Age," *Proceedings of the British Academy*, Vol. 27 (1941), pp. 221, 200, 204.

29. *E.g.*, C. Blitzer, "Introduction" to *Selections from the Writings of James Harrington* (New York, 1955), pp. xi–xxxix; C. J. Friedrich, *The Age of the Baroque* (New York, 1952), pp. 33–34; C. Hill, "Recent Interpretations of the Civil War," *History* (N.S.) Vol. 41 (1946), pp. 70–71; G. H. Sabine, *A History of Political Theory* (New York, 1951), pp. 498 and 507.

30. *Oceana*, pp. 124–125, 48–50, and 53; *Works*, pp. 365–367.

31. *Oceana*, pp. 38–39; *Works*, pp. 367, 408, and 465.

32. *Oceana*, pp. 36, 39, 85–99; *Works*, p. 368.

33. I am very much indebted to the analysis of J. G. A. Pocock, *The Ancient Constitution and the Feudal Law* (Cambridge, 1957), pp. 128–130, and to his letter to *Encounter*, July, 1958.

34. *Oceana*, p. 14.

35. *Ibid.*, p. 16.

36. *Works*, p. 466.

37. *Works*, p. 363. The fundamental law in a state is the law that settles what is a man's "own." *Oceana*, p. 185.

38. Koebner, "Oceana," *loc. cit.*, p. 367.

39. I suspect that Harrington's description of the Gothic-balance of pre-Norman England was directed at the Levellers' myth of an Anglo-Saxon paradise. *Oceana*, pp. 43–45. I shall not here discuss either the adequacy of Harrington's historical scholarship by the standards of his own time, or even his basic historical concepts, since these subjects have already been treated exceptionally well in Pocock's *Ancient Constitution*, pp. 124–147.

40. C. H. McIlwain, *The Development of Political Thought in the West* (New York, 1932), p. 394.

41. *Oceana*, 15, 30–32, 47–48, and 187; *Works*, 226–228, 248–262, 270, 363–364, 553.

42. Pocock, *Ancient Constitution*, pp. 128–130 and 143; *Oceana*, 51–52; *Works*, pp. 364–365.

43. Polin, *loc. cit.*, pp. 27 and 30–31; F. D. Wormuth, *The Origins of Modern Constitutionalism* (New York, 1949), p. 135.

44. Koebner, "Die Geschichtslehre James Harringtons," *Geist und Gesellschaft* (Breslau, 1927), pp. 17–18.

45. In fact, Harrington defended Hobbes against the attacks of the divines, *Works*, p. 354.

46. *Oceana*, pp. 12–13, 50; *Works*, pp. 553, 558–561. Other writers have been only too ready to take his word for it, *e.g.*, Maitland, *op. cit.*, p. 21; Sabine, *op. cit.*, p. 499.

47. *Leviathan,* ed. Oakeshott (Oxford, 1947), pp. 435–436.

48. *Ibid.,* pp. 50–64.

49. *Oceana,* p. 30.

50. *Ibid.,* pp. 14, 20–21, and 24.

51. *Ibid.,* pp. 15–17; *Works,* pp. 362, 457, and 477.

52. *Oceana,* pp. 30–34 and 207.

53. *Behemoth, English Works* (London, 1840), Vol. VI, pp. 167–218, 362; *Leviathan,* pp. 140–141 and 214.

54. *Behemoth,* pp. 166–169.

55. *Oceana,* p. 50. It was not, thus, that his friend Charles I had been *bad,* just helpless. *Works,* p. 367.

56. *Oceana,* pp. 49–50; *Works,* pp. 364–367, 408, and 467.

57. *Oceana,* pp. 53–54, 185–186; *Works,* p. 456.

58. *Oceana,* p. 56; Machiavelli's *Discourses,* Bk. I, chs. 1, 2, 18, 37, and 39; Bk. II, "Introduction"; Bk. III, ch. 1; Pocock, *Ancient Constitution,* pp. 145–147; Koebner, "Geschichtslehre," *loc. cit.,* pp. 13–14 and 19.

59. J. H. Hexter, "Storm over the Gentry," *Encounter,* May, 1958, pp. 22–34.

60. H. R. Trevor-Roper, "The Gentry, 1540–1640," *Economic History Review Supplement* (1954); "The Country-House Radicals, 1590–1660" and "The Outbreak of the Great Rebellion," *Men and Events* (New York, 1957), pp. 179–188 and 195–205.

61. See R. Aron, *The Opium of the Intellectuals,* tr. by T. Kilmartin (New York, 1957), *passim,* for a discussion both of the obsolescence of these ideas, and the passions which they can stir among café-politicians.

62. I am happy to see that I am not alone in this suspicion; see M. Beloff, "Another Fallen Idol?" *Encounter,* January, 1959, p. 74.

63. *Oceana,* p. 10.

64. Smith, *op. cit.,* pp. 75–112. For the friendship between Neville and Harrington see *Aubrey's Lives,* ed. O. L. Dick (Ann Arbor, 1957), pp. 124–127.

65. *Oceana,* pp. 410–411. I am particularly indebted to Blitzer's thesis for drawing my attention to this.

66. *Ibid.,* pp. 10 and 169; *Works,* pp. 279–280.

67. *E.g., Oceana,* pp. 38–39, 118, and 173–174.

68. J. A. Froude, *Oceana* (London, 1886), pp. 1–4.

69. *Oceana,* pp. 11, 33, 133, 185–187, and 194–198; Z. Fink, *The Classical Republicans* (Evanston, 1945), pp. 83–85; C. Firth, *Cromwell and the Rule of the Puritans in England* (Oxford, 1953), pp. 382 and 386; Koebner, "Oceana," *loc. cit.,* pp. 372 and 374.

70. *Oceana,* pp. 148–149; *Works,* pp. 456, 562–563, 577. Tawney, "Harrington," p. 212.

71. *Oceana,* pp. 34–35.

72. *Ibid.,* pp. 17–18, 118–125, and 142; Machiavelli, *Discourses,* Bk. I, ch. 55.

73. *Oceana,* pp. 176–177; *Works,* pp. 409 and 465.

74. C. Weishofen, *James Harrington und sein Wunschbild vom Germanischen Staate* (Bonn, 1935), pp. 37, 45, and 70–71.

75. *Oceana,* pp. 18, 34, 118, and 122.

76. Hexter, *loc. cit.*

77. In the words of an older commentator, he was "to the right of the left and to the left of the right," T. W. Dwight, "James Harrington," *Political Science Quarterly*, Vol. 2 (1887), p. 6.

78. H. Gerth and C. W. Mills, *Character and Social Structure* (New York, 1953), pp. 14 and 26.

79. This might as well be called post-Marxism, in contrast to Mr. Pocock's neo-Marxism which limits itself to strictly *social* experiences and situations. Letter to *Encounter*, October, 1958.

80. Unlike Karl Popper I do not regard the personification of historical categories as analogous to medieval realism. His own medieval nominalism would make the writing of any sort of history impossible. How little he has understood the real problems of historical explanation and especially those created by generalizations on different levels of abstractness can be seen in his claim that the First World War is an "individual thing" just like Alexander the Great. *The Poverty of Historicism* (Boston, 1957), pp. 17–34, 76–83, 143–152.

81. Krieger, "Marx and Engels," *loc. cit.*; K. Mannheim, *Ideology and Utopia* (Harvest Books, New York, n.d.), *passim* and pp. 56 and 93–97.

82. Hill, "Recent Interpretations," *loc. cit.*, p. 74.

83. Bernstein, *op. cit.*, pp. 1–7; Hill, "Marx and Engels," *loc. cit.*, pp. 132 and 154; *The English Revolution*, pp. 13 and 17; Petegorsky, *op. cit.*, pp. 22 and 25.

84. Hexter, *loc. cit.*; see also Firth, *op. cit.*, p. 71, or G. M. Trevelyan, *op. cit.*, pp. 195–196 and 228–231, where it is said, "in motive it was a war not like the French or American of classes or of districts, but of ideas," p. 229.

85. I am aware that there are plenty of philosophical problems in describing individual behavior in this way too, but I do not think this is relevant to the everyday discourse of historical writing. I am much indebted to P. Gardiner's *The Nature of Historical Explanation* (Oxford, 1952), especially pp. 60–61, 99–112, and 114–127, for these considerations. However, I think that while Gardiner rightly emphasizes the abstractness of words like "revolution" or "class," he treats these as "events" capable of being explained causally. I think that as pure "cover-words" they cannot be treated in this way, especially when one is analyzing social factors. This, however, does not apply to more purely narrative history where the antecedent event simply serves as the cause of subsequent ones, and more limited entities are involved. Of such writing C. V. Wedgwood's *The King's Peace* (London, 1955) is clearly a fine example, even if it tends to be the history only of conspicuous persons and highly articulate speakers.

86. Letter to *Encounter*, October, 1958.

87. He makes no complaint against these writers, "Gentry," *loc. cit.*, p. 44.

88. Aubrey, *op. cit.*, p. 125.

89. G. Burnet, *History of My Own Time*, ed. O. Airy (Oxford, 1897), Vol. I, p. 120; Cromwell treated *Oceana* as too unimportant and fanciful to matter, then took care to condemn its paganism, Smith, *op. cit.*, pp. 75–76, 113–117; Toland, pp. xvi–xvii. See also C. J. Friedrich, *Constitutional Reason of State* (Providence, 1957), pp. 35 and 110.

90. If it was Hobbes's mistake to forget that "no society can survive without its myth," it was also Harrington's. Presumably that is why John Bowle does not even mention him among Hobbes's critics. *Hobbes and his Critics* (London, 1951), p. 45.

91. M. James, "Contemporary Materialist Interpretations," *loc. cit.*, p. 86;

Tawney, "Harrington," p. 203; "The Rise of the Gentry: A Postscript," *Economic History Review*, Vol. 7 (1954–55), p. 96; Blitzer, "Introduction," *loc. cit.*, p. xv; Trevor-Roper, "The Gentry," p. 22.

92. Smith, *op. cit.*, pp. 2–3.

93. Aubrey, *op. cit.*, p. 125; Blitzer, "Introduction," *loc. cit.*, pp. xxiii–xxiv; Smith, *op. cit.*, pp. 101–108; Tawney, "Harrington," p. 205; Toland, *loc. cit.*, pp. xxv–xxvi.

94. *Ibid.*, p. xiii; Smith, *op. cit.*, pp. 1–11; Koebner, "Oceana," *loc. cit.*, pp. 370–371; "Geschichtslehre," *loc. cit.*, p. 19.

95. Toland, pp. xi–xiii and xxx; *Works*, pp. 219 and 367.

96. *Ibid.*, p. xxx.

97. *Oceana*, p. 177.

98. *Works*, pp. 470 and 578.

99. For Machiavelli's own historical unrealism, see F. Chabod, *Machiavelli and the Renaissance* (London, 1958), tr. D. Moore (London, 1958), pp. 20–21, 85–104, 119–120, 137, and 143–147.

100. Fink, *op. cit.*, pp. 53–55 and 62–67.

101. Hill, "Recent Interpretations," *loc. cit.*, p. 73.

102. Firth, *op. cit.*, p. 72.

103. *Oceana*, pp. 55–56; *Works*, pp. 156, 457–458, 469, and 574.

104. *Oceana*, pp. 158 and 220–221.

105. *Patriarcha and Other Political Writings*, ed. P. Laslett (Oxford, 1949), pp. 207–208 and 221–222.

106. *Oceana*, p. 173. Gough, I think, is quite mistaken in treating Harrington as no more "irreligious" than the radical Puritans. The use of religious arguments signifies a no greater degree of religion in him than in Hobbes. The radical Puritan arguments based on rights were *secularized* religious conceptions, whereas Harrington returned to the *pagan* notions of social order and civic liberty. I should therefore agree that Harrington was not a *secular* thinker in that sense, but insist on his utter indifference to religious faith. Gough, *loc. cit.*, pp. 395–404. In contrast, see A. S. P. Woodhouse, *Puritanism and Liberty* (Chicago, 1951), "Introduction," pp. 38 and 82, where this distinction is very clearly drawn.

107. *Discourses*, Bk. I, chs. 11–12, and Bk. II, ch. 2.

108. *Oceana*, pp. 38, 55, 69–70, 109–110, and 169–173; *Works*, pp. 420–423, 474–476, 484–485, and 594–596.

109. *Spirit of the Laws*, Vol. II, Bk. XXVI, s. 2.

110. *Oceana*, pp. 10–11.

111. *E.g., Oceana*, pp. 32, 135–137, and 185–186; *Works*, 218 and 370.

112. Blitzer in his thesis gives a very convincing point-by-point comparison of the institutions of the *Laws* and *Oceana*.

113. Fink, *op. cit.*, pp. 3–27 and 54–57.

114. *Oceana*, p. 17.

115. I borrow this term from C. J. Friedrich, *Constitutional Reason of State*, pp. 34–54, though I give it a broader meaning than he intended.

116. On the strength of his remark that it was impossible to keep colonies—that is, to feed soldiers—when the native population owned the balance, everyone from Otis on treated him as a prophet of American liberty, forgetting that *Oceana* was to be a second Roman Empire. See Smith, *op. cit.*, pp. 185–200. See Levett, *loc. cit.*, pp. 189–191, for a criticism of this Americanized Harrington.

117. *The Selected Writings of John and John Quincy Adams*, ed. A. Koch and W. Peden (New York, 1946), pp. 44–45.

118. *Ibid.*, p. 52; *Works*, ed. C. F. Adams (Boston, 1850–1856), Vol. IV, pp. 395–360, 521, 551; V. L. Parrington, *Main Currents in American Thought* (New York, 1954), Vol. I, p. 274.

119. Parrington, *op. cit.*, Vol. II, p. 5; Smith, *op. cit.*, pp. 160–185.

120. For a contemporary restatement, see Wormuth, *op. cit.*, pp. 3–9, 211–215.

121. Adams, *Selected Writings*, pp. 23, 36, and 208.

122. Adams, *Works*, Vol. IV, pp. 413–414; Dwight, *loc. cit.*, p. 19; Z. Haraszti, *John Adams and the Prophets of Progress* (Cambridge, Mass., 1952), p. 35; Parrington, *op. cit.*, Vol. I, pp. 324–325; Smith, *op. cit.*, pp. 191–199.

123. *Oceana*, pp. 59, 61, and 142–149; *Works*, pp. 214, 472, and 490.

124. I am much indebted to L. Hartz, *The Liberal Tradition in America* (New York, 1955), pp. 46–47, for this and most of the ideas presented here.

125. For a good criticism of current practices in this field, see K. R. Minogue, "The Language of Comparative Politics," *Political Studies*, Vol. VI (1958), pp. 267–270.

126. The quarrel here was not between those who wanted to treat constitutions as if they were "pudding to be made by a receipt" and those who did not want to make them at all, but between different kinds of cooks, receipts, and diners. See C. H. McIlwain, *Constitutionalism Ancient and Modern* (Ithaca, 1958), pp. 1–22 and *passim*.

127. Haraszti, *op. cit.*, pp. 34, 45–46, and 258; Parrington, *op. cit.*, Vol. I, pp. 273, 284, 323, 328.

128. *Works*, Vol. VI, p. 218.

129. Parrington, *op. cit.*, Vol. I, pp. 25–26; Vol. II, pp. 296–297; C. Beard, *The Economic Basis of Politics*, ed. W. Beard (New York, 1957), pp. 37–40 and 53, for quotations from Webster in praise of Harrington.

130. M. Oakeshott, "Rationalism in Politics," *Cambridge Journal*, Vol. I (1947), pp. 83–84, 88–91, and 145–157. See Harrington's *Oceana*, pp. 62 and 207; *Works*, pp. 214–215, 367, 463, 470, 472, 477, 480–482, and 488, for his addiction to the politics of technical invention and "reason of state."

131. Blitzer, "Introduction," *loc. cit.*, pp. xxvi–xxvii.

132. *E.g.*, *Oceana*, p. 107.

133. Blitzer, p. xxvii.

134. *Ibid.*, pp. xxvi–xxviii and xxix.

135. *Oceana*, pp. 13 and 62; *Works*, pp. 214, 232, 402–403, 463, 470, and 560.

136. This failure to distinguish between the logic of discovery and technology lies behind most of the current concern for "measurement," "certainty," and "methodology" in the social sciences. Moreover, I agree with those who see in this development the ideological expression of a pervasive concern for security—political, social, and intellectual. See *e.g.*, B. Moore, Jr., *Political Power and Social Theory* (Cambridge, Mass., 1958), pp. 92–94. I have in mind exactly what C. W. Mills calls "abstracted empiricism." *The Sociological Imagination* (New York, 1959), pp. 50–75.

137. Beard, *op. cit.*, pp. 16, 36, and 40.

138. *Ibid.*, pp. 93 and 103–104.

139. *Ibid.*, pp. 83, 93, 98–99, 103–104, 122–123.

140. *Ibid.*, pp. 99–100.

141. *E.g.*, R. Aron, "Social Structure and the Ruling Class," and R. Bendix, "Social Stratification and Political Power" in R. Bendix and S. M. Lipset, eds., *Class, Status and Power* (Glencoe, 1953), pp. 567–577 and 596–609; J. E. Meisel, *The Myth of the Ruling Class* (Ann Arbor, 1957), pp. 345–381; C. W. Mills, *The Power Elite* (New York, 1956), pp. 269–324; F. Neumann, *The Democratic and the Authoritarian State* (Glencoe, 1957), pp. 3–21 and 233–269. Note particularly the latter's appreciative analysis of Montesquieu, pp. 96–148.

142. See, *e.g.*, C. A. R. Crosland, *The Future of Socialism* (New York, 1957), both for the recognition of power, status, and ideology as social factors, and for the values of an "Americanized" social atmosphere and constitutional government, by a not untypical socialist, pp. 29, 38–41, 71, 97–116, and 169–217, 220–221, 232–237, 245–248.

CHAPTER THIRTEEN

Montesquieu and the New Republicanism

Montesquieu did for the latter half of the eighteenth century what Machiavelli had done for his century, he set the terms in which republicanism was to be discussed. It goes without saying that it was a significantly different republicanism, not so much because of Montesquieu's doubts about Machiavelli's scholarship, but because their aims were not the same.[1] To be sure, like all republicans they shared at least one polemical object, hostility to the Roman Catholic Church, but even here the reasons for their respective hatred were quite different. Machiavelli objected to the papacy's interference in Italian politics, and Christianity's lack of martial spirit. Montesquieu hated the Church for the cruelty of its persecutions, its intolerance, its obstruction of scientific learning and its superstitious practices and prejudices. Paganism did not therefore seem like an attractive alternative to him and he had no more use for political than for theological religiosity. This was thus not an aspect of Roman republicanism that was significant for him, as it certainly was for Machiavelli.

The two authors also had different political enemies, even though republicanism might stand as a reproach to all of them. Machiavelli's contempt was directed at the incompetence of the petty rulers of the Italian city states, while Montesquieu excoriated the absolute monarchy created by Louis XIV. His great fear was not political impotence, but despotism, a regime to which Spain was rapidly descending and to which even France might fall prey. This had an extremely impor-

Reprinted from *Machiavelli and Republicanism*, edited by Gisella Bock, Quentin Skinner, and Maurizio Viroli (Cambridge: Cambridge University Press, 1990), with permission of Cambridge University Press.

tant bearing on the character of his republicanism. Indeed most republican ideologies after the Reformation found their inspiration and structure in revolts against monarchy, rather than in an unbroken adherence to the Florentine tradition. Montesquieu, however, was to present a wholly new case against the political mores of the monarchical order. Among the several ideologies which sustained the *ancien régime* there was what one might call the Augustan charade. It was certainly used by Augustus himself, and eventually by Seneca in *De Clementia*. It consisted in simply transferring the ancient Roman virtues to the new ruler and his court. He and his successors continued to distinguish themselves drastically from the primitive kings of Rome, and posed as the saviours of the republic. Something analogous was, surely, perpetrated by the panegyrists of the monarchy of Louis XIV and certainly by the fascist ideologies that flourished in the years between the two wars in our century. In the seventeenth-century version of the Augustan pretence, a good prince not only possessed all the great stoical and republican virtues of selfless patriotism, abnegation of all personal inclinations in favour of the public good, stern repression of all ambitions other than public ones, impartial justice for all, and so on, but the courtiers also displayed republican virtues by just serving him as selflessly as he serves the state. For he is the republic now. That is what the young were taught as part of the classical curriculum and that was what the finest drama put on the public stage. Consider Corneille's *Cinna,* where Augustus not only gives up justifiable personal vengeance and weariness as well, because he now *is* Rome. In Racine's *Berenice* Titus gives up a woman he loves because she is a queen and Roman republican mores do not allow a marriage to a princess, it is just too monarchical. And Nero's unlucky tutor in *Britannicus* tries to persuade the young emperor to restore the practices and mores of the republic under his absolute, omnipotent rule. As a determined critic of that monarchy, Montesquieu's first task was to delegitimise this ideology by exposing it as essentially fraudulent. To this end he had to demonstrate that republican virtue was possible only in genuinely popular nonmonarchical republican regimes and that political virtue had never been the effective ideology of any monarchy, whose "principle," that is, active political ethos, was that of personal honour, and not virtue.[2] That is, in fact, one of the main themes of *The Spirit of the Laws.* Moreover, even on purely scholarly historical grounds, he would show that the republic was a political form that had no place in the modern age. It was a thing of the past. It had been admirable, in its time, but now it was an object of scientific historical study and curiosity, not of emulation. Unlike

Machiavelli he did not for a moment dream of a new Roman republican order to replace the monarchy, and that is, of course, a very great difference. Even though Montesquieu eventually wrote two different accounts of the character of ancient republics, he never wavered in his conclusion that they were utterly remote from the political world of modern Europe. The differences between then and now were numerous, but they could be summed up in one word, size. The modern state was large, its culture diffuse, while the ancient republic had to be small and governed by a shared civic ethos. If a republic tried to expand, it simply lost its soul and decayed as Rome had. That meant that if the republican past was not to become irrelevant it would have to be imaginatively recreated or to be explicitly replaced by a new expansive republicanism to fit the modern political world. Rousseau responded to the first of these intellectual possibilities, while the authors of *The Federalist* pursued the second one. Both were deeply indebted to Montesquieu.

The opening sentences of Montesquieu's first published work on classical antiquity, *Considérations sur les causes de la grandeur des romains et de leur décadence*, tell us that Rome was not even a city in the modern sense of the word. Its private dwellings were insignificant, because it was a place of public structures for public activity.[3] In *The Spirit of the Laws* we are reminded that with the discovery of the compass, the symbolic significance of which did not escape him, Europe was so transformed that it had become wholly unlike anything that had ever existed in the past.[4] New directions, communications, discoveries, new wealth and above all new power, had made it completely unlike the earlier world. The great danger in this, Montesquieu thought, was that it tempted princes to strive for a world monarchy, like the Roman empire. They could not achieve it, but their efforts would certainly ruin Europe.[5] Empire was on the agenda of every European state and Montesquieu meant to deglamorise it. The Roman empire was to serve as an awful example and the republic that had preceded it and led to it could, therefore, not be painted in altogether glowing colours. We are never allowed to forget the inveterate bellicosity of the Romans. Rome was always bent on war and conquest was its only passion.[6] And so he took the story right up to its bitter end, the fall of the Eastern empire. Machiavelli, while he does mention later events, wisely quit with the Punic Wars. But as part of this debunking enterprise Montesquieu went all the way to the final decline and fall. Also his naturalistic approach to history, so unlike Machiavelli's, led him to brush aside that staple of heroic republican history, the great military and political hero. In his history great men were insignificant except at the very beginnings of cities. Later they scarcely mattered. If it had not been Caesar some other general would have done the republic in.[7] Fortune therefore plays no part at all, since it is not required to account for the failures of great leaders, as it does in Machiavelli. History is about deep, determining causes and immediate precipitating ones. To know them is to explain the past.[8]

In other respects Montesquieu's history of Rome is more conventional. Martial virtue is appreciated for its civic qualities and it is not denied that the republic was a free and popular state. Nor did the people fail. It is leaders who corrupt the people, not the other way around, so that we are not led to believe that the popular basis of republican rule was at fault.[9] Military success was itself, however, bound to lead to corruption, and it is conquest that led to the influx of wealth and avarice, and to luxury and effeminacy. But these were not in themselves the most serious causes of decline. Rather, it was the independence of local military commanders and their rivalries that were the real cause of the fall of the republic. The scenario is one in which the martial vigour that had made the city virtuous also killed its spirit and freedom, as it succeeded in its objective, the conquest of the known world. Rome was bound to commit civic suicide because it was first and foremost an expansionist military state. A tragedy of character, not of fate, in short.[10]

The analysis of republican government in *The Spirit of the Laws* is far less harsh and more traditional. Even the Polybian cycle is resurrected though it was not, in fact, Montesquieu's only theory of political decline. The purpose of that work was in any case far more scientific than polemical. The great question was to determine what made various regimes survive or fail, and to construct a comprehensive theory of comparative law. The positive features of republics are therefore stressed, especially their equality. Virtue is the love of equality, and while it does create a dreadful danger of anarchy that is not inevitable. The account of Athens in *The Spirit of the Laws,* the most democratic of cities, is especially notable, for Montesquieu attributed all the commercial virtues to its citizens, as well as the normal republican ones of patriotism, in this case love of equality itself. Frugality, prudence, honesty, caution, these are the commercial traits of character, and a democratic republic needs them especially.[11] Athens' failure was military, because its citizens had too good a life to sacrifice themselves to the demands of war. A federation of small republics should in principle have rendered them more secure, Montesquieu thought, but the evidence was discouraging.[12] Like a martial republic, an egalitarian one requires intense education, a small face-to-face society, and inviolable traditions, mores and personal habits, all directed towards public objectives. Censors must reinforce the informal restraints that citizens impose on each other, and if small size is a military liability, republics can always federate. However, the demands of the virtuous, egalitarian republic seemed overwhelming, and Montesquieu thought that they were very frail and likely to slip into other forms. The aristocratic republic depends on the moderation and intelligence of its ruling class, and with the example of Venice before him, Montesquieu did not rate its chances of success very highly. What is most significant in this picture of republicanism is the stress on equality and the sense that these regimes were not very durable. At no time did Montesquieu present them in such a way as to make them appear as anything but irretrievable memories of the past, objects of historical understanding.[13] They acted as contrasts, not examples to be copied. And there was no nostalgia at all here. Let us recall that the celebrated Eleventh Book of *The Spirit of the Laws* is not merely about England, but a *comparison* between England and Rome, and that Rome is presented as less self-correcting and less just than England.[14] For while the life of every citizen was precious and capital cases were very carefully tried, Rome did not have an independent judiciary. The people, the Senate and the magistrates, all three, had judicial functions, and that made the separation of powers and its cornerstone, a wholly independent judiciary, impossible. It was England's achievement to have such a judiciary which alone could secure the personal, as well as the political liberty of its citizens. The Romans enjoyed only the latter. The classical republic was, in sum, not only gone forever, it was for all its many remarkable qualities not to be regretted. The model for Europe now was a commercial, extensive, non-military representative "democracy disguised as a monarchy," England, ruled by legislation, not mores.

In the Thirteen Colonies of North America this was a tune that was going to play extremely well. Not virtue, but interest, and not unchanging customs, but consciously made laws keep a modern free state like England going. It was certainly a more stable and less oppressive form of government than any other, even if it was less than edifying. Above all it raised the prospect of an extensive republic that would not be a conquering imperial power. In 1787 no writer was quoted by all sides more often than Montesquieu.[15] It was his hour of vindication, for many French readers had not appreciated his doctrines. To some readers, indeed, Montesquieu's new political science was nothing but an intellectual obstacle, not because it was untrue, far from it, but because it seemed to eliminate republicanism from relevant modern political discourse. Democratic readers might well wonder whether he had succeeded in making equality and virtue politically obsolete ideas. Rousseau certainly feared that he had, and it forced him into a life-long struggle with the modern author whom he respected the most and quoted most often. That accounts for the otherwise incomprehensible and absurd remark in the Fifth Book of *Emile,* that only "the illustrious Montesquieu" might have created "the great and useless science" of political right, but that "he was content to discuss the positive right of established governments."[16] In short, he had chosen to discuss what is, rather than what ought to be, or to be exact, what Rousseau thought "ought" should be. He did not disagree with Montesquieu about the prospects for republicanism in Europe, his pose as the citizen of Geneva did not last, and eventually, in his enraged *Lettres écrites de la montagne,* he reminded the citizens of that city that they were not Spartans, or even Athenians, but just a bunch of petty, selfish merchants and artisans.[17] Corsica, happily underdeveloped, was the last faint hope that some remote corner of Europe might remain uncorrupted by civilisation, but that did not amount to a refutation of Montesquieu's analysis of the modern world. On the contrary, it only proved how far Europe had strayed from the republican ideal.[18] The problem for Rousseau was therefore to find a way to bring the egalitarian ethos of republican regimes back into modern political theory, if not into practice.

In some ways the distance that Montesquieu had created between ancient and modern politics served Rousseau very well. It allowed him to condemn modernity by comparing it to an idealised republican antiquity. It was only when he wanted to construct a model of a truly just egalitarian society that Montesquieu became a threatening presence. Nevertheless, Rousseau was able to work his way around his predecessor and to use him for his own purposes. It was done in three ways: first, by using Montesquieu's version of the egalitarian republic as a critical mirror for modern society as a whole, secondly, by showing that the old republic, especially Sparta, was the only fit model for a just society and finally, by universalising republicanism as a preventive psychotherapy for the anguish created by inequality and indeed by all social encounters. It comes as no surprise, therefore, that Rousseau admired Machiavelli without reservations, and probably wished that it were possible to return to his relatively simple stance.[19]

To illustrate these three uses of republicanism one need consider only three of Rousseau's works: *The Discourse on the Arts and Sciences,* his first published essay, "Political Economy," written for the

Encyclopédie and in some ways a first draft for the *Social Contract*, and lastly the first chapter of *Emile*. In the *First Discourse* the classical republic is a mixture of Sparta and Rome and it is seen as a culture, as what Montesquieu would have called the spirit of a people. Physically and morally healthy, the republican citizen endures hardship joyfully. Virtue, "the sublime science of simple minds," flourishes, as there are no arts, no sciences and no scepticism. Cato had thrown out the Greek intellectuals, and Spartans were taught only courage in war, religion, physical fitness and to repress cupidity. Virtue is first and foremost anti-intellectual. It must be so, since the difference in human talents has been the origin of "the sinister inequality" that has ruined European society. Sparta, in stark contrast, was a wholesomely mindless, single-value society. In their happy ignorance the Romans, who shared this virtue, conquered the world. Their forced marches cannot be repeated in the modern world which consists of happy slaves, whose arts disguise their chains, who live in a divisive inequality, racked by vanity, curiosity and doubt, which have as debilitating an effect on their moral as on their physical well-being.[20] It is a clear answer to the question of whether art and science improve us, but it is so colossal a critical over-kill, that no hope for any recovery for modern Europe is imaginable. The effect of the distance between republican virtue as health and modern vice as terminal decay is so great as to leave no plausible way of making the ancient republic politically relevant except as a blunt instrument of moral aggression. It also put Rousseau in a very equivocal position to Montesquieu, because he praises everything the latter found most questionable in classical republicanism, especially the spirit of conquest, but yet stays within the confines of Montesquieu's historical paradigm.

In "Political Economy" we discover that the ultimate moral justification of the republic is that in it "man is not in contradiction with himself," because the laws succeed in making his personal wishes identical with the just aims of society.[21] The personal self is utterly absorbed by the public self in a genuine republic. Indeed all erotic energies are directed towards the republic as the citizens do not just obey the laws, they *love* them. There are no partial societies, for these would tend to divert love and loyalty from the state. The education of the young is not left to the family, but conducted by retired magistrates and soldiers who have already proven themselves in the service of the republic. The children "do not perceive their own existence except as part of the state." This would not be possible if this were not a just society, whose laws exist to protect the life, the goods and the freedom of the citizens. Their freedom, moreover, is based on both material and political equality. The government administers the laws and makes them conform to the "general will," a phrase drawn from Montesquieu but given a new meaning. It was Montesquieu's assumption that the British House of Commons spoke for the general will, while Rousseau did not think that it could be represented, that indeed representative institutions made a mockery of republican freedom.[22] The effect is that the socially informed consent of all prevails and both the spirit and actuality of social equality are maintained by a system of graded taxation. Here the republic is more Spartan than Roman and the dangers of a policy of conquest are stressed, because the whole purpose of republican government is to create a small, cohesive community whose citizens will be almost identical. If there is competition here it is athletic, both in the physical and moral sense, as men compete for public approbation, which depends on displays of public not of personal qualities. The magistrates of the republic have basically only one task, to maintain equality, by the laws and by education. The laws being loved are spontaneously followed, and it is they that are "the miracle" of the just society, because they treat all citizens identically, and indeed see to it that they in fact *are identical*. As he was to say in the *Social Contract,* liberty cannot prevail without equality, because the dependence of one person upon another is inevitable in all unequal relationships. And such dependence "est autant de force ôtée au corps de l'Etat."[23] Whatever the liberty within the body of the state might be it was not the individualism that prevailed in Montesquieu's idealised England.

To see the full implications of the specifically republican institutional order that Rousseau favoured one must turn to the last section of the *Social Contract.* These pages are directed not just against modern practices in general, but against Montesquieu in particular. Because representation was no substitute for democratic participation, Rousseau had to show that a large population might be able to govern itself directly, after all. He therefore set out to show that the Romans proved that 200,000 citizens could be assembled to legislate for themselves. In the synopsis of this section of the *Social Contract,* in the section "On Travel," in *Emile,* Rousseau said that one of the questions he dealt with there was whether the democratic Roman republic was a large state.[24] In fact he never tells us whether 200,000 citizens are or are not a large population. Obviously, 200,000 people are quite a crowd, but by eighteenth-century standards it was clearly a small state, which would prove Montesquieu right, which was very troublesome. If republics must remain small to function as politically egalitarian regimes, then they have no place in modern Europe, and it is not at all clear that this is the conclusion Rousseau wanted his readers to draw at this point. He certainly wanted to embellish the picture of Roman institutions that Montesquieu had so convincingly drawn. So in the last part of the *Social Contract* what he first of all set out to deny was that block voting was weighted in favour of the rich in Rome, as Montesquieu had argued, but it was not the main issue for him. The heart of the matter was that as long as tribunes and censors and other magistrates saw to the virtue of the Romans, they had governed themselves more directly and perfectly than Montesquieu had suggested.[25] Finally, there was the matter of religion, which more than any other part of the *Social Contract* was meant to speak to contemporary Europe. For the civil religion not only completes the institutional design of the just and virtuous republic, it also presents a modern substitute for paganism.[26] Rousseau had first presented this notion in a letter to a horrified Voltaire, and we can be sure that Montesquieu would have been even more repelled by it.[27] As is entirely clear, the civil faith is a religious programme for a post-Christian society, not a simple reversion to paganism. In his view of religion Rousseau was very close to Machiavelli, but unlike the latter he could imagine a modern alternative to both a lost paganism and a decadent Christianity. Its effect would be to emulate the republican martial ethos by removing the deepest source of our inner division. Rousseau often said that we are what we believe, that opinion makes us. Give Europe a new civic religion of public loyalty, and maybe it could yet attain a republican future.

A revival of republicanism, especially in the absence of a new Lycurgus-Moses figure was not likely. And for Rousseau as for his Plutarchian models, everything depends on great, creative authority figures, from Moses to Calvin and his own vision of a Great Legislator. That such a miracle should recur was not likely and psychologically little could be hoped for without him. The *Discourse on the Origins of Inequality* had given such a harrowing account of the depth of the psychological damage that we suffer in any society and of the encompassing deformity we suffer at its beginning, at the most primitive level of our experience, that inequality and all its vices seem wholly insuperable. Health is not possible, even in those rustic societies where people see each other very rarely and only in order to quickly conduct their public business. The republican regime in the face of this disastrous psychological reality acts as a possible preventive psychotherapy. It denatures us to such an extent that we lose all our natural instincts and respond only to social stimuli. In Rome a man was neither Caius nor Lucius, he was only a citizen, and Spartan mothers rejoiced in military victories in which they had lost all their sons. What they do not suffer from is the dreadful inner tug of war between nature and culture that renders civilised humanity so neurotic and distraught. In a republic early and complete training avoids it. The citizen does not "float between inclination and duty," he has been wholly denatured.[28] It is not a plausible defence of republicanism on Rousseau's own showing. Our corruption is rooted so deeply in our psyche that no amount of patriotic fervour or civic reinforcement can really touch it. If the very proximity of others arouses our *amour propre,* our tendency to see ourselves through the eyes of others and to torment ourselves because in *no* society can our natural differences fail to lead to a degree of inequality, then republicanism cannot repair the pain of *all* association. It might be palliative at best.

Such then were the uses of republicanism for Rousseau. He was not able to make a contemporary programme out of republicanism in the way that Machiavelli had been able to do, because he could not and did not wish simply to discard the historical confines within which Montesquieu had placed that model. What he did recover was the absolute primacy of the idea of virtue, of egalitarian patriotism, as the essence of the republic. It gave his theory of equality its most characteristic feature and restored it to a second life in the vocabulary of modern radicalism. He thus opened a new chapter in its uses. First it became a weapon against modernity, especially against scepticism and modern intellectuality. Secondly, it could be used as a way of highlighting the psychological tensions inherent in all social life, but especially in complex, stratified and inegalitarian societies. And, most fatefully of all, in the most directly political of his essays, one sees republicanism as a new and powerful ideology for modern Europe. It was to offer both a democratic and a spiritual regeneration. We should not, however, place him too hastily. We ought to remember that Rousseau never lost sight of the ordinary individual for whom the republic exists. The best test of a good society, we are told in the *Social Contract,* is to see whether people have big families. If they do, it means that they are secure and content. That is why Rousseau's republicanism is popular and not heroic in its ultimate character, even if he resorted to all the Plutarchian myths of great men. For all their divergences, and they are very great, Rousseau accepted more of Montesquieu's theories than he rejected. He certainly turned them to unexpected and utterly new uses; not those of Machiavelli after all, but of a new democracy with a will to equality.

The bridge that leads from the republicanism of Machiavelli to that of the French Revolution does not stand alone. There is another one that ends in the United States Constitution of 1787. After a heated debate about the possibility of an extensive republic Americans discovered that they were actually living in such a polity and that they needed to explain it to themselves. That was the task that Alexander Hamilton and James Madison, writing under the name of Publius, accomplished in their celebrated *Federalist Papers*. Their first object, however, was to reply to the numerous critics of the proposed constitutional plan. Many democratically inclined Americans shared Rousseau's fears, and one journalist in Newport, RI, even quoted him correctly to demonstrate that representation on the English model was not freedom, but a charade.[29] Other less original anti-federalists argued, quoting Montesquieu copiously, that no large territory could be a republic, that the government was so remote from the people that it must soon degenerate into a distinct political class, and become despotical. The electoral districts were so large that only the rich and clever could ever be elected to the House of Representatives, and that they would certainly not speak for the general will. The culture of the North, with its industrious traders was wholly unlike that of the slave-owning, idle planters of the South. Had not Montesquieu said all there was to say about the differences created by the climate? No government could possibly suit such diverse populations and one must dominate and oppress the other, soon there would be Georgian militiamen in New England and Pennsylvania. Finally the separation of powers was not as complete as was required by Montesquieu, nor did the provisions for a safe criminal law and jury trials meet his or their standard for a free government.[30] As we know, half the amendments of the Bill of Rights are about the rights of the accused in criminal cases, so the point was well taken. For us the most relevant issue is, however, about republican government. The radical Pennsylvanians clearly believed that the individual states were small societies in the classical pattern, and that egalitarian virtue could survive only under democratic political arrangements in which the sovereignty of the people expressed itself in fairly direct, participating ways, and the distance between voter and representative was slight. It should be added that there was no trace of martial breast-beating among the Pennsylvanian anti-federalists, some of whom were, of course, Quakers.

Such were the arguments Publius had to answer. He was, however, determined to do more than merely assuage the fears of his opponents; he meant to show that the new constitutional order would be in every way superior to all other republican governments, especially those of classical antiquity. It was intrinsically better because it would offer its citizens stability and freedom such as no city-state had ever known. Moreover, it would be a real republic, not in spite but because of its size. Without a monarch, or a hereditary nobility, or a mixed regime it would be an entirely popular state based on the consent of the governed. The very divergences among its many citizens would, moreover, create a system in which no party would impose its will upon the public to destroy the republic in the suicidal manner of the ancient city-states.[31] To that end Publius had to put the greatest possible distance between modern America and classical antiquity. The illusion that any of the thirteen states resembled republican Rome or Athens was to be dispelled once and for all. They were simply far larger already. However, the old city-states were in any case an unworthy example to follow. Publius had far less affection for them than Montesquieu had displayed. Their main use for him was negative, as awful examples of political failure. The only time Rome is mentioned with full approval in *The Federalist* is to demonstrate that two concurrent taxing authorities are compatible with achieving greatness. The power of both the states and the Federal Government to tax the same citizenry does not, therefore, have to lead to any dire consequences at all.[32] With that exception, the institutions of antiquity were treated as suggestions to be discarded or as examples of everything that was to be avoided.

The rejection of the example of antiquity begins very early on, with a reminder of their endless wars. Unlike Montesquieu and most liberal political theorists Publius did not think that commercial states were particularly peaceful. Commercial republics he noted, pointing to Athens and to Carthage, were inclined to go to war. And they did so for no good reason. War is always an option. Pericles apparently dragged Athens into war in order to please a prostitute.[33] There was no need to dwell on the conduct of military republics, since they were completely irrelevant to the civilian ethos of America.[34] The message of antiquity was, however, clear. Unless the states accepted the proposed constitution and united under it, they would sooner or later go to war against each other. That was not the only classical disaster that would be averted. The internal divisions of the ancient republics had been a perpetual invitation to foreign intrigue and to treachery on the part of the very men to whom the people had entrusted the powers of government.[35] "It is impossible to read the history of the petty republics of Greece and Italy without feeling a sensation of horror and disgust at the distractions with which they were continually agitated, and at the rapid successions of revolutions by which they were kept in a state of perpetual vibration between the extremes of tyranny and anarchy," wrote Publius. All of this could be avoided only if the states were to be united into a modern extended republic, built on principles of an improved political science that was unknown to the ancients, for the latter knew nothing of self-correcting representative federal government that was both energetic and free. Should the constitution be rejected, however, the states would also become "little, jealous, clashing, tumultuous commonwealths, the wretched nurseries of unceasing discord and the miserable objects of universal pity and contempt." Just like the classical republics. A genuine federal republic would avoid all that, for it would have the resources to quell any uprising in any of the States as well as to provide for the common defence.[36]

When one considers the scorn that Publius heaped upon the endemic disorders of the republics of antiquity, one might suppose that unity was his highest political aim, which would scarcely be compatible with his ardent championship of liberty. That was not the case, however. It was his view that America could overcome the tension between freedom and unity thanks to the practices of representative government. In this it was again ahead of the ancient republics, for although the Athenians had understood representation, they did not use it fully, and so fell prey to personal tyrants.[37] There was far too much direct participation by the entire body of citizens in every branch of the government, and especially in Athens' popular assemblies. "Had every Athenian citizen been a Socrates, every Athenian assembly would still have been a mob." Such a crowd is bound to give way to unreasoning passions and is invariably manipulated by some wholly unprincipled leader.[38] In contrast to this lamentable spectacle, "is it not the glory of the people of America" that "they have not suffered a blind veneration for antiquity?" Though they have shown "a decent regard for the opinions of former times," they have now embarked upon "the experiment of an extended republic" and posterity will be grateful for this innovation. "Happily for America, happily we trust for the whole human race" they have rejected the past and "pursued a new and more noble course."[39] To legislate for one's own needs as they arose and to favour political change, rather than merely to preserve one's institutional patrimony, was clearly one of the greatest departures of Publius from classical political theory and even from Montesquieu's caution. Above all, it reversed the belief that republics had to be bound by ancient mores, rather than by innovative legislation. Publius had, after all, absorbed the lessons of a successful revolution, and if his faith in human nature was not great, he certainly had a lot of confidence in modern science, not least the political science learned from Montesquieu. That science had taught him that freedom and virtue were not necessarily tied to each other. The English, as they make their second appearance in *The Spirit of the Laws,* are presented as selfish, irrational, debauched and devoid of any religious beliefs whatever. Yet they will bear any taxes and give their lives for their freedom.[40] Joined to what he had said about the excellences of the British constitution, Montesquieu's American readers, who thought of themselves as the last true Englishmen, could now understand just how different their world was from that of ancient Sparta and its like. The political qualities that they had to cultivate did not in any way depend on the educative forces of the small, watchful city. They appreciated virtue, but its requirements were not those of Rousseau. A respect for the property and rights of all citizens and a willingness to do one's best for one's constituents was all that was required of those who ruled. Nor should one rely on great men. Even "enlightened statesmen" were a rarity, and a good constitution was built on their absence or political insignificance. What counts is to get reasonably able representatives into office, and here the larger the constituency, the greater the pool of able people who might be candidates for election. Extensive republics are simply "more favorable to the election of proper guardians of the public weal."[41] Moreover, as long as elections are popular the essence of republicanism is preserved, for it is not size or immediacy that counts, but the ultimate source of authority, which remains the people. This was no monarchy or aristocracy, but a republic, that realised the permanent will of the people because both the states and the proposed federal republic had constitutions that were designed to preserve their liberty and property.[42] The new extended republic, unlike the little republics of antiquity would, moreover, be able to protect the public against the local factions that threatened freedom and property precisely because it was both large, powerful and overtly grounded in the consent of the entire American people, "the only legitimate fountainhead of power."[43] After all, the constitution Publius was defending does begin with the words, "We the People" and it did not mean the plebs of Rome or the Commons of England or the Third Estate of France. It was everybody. The mixed constitution had, in fact, died early on in the Convention, when Charles Pinckney got up and said what everyone knew, that there was nothing to mix in America, the difference between the rich and poor was not so great as to require any institutional recognition. Neither Polybius'

Roman constitution, nor its equally mixed feudal successor had any relevance. Even England was not to be treated with the reverence that Montesquieu had heaped upon it.[44]

If the mixed constitution was gone, direct democracy and its ethos were even more irrelevant. Modern representative government in an extended republic was a vast improvement because, unlike classical democracy, it has a built-in remedy against the ruinous conflicts of factions. Far from having to crush differences of interest or political and religious opinion, diversity was encouraged to flourish in an extended republic. The greater the multiplicity of religious sects and of more tangible property interests, the more likely these groups are to form changing and flexible electoral coalitions, none of which has a motive for crushing the others.[45] Bargaining replaces the tumult of popular assemblies, as order and freedom are reconciled prepolitically just as among free sects, in society generally. As every group has a chance of being part of a majority at some time, but also in the minority at others, none has an interest in oppressing their opponents. The representatives of the people act according to the same expectations. They can, moreover, deliberate calmly and save the people from occasional follies, and still remain close enough to the electorate to maintain their trust. Any temptation to behave despotically must die as they remember that they must face the voters soon and eventually become ordinary citizens again. With federalism the need for what Montesquieu called "intermediary powers" is satisfied, and together with the separation of powers, any concentration of authority in too few hands becomes impossible. Indeed the separation of powers in the federal government was greater than Montesquieu, with his English model, had prescribed. Not only was the judiciary given all the independence it needed, the balance of powers was psychologically perfectly equilibrated; "ambition had been made to counteract ambition." To be sure, in a republic the legislature must predominate, but in an extensive republic the multiplicity of interests will be reflected there as well, and "the security for civil rights must be the same as that for religious rights," which were in principle at least fully protected.[46] Finally, as a trump, Publius recalled the military inefficiency of small republics which would now be overcome in a federation that really worked. That was more than all those ancient leagues had been able to do. The latter only showed the costs of smallness, an awful warning to the States.[47]

Turning from the general structure to the specific institutions of the ancient city-states Publius found that they also failed to pass muster. Rome had so feeble an executive that it had to resort to dictators in moments of danger, which was a dangerous expedient.[48] The consuls who made up its plural executive, were often at odds and would have been so more often if, as patricians, they had not been united by their fear of the people.[49] And finally, worst of all, ancient politicians did not really know how to put a constitution together. They had to find individual legislators who were driven to resort to violence and superstition to impose a basic law upon their republics. The men who together had written the proposed constitution of the United States were in every way their intellectual and ethical superiors. They had managed to introduce stability and energy into a limited republican government designed for a free people.[50] And they had done this by "quitting the dim light of historical research" and following "reason and good sense."[51] Antiquity had very little to teach them, except to remind them of its many errors.

This then is the second bridge from Montesquieu to a wholly new notion of republicanism. Clearly Publius used Montesquieu's account of republican government to suit his own purposes. He had to denigrate the old republics far more than Montesquieu was inclined to do, and while the latter did constantly speak of legislators, the very idea of a constitutional assembly writing out a future scheme of government had not occurred to him. Cromwell's failed attempt was, after all, the only predecessor of this American political practice. Nevertheless, the extensive republic, short on virtue and dedicated to securing "the blessings of liberty" was deeply indebted to him. If Rousseau was able to rescue the virtuous, small republic from the assaults of modern politics, Publius managed to make the expansive republic respectable and to devise a model of government that was neither oppressive nor given to the militaristic Augustan ideologies which Montesquieu set out to unmask and destroy. In either case republicanism survived thanks to him even though in forms that were notably different from the Renaissance version and its classical archetype.

Notes

A version of this essay was presented as the Samuel Paley Lecture in the Hebrew University of Jerusalem in 1987.

1. *Dossier de L'Esprit des Lois, Montesquieu. Oeuvres complètes*, ed. Roger Caillois (Paris, 1951), vol. II, p. 996.

2. *De L'Esprit Des Lois*, Bk III, chs. 5–7. (I do not cite pages here since there are so many scholarly editions and as the chapters are very brief.)

3. *Oeuvres*, vol. II, p. 69.

4. *Esprit*, Bk XXI, ch. 21.

5. *Romains*, pp. 193–4; *Esprit*, Bk IX, ch. 8.

6. *Romains*, pp. 70–4, 80, 122.

7. *Ibid.*, pp. 70, 124–32.

8. *Ibid.*, p. 173.

9. *Ibid.*, p. 139.

10. *Ibid.*, pp. 116–20, 151.

11. *Esprit*, Bk v, ch. 6; Bk xxi, ch. 7.

12. *Ibid.*, Bk ix, chs. 1–3.

13. *Ibid.*, Bk ii, ch. 2; Bk iii, ch. 3; Bk v, chs. 2–7; Bk viii, chs. 2–4, 16.

14. See also *Romains*, p. 116.

15. Donald S. Lutz, "The relative influence of European writers on late eighteenth-century American political thought." *American Political Science Review*, 78 (1984), pp. 189–98.

16. J.-J. Rousseau, *Oeuvres complètes* (Paris, 1969), vol. iv, p. 836.

17. *Oeuvres*, iii, p. 881.

18. *Du Contrat Social*, Bk ii, ch. 10.

19. "Le Prince de Machiavel est le livre des républicains," *Contrat Social*, Bk iii, ch. 6. *Oeuvres*, iii, p. 409, can stand for many similar remarks.

20. *Oeuvres*, iii, pp. 6–30.

21. *Discours sur l'économie politique, Oeuvres*, iii, pp. 241–78, *passim*.

22. *Contrat Social*, Bk iii, ch. 15.

23. Untranslatable. *Contrat Social*, Bk ii, ch. 11, p. 390.

24. *Emile. Oeuvres*, iv, p. 843.

25. *Contrat Social*, Bk iv, chs. 4–7.

26. *Contrat Social*, Bk iv, ch. 8.

27. *Lettre à Voltaire*, August, 1756. *Correspondance complète de Jean-Jacques Rousseau*, ed. R. A. Leigh (Geneva, 1967), vol. iv, pp. 37–50.

28. *Emile*, Bk. i, pp. 249–50; Bk ii, p. 311.

29. *A Newport Man*, Newport Mercury, 1788, *The Complete Anti-Federalist*, ed. Herbert J. Storing (Chicago, 1981), vol. iv, pp. 250–4.

30. See especially, *Essays of John DeWitt*, and *Letters of Agrippa* for New England anti-federalism, and for Pennsylvania, *Essay by Montezuma* and, most important of all, *The Address and Reasons of Dissent of the Minority of the Convention of Pennsylvania to their Constituents, The Complete Anti-Federalist*, vol. iv, pp. 15–40 and 68–116; vol. iii, pp. 53–7 and 145–67.

31. See especially *Federalist*, 10, 39 and 51. Because there are so many editions of *The Federalist Papers*, and since the individual papers are so short, I shall cite them only by number.

32. *Federalist*, 34.

33. *Ibid.*, 6.

34. *Ibid.*, 8.

35. *Ibid.*, 22.

36. *Ibid.*, 9.

37. *Ibid.*, 63.

38. *Ibid.*, 55.

39. *Ibid.*, 14.

40. *Esprit*, Bk xix, ch. 27.

41. *Federalist*, 10.

42. *Ibid.*, 36.

43. *Ibid.*, 49.

44. *The Records of the Federal Convention of 1787*, ed. Max Farrand (New Haven, 1966), vol. I, pp. 396–404.

45. *Federalist,* 10 and 51.

46. *Ibid.,* 51.

47. *Ibid.,* 17 and 18.

48. *Ibid.,* 69.

49. *Ibid.,* 70.

50. *Ibid.,* 37 and 38.

51. *Ibid.,* 70.

CHAPTER FOURTEEN

Reading the
Social Contract

Rousseau's writings have, from the day of the their first appearance, been subjected to every conceivable interpretation, both
friendly and hostile. They were never ignored or read with
indifference. One could indeed write an interesting monograph on
the history of these readings. Most of them have been too crudely
ideological to be of much intellectual worth in their own right, but
they might well add up collectively to a chapter in the history of opinions. A more substantial group of interpretations traces the line
of influences on Rousseau and those to which he, in turn, contributed. These efforts belong to a tradition of intellectual history
that strives to remain as close as possible to the general study of the
past, and so treats influences as a chain of causes and effects. Others
have tried to put Rousseau in his age and place. They are preoccupied generally with social and economic history and so "use" him.
Psycho-historians have found Rousseau a natural subject. Political
theory, in spite of all these efforts, is not, however, easily reducible
to historical thinking. Literary and philosophical analysis also have
claims on its attention. The archetypes, metaphors, and rhetoric
of a given text and the structure of argument cannot be ignored. In
fact they must precede any other work of understanding, for if we
do not know the works we discuss, we simply do not know what we
are talking about, or why it is worth doing so at all. Thus the line
that has conventionally linked Rousseau to Kant, for example,
may be a far from certain one, but we do want to know what it was
about *Emile* that kept Kant glued to its pages. He was, of course,

Reprinted with permission from *Powers, Possessions, and Freedom,* edited by Alkis Kontos
(Toronto: University of Toronto Press, 1979).

an extraordinary reader, but then he was not reading an ordinary book.

Emile is surely Rousseau's masterpiece, but the *Social Contract,* even if it is a far less accomplished work, has driven a wedge into every literate consciousness since the French Revolution. Why does it impinge so heavily on one's mind? There is probably no single satisfactory answer to the question. Perhaps there are as many reasons for the effect of the *Social Contract* as there are readers. A serious but puzzled reader may find that he is moved in two ways. Certainly he cannot help being stirred, one way or the other, by the pervasive tone of indignation that Rousseau made uniquely audible. Beyond that, however, he may find that each re-reading of the book reveals new meanings and different messages, and the exact character of Rousseau's intentions becomes problematical. The inherent unity of Rousseau's mind has often been shown. It is the complexity of his design that makes him fascinating. If, after several readings, one sees that the *Social Contract* is written in counterpoint one learns to read it both for the different lines of thought and feeling and for their ultimate relatedness. The trouble is that many listeners are not able or willing to follow fugues. They will listen selectively, so that only the very simplest tunes, the most obvious harmonies, will come through, and though they may well enjoy the music, they will never know the score.

To illustrate, though only partially, some of the voices that appear in the *Social Contract,* one may read it, book by book, chapter by chapter, to find egalitarian, democratic, and populist themes as well as one of dire tragedy. The first three can, for the sake of brevity, be grouped into one section, the last one is to be treated apart from them. That makes for only two readings, and they do not suffice, but only indicate how one might go about unravelling the whole text. There are surely other possibilities, but one must begin somewhere.

> What though on homely fare we dine,
> Wear hoddin gray, an' a' that,
> Gie fools their silks and knaves their wine,
> A man's a man for a' that!

> For a' that an' a' that,
> It's coming yet, for a' that,
> That man to man, the world o'er,
> Shall brothers be for a' that!

When speaking of egalitarian motifs in the following pages, a generally equal distribution of the burdens and advantages of society is meant. Democracy is taken to be a government in which the entire adult population takes part. *Populism,* the most elusive of these words, is used to refer to the demand for the social recognition of the common decencies and communal cohesion of simple people as the highest of human values, and therefore as worthy of the greatest respect. That there is a note of truculence in populism is inevitable, but that does not render it any less powerful a feeling. The best illustration of populist sentiment is Robert Burns's celebrated poem, from which a few lines are given above, but the whole should really be recalled for full effect—both for its resentments and its hopes.

What evidence is there in the *Social Contract* for arguments on behalf of these three political assertions? What is the case for this sort of Rousseau in the *Social Contract?* Even a very partial account, such as this one, shows that the case for treating the work as a charter for the claims of the common man is a powerful one, and that those who have read it thus were by no means mistaken. Whether it is the sole meaning is another question.

The topics of the four books of the *Social Contract* are relatively clear. Book One defines, describes, and explicates the social contract on which all societies rest; Book Two is about sovereignty, specifically that of the people; Book Three deals with forms of government; and Book Four discusses the mores which a republican polity requires.

The Introduction sets the question, whether a legitimate governance of civil society is possible. Given "men as they are," and "laws as they might be," can justice and utility be made one? That is, can the rules of society be made in such a way that both the moral and physical needs of those who are obliged to obey them are satisfied? We are then, in true populist vein, reminded that this is not what prevails and that everywhere men are in chains. The next call is, however, not one for shaking off the bonds, which would be acceptable only if force made right, in which case both the chaining and unchaining would be acts of superior power. We are, rather, to look for the social conventions that justify the chains (chap. 1). Nature is certainly not the source of this or any other social law. It only teaches self-preservation. The basis of every political order is therefore not to be found in nature, or even in the most natural of human associations, the family. Those who argue that it is, do so with evil intent. They picture men as a herd of sheep protected by a fatherly shepherd. This seductive picture mistakes the results of social practice for its origin. Slavery makes sheep-slaves, not nature. So much for Grotius, Hobbes, and Aristotle in their naturalistic paternalism or monarchism (chap. 2). The specifically Hobbesian form of legitimization as a prudential resort is dismissed as just another variant of the might-makes-right argument. It does not make for duty, only for calculation (chap. 3).

With nature eliminated, only art or agreement remains as the source of obligation. What can pass for agreement, however? Conquest, as Grotius had argued? Certainly not. The peace of the dungeon at the end of war is a dangerous fiction. Men are asked to renounce their responsibilities as men by reducing themselves to things, to slavery, to avoid wars. Wars, however, are not pre-social; only personal conflicts are that. War is over some object of possession, fought in order to appropriate something. And that itself requires the social institution of property, an artifice, in short. Above all, Grotius's theory defies all common sense. Conquest cannot yield anything like consent, for no one would accept a bargain as self-destructive as that of slavery. Even if he did, he could not impose this "agreement" on his offspring (chap. 4). If one goes back far enough one does not find the degrading situation of herds, slaves, shepherds, and conquerors, but discrete individuals with no bonds to tie them into a people as yet, undefiled men as populism sees them, in short. To say that they make the body politic does not, however, mean that they may unmake it. That only follows from the might-is-right formula. On the contrary, as we now discover, the fundamental convention on which all things—good, bad and indifferent—are based, is indissoluble and is tacitly recognized everywhere. This is the agreement by which each one gives up all his rights and powers to society as a whole in exchange for social protection under conditions identical for all. Nothing could be more in keeping with equality (chap. 6).

Since all abide by the same rules and are equal parts of the whole, no one can have any interest in injuring the community as a whole. That would be a sort of self-injury. Of course, this says nothing about private hostilities nor does it prevent disobedience (chap. 7). The right of society to punish its delinquents is part of the contract and to the advantage of each and all. In deciding to punish murderers the original contractors agree to be punished if any one of them should commit that crime and in being punished one is merely "forced to be free." For the real meaning of the pooling of resources and submission to a single social will is that dependence of one person upon another is ended in favor of the subjection of all to the general will. The "will" reminds us again that laws are made, not discovered (chap. 7). Impersonal though the general will is in its application, will remains a psychic function and as such a personal act. That is why society is a transforming experience. Each natural brute becomes a moral being. Only now does duty acquire any sense, intelligence any scope (chap. 8).

Civil liberty and property remake us. Because our own in a presocial state is at worst mere possession by the strongest, at best the right of the first possessor, it is neither secure nor irrevocable. By making it all over to the sovereign whole we create a power capable of defending mine and thine, and moreover alter these into a public institution, property. For though property is a social right and a public trust, it brings with it defence against foreign aggressors and wrongful encroachments by one individual on another's right. What each one has, he has as a right, held as a grant from the sovereign, and he enjoys it in perfect security. In short, property is subordinate to the rights of the community and is not a private natural right, but it is held far more safely and equally. For social equality has now replaced the inequality of nature (chap. 9). The last sentence of Book One affirms the social equality of citizens under the law they have created by and for themselves in order to escape from the defects of the natural state. Equality is the only condition worth more than natural freedom. A footnote at the very end reminds us that it is bad governments that lead to gross inequality and that society is beneficial only when everyone has something and nobody has too much. The tone of resentment is as clear as that of the egalitarian arguments. Rousseau's anger is, moreover, directed against both the actual political order and its intellectual defenders.

Book Two. We have seen what the social contract should logically imply but never seems to mean in political practice. The common good, which is the common interest and the general will, tending to equality, cannot be alienated. In short, no one but the people, even if it does so tacitly, has the right to act as sovereign (chap. 1). However, only the original compact itself requires unanimous assent. Those who do not agree simply do not joint the association. Thereafter majority decisions are binding. Everyone must be counted, whether for or against, and no one may be excluded from the general will, if its universality is to be maintained. This is the meaning of indivisible sovereignty from which alone binding laws can issue. It is the task of men like Grotius to deny it, of course, because kings, and not the people, give out pensions and professorships. We note the populist and egalitarian emphasis (chap. 2).

The people's will, being the sole possible measure of right, must be allowed to express itself in such a way that the falsifications of dominating parties cannot overcome and mislead it. Voting must be entirely individual and factions must be prevented. If that is too much, let all groups at least be equal in strength. Otherwise some cabal is bound to become excessively powerful and certain to impose its own will. Individual wills cancel each other out, so that the public will emerges out of the rejected private wills. When groups vote that does not happen (chap. 3). The danger to be avoided at all cost is then usurpation of sovereignty by some special interest group. That does not mean that the community as a whole should absorb those goods and powers which are not needed for public purposes, but it is up to the sovereign to decide what is and what is not public. The private domain is set by a public decision. Since it is an agreement which binds all mutually to each other, there is no partiality in all this. What is done for the public is also done for oneself, as part of the community. As long as all public decisions are general, affecting all equally, no one can feel endangered (chap. 4). Justice can, indeed, come about in no other manner, for we are not able to know the word of God. When the people as a whole makes rules for the people as a whole, justice is created. Thus while the people may choose to institute privileges, the sovereign, which by definition only makes general rules, cannot favor or hinder specific individuals. That is the task of government, not of sovereignty (chap. 6).

It is possible for a people to achieve justice with the aid of an educative lawgiver or after a revolution when, like the Dutch, a society begins with a clean slate (chaps. 6, 7, 8). It is also necessary that states be small, because otherwise there is bound to be an impersonality in public life that drives people apart (chap. 9). Where unity prevails, shared objectives are before the eyes of all, and anyone can understand them. Finally, a just state must be wealthy enough for autonomy but not so rich as to attract hungry conquerors (chap. 10). Individually each one is interested in preserving his freedom from domination. To that end there must be equality. No one may be so rich as to be able to buy another, and no one so poor as to be forced to sell himself. To maintain this equality, the richer people must exercise moderation in their goods and influence, while the less well off must moderate their envy and avarice. It is likely to be a considerable moral task, but the laws can encourage men to attempt it (chap. 11). It is above all a matter of forming good habits, especially customary simplicity. Book Two then demonstrates the inescapability of popular sovereignty, once it is really understood that men enter society for their own benefit and should agree only to such laws as serve their interests as social beings and citizens. All laws, to be legitimate, must be such as any people would agree to, if they had only those ends in view which made them prefer society to nature in the first place. That implies the equal protection of the laws for each and all, and an equal obligation to obey them. Nothing is due to persons, only to the law. This supremacy of the law, which is what sovereignty means, originates in the people and falls on the entire people identically. The egalitarianism that is involved here is extensive and intense.

The nature of government comes next, in Book Three. The most important thing to remember is that government is not sovereignty. Governments are the mere agents of the sovereign and law-making people. Governors exist to execute the law, and can be recalled or recommissioned at any moment by the sovereign. There is obviously no contract involved here (chap. 1). Democracy can be either the rule of all or just majority rule, but in one respect it is always the best form of government. For those who make the law are sure to be its best interpreters (chaps. 3, 4). The case for democracy as good government is therefore a strong one, even if not all peoples are up to it, for only a small state with simple manners, equality of social rank, and above all no luxury can even try it. On the moral plane, there must be no vanity to make men slaves of opinion (chap. 4). Secondly, there are aristocracies that are all but democratic in form. There is the rule of the old which is natural and works very well among American Indians. Again, elective aristocracies, chosen for merit, are not to be despised. The trouble is that inequality does tend to increase and sooner or later aristocracies become hereditary, which is a disastrous form of government (chap. 5). Finally, nothing can really be said in favor of monarchy. Succession crises speak in favor of the hereditary principle, which gives young princes an education designed to produce bad kings (chap. 6). In view of all that, clearly a republic is bound to be better than a monarchy and a free state superior to a despotism. However, there is really no point in looking for the best form of government, since conditions differ (chap. 8). What is permanent is not the structure, but the purpose of government. Is the people well off or not?—that is the question. It is quite easy to tell. If they choose to have large families, they are content. A simple test applied to ordinary peasants is really all one has to look for; there is no need to be over-elaborate about forms of government. Nor should one look to stability as a standard. Wars, civil war, and the like do not affect most people very much. It is just the ruling classes that get involved. As for the arts and sciences, their baleful brilliance contributes nothing to good government; quite the opposite, in fact. Simple benefits for simple men, in short, are what one should look for in judging the success of governments (chap. 9).

If Rousseau can afford to sound almost like Pope about forms of government, it is because he had such a clear and democratic notion about the ends of administration and because the exercise of sovereignty is what really matters. It is the sovereign's task, after all, to see that the rules be maintained and enforced in keeping with their spirit and letter. The people must be frequently assembled to impose its sovereign supervision over the government. The latter is suspended as soon as such an assembly has gathered. Assemblies have only one function, to act as watchdogs, to see that the original law is preserved in every way by the government. The Romans had these assemblies and so did the primitive Frankish monarchies. At their best the citizens of a town act together for themselves. If there is more than one town, let the citizens of each town successively act for all; in that way you get no capitals (chaps. 12, 14). As in the case of civilization generally the tone here is as populist as it is democratic: no fancy values and no luxurious ways to outshine the honest citizen. That must be so, for otherwise the citizens will become indifferent to their civic existence: they will pay taxes with money, rather than by labor or in kind; they will prefer representation to direct participation, a feudal sham to self-government; and their freedom will be gone (chap. 15). Ultimately they will cease to keep a stern eye on the government. They may forget that they can dismiss, establish, and alter governments by simple law. When they do so they act as a simple democracy, thus closing the gap between the people, their laws, and their government (chaps. 16, 17). We have returned to the democratic voice.

Quite naturally Book Four moves into the mores that are capable of sustaining democratic polities. Clearly Rousseau has been considering democracy in two ways, as a form of political activity and as a social result. He concedes that the contentment of the common man is an adequate sign of good government. We are, however, also forced to conclude that, unless people assemble frequently to keep a sharp eye on their government, they are not likely to prosper. It is not the form of government, but its fidelity to the laws, that counts. That is why people if they are to exercise their sovereignty effectively must possess the appropriate republican *mores*, as we have already been told. So the last book of the *Social Contract* begins with that most democratic of all images—solid peasants sitting under an oak, making their own political decisions. It is the greatest possible contrast to all ill-governed states. Here harmony prevails and magistrates can be chosen by lot, the most egalitarian of all elections, since office is a civic burden, not a privilege (chaps. 1, 2, 3). The evidence of history is not perhaps encouraging; not even Roman politics conformed to this happy vision. However, they did have censors and they do remind us that it is custom that rules a people's pleasures, not nature. And customs can be molded by law (chap. 7). In sum, men do make themselves as they make their laws. Perhaps the group under the oak is not quite real, but republican virtue and a civil religion designed to support it are entirely thinkable. It is this set of beliefs that really matters. Without it majoritarianism makes no sense. Unanimity is required only for the original compact; for subsequent decisions a majority will do. It is sufficient because an assembly only has to assert the original laws and to ask whether the general will is being followed. If a few people differ, they are merely a mistaken minority, as long as republican virtue prevails. When it no longer does, then the majority may be in error, and then all is lost. When the majority is patriotic its rule can safely be accepted as correct and the minority can be tolerantly ignored as showing nothing but a human weakness. It is not numbers but its spirit that guarantees the sovereignty of the people and that gives a majority its weight in a republic. It has nothing to do with rights, social or natural (chap. 2). For the great problem of an egalitarian, democratic, popular polity is not the rights and privileges of the few, but the well-being, both civic and personal, of the whole people or at least of the majority; that is, "peace, unity, equality . . . [the] enemies of political sophistication" (chap. 1). It is a powerful case and no one who reads the *Social Contract* honestly can miss it. This is a book in defense of equality in all its aspects. That is not, however, its only significant message; it may not even be its major argument.

> Sing of human unsuccess
> In a rapture of distress.

The egalitarian and democratic aspects of the *Social Contract* are really the coherent working out of the implications of a single idea. Since convention, and not God or nature, is the origin of all societies, and since conventional rules are made, openly or tacitly, by all those who choose to join a society, the only justifiable political order is one that serves the interests of all, or at least of most of those who are thus associated. Democratic and populist government and *mores* follow from that. To be sure, it is perfectly clear throughout that actual institutions fail to meet these standards of legitimacy, and this provides Rousseau with frequent occasions for the expression of populist indignation. So far so good. The trouble is that men "as they are"

are quite obviously unable to live under laws "that might be" and that the evidence of actuality proves men to be irremediably warped.

Mankind is simply a mistake. Human nature is fit only for solitude, but human needs make association a necessity. The two cannot be harmonized and the *Social Contract* demonstrates that even the most reasonable of legal orders can do nothing against the corrosive effects of self-oriented and inegalitarian human drives. The chains men bear cannot be rendered legitimate, because men are incapable of supporting a just yoke. Rousseau's theme is the tragic encounter between man's character and man's fate, between the self-absorbed ego and the co-operation that survival, even at its least elaborate, demands.

It is precisely because all social rules are made by men for men that the situation of social man is so hopeless. The master is no less enslaved than the slave, for both are locked into a mutual dependence from which neither one can free himself. Each has enchained himself (Book One, chap. 1). There is no one to blame. It may be true that slavery makes slaves and that nature does not create these abject herds, but it is men who enslave each other, and men who submit to it (chap. 2). The reason why men must alienate everything to the sovereign and endow it with such overwhelming power is that any vestige of extra-social freedom will be used by the strong to subject the weak to that condition of personal dependence from which association is supposed to save them. As we know it does not (chap. 6). That is why people have to be forced to be free. Their private self is always apt to be asocial (chap. 7). And while life under a contract may indeed transform that stupid animal into a moral being, the advantages to him are obscure. Justice may replace instinct, but not sufficiently to rule unchallenged (chap. 8). For while law may indeed treat all men as equals, bad governments do manage to make the rich richer and the poor poorer (chap. 9). Nature may be molded by art, but it obviously cannot be destroyed, and a private will always remains to compete with the public will, not only on the political stage, but within each man. The message of Book One is, therefore, not unambiguous. It may be rousing to tell men that they can make their society such as it ought to be, in order to secure safety and justice. It is also true that one must face the realities of man's failure even to approach these goals.

Book Two begins with a simple statement, explaining the inescapable and destructive tension in political society. The general will tends to equality while the personal will moves men to inequality (chap. 1). Something else also begins to emerge. Some of the most basic political decisions cannot be left to the sovereign people. War and peace are questions of prudence and therefore fall into the sphere of government, not of sovereignty (chap. 2). Moreover, groups form spontaneously, and someone wiser than the people is needed to prevent faction. There is a need for wise men, and those named belong to myth, not to history, Lycurgus most of all (chap. 3). We are becoming aware that stupidity and incompetence are not to be discounted and presently the people is no longer nobly engaged in acts of social self-formation, but is openly called "a blind multitude" that needs a law-giver (chap. 6). The figure of the law-giver is a study in despair, and for two reasons. He is a desperate device demanded by the incapacity of men to make rules for themselves; and he does not exist. His powers of mind and soul must be "super-human," and that is all we need to know about him really. He is needed to de-nature men so that they can become citizens, and that is impossible. Even if it could be done, there is no human being capable of performing this miracle. Moreover, nothing can tell us more about Rousseau's opinion of the political talents of most men than the fact that they must be systematically and continually duped and mystified if they are to be shaped for social justice (chaps. 7, 8).

The self-cure of revolution is, moreover, only a qualified one. If it is a real founding it may succeed, but unless there really is a clean slate it is hopeless. Liberty cannot be regained (chap. 8). Revolutionary turmoil is no time for legislating in any case. Turbulent moments are exploited by tyrants, but not by true law-givers, who will act only in calm periods with docile people (chap. 10). The equality which the general will strives for is therefore only a hope, something men may long for; but the moral strength for it can be found neither among the people, who are stupid as well as egotistical, nor among legislators, who are usually bunglers like Peter the Great or tyrants. The great law-giver, like the just law and like equality, is a myth. Clearly also the psychological basis of participatory democracy and social equality cannot be found in nature or in art. Popular resentment alone would seem to survive.

If Book Two introduces the tragic theme, it is Book Three that develops the entire scenario. Government is absolutely necessary and it must be strong. It is the physical power that society needs to move at all. Because it must be strong, it is inevitable that government will aggrandize itself at the expense of the sovereign people. To this there is no simple solution. Any form of government has its weaknesses, and there is no best regime for all men at all times. Indeed, the relativism here is so strong that it amounts to saying that people have the governments they deserve (chap. 1).

The reason why governments must corrupt society is that they all have three wills, the general will, their own corporate will as a body of magistrates, and their private oligarchic wills. In theory the first will should rule; in practice it is the third. To be effective there must be specialized functions for governors, but special political skills lead to concentration of power. Governments must be bold and know how to act at the right moment. The fewer the members of a government the more likely they are to recognize their chances (chap. 2). That is fine if these "chances" benefit society, but that is not usual. In sum, the victory of the clever and unscrupulous few over the dull multitude is inevitable.

Democracy is the name of the political escape from this treadmill; but it is only a name. For if men were able to govern themselves, they would not need governments at all. Therefore there are no true democracies among "men as they are." Even to try it is dangerous. For if the people in its capacity as government is, as it must be, corrupted, then the sovereign is also destroyed. There would be no reservoir of restraint left at all. The prevalence of civil war in such democracies as have been attempted proves as much (chap. 4). If true democracy makes excessive demands on the people, natural and elective aristocracy ask too much of rulers. The trend of inequality is toward its own enhancement and in due course aristocracies become hereditary (chap. 5). The movement of all governments is toward contraction and concentration of power and, in any case, few people are fit for freedom (chaps. 7, 8).

Science is helpless here, moreover, because one cannot measure the exact needs of a society for government. And so one cannot really expect to stop the well-known but irresistible slide into usurpation and general corruption (chap. 9). As old age creeps up on each individual, so does decay on societies (chap. 10). Art is what makes polities, but it is not enough to brake the forces of nature. Medicine may prolong a life, but death cannot be averted. If Sparta and Rome perished, how can historical polities expect to survive? The claims of tradition are therefore very great. Antiquity is a proof of utility and one had better obey the oldest laws, since change is itself a sign of decay. The movement of societies is all in one direction—downhill (chap. 12). The final nail in the coffin of hope is in Rousseau's destruction of his own favorite myths. Sparta and Rome offer little ground for expectation; Rousseau never denied their largely imaginary character, but he wants finally to prove that even human fancy cannot devise a vision of perfection. The ancient republics, so virtuous and free, were all grounded in slavery; the liberty of the few was paid for by the enslavement of the many. Slavery is, however, a wrong and a denial of a man's humanity. It cannot be justified and it proves that the past was no more perfect than the present. Only the forms of unfreedom differ (chap. 15). In conclusion we are reminded that all governments degenerate—as if we could by now have forgotten (chap. 18)!

The last Book reverts to some of the themes of the second one. Compared to the Third Book its tone is one of muted, rather than of outright, tragedy. The opening image of simple men under their oak-tree is immediately followed by the reminder that, compared to that picture, Europe is indeed politically *in extremis*. The private will has now obliterated the general will (chap. 1). We are again reminded that there is no true democracy (chap. 3), and then we are shown what is at best possible, Severus's laws for Rome. This model of a possible law-giver dupes the people into a six-class division according to wealth. The Senate perpetuates the duplicity, and in the absence of luxury a sort of stable client-patron relationship keeps this wholly unequal society stable. To be sure, even this order degenerates (chaps. 4, 5). The art of politics, the conditioning of *mores,* is clearly the art of deception and, while it can hold nature at bay for a while, it is doomed to ultimate failure. Men "being what they are" cannot be made to obey good laws that "might be" invented. The reason why there is no legitimate political rule is quite simply that it is impossible. The tragedy is that we can imagine a world better than the one we can make. We are therefore in a position to judge actuality, but not to improve it.

When these two Rousseaus are placed next to each other by an impartial recorder rather than by a pair of competing advocates, the *Social Contract* does not seem incoherent. At no point does Rousseau look forward to a day when men "shall brothers be for a' that." He does not concern himself with the future at all, nor can it be said that he is telling his readers what to do or feel. He is not asking them to be hopeful. As Emile was told that political principles, such as those of the *Social Contract,* are to be used to judge the states he is about to visit, so the reader has been supplied with a yardstick. The system of measurement is egalitarian, democratic, and populist. The historical world falls short of every principle of justice against which it is measured. As a psychologist Rousseau was bound to ask himself why that should be so. Since he did not believe that one could remake men and indeed considered education overwhelmingly difficult even when only a single child was involved, he held out no prospects of reform. However, he did not preach resignation either. We emerge with a picture of social possibilities that mirrors the same confusion that appears in our hearts. We are capable of seeing the good, but we are too feeble and too stupid to act upon it. The result is self-deception and, like all good philosophers, Rousseau meant to rob us of our illusions.

CHAPTER FIFTEEN

Jean-Jacques Rousseau
and Equality

"Je conçois un nouveau genre de service à rendre aux hommes: c'est de leur offrir l'image fidelle de l'un d'entre eux afin qu'ils apprennent à se connoitre."[1] Rousseau's mirror was meant to reflect both our private and public faces, and without disguise. What were we to see? The image of man as a self-made victim. Rousseau was preeminently the philosopher of human misery. His entire design was to show how mankind had built a social prison for itself. In the course of this enterprise Rousseau produced a veritable encyclopedia of egalitarian ideas, unique both in its scope and in the personal passion that informs it. For Rousseau chose to write from the vantage point of the wretched. He was not, however, blind to the intellectual difficulties of the very idea of equality, and it is the blending of emotion and intelligence that gives his pages their unique quality. He did not invent the secular idea of equality, but he was its most complete and eloquent defender.

Rousseau chose to speak for and as one of the poor, but he did not share the limitations of their condition. He knew the privileged well and could address them with extraordinarily, perhaps surprisingly, great effect. Certainly he still moves that public. One of the more notable aspects of contemporary egalitarianism is that it is usually promoted by the competent and relatively rich for the sake of the feeble and poor. To say that it is merely the ideological vehicle for the politically ambitious does not suffice to explain the prevalence, especially among the young, of the conviction that inequality must

"Jean-Jacques Rousseau and Equality" is reprinted by permission of *Daedalus, Journal of the American Academy of Arts and Sciences,* from the issue entitled "Rousseau for Our Times," 107, no. 3 (Summer 1978): 13–25.

go. The style of argument may be dry and pedestrian often, but the real inspiration is not revealed by words alone. It is compassion, pity, guilt, and shame or an aesthetic disgust at the very thought of so much man-made misery that forces men and women to abandon class, caste, and self-interest "to cast in (their) lot with the victims," in William Morris's words.[2] Wave upon wave of social outrage has swept over successive generations of Anglo-Americans moved by evangelical protestantism, utilitarian benevolence, and simply an immense pity.[3] Pity itself is old as mankind, but as a political force it is new. Rousseau did not invent it, perhaps, but he was the first to explain, to diagnose, and finally to judge it. That is because he made no attempt to disguise the personal and emotional aspects of his whole argument. Equality was not a quasilegal fiction for him, and inequality not something that others suffered. When he announced to his shocked readers that all our vices had their origin in inequality, he meant to take a wholly new view of the moral world: the way it looks from the very bottom of society.[4]

The enduring source of Rousseau's insight into the condition of inequality was personal experience. His fateful decision to make his private life into a public document was grounded in the belief that his existence was politically significant. He alone had lived in every class of society without belonging to a single one of them. He had dined with princes and supped with peasants on the same day. Although born a citizen of a republic, he was ending his days as a refugee, enjoying "la célébrité des malheurs."[5] He was "the watchmaker's son" against whom all the states of Europe had formed a league. It was therefore he alone who could and did speak of equality as only a universal victim could. In this also he felt alone, especially in France, where "only masters and valets were wanted and where equality was held in horror."[6]

Masters and valets were the two poles of Rousseau's society. He had been a footman in several households, and he could speak of this peculiarly degrading situation as an insider. It was here that he learned to hate violently the ruling classes whose cruelty, pettiness, prejudices, and vices revolted him to the end of his days.[7] It was here also, more significantly, that he acquired his numerous vices. All valets are rogues and cheats. It is inherent in their position, and Rousseau was no exception. Envy, lying, dissimulation, dishonesty, and disloyalty to one's fellow servants are normal for valets. That is the wage for being dependent on others. The master is, in turn, corrupted by power. He becomes cruel and brutal.[8] As a general rule, for there are always a few exceptions, "la canaille des valets" is the lowest form of humanity—except for their masters.[9] There was little difference between domestic service and slavery for Rousseau. The two were separated only by the extent of personal dependence. That was the real evil, and it was morally devastating. No bonds of duty or of mutual obligation can be formed where one is completely helpless, the other omnipotent to all intents and purposes.

Rousseau was far more radical than *Figaro*. Beaumarchais's hero has long been recognized as a revolutionary figure. The servant who is smarter than his master had always been a stock figure of the comic stage, but *Figaro* was the first to resent it. That a gifted, competent, and honest man should serve a decadent nobleman was, suddenly, an outrage. That the likeable countess should have a maid, however, was not at all objectionable. For it was not the very existence of domestic service that was wrong. *Figaro* was rebelling against a system that subordinated useful talent to mere birth. He personified a circulation of elites. Rousseau clearly implied more, but he also had had a *Figaro*-like experience. Once, while serving at table he was able to demonstrate to an assembled aristocratic family that he was far better educated than the son of the house. He never forgot the sweet delight of that moment when things were for once "put in their natural order."[10] The unnatural order was, however, what prevailed, and Rousseau's response to it went beyond *Figaro*'s. It reached that revolutionary point that Tocqueville located halfway between an aristocratic and a democratic régime.[11] In the ancien régime the world "downstairs" mirrors that of "upstairs," and the servant identifies himself with the master so completely that he may well lose any sense of selfhood. Such was the faithful domestic retainer. In a democracy the servant is an employee who receives wages for services in an impersonal quid pro quo exchange in which the opinion of mutual equality prevails. In the period of transition, however, the master is "malevolent and soft," while the servant is "malevolent and intractable." Tocqueville had his reservations about the arrangement that created trusted retainers, and he knew that the democratic equality between servants and masters was only a sort of "fancied" opinion, not an actuality. He thought, as did Rousseau, that contracting for services was an improvement over a wholly servile state. The ex-slave in the North was very much like the base laquays, at the bottom of the old domestic order. They were "obstinate and cringing." The intermediary condition of revolution he deemed the worst. It had been Rousseau's own state, and he did not deny that it had brought him to the lowest moral point, as well as to a state of intolerable resentment.

The slave is only one degree below the valet. In slave households neither master nor slave belongs to a family, but only to a class.[12] The demoralization is the same for all domestic servants, but slavery is, in addition, totally unjust, or to be exact—antijust. It is a situation which cannot be mitigated, because the master cannot be a master without a slave, while the slave has no self at all.[13] The two are locked into a situation of total mutual dependence. That is why slavery is a paradigm for all the lesser states of personal dependence: it reveals so starkly what is wrong with all of them. The social contract is the only cure for them, because it alone depersonalizes, and so moralizes obedience.[14] The necessity for such a step becomes clear when one considers slavery. To begin with, it is wrong, because no man can have the right to sell his life. Only property can be bought, and property is a social creation, while one's life is a gift of nature. As suicide is wrong, so is selling oneself, since in both cases one is trading away something that is not wholly one's own. Certainly the life of children cannot be alienated by their parents. The Aristotelian argument that some people are naturally born slaves mistook the effect for the cause. It is enslavement that makes imbeciles, not the other way around. The most important reason we cannot sell ourselves is, however, moral. No one may simply give up his moral responsibilities, but the slave does just that. Without the power to make choices, he loses his moral personality.[15] His existence is antijust, an offense against the moral order. For enslavement is an assertion of pure force, which can give rise to no ties of duty or obligation, and the slave may rebel, if he can, in a simple act of counterassertion. Slavery is that ultimate point of personal dependence where right and wrong cease to apply.

Unjust, false, and degrading as slavery is, Rousseau did not forget that the finest of the classical republics depended on slave labor so that its citizens might have the leisure for self-government. That did not prove that slavery could be right, but merely that all civil institutions are subject to imperfections.[16] For slavery, like all the lesser kinds of social dependence, is systematic, not incidental. All the various degrees of inequality create the given social pattern to which individuals adapt. People had sympathized with Rousseau when he was sacked, but it was part of his position to be subject to that injustice, and so no one did anything. The poor are sacrificed to the rich by the maxims of all actual societies and by all legal systems, since these exist to stabilize inequalities of wealth.[17] For in the end, all inequalities can be reduced to rich and poor.[18] Even slavery is possible only because of that difference. That is why there is only one way to root out slavery: no one may be so rich as to buy another and no one so poor as to be tempted to sell himself. That is the basic minimum of equality required for personal freedom.[19] It is not enough to achieve justice. For that, another kind of equality is needed. "Moral and lawful equality" must replace the inequalities, both physical and intellectual, "that nature may have imposed upon mankind."[20]

What did Rousseau mean by natural inequality and "moral and legal equality?" Obviously he did not believe that men were "created equal" or alike. Human beings differ from one another at birth and throughout life.[21] However, in their natural presocial condition, when they are isolated and perfectly free, men's talents do not manifest themselves, nor do they matter. Only when men congregate and their intelligence develops do differences in natural endowment become significant. Then competition replaces egoism, and newly acquired skills and needs bring on the division of labor, mutual dependence, and accumulation of possessions. Inequality now is an established given among associated men, and the institutions of property, law, and government follow.[22] The cement that holds all this together is not egoism, which is a perfectly healthy instinct, but vanity, the desire to shine in the eyes of others and to climb up the social ladder. Otherwise those who benefit least from this system would not accept it so readily.[23] Men are not just oppressed but also deluded. They are, moreover, deeply divided within and among themselves, because the impulses of nature survive in the social state.[24] The exercise of power is an assertion of natural inequality, but might cannot make right. Physical prowess cannot make obligation, only submission. As soon as the oppressed can fight back, they will do so. Conquest, like slavery, is a harsh fact of life, and so is rebellion.[25] To become socialized we need to do more than just cease to be "stupid and limited animals"—we need a moral life.[26]

Even the worst societies have some standards of right and wrong, which create some notion of duty. The trouble is that the rules have no other purpose than to freeze people into positions of such inequality that only bonds of fear, not obligation, can develop. How can one have social rules that really serve the interests of all men? How can men be made to obey without anyone commanding, given "men as they are"?[27] If everyone openly agrees to a single set of rules to be equally and impersonally applied to all, then the citizens are all perfectly free, for they obey only themselves. To achieve that impersonality of legal rulership, the "total alienation of each associate of himself and his rights to the community" is the first step.[28] Nature must be really abandoned, so that each one can put himself in an identical relation to the whole. That way no one has an interest in making the rules onerous. Everyone receives the same rights and all oblige themselves to obey and to receive the protection of the laws under the same conditions.[29] It is a wholly artificial equality. The criminal is not the equal of the good citizen, but both are measured by the same yardstick. Just as money is a neutral standard which allows us to compare widely different commodities for purposes of fair exchange, so the law allows us to make fair judgments of civil worth.[30] Absolute equality is unthinkable in any society. All have standards, which some men meet and others do not. The question is how to have just rules of distribution according to which we judge some to be good and others bad. Rousseau thought this so obvious that he put it in a footnote.[31] The argument is, however, still offered with considerable flourish by the defenders of inequality. That is because it is incompatible with such rejections of all distributive justice as the communist formula, "from each according to his abilities, to each according to his need." That may, in fact, provide the basis for new kinds of rules, but not, as Marx knew, for "men as they are" here and now.[32] The issue is not really equality here, and Rousseau's point is elementary. Since no society can exist without rules, the great question is which are the least onerous.

How much equality is needed for the rule of law? The people know well enough that equality before the law is in their interest, that when exceptions are made it will not be for the benefit of the many.[33] Nevertheless "the force of things" is always against equality, even though it is so obviously best for most men all of the time. Equality is not self-perpetuating, and the problem is therefore not how much equality, but how to maintain the degree of equality necessary to prevent injustice.[34] The point to be avoided is when the rich can bend the law in their own favor. There is no easy way to that end, for although the general will, the will of society considered as a single whole, always tends to equality, each one of us has a particular will which yearns for privilege. This unsocialized self would not in itself be dangerous if it were not organized. The perpetual threat to equality comes from factions, combinations, special associations, all of which become dominating castes.[35] There is a familiar populist sense of conspiracy here, all the more so since Rousseau was personally obsessed by it. Who was to rescue mankind from these multiple threats? The state as a paternal savior was the only possible hope. That introduces a new idea of freedom. Partial associations are bound to create personal dependencies, and these are so much power withdrawn from the "body of state."[36] Freedom is defined, here, as the unimpaired strength of the state, not as personal choice. Dependence on private persons is a loss of freedom now, *because* it diminishes the state, not because it enchains the subordinate. Freedom is in reliance on the state's laws which one has made. For one then is *not* doing anything one does *not* want to do, which is Rousseau's definition of freedom in society. It is exceptionally negative. Obeying one's socialized public ego is *not* being forced by anyone else.[37] To that end equality is absolutely necessary, because one cannot identify with the law fully in its absence.

Equality, however, is not enough to ensure that the force of the state be recognized as a liberation. Heavy doses of civic education and manipulation by a great legislator and by censors are needed to keep the civic self alive. Rousseau's medicine may well have been worse than the disease. It is, however, absurd to overlook the psychological truth to which he points. He and many other people who have no self-confidence experience paternal rule as liberating. Protection is not freedom, but it certainly may feel just like it. Nevertheless, anyone who thinks that pluralism and diversity of views and manners are the very core of freedom will look upon Rousseau's definition of freedom as a simple abuse of the word.[38] The liberty of those who can cope on their own is one that rejoices in conflict and competition. To those who see themselves as unalterably weak and subject to oppression by an endless army of predators, this prospect is a nightmare. Rousseau chose to see society from their perspective, and his view of freedom follows from it.

In fact Rousseau was not oblivious to some of the difficulties that a policy of preventing inequality might create. To suppress potentially dangerous particular associations requires a strong government. That immediately creates a problem, for the government is also a "particular association." It has, like all the others, whether they be military or religious, loyalties and interests that are at odds with those of the general public.[39] The means of domination are always readily at hand. The purposes and the actual tasks of governments are therefore usually incompatible. Governments are necessary to enforce the law, not to make it; that is to be done by the sovereign people.[40] As executive agents, governments should in principle have no arms of their own. However, their work is such as to make them the masters, rather than the servants of the people. They must prevent the rise of wealth and poverty which would quickly make a mockery of the social contract. For once there are rich and poor, every law serves the former. To achieve equality the government must command ample forces, and with that the awful equality of despotism may eventually come.[41]

For all their defects, Rousseau could imagine governments that could successfully impose and maintain equality. The conditions that he set might seem utopian, but in fact they amount to the very opposite: an exact estimate of the full cost of equality. There would be very little division of labor in a subsistence economy with no foreign trade as part of a society that would have no arts or sciences or any civilization to speak of. The price of equality is the elimination, preferably through taxation, of any surplus. Rousseau knew perfectly well that no modern European, certainly not any of his Genevan fellow citizens, was interested enough in equality to accept such harsh terms. Corsica might try to create equality at such a cost, but no one else would. Rousseau was exceptionally honest here. He had no intention of claiming that equality could be had cheaply, or that civilized people could really afford it. If Corsica was to attempt a policy of equality, all opportunities for the accumulation of riches must simply be eliminated. In a permanently underdeveloped, agrarian society, that is readily avoided. Under this "rustic system" each one produces enough for himself and his family and is discouraged by taxation from doing more. Under primitive noncommercial conditions there will be no atrophy of incentives to work, for self-sufficiency requires a lot of hard labor. The state will be rich, the people poor, and there will be a minimum of inequality.[42] Contemporary political theorists who see Rousseau as the prophet of Third World democracy have not taken full account of these views. The hope that Third World countries might retain enough traditional social cohesion to avoid the class divisions of the former colonial powers may, or may not, be reasonable. Since these countries are determined to become developed technological societies, however, they are not taking Rousseau seriously. He at least took it for granted that the equality of rustic systems such as Corsica's could not survive even commerce and money, not to mention industrial economies. Whatever the rhetoric, the elites of these countries and their Western champions owe little to Rousseau's vision of agrarian equality.[43]

Rousseau's preference for the rustic system was inspired not only by his egalitarianism, but also by a deep moral distaste for luxury. To be sure, luxury was, in the first instance, the effect of inequality, but once superfluity existed, it was a powerful stimulus to ever greater inequalities. That was not all. Luxury was directly corrupting. It made men soft and self-indulgent. It destroyed the martial spirit and eroded civic virtue.[44] These views had long been a standard feature of that civic humanism which was central to early modern radicalism.[45] Robespierre was to be both its epitome and nemesis, whereas Rousseau was perhaps its last genuine prophet. If any remnants of this Spartan moralism survive, it is among those who revile the consumer society as demoralized and politically debilitating. Rousseau was, however, far more severe than these contemporary critics. Luxury included the arts and sciences, and not only soporific *Kitsch*. It was high culture that provided the garlands to hide the chains which imprisoned the people. It entertained the ruling classes and gave artists a means to gain public reputations. It kept citizens from their social duties, and ruined their private morals. Art as a spectator sport was isolating and ruptured the ties of social life. Finally it provided audiences with a pseudomorality. After weeping at the spectacle of suffering, they felt that they had actually done good deeds. The best that could be said for the theater was that in a corrupt city, like Paris, it kept the dissolute off the streets, where they would commit crimes. Rousseau thought that art alienates people, because it provides an imaginary world to which one can escape, away from family, work, and social duty.[46] Nothing could be more opposed to this than Marcuse's complaint that the rationalized domestication of art has robbed us of its revolutionary antibourgeois power. For him it is precisely high art that enables one to recognize the shoddiness of all actuality.[47] To Rousseau art looked like a mere escape from actuality, which is our one and only world. But then Rousseau did not look forward to revolution from above. In fact he did not look forward to anything. Change is always a disaster: for societies, because the normal course of history is from bad to worse, for the individual, because social mobility is psychologically destructive.[48]

Science, Rousseau thought less harmful than high art. For most men it is an unsuitable waste of time, but the great scientist is not corrupted as artists and writers are. Scientists are not mere peacocks and flatterers of the great. Moreover, Rousseau could imagine popular art that was not destructive. The Swiss peasant locked in his cabin might sing, fiddle, and do a little science without harm. On the contrary, it kept him and his family happy and united.[49] Finally there were the public festivals. The Greek drama was a national spectacle uniting citizens in common remembrance of their past. Modern country fairs again provide a lot of communal pleasure and renew ties of friendship among hardworking people.[50] This is certainly not a full-blown ideology of popular culture, but it is its beginning and it stems from Rousseau's own experience as both a successful artist and a failed citizen.[51]

In the end luxury was part of the system of rich and poor. Intellectual luxury was an excess of self-development, as material luxury was the production of superfluities. Neither would arise if men did not wish to be superior to their fellows. The best answer to it was civic education and sumptuary laws, imposed especially on the well-to-do.[52] That returns us to the difficulty of governmental usurpation. It is an unavoidable evil, but it can be postponed. Both the form of the government and the vigilance of the sovereign people can do much to put off the fate that overcame even the best of republics.[53] The best form of government varies from place to place, in keeping with the considerations that Montesquieu had discussed. In principle, however, the most just government is the one that departs least from the general will which seeks equality. That would be direct democracy, but it is possible, if at all, only in a primitive Swiss Canton—not generally. Men fit to govern themselves would need no government at all.[54] The best alternative is an elective aristocracy chosen for brief periods of office by the whole people. In general that would mean that the wealthier members of society will be elected, but from time to time a poor man should be chosen to prove that merit is not ignored.[55] This system is not to be confused with representative government in which deputies make laws, which is a destruction of popular sovereignty, since political justice and freedom depend on popular legislation.[56] Representation may be one way to govern large polities, but these cannot enjoy much freedom. The citizen is an insignificant cipher, and the rigor of the law must be severe to reach a great, dispersed population.[57]

Given the difficulties of democratic government, there is always the potential for tyranny, and only a watchful citizenry can prevent its emergence. This is why active political participation is necessary.[58] The people do not assemble to make new laws. That is to be avoided, as is all change. The popular assemblies exist to preserve the republic, not to alter or adapt its laws.[59] Their chief purpose is to express their confidence in or dissatisfaction with the magistrates and to reconfirm the original laws. Sporadic and limited as these gatherings are, they clearly are designed to protect the interests of the people at large, and everyone is expected to attend and to take an active part in the proceedings.[60] They are clearly very democratic, but they do not aim at the sort of politics today called participatory democracy. First of all, Rousseau's assemblies do not govern and do not frame policies; that is left entirely in the hands of the elected magistrates. The function of participation is also different. It does indeed aim at forming a new and better individual citizen, but not by encouraging the "realization of his creative capacities."[61] The citizen is to be relentlessly socialized, to remain patriotic, and to achieve personal and social integration by identifying directly and constantly with the polity. He is to be made and kept a patriot all the time. When the citizens no

longer rush to the assembly, all is lost.[62] Civic commitment also expresses itself in unanimity. When there is a small minority vote, it
does not matter; a few individuals have erred, and a large majority
is likely to be close to the general public will. The real disaster is
when a majority has lost its general will. Then the republic is dead,
killed by the particular wills to inequality—for men may agree to
that also.[63] Mutuality of obligation tends to evaporate, but assemblies
can halt that.

Rousseau's democracy was not designed to promote a long conversation in a "public space," bringing compromise, social change, self-
fulfillment, and power to one and all. It was far from being eccentric.
New England town meetings in the eighteenth century were also
meant to achieve consensus. Differences were generally called unhappy, and the primacy of peace rendered discord, argument, and
parties unacceptable. The meetings were not presented with a choice
of competing interests or opinions. They met to reassert the unity
of townsmen. In the absence of coercive authority the town meeting
shaped obedience by creating harmony, which was achieved by careful compromises and pressures well before the meeting took place.
Neither the defense of private interests nor the projection of personal
ideas was welcome.[64] Given the small size and exclusiveness of the
towns, these meetings were not, however, extensively "managed."
The advocates of participatory democracy today tend to accept far
more specialization of functions, and to provide a great deal of direction to those who are to be improved by participating. Its educative
ideal is, moreover, highly personalized and dynamic. There is none
of that in Rousseau. His civic-soldierly peasants may not be plain
New Englanders, but the psychic benefit of participation for them is
also social integrity and mutual peace. The elimination of emotional
and social conflict is the great objective. Why this requires so much
civic heroism is not altogether clear, but at least Rousseau did not
expect the poor to become a heroic proletariat. Certainly creativity,
individual self-fulfillment, and personal completion were not what he
had in mind. In the end the simple domestic contentment of the peas-
ant-citizen was his ultimate test of good government, and he in fact
expected men to remain "as they are."[65] That did not mean pluralism
or freedom, but censors, tutorial legislators, civic religion, and mutual watchfulness. To Rousseau it seemed a price worth paying for
political cohesion and emotional peace.

The emphasis on political unanimity and on common mores and
beliefs and on an essentially plebiscitary system, reveals the distance
between Rousseau and the New England towns of his time. It is a

difference rooted in Rousseau's low opinion of the social capacities and general intelligence of most people. Community is therefore not an independent ideal for him, the end which equality is meant to serve. Indeed if by community we mean not only shared attitudes, but also constant interaction between individuals, Rousseau was against it. The benefits of solitude were, in his eyes, too great for that. One of the advantages of the Swiss mountain cantons was that its people were kept indoors and apart by the weather for almost half the year.[66] To avoid parties or any divisive ongoings each member of the assembly must, before voting, isolate himself to seek only his own opinion.[67] Each citizen is inextricably bound to the state, but each one is alone, a discrete unit in relation to the whole. There are indeed to be plenty of festivities in a good society, but the main purpose of these, beyond fun and games, is to arrange marriages.[68] The community is one that has only private and no public functions. It enhances ties of affection in hours of leisure, but work and politics are individualized; for relations of dependence and exploitation would otherwise arise. There is, moreover, one community in which there is no equality at all—the family. Women are to be inferior to their husbands. Equality is between households, not between spouses.[69] That had something to do with Rousseau's fear that women tended to dominate men. Indeed the primacy of isolation expresses a profound sense of weakness and inadequacy. In solitude one is at last safe from the domination of others. This is not the solitude of Prometheus, but the self-protective flight of the incurably weak who are afraid of being bossed.[70] Mutuality is achieved by avoiding face-to-face relationships, and the impersonality of legal relations becomes a substitute for politics.[71] That may not appeal to those who feel a great deal of confidence in their ability to hold their own in a free political arena, but it may have an obvious advantage for those whose chief hope is to escape subjugation, especially in the form of personal dependence.

Not only are most individuals too weak to protect themselves against the strong among them. They are not even able to see and pursue their own best interest. The general will, the public will of the people does tend to equality, but alas, "the force of things is always against it."[72] That is so because "the people are stupid."[73] The people are simply a collection of potential victims. They are nevertheless better, healthier, and more decent than the rich and powerful. They are also all that matters. Let all the kings and philosophers disappear and everything would go on much as usual.[74] These are indeed the perennial attitudes of "populism," and Rousseau was surely its original voice. American agrarian populism shared his truculence, the demand that the simple decencies should receive the respect they deserve, and a certain moralistic distaste for intellectuals. But the hope that, given the opportunity, each man could rise by his own efforts was there also. It was wholly absent in Rousseau and in most European populism.[75] Indeed Rousseau was far better able to accept failure and rejection than his overwhelming success. "Let no one say that my life is of no interest because I am a man of the people," he wrote about his *Confessions*.[76] He knew of course that he had made his life sensationally fascinating, but he preferred to present himself as not only the spokesman, but also as one of the people. He had, after all, begun as "the son of a watchmaker."

The picture of the people as an undifferentiated mass which must be protected against the depredations of financiers and tax-gatherers is certainly inspired by the most intense feelings of class hatred, but it is not the militancy of the Marxian proletariat. Rousseau's people are to look backward from technology and development to a harmony that history has always missed. To be sure Rousseau knew as much about social alienation as the author of *On the Jewish Question*. Marx was, however, right not to acknowledge any affinity for Rousseau, who was ahistorical and only wanted to escape from, not to transform, the new world that was coming into being. Rousseau's egalitarianism did, however, serve that all-purpose antiestablishment fervor which has colored every subsequent ideology and has survived them all. Populism is a sort of trade-unionism of the victimized, a response to the people seen in terms of its sufferings, but there are also far less structured reactions. Pity is likely to be the most immediate feeling, and Rousseau certainly meant to arouse it in his readers.

It has lately been argued that Rousseau invented political pity, and that he supplied Robespierre and Saint-Just with the rhetoric of "compassionate zeal" on behalf of the wretched.[77] That may be something of an exaggeration, but there is no doubt that Rousseau did much to advertise pity as a means of creating bonds of solidarity. He did, however, have much more to say on the subject.[78] Pity is one of man's natural feelings. Natural man identifies immediately with the suffering being, whether it be another man or an animal. He knows intuitively that he too is a potential sufferer, and he feels briefly the pain he sees. That is to be expected, because suffering is the universal experience. To be human is to suffer. In simple people, whose passions are not overwhelming, and whose intelligence is limited, this capacity for compassion survives in society. Among the rich and clever it atrophies. When there is a street fight the market women will separate the brawlers; the scholar just shuts the noise out. Nevertheless, pity remains a sweet emotion in society; but it is not quite the same sentiment that it was in nature. Now that we compare ourselves to each other all the time, there is always an element of self-satisfaction in pity; we are glad that it is not we who are suffering when we pity another person. That does not render pity socially worthless. On the contrary, even though it be flawed, it is still the only feeling likely to bind us to one another. It serves among the people to bring them together, and it would render the wealthy less odious if they would not bear the sufferings of others quite so patiently. It is, in fact, common among the rich to claim that the poor are too stupid to suffer, and so to absolve themselves from the pangs of pity. That is the mature, adult response. In our society adolescence is the only age when pity is felt intensely; later, callousness is rationalized. Education might attenuate that, but in the long run there must be less inequality, so that only the people remain, if pity is to accomplish its binding task.[79]

The place of pity in society is socially ambiguous. It is a tie between the dissociated, but it is no substitute for duty. Without duty there can be no polity, but there would be no impulse to treat people fairly without mutual identification, which requires compassion. Indeed, Rousseau's own enduring hatred for injustice had its germ in a compassionate encounter with a hospitable peasant who lived in fear of tax agents.[80] It is, however, very dangerous to let pity degenerate into weakness. Compassion must be generalized and depersonalized until it is transformed into justice. Pity cures us of hatred, cruelty, and envy, but it is no replacement for justice, which depends not on feeling, but on an unremitting adherence to rules. Moreover, the kindness that pity expresses creates ties of dependence. The feeble cling to their benefactors without gaining strength, while the latter soon feel intolerably burdened by the objects of their generosity. Rousseau for once spoke as a patron and admitted that he had been too weak and too inconstant to endure the obligations that he had incurred by his casual acts of benevolence. He simply ran away from his charges.[81] Pity is too uncertain and fluctuating to guide us in society. We need duty and justice that depend on law, not sentiment, which reduces the weak to suffering clients. In nature we do not need attitudes that support enduring relationships. Pity is fleeting there also, lasting only as long as the sight of suffering is present. Then it goes away. It creates no bonds and can be evoked as readily by an animal in pain as by another human being. It is no more enduring among socialized men. Rousseau had been patronized often enough to know the difference between friendship and justice among equals and the benevolence that the strong may lavish occasionally on those whom they wish to help.

Justice, unlike pity, makes the weak independent. By belonging to a polity, they gain the strength of citizens, which protects them against the strong in body and mind. Compassion binds the weak together, as vanity tears them apart, but these ties of natural emotion are quite inadequate in society. They cannot protect legitimate interests, nor sustain the public good. Without pity we would not be joined, but once we have come together, only justice can make society tolerable. That is why the poor must be protected even against pity, lest they fall prey to the vices of helplessness. Beggars are the support of tyranny. If the poor, who are never disguised, are far from amiable, the rich, when they are seen as they really are, are horrible. Rousseau had little use for the consumers of pity, but he hated far more those who refused to respond to suffering. Without equality there could be no healthy compassion, just as without pity there could be no justice.

Political pity has been with us for more than two hundred years, fired by religious revivals, sentimental literature, guilt, and much else. That it is no substitute for justice will come as no surprise to those who know the history of America's exslaves. Rousseau is not to blame for the inadequacy of pity, which he both stimulated and dissected. On the contrary, by identifying with the dispossessed, he could shudder at the harshness of the rich and yet know perfectly well that this was not the great question of politics. The real issues clustered around the historically inevitable experience of inequality. What makes his account of the majestic progress of inequality and oppression so complete and compelling is his refusal to abandon the source of his energy, his unquenchable sense of personal injury. He was with matchless success able to reveal the experiences of the endemically unsuccessful. Other philosophers write about those less fortunate than themselves in measured sentences, and they often do persuade us of their case. But they do not shake us, as Rousseau does, with his epic prose. He alone is the Homer of the losers.

Notes

1. Jean-Jacques Rousseau, *Mon Portrait,* in *Oeuvres complètes de Jean-Jacques Rousseau,* ed. Bernard Gagnebin and Marcel Raymond, 4 vols. (Paris: Gallimard, 1959–1969, Bibliothèque de la Pléiade), vol. 1, p. 1120. Unless otherwise specified, all references to Rousseau's works are in the Pléiade edition.

2. William Morris, *Art and Socialism, Work XXIII* (New York: Russell and Russell, 1966), p. 213.

3. E.g. Stanley H. Elkins, *Slavery* (New York: Grosset and Dunlap, 1963),

p. 173, and George M. Frederickson, *The Inner Civil War* (New York: Harper and Row, 1965), pp. 15, 81, 86, for what *Uncle Tom's Cabin* achieved before the Civil War.

4. *Discours sur les sciences es les arts*, vol. 1, p. 25; *Observations sur la Réponse qui a été faite à son Discours*, vol. 1, pp. 49–50.

5. *Ebauche des Confessions*, vol. 1, pp. 1150–1151.

6. *Lettre à Christophe de Beaumont*, vol. 1, pp. 932, 980.

7. *Lettres à Malesherbes*, vol. 1, p. 1145.

8. *Les Confessions*, vol. 1, pp 31–32, 82–87, 514–515.

9. *Emile*, vol. 4, p. 326; *Lettre à M. d'Alembert*, ed. M. Fuchs (Lille Geneva: Giard and Droz, 1948), p. 47.

10. *Les Confessions*, pp. 95–96.

11. Alexis de Tocqueville, *Democracy in America*, trans. George Lawrence (New York: Doubleday-Anchor, 1969), pp. 572–580.

12. *Emile*, p. 764.

13. *Discours sur l'origine et les fondemens de l'inégalité parmi les hommes*, vol. 3, p. 175; *Discours sur les arts*, vol. 3, p. 80; *Contrat social*, vol. 3, book 1, chap. 1.

14. *Emile*, p. 311.

15. *Contrat social*, book 1, chaps. 2–4; *Discours sur l'inégalité*, vol. 3, pp. 183–184.

16. *Contrat social*, book 3, chap. 15.

17. *Les Confessions*, pp. 325–326.

18. *Contrat social*, book 1, chap. 9; *Discours sur l'inégalité*, pp. 177–178, 189; *Lettres de la Montagne*, vol. 3, book 9, pp. 891–892.

19. *Contrat social*, book 2, chap. 11.

20. Ibid., book 1, chap. 9.

21. *Emile*, pp. 324–325; *Notes sur "De l'esprit,"* vol. 4, p. 1129.

22. *Discours sur l'inégalité*, pp. 160–162, 170–174.

23. Ibid., p. 188 et passim; *Contrat social*, book 1, chap. 2; *Emile*, pp. 491–492, *Rousseau juge de Jean-Jacques*, vol. 1, pp. 811–812.

24. *Emile*, p. 251.

25. *Contrat social*, book 1, chaps. 1–3; book 3, chap. 10; *Discours sur l'inégalité*, pp. 177–179.

26. *Contrat social*, book 1, chap. 8.

27. Ibid., book 1, chap. 1; book 2, chap. 6; *Discours sur l'économie politique*, vol. 1, p. 248.

28. *Contrat social*, book 1, chap. 6.

29. Ibid., book 1, chap. 7; book 2, chaps. 4, 6; book 3, chap. 16.

30. *Emile*, p. 461.

31. *Discours sur l'inégalité*, pp. 222–223, note 29; Ralf Dahrendorf, "On the Origin of Social Inequality," in *Philosophy, Politics and Society* (2nd series), ed. Peter Laslett and W. G. Runciman (Oxford: Basil Blackwell, 1962), pp. 88–109.

32. Lucio Colletti, "Rousseau as Critic of Civil Society," in *From Rousseau to Lenin*, trans. John Merrington and Judith White (London: New Left Books, 1972), pp. 143–193.

33. *Lettres de la Montagne*, vol. 3, book 9, pp. 881–890.

34. *Contrat social*, book 2, chaps. 1, 11; *Discours sur l'inégalité*, pp. 176–181.

35. *Contrat social,* book 2, chap. 3; book 4, chap. 1.

36. Ibid., book 2, chap. 11; *Projet de Constitution pour la Corse,* vol. 3, pp. 909–910, 939.

37. *Contrat social,* book 2, chaps. 12, 13; *Lettres de la Montagne,* book 9, pp. 891–892.

38. E.g. Isaiah Berlin, *Two Concepts of Liberty* (Oxford: Clarendon Press, 1958).

39. *Economie politique,* pp. 245–246; *Contrat social,* book 3, chap. 2.

40. *Economie politique,* p. 244; *Contrat social,* book 2, chap. 2.

41. *Economie politique,* pp. 258, 272–277; Corsica, pp. 924, 931; *Discours sur l'inégalité,* pp. 176–181, 191.

42. *Economie politique,* pp. 262–263, 272–273, 276–277; *Corsica,* pp. 916–917, 920, 924–925, 931.

43. E.g. C. B. Macpherson, *Democratic Theory* (Oxford: Clarendon Press, 1973), pp. 157–169, and *The Real World of Democracy* (Oxford: Oxford University Press, 1972), pp. 23–24, 56–67.

44. *Discours sur les arts,* passim; *Observations,* pp. 36–79.

45. See J. G. A. Pocock, *The Macbiavellian Moment* (Princeton, N.J.: Princeton University Press, 1975).

46. *Lettre à d'Alembert,* pp. 20–21, 33–34, 77–79; *Préface à "Narcisse,"* vol. 2, pp. 963–972.

47. Herbert Marcuse, *One Dimensional Man* (Boston: Beacon Press, 1964), pp. 56–74.

48. *Lettre à d'Alembert,* pp. 99–100; *Corsica,* p. 925; *Emile,* p. 251; *Economie politique,* p. 264.

49. *Lettre à d'Alembert,* pp. 80–82; *Discours sur les arts,* p. 29; *Observations,* p. 52–53; *Dernière réponse,* vol. 1, pp. 72–73.

50. *Lettre à d'Alembert,* pp. 44, 103–105, 168–176.

51. *Préface à "Narcisse,"* pp. 952–963, 972–974.

52. *Corsica,* p. 936; *Economie politique,* pp. 259–261, 276–277.

53. *Contrat social,* book 3, chaps. 10, 11, 18.

54. Ibid., book 3, chaps. 2, 4, 8; book 4, chaps. 1, 3.

55. Ibid., book 3, chaps. 5, 6.

56. Ibid., book 3, chap. 15.

57. Ibid., book 2, chap. 4; book 3, chap. 6.

58. Ibid., book 3, chaps. 11–13; book 4, chap. 5.

59. Ibid., book 3, chap. 3; book 4, chap. 1.

60. Ibid., book 3, chap. 18; book 4.

61. Macpherson, *Democratic Theory,* p. 184, is one example among many.

62. *Contrat social,* book 3, chap. 15.

63. Ibid., book 4, chaps. 11, 12.

64. Michael Zuckerman, *Peaceable Kingdoms* (New York: Vintage/Random House, 1970), pp. 65–72, 93–102, 154–156 et passim.

65. *Contrat social,* book 3, chap. 9.

66. *Lettre à d'Alembert,* pp. 80–82; *Corsica,* p. 914.

67. *Contrat social,* book 2, chaps. 3, 12.

68. *Lettre à d'Alembert,* pp. 168–171, 179–184.

69. E.g. *Economie politique,* p. 242.

70. *Les Rêveries,* vol. 1, pp. 1040–1049, 1159.

71. See John Charvet, *The Social Problem in the Philosophy of Rousseau* (Cambridge, England: The University Press, 1974) for an excellent critique of this aspect of Rousseau's thought.

72. *Contrat social,* book 2, chap. 11.

73. *Lettre à Christophe de Beaumont,* pp. 950–951; *Contrat social,* book 2, chap. 6.

74. *Emile,* pp. 509–510.

75. Richard Hofstadter, "North America," and Peter Wiles, "Symptom not a Doctrine," in *Populism,* ed. Ghita Ionescu and Ernest Gellner (London: Weidenfeld and Nicolson, 1969), pp. 1–27, 166–179.

76. *Ebauches des Confessions,* p. 1150.

77. Hannah Arendt, *On Revolution* (New York: Viking, 1965), pp. 68–76, 83–87.

78. I am much indebted to Clifford L. Orwin's unpublished Harvard Ph.D. dissertation, "Humanity and Justice: The Problem of Compassion in the Thought of Rousseau" (1976).

79. *Discours sur l'inégalité,* pp. 154–156, 170, 176–177; *Emile,* pp. 503–548.

80. *Les Confessions,* pp. 163–164.

81. *Les Rêveries,* pp. 1051–1055.

CHAPTER SIXTEEN

Jean D'Alembert and the Rehabilitation of History

One of the great problems of Enlightenment thought was to find an appropriate place for history among the sciences. This preoccupation has often been dismissed as a sign of a lack of "historical spirit" in most *philosophes*. The absence of "historism" did not, however, imply an indifference to or a willful ignorance of the past.[1] On the contrary, they were deeply interested in accurate information about other ages and in the possible uses of such knowledge. History was, however, both an epistemological and moral puzzle because there was no obvious location for it on the map of the sciences. It was difficult to justify history in the eighteenth century because genuine knowledge was supposed to be both certain and useful, and it was far from obvious that history was either one.

Jean d'Alembert (1717–1783) has been long recognized as particularly important among those who tried to offer answers to the pressing questions raised by history, but his contribution to the theory of history has not been fully appreciated.[2] That is partly due to his general eclecticism. He was above all a mathematician, and only secondarily a man of letters. While he wrote some remarkable essays about historiography, he composed no concentrated treatise on the subject. And while he considered the history of any subject he treated, he did not write a single work of historical scholarship. Nevertheless, as part of his work as an encyclopedist and as a theorist of science he was forced to confront the history of ideas directly. In his capacity as the permanent secretary of the Académie Française he felt, moreover, obliged to memorialize the life and work of its recently deceased

This chapter is reprinted with permission from the *Journal of the History of Ideas* 41 (1981): 643–64.

members. That unavoidably forced him to defend both the scientific and social status of biography and of the history of ideas generally. For not only did a significant part of his public doubt the value of these endeavors, d'Alembert himself at times showed little respect for history. Yet, he did ultimately restore history to a more secure and dignified position in the world of learning than any that it had occupied for over a century.

By the middle of the eighteenth century traditional history had suffered a century of massive abuse. D'Alembert's occasional contempt was quite normal and owed much to his admired predecessors, Descartes and Locke. When he spoke of history as idle entertainment suitable at most for teaching moral lessons to children, he was only repeating what he had learned from some of his forebears.[3] However much these two differed on other subjects, they were remarkably at one in their views on history. Most books on history were nonsense and, in any case, most book-learning was a waste of time. The only knowledge worth acquiring was self-generated. Of the two charges the latter was the more devastating, since even sensible history is largely second-hand information, but the first was damaging also. What could be more condescending than Descartes's remark that a little history is good for us because it saves us from a narrow parochialism? A little learning is quite enough, however, for even the most truthful historians are so given to exaggeration that they endanger one's realism and common sense.[4] Locke at least thought that an english gentleman who expected to enter public life should know the history of his own country. History is, after all, "the great mistress of prudence and civil knowledge." Nevertheless, he was unhappy about the moral impact of historical literature. It glorified cruelty. For what were all those celebrated conquerors but "the great butchers of mankind"?[5] Severe as these strictures may seem, they do not utterly condemn all history to oblivion. The possibility of a reliable and morally useful history remains open. Even Descartes implicitly accepted at least the historical element inherent in the very pursuit of science. He expected future scientists to build on his work. Science is a collaborative effort in which scientists depend on their predecessors even though they must critically re-examine the latter. It is indeed a pity that ancient philosophy had been so falsely represented to us, but if one now reports one's own work carefully, such errors could be avoided in the future. That is why he, Descartes, had after much inner doubt decided to publish his researches. Science, in short, writes its own history and so forms a link between past, present, and future.[6] Descartes may not even have recognized this continuity or scientific heritage as a form of history. It was altogether new, but it was to be one of the overt objectives of the *Encyclopédie* as a work of history, according to d'Alembert. Characteristically, he added that there was much curiosity and sheer vanity in that hope.[7] The lure of fame was clearly not unknown to scientists, but it might be a good thing. The notion of a new epic had already occurred to Locke. Political society may be dominated by "butchers," but "the commonwealth of learning is not . . . without its master builders." They were Boyle, Sydenham, Huygenius, and, of course, "the incomparable Mr. Newton."[8] Without the ancestral piety of the Romans there was no reason to write their kind of monumental history, but to praise these truly great men, scientists all, might be as edifying as the record of battles was degrading. That also was to be one of the aims of the *Encylopédie*. The victory of the moderns over the ancients did not mean the end of memory, but rather its redirection. The critique of traditional history did not preclude the creation of a new kind of history, new in its subject matter, in its greater reliability and, above all, new in its aims. Contemporary history thus became very important. It would secure for future generations history worth knowing.

The most serious obstacle to any possible history was raised by the doctrine of systematic doubt. History is not direct experience. It depends on information, on documents and artifacts that must, to some minimal degree at least, inspire trust in the historian. It is derivative knowledge and it is neither clear nor certain. For Descartes that was a decisive flaw. His program for the future of knowledge had no room for political history. Custom must be rejected entirely and everything be grounded solely on one's own opinions. These could emerge only after one had washed all received opinions out of one's mind. The world must be thought anew and one begins with knowledge of self to read the great book of the world.[9] History cannot survive such a declaration of individual self-reliance. One can repeat scientific experiments, but history is a matter of trust. This part of Descartes's philosophy flourished, for it was reinforced by Locke at every turn. Who ever scoffed more effectively than Locke did at those who "read, and read and read on yet make no great advance in knowledge?" Because they depend upon the erudition of other men, they let their poor minds be "bound by citations and built upon authority."[10] Indeed, "the floating of other men's opinions in our brains makes us not one bit more knowing, though they happen to be true."[11] The trusting man is simply a fool. This was independence indeed. Knowledge was not worth having unless it began in direct experience. Then it could be stored in one's memory to form one's intellectual capital, honestly acquired and entirely one's own. That it must be merely probable knowledge did not trouble Locke as it would have disturbed Descartes. Probable knowledge was "sufficient to govern our concernments."[12] A Lockean might endure the relative uncertainty of historical knowledge at least, but he could not bear its submissiveness, its dependence on other minds. History had been expelled from the "commonwealth of learning" only to await further blows.

Descartes's and Locke's polemic was certainly directed at sacred history, but not exclusively or directly. That task was reserved for Bayle and biblical criticism generally. From the critical examination of traditional ecclesiastical history it moved on to what Bayle called "historical Pyrrhonism." His review of all that was unreliable and unbelievable led him to doubt everything except a few basic historical facts. The same impulse led more pious historians to reject everything save the revelations of the Holy Spirit.[13] It was also shared by Voltaire, d'Alembert's immediate predecessor as heir to Descartes's doubts and Locke's hopes for an alternative history. Although he claimed that he was not an "outré" skeptic, Voltaire was certainly haunted by Bayle's skepticism. He saw no particular reason to doubt that a city called Peking existed, but he would not wager his life on it.[14] Because he put so much passion and effort into the discrediting of miracles and every other sort of traditional religious and classical lore, he fell victim to an overwhelming state of suspicion. As an historian Voltaire often could not bring himself to believe anyone or anything. The mission of his age, as he saw it, was to destroy error.[15] Nevertheless, he did write history because he recognized that the means of recovery were at hand. Voltaire did much to establish rational procedures for historical research. Because he found it so very difficult to accept mere probability, he devised rational ways to mitigate it. One must authenticate documents, judge the reliability of witnesses, doubt all oral evidence committed to writing long after the event, and one must never accept accounts of events that are out of the common course of nature.[16] Methods for the protection of the historian against fraud were also safeguards against the despair of perfect doubt. Moreover, Voltaire had hoped to be the creator of a new kind of history, social and intellectual, which would be broad in scope, elevating and accurate. It would deal with the experiences of peoples rather than wars.[17] In practice his historical writings fall very far short of his proclamations. The arts receive far less space than the wars of the great patron-king in *Le siècle de Louis XIV*. There are only a few pages devoted to daily life and customs and a very great many to popular superstitions and to royal politics in *Essai sur les moeurs*. That is not really surprising, since Voltaire admired "the great" and especially kings. He could never believe that Tacitus was reliable because it seemed to him incredible that emperors should be so monstrous.[18] But d'Alembert was perfectly ready to believe the worst about rulers. He deeply admired Tacitus's message and translated him carefully even though he thought him too rhetorical.[19] Kings and courtiers were, in his eyes, a corrupting menace as patrons of the arts. He was therefore never tempted to write their history as his older friend had been.[20] In fact, throughout their gossipy correspondence history is never seriously discussed, and although d'Alembert often praised Voltaire's historical writings, he never explained their merits in any detail.[21] He did share Voltaire's severe skepticism and the urgent need to overcome it, but he looked to other intellectual models for practical instruction.

Voltaire was not the only advocate of a renovated history. Leibniz, Fontenelle, and Condillac proposed the same program without suffering from debilitating doubts, and d'Alembert learned much from them, directly and indirectly. Fontenelle (1657–1757) especially had done as much as Voltaire to discredit the fables that passed for historical facts. He was, however, perfectly confident that reliable history could be, and indeed had already been, written, most notably by Leibniz. In extending the scientific spirit to historical studies Leibniz had, according to Fontenelle, provided so sound an account of the past that it provided the means for making predictions about the future.[22] History had, in short, already joined the other advanced sciences. Nor did Fontenelle entertain doubts about the usefulness of history. A mere recital of the facts was not enough, but historians who linked natural causes and effects explicitly could tell us much about human motivation. History was applied psychology. To achieve that it must learn to deal with ordinary people. For the scientific study of conflict, Fontenelle noted, a lawsuit between two bourgeois is just as important as a war between princes.[23] D'Alembert was to agree with most of these views, but he could never share Fontenelle's or Leibniz's serene optimism.[24] The notion of history as a predictive science plays no part in his thought.

Fontenelle's real importance was his contribution to the history and glorification of science. As permanent secretary of the Académie des sciences he not only contributed to the writing of its history but also wrote the *éloges* of those of its members who had died since 1699. These memorials were entirely his own invention. The history of other academies, notably Bishop Sprat's, existed and speeches in honor of academicians were not unknown. There had, however, never been anything quite like Fontenelle's regular series of reviews of the achievements of notable scientists. Other academies did not have them, his predecessors did not deliver them, and he was not obliged to write them as part of his official duties. The genre was entirely the invention of this gifted nephew of the great Corneille. The fact that the Académie had just become a more open society with sessions open to the public probably inspired him, for it gave him the opportunity to promote the fortunes of science and to present scientists as heroes of the intellect.[25] He certainly knew that these were "lay funeral orations" designed to replace a solemn religious rite.[26] They were clearly intended to raise the intellectuals to a new and superior social level, one comparable to that of the highest clergy. In setting out and praising the characteristic virtues of scientists these *éloges* were also meant to encourage solidarity and cooperation within the republic of science. Finally, Fontenelle hoped that young scientists would be moved to emulation by the example of their distinguished elders and so ensure the progress of science and the triumph of the moderns over the ancients.

The style of these *éloges* mirrored the very qualities that Fontenelle expected scientists to cultivate: seriousness, simplicity, refinement, and an impersonal, selfless devotion to science. Sainte-Beuve quite justly admired them for their "grandeur of spirit spent on great matters." They were "exact, spiritual, and serious," as Fontenelle claimed his subjects had been.[27] Theirs were not, very obviously, the aristocratic or princely virtues. Cassini cared more for the progress of science than for personal glory, while Homburg's style was notably simple, methodical, and without superfluity. Viviani's Régis', and Lémery's *éloges* mentioned the simplicity of their manners.[28] These were the social virtues needed for unity among scientists, the end which the academies were meant to achieve and which became constantly more urgent as specialization advanced. With less optimism d'Alembert as usual came to share Fontenelle's program for ordering the social world of the intellectuals.

The social cooperation of scientists and the use of history as a way of promoting intellectual unity among the sciences became particularly important when the belief in the inherent oneness of science waned. Leibniz had still believed in the Cartesian notion of a single truth, a universal science, from which all others would be deduced. He thought, however, that until that unity was known, all existing kinds of knowledge should be organized in a convenient encyclopedic form. For d'Alembert the metaphysical unity of science remained a very faint hope, probably beyond human intellectual powers. He therefore turned to the encyclopedic scheme as the only practical way to preserve a semblance of order among the sciences.[29] The history of science—both as a way of unifying the diverse sciences and of celebrating the fame of the great genii of science—replaced the now untenable metaphysics of a universal science. History for d'Alembert had both a moral and an intellectual function in the republic of learned men. The history of science, accurate in form, with the pursuit of truth as its content was obviously worthwhile, even if it was limited in scope.

Voltairean skepticism and Fontenelle's confidence in history generally and in its uses for the enterprise of science particularly were not d'Alembert's only inheritance. It was complicated by a third author whom he admired far more, Montesquieu, "the legislator of nations" as he was to call him.[30] As that compliment implies, Montesquieu was not interested in the history of daily usages and customs for their own sake or as an alternative to the history of governments. They were to be studied as part of the rise and fall of states. His broad generalizations were remote from the specificity that Voltaire and Fontenelle demanded. Lastly, Montesquieu was not interested in praising great men, least of all intellectuals. L'Esprit des lois is highly impersonal and is addressed to lawmakers and to their critics. It was not compatible with Voltaire's or Fontenelle's purposes, yet d'Alembert was wholly convinced of its usefulness and philosophic importance. It was the great textbook of applied psychology and of "moral causes," and if it was neither predictive nor certain, it was an immensely instructive book. It did not deal with men who pursued truth; it was not exact. On the contrary, it was a tale about errors and it was often vague. Epistemologically it did not meet the standards for a respectable science. It did, however, fulfill one task of history admirably: to warn men against tyranny and superstition and, above all, it made sense out of the chaos of politics.[31] Nevertheless, it rendered the science of history more problematic for d'Alembert. History was supposed to meet two philosophical ends, certainty and utility, but the two were not identical.[32] The new Tacitus seemed to demand a reconsideration of the nature of historical knowledge because he widened the gap between them.

Montesquieu had never been troubled by the doubts that tormented Voltaire. He had chosen an intellectually far less hazardous course. He could escape unending self-interrogation because he did not devote himself to the systematic destruction of historical errors. He could concentrate on the creation of his kind of new history, sociological and philosophical, without incessant doubts. That did not earn him Voltaire's admiration.[33] It also disturbed d'Alembert who was only too familiar with Descartes's, Locke's, and Bayle's misgivings, both philosophical and practical. His first reaction to *L'Esprit des lois* was, therefore, predictably hostile. Montesquieu's book, he wrote to a friend, "resembles those physical dissertations . . . where the author explains phenomena so easily that he could just as well have explained completely different phenomena by the same principles."[34] He eventually absolved Montesquieu from that mistake, but he thought that all other authors who attempted to write about the rise and fall of empires were given to just such abuses. They were like "demonstrative chemists" whose causes can produce any set of effects whatever.[35] How can one know historical causes at all? The smallest incident which no contemporary would notice or bother to record might produce the most momentous consequences. That certainly is one of the difficulties of Cleopatra's nose. Given the defective materials with which historians work, how can effects be traced to their causes? It is all highly conjectural.[36]

Then there is the problem of distinguishing moral from physical causes. D'Alembert entirely agreed with Montesquieu that there were moral causes at work in history. Climate was far from accounting for everything. The only way, however, one can impute moral causes to events is by observing their physical manifestations, that is, human actions, which may have any number of psychological origins. How does one get to moral causes then? D'Alembert saw the difficulties of social history clearly enough, but could find no way of overcoming them.[37] His admiration for Montesquieu's work was, nevertheless, intense once he could accept its inevitable guesswork. Mainly he was impressed by the historical use of physical psychology, and by its moral and political implications. He was obviously convinced by the theory of climate and the related notions of national character. The article he wrote for the *Encyclopédie* on these topics is essentially a summary of and a tribute to Montesquieu. The theory of climate had a sound empirical basis, and one of d'Alembert's collaborators was to give a more detailed review of it than Montesquieu had.[38] There was plenty of medical evidence to back up the latter's observations. Even *Sauerkraut*, it seems, is healthful for some people in some places! The study of populations that Montesquieu presents is thus a contribution to physiology. It also helps one to separate long-term general from short-term particular causes in history. The immediate causes are clearly more "moral," political in character, and therefore more open to speculation than the climatic influences.[39] Given a man of impartiality, circumspection, and probity, however, even this part of history can be of immense value, "a series of experiments on mankind." We are in the realm of group psychology here, but it is not the scientific accuracy but the utility of this kind of history that continued to earn d'Alembert's praise. Scientifically, he observes, it is just as unreliable as medicine and just as necessary. It also holds out the same hope: we need both as our only chance for finding a cure for our afflicted condition.[40]

Montesquieu's glory is political and moral rather than scientific, for like a good physician he has to be content with hit-or-miss methods. The more facts a physician or a historian has, the better off he is, but facts without theory are simply pointless. The mere recital of data, history uninformed by philosophy, is the very least of "the human sciences" in d'Alembert's view.[41] His approach is not, to be sure, an invitation to forget the evidence but to remember the purpose of history: to know mankind, not to gather information for its own sake.[42]

Merely piling up accurate information, especially about antiquity or the past generally, d'Alembert regards as useless erudition. At times he thinks one should respect all forms of knowledge; at other times he is sure that we already know all that is worth knowing about antiquity.[43] Surely we should be more selective in what we choose to remember. Perhaps one should pick out the really useful facts every hundred years and burn up the rest.[44] In the history of the exact sciences, this process takes place spontaneously. Errors are simply forgotten. That is why, as the sciences become more perfect, the history of science becomes shorter. Who records mere opinions and errors in mathematics? It does not have a history of sophisms.

Montesquieu's history was certainly speculative, but it was not random, for as Condillac had said of his own history, "the art of conjecture has its rules."[45] When d'Alembert raged against the practices of current historians, it was not their selectivity that he deplored but their aimless erudition. If the moral and political lessons of history were compensations for its lack of rigor, then intelligent selection, such as Montesquieu's sophisticated real order amid apparent confusion, must be the model.[46] The trouble with most readers of history was that they were not ready for that kind of history. They were people who were unwilling to think, even if they were not prepared to vegetate entirely. They tended to turn their backs on the good historians in favor of unedifying recitals of errors and wars that were simply not worth remembering.[47] At times d'Alembert was utterly exasperated. History was good only for children whose moral principles were not yet set. After thirty it was useless. To the young it should, moreover, be taught backward, from the present to the past, so that they might see its relevance to their own time.[48] For the rest, history was just idle curiosity.

Even though most of what the public received was of obscure origin or made up by authors, history could be reformed.[49] D'Alembert would not join those "sad Diogenes" who shunned history altogether because he recognized that philosophical history "instructs, consoles, and encourages us."[50] His answer to the "bitter critics of history," however, also suggested that "facts not verbiage" would effectively reform historical literature.[51] Rigorous history based on accurate chronology, geography, authentic documents, artifacts, monuments, and especially memoirs and letters would render it truthful. And still following Voltaire, an elevating content would dignify it. The *Encyclopédie* explicitly omitted saints' lives, genealogies of noble houses, and the lives of conquerors, all of which low subjects were of no use.[52] D'Alembert never tired of calling the roll of great names from Galileo to Boerhaave. These were the real heroes of the human spirit that history was to celebrate.[53] He agreed with all that Fontenelle had claimed for them. Their history could be both true and useful. The history of science is the history of a very few men of genius in each epoch. They are an inspiration to new scientific experiments and their history a direct service to science, to the pursuit of truth. Science is a self-correcting process, slow work, possible at all for only a very few men, and work that becomes ever more difficult as the sciences advance.[54] Most of the history of science is recent history, and as scientists leave accurate accounts of their labors it is easy to write true history. In all these ways the history of science is true and good.

Accurate and improving as the history of science is, it does not and cannot touch our public consciousness. In what ways does rigor console us, or even broaden our sympathies? Diderot drew the obvious conclusion. He did not care how good or bad the evidence was if history turned its readers into heroic defenders of freedom.[55] Rousseau began his inspired account of the origins of human inequality by simply putting the facts aside.[56] For d'Alembert such an easy solution was impossible; he was certain that truthfulness and utility would have to be combined. The easiest way to achieve that was to argue that enlightenment was bound to ensure general progress. The more men knew the better they would become. D'Alembert did in fact hope that this was the case, but he did not see it as a law of development or a certainty. It was only a possibility, and history was not the record of past gains and the vision of future glories. He was given to neither gloom nor hope about the future of mankind. Civilization was thin ice. He welcomed amateurs, he once noted sardonically, because they make it less likely that we shall relapse into barbarism, "our natural element."[57] Even without a complete relapse, civilization was a matter of ups and downs, an exchange of gains and losses. The image of the ocean waves that deposit something on the shore, but also take something out again, appealed to him. New knowledge could often be destructive. The growth of the critical spirit, for example, so good for the sciences had stifled poetry.[58] Truth was certainly preferable to error, but its moral and social advantages remained to be proven.[59]

What was the moral place of rigorously factual history? The Voltairean program applied to the history of science and of learning generally had its own distinct moral advantages, different and apart from the political lessons of Montesquieu's conjectural history. The former stimulated intellectual growth while the latter educated political man. For d'Alembert there was another moral benefit. He did not want merely to promote the reputation and social standing of intellectuals, as Fontenelle and Voltaire had, but also to raise their standards of conduct. The pursuit of truth has immediate effects upon the character of scholars; it makes better persons of them. The impact of geometry upon the mathematician is direct. It molds his mind into a finer form. That much was implicit in Descartes's *Discourse on Method,* and d'Alembert greatly expands upon it. Mathematicians, unlike artists or men of letters, do not depend upon the public for approval. They are their own judges and so are peculiarly self-sufficient. They pursue the truth for its own sake and for the certainty it imparts, and they would be as happy with that on a desert island as in Paris. Of all men, they, and they alone, achieve a rational autonomy.[60] The rest of the republic of letters is not fortified against the temptations of patronage. Artists and authors work for an audience, which tends to degrade them to a servile dependence on their public, especially the rich and powerful. Scientists are not amusing and so do not attract the interest of idle patronage. The frivolous do not pursue mathematicians.[61] These happy circumstances are not, however, all; it is not just the absence of temptation that preserves the independence of mathematicians. Mathematics is inherently purifying. "La géométrie," he wrote in his eulogy of Jean Bernoulli, "est pour ainsi dire la mesure la plus précise de notre esprit, de son degré d'étendue, de sagacité, de profondeur, de justesse. Si elle ne peut nous donner ces qualités, on conviendra du moins qu'elle les fortifie, et fournit les moyens les plus faciles de nous assurer nous-mêmes et de faire connaître aux autres jusqu'à quel point nous les possédons."[62] The great mathematicians deserve to be remembered because they embody the essence of what is good in the human spirit. If material utility were really what we prized, d'Alembert went on to say, we should honor manual laborers and soldiers. If we were really to do that and forget the great mathematicians, then we would put an end to civilization. Geometry may be of no obvious use, but mathematicians are far from frivolous in their profession. They are all that stands between us and barbarism which is so natural for us. What emerges here is that personal autonomy and civilization are ends in themselves to which the pursuit of truth contributes. That is how truth becomes morally useful.

D'Alembert did not think that the probity that marked the pure mathematician could be shared in its entirety by other intellectuals. That was because geometry is our only example of what perfectly certain knowledge is like. Geometry is our sole intimation of what perfected science might be. D'Alembert could not give up the idea of a single truth from which all others must follow. His empiricism was therefore always uneasy. It is because we are intellectually too feeble to perceive that one truth that we can only hope to approximate it by pursuing individual sciences in terms of the principles inherent in each. The more facts we can gather and organize, the more complete the sciences become. That does not, however, alter their inherent instability. If we could see the truth whole, it would be like geometric knowledge in its clarity and certainty, but such omniscience must elude us forever.[63] What we can and should do is to imitate and approximate the geometric model. The *Encyclopédie* was meant to do just that. By showing all the interconnections among the individual sciences it would give us a vision of the whole, even though it was a very imperfect one. To be sure, it was also to remind us of the purely conjectural state of most of our knowledge. Even the highest degree of probability is not a demonstration of truth. For historical knowledge that means that even its high level of uncertainty is not a difference in kind from the other empirical sciences. There is no special reason to worry about whether Caesar existed. It also meant that historical knowledge, however speculative, had its place in a whole that we could never quite reconstruct. Finally, there was a political message in this acceptance of the merely probable. As long as no one knows, everyone has a right to enjoy the most "extreme liberty" of expressing his own opinions.[64] Geometry remains a moral and intellectual beacon in this wilderness because of its certainty. It disciplines scholars and sets the standards for all scientific work.

Conjectural knowledge, however, also has its moral advantages. It teaches us our limitations and invites moderation.[65]

D'Alembert's commitment to certainty has often been misunderstood.[66] It is said that he was so infatuated with certainty that he could accept nothing between it and utter skepticism. In fact, d'Alembert saw himself as the guardian of conjectural knowledge not only in his encyclopedic labors but also in his defense of the less rigorous kinds of history. What really disturbed him was the tendency to treat probable knowledge as if it were certain. That did not mean that conjectural knowledge was of small value. Montesquieu's kind of history and medicine were necessary if they were appreciated properly and not misused. But uncertain knowledge should inspire caution, especially when applied to public policy.

D'Alembert was not alone in drawing a very sharp line between certainty and probability. Voltaire did so also. He took the Abbé de Prades severely to task for arguing that if all Paris claimed to have witnessed something, a miracle for example, then it was a certain truth. Only mathematicians are certain and truth is not a matter of majority votes.[67] Voltaire did, however, regret that probability was all one could achieve, and he would have liked to render all knowledge immediately more nearly certain. D'Alembert, on the other hand, was afraid of premature mathematization of probabilities and of the pseudo-certainty that it might engender. Undoubtedly, his low esteem for literary men in general did nothing to lessen his worry about their hasty desire to apply the newly discovered calculus of probability to daily life. He knew that our only hope for fairness in courts of law, as in daily life, depended on the probity and decency of the judges, not on mathematical calculations. Voltaire, however, could not settle for that, and he was immediately anxious to see that the new calculus of probability be applied to judicial evidence. In practice, these efforts to attach mathematical weights to evidence in judicial proceedings were no better than the old system of fractional proofs against which he and Beccaria had so rightly protested.[68] Doubt was for Voltaire a weapon against the Church, not a principle to live by. He railed against d'Alembert's lack of zeal even though the latter was, in his quiet way, a very determined *philosophe*.[69] Condorcet, in his eulogy of d'Alembert, continued to reprove his dead friend for his caution in attacking prejudice. D'Alembert was in fact singularly devoid of autocratic impulses. He did not like to dictate, which was quite in keeping with his acceptance of all the psychological and social implications of living in a permanent state of doubt. If everything is conjectural, one must respect common sense, be sure of one's facts, practice forbearance, and be perfectly tolerant. Condorcet did not particularly care for such a temper. D'Alembert, he noted, pushed rigor and fact-finding too far. He was too fond of geometry and its manner of thinking and therefore thought of the human spirit as too limited in its scope, especially in matters of morals and politics where there were few if any certain principles. It was not a very generous eulogy.[70]

Condorcet's strictures had their roots in d'Alembert's critique of the calculus of probabilities. D'Alembert had noted that the connection between mathematical and physical probability was assumed, not proven. From this he concluded that the mathematical calculation of probable truths did not render them more certain or make them a surer guide to practical conduct. In the art of practical conjecturing, mathematics is useless.[71] He even criticized Bernoulli for a futile effort to apply mathematics to human physiology.[72] It is now generally agreed that however poorly he presented his argument d'Alembert was quite right: there was no proof that the laws of mathematical probability accurately describe the physical world. The moral and social implications were for him especially worrying, for he knew where to expect trouble. The application of the calculus of probability to social policy was not limited to the judicial process. It was also suggested that it justified making inoculation against smallpox compulsory. The chances of dying from the disease could, after all, now be exactly proven to be so much higher than the likelihood of dying from the inoculation. The theory of infection being still unknown, this was not a proposal to prevent the spread of the disease but to save the ignorant and superstitious from themselves. D'Alembert strongly approved of inoculation, but he was utterly opposed to the use of compulsion. When one's own life is at stake, everyone must be left free to make his own decision as he may see fit. He warned especially that orphans and abandoned children under public care should not be made the object of medical zeal.[73] Even Condorcet was moved by the plea to recognize that in this case an "exaggerated patriotism" would have infringed upon the rights of the individual.[74] It was not he, however, but d'Alembert who raised his voice against this proposal, one may assume because his own helpless childhood made him more sensitive. That may also have contributed to his dislike and fear of the social and political ambitions of the intellectuals, whose general outlook he shared in most respects and with whom he lived amicably enough.

Such views about the art, rather than the science, of conjecturing have considerable bearing on history such as Montesquieu's. Common sense was everything in this highly conjectural field, and mathematics could do nothing here. The philosophy which d'Alembert urged upon historians was really only a general critical spirit, with which Montesquieu was already amply endowed. Philosophy can teach careful methods of weighing evidence, but history also teaches philosophers how to make the most of insufficient factual materials. If history cannot compete with the sciences, given its low store of reliable facts and the unlikelihood of making new discoveries, it remains valuable as an incomparable school of wisdom. It shows us what men are by revealing to us what they once were.[75] It is the master of common sense, and it is of supreme importance that we develop that faculty because we must not overstep it. Hence the greatness of Montesquieu whose inspired guesses did not need the misapplied support of mathematics.

These precepts also guided d'Alembert's own practices as an historian. His task was, like Fontenelle's, to write notices of the life and work of former members of the Académie Française of which he was the permanent secretary. While he recognized Fontenelle's achievement as the real inventor of these panegyrics, he did not wish to imitate him entirely. He found Fontenelle's style mannered, too familiar, and too informal.[76] The real difference was, however, that d'Alembert had to eulogize many people who were completely undistinguished. The members of the Académie des sciences were all bona fide scientists, while the Académie Française, like most purely literary societies, was not so selective. The question of how truthful he should be was therefore a far more pressing one for d'Alembert than it had been for Fontenelle. The obligations of an historian to posterity were for him a real burden. He could not simply sing the virtues of scientific man. In fact, he wrote the *éloge* of only one mathematician; all the others were more or less literary men. D'Alembert was determined not to prevaricate under any circumstances. If the work of a dead member was bad or his life disgraceful, just pass over it in silence, he advised.[77] Leave out the bad, but do not invent virtues. The Abbé de Saint-Pierre was remembered for his total lack of common sense and his poor style as much as for his good intentions.[78] Other *éloges* are tellingly brief. "I write your history and not your eulogy," he wrote of Jean Bernoulli.[79] The Abbé Dubos's only notable achievement was to have been refuted by Montesquieu.[80] Fléchier was only a second-rate orator.[81] Truthfulness, even when tempered by tact, was not d'Alembert's only achievement. He knew that he was using history as a replacement for a religious rite. He even claimed that Massillon would have preferred to write history instead of his celebrated *oraisons funèbres.*[82] The two were for d'Alembert competing ceremonies, defining two wholly incompatible views of man's destiny. History was meant for posterity, and it demanded accurate biographies in order to study mankind carefully and scientifically. On occasion d'Alembert, perhaps remembering Tacitus's biography of Agricola, parts of which he had translated, dwelled on the pettiness, especially that of the court, which threatened but did not overwhelm remarkable men such as Bossuet or Fénélon. These were, however, not models to be emulated by the young, such as Fontenelle's subjects had been. The biographies of intellectuals should be just as unflattering as those of kings if that was deserved.[83] D'Alembert was not only serving future historians, he was also reminding intellectuals to consider their future reputations. History had its disciplinary uses. Here accuracy and didactic purpose meet.

The history of science, the history of men of learning, and philosophical political history all have their diverse uses and aims. In the *Encyclopédie* all were to come together, the certain and elevating as well as the psychologically and politically conjectural, for d'Alembert here developed a new notion, history as the science of man, that could embrace them all. In the end he was able to bring a measure of coherence into the conflicting tendencies he had inherited. History as the science of man illustrates the pattern by which men learn. Everything that can be called knowledge at all, whether certain or merely probable, has its place here. That makes history more than a form of moral education. The notion of an encompassing history may well have come to d'Alembert from Condillac's belief that change begins in the human spirit and is then reflected in mores which in turn determine politics.[84] In d'Alembert's version the process of learning is a psychology of intellectual change which, with all its ups and downs, is an historical framework within which all knowledge and conduct find a place. As an encyclopedic umbrella, history is not merely good for us. History can make an integral contribution to knowledge in general. It can serve as a method of organization, a way to order our otherwise overwhelming stock of facts.

History is our collective remembering and that mental faculty is a far from passive one. Memory is passive, a mere attic, but without it all our other knowledge is useless to us. Remembering is active. The retrieving from memory what has been stored up is, like perception, an activity of the human mind without which there could be no human understanding. Memory is indeed the mother of all the muses, as the ancients had said, d'Alembert recalled.[85] It inspires work. Considerations such as these led him to assign to history, as active remembrance, a central place in the universe of knowledge. These new functions were not related to the moral and political uses of history, but they were scarcely less important. The sheer amount of history in the *Encyclopédie* is staggering. Most topics seem to have their history. D'Alembert and Haller introduced their discussions of individual sciences with a brief historical outline even if other authors did not do so. Some sciences did not have much of a history to recite, and most of d'Alembert's articles dealt with aspects of specific sciences that required merely definitions. However, whenever possible, he did mention the work, especially of antiquity, that preceded the present state of a science.[86] Even the history of previous encyclopedias and the debt the latest one owed to them received due attention.

Whether he discussed physics, literature, academies, or the expulsion of the Jesuits from France, d'Alembert had always found it necessary to begin with a history. How can one understand the character of a religious order, or a system of patronage, or the structure of a learned society without first presenting its history? How else can one organize what one knows about it? How else is one to place it and explain its present status?[87] The need to write history, whether of the sciences or of social groups, was forced upon d'Alembert by the imperatives of systematization, of which the *Encyclopédie* was the ultimate and most expansive expression. It was history designed to retrieve all knowledge and to situate its individual forms. As such, it assumed the very style of its subject matter. D'Alembert strove to eliminate every trace of rhetorical embellishment from his narrative and to make it as plain, as unadorned, and as close to scientific exposition as possible.[88] Here his debt to Fontenelle's style became very evident, for their intentions coincided.

Encyclopedic organization required more history than prefaces to the main subjects. Active memory, remembering, was needed to grasp the totality of available knowledge. The Baconian universe of knowledge followed the three main faculties of the human mind: memory, reason, and imagination, which engendered history, philosophy, and the arts respectively. The first, however, played a part in each of the others. It was the storehouse of each, and in the act of remembering it played a decisive part in every development.[89] It also had the very special task of organizing the unified whole. From a purely philosophical perspective all knowledge should be seen as a single interconnected whole, as a chain. The philosopher stands above the whole and gets a bird's-eye view of all the relationships that bind the sciences into a single unit. He can do that even without knowing that single truth that forever escapes us. The encyclopedic organization of knowledge follows this pattern through a system of exhaustive alphabetical listings which are linked by a complete system of cross-references. And each link and each branch of knowledge has its history, thus giving history an expansive character that d'Alembert had not originally foreseen. It could not be confined to one of the three categories into which he had tried to divide all knowledge.[90]

When he defined history directly, d'Alembert had sliced it into three segments. First there was sacred history, then the history of man, civil and intellectual, and finally natural history. The last covered both the order of nature and the use man made of it. The history of the human intellect was, however, of a peculiar kind, since it embraced all knowledge whether it be imaginative, mnemonic, or rational. Art, history, and science properly so-called all fell within its realm. Indeed, they fell into both an historical and a parallel psychological sequence. The arts, most sensual, come first, then imaginative belles-lettres, and finally, philosophy and science, expressions of the critical spirit. This series does not show any sort of progress; indeed, there are real losses here as dry reason seems to destroy the inspiration of the fine arts. The work of history, it becomes clear, escapes definition as a separate or isolable topic because remembering is not just memory—it is active. Any reasoned dictionary, even a purely grammatical one, must be a philosophical history pursuing its subjects from their infancy to their maturity, and on to their old age and decline.[91] The tree of knowledge grows, whether as the accumulated work and virtue of great men of science or as the work of obscure mechanics; knowledge increases through the ages and acquires an even longer past. Remembering these achievements, the historian in his work provides the only way to bring the growth of knowledge to our present consciousness, to give us any view of the whole and all its parts.

D'Alembert's replacement for a discredited tradition of history has its peculiarities. In the history of science there is no enduring place for the history of fraud and errors which become eliminated as non-knowledge. Such centennial discarding of useless facts that d'Alembert had suggested makes perfectly good sense here. His new history was not to be confused with mere traditionalism, as much of nineteenth-century "historism" was. Philosophical history was to be a master science.[92] As the organizer of human knowledge generally, it could not just preserve the whole past as equally precious. It had, moreover, to embrace an endless future, for the childhood of the sciences is long, or to be exact, eternal.[93] History cannot, given its purpose, keep such a mass of matter in perpetual consciousness. If one knows, as d'Alembert did, what the uses of history are, then one can choose information that is worth remembering and periodically eliminate the worthless from the scholarly memory. There are things that might well be fit for forgetting if they do not help us to order our moral and intellectual conduct.

The intense concern for the usefulness of history may not, in practice, be helpful to the working historian, but it led d'Alembert to find a commanding place for history among all the other forms of knowledge. He provided an answer to the outstanding questions about historiography, an answer which allowed history to survive and grow in a scientific intellectual climate. He also suggested reasons why the history of ideas generally, and of science particularly, has a special function in the world of knowledge, where it was not only a member but a master.

Notes

1. For the notion of Enlightenment historiography as merely preparing the way for genuine history: Friedrich Meinecke, *Historism*, trans. J. E. Anderson (New York, 1972). The *philosophes* were not concerned to explain the growth of such "individual" wholes as nations and classes within the development of world history, which was to become the mark of post-Napoleonic historiography, as particularly well described by Otto Hintze, "Troeltsch and the Problems of Historicism" in *The Historical Essays of Otto Hintze*, ed. Felix Gilbert (New York, 1975), 368–421. The defense of the Enlightenment's approach to history, on which I have relied, is to be found in Ernst Cassirer, *The Philosophy of the Enlightenment*, trans. F. C. A. Koelln and James Pettegrove (Boston, 1951), 197–233. Peter Gay, *The Enlightenment*, 2 vols. (New York, 1966 and 1969), and esp. Georges Gusdorf, *L'avènement des sciences humaines au siècle des lumières* (Paris, 1973).

2. Cassirer, *op. cit.*, singled him out, but mostly as a step toward Kant's philosophy of history. The best treatment of d'Alembert as a historian of science is Georges Gusdorf, *De l'histoire des sciences à l'histoire de la pensée* (Paris, 1966), 47–92.

3. "Collège," *Encyclopédie ou Dictionaire raisonné des sciences, des arts et des métiers* (Paris, 1751–65), III, 632–38; "Erudition," *ibid.*, V, 914–15.

4. René Descartes, *Discours de la méthode* in *Oeuvres et Lettres*, ed. André Bridoux (Paris, 1949), 95.

5. John Locke, *Some Thoughts Concerning Reading and Study for Gentlemen* in *Works* (London, 1823), III, 296–97; *Some Thoughts Concerning Education*, IV, 182–84, 116.

6. *Discours de la méthode*, 134–44.

7. *Discours préliminaire de l'Encyclopédie* in *Oeuvres Complètes de D'Alembert* (Geneva, 1967), I, 36.

8. *An Essay Concerning Human Understanding* in *Works*, I, 1.

9. *Discours de la méthode*, 97–98, 101–04, 110–11; *Règles pour la direction de l'esprit, ibid.*, 7–19 *et passim*.

10. *On the Conduct of the Understanding* in *Works*, III, 24, 250–52.

11. *Essay*, I, Bk. I, ch. IV, 2–3, 79.

12. *Ibid.*, Bk. I, ch. I, 6, 4–5.

13. For the historical doubts of believing Christians, see R. R. Palmer, *Christians and Unbelievers in Eighteenth Century France* (Princeton, 1947), 67–76, and generally Paul Hazard, *The European Mind*, trans. J. Lewis May (New Haven, 1953), 29–52, 106–14, 162–67, 185–97.

14. "Le Pyrrhonisme de l'histoire," *Ouevres Complètes de Voltaire* (Paris, 1877–85), XXVII, 235; "Histoire," *Dictionnaire Philosophique*, XIX, 346–70, and "Certain/Certitude," *ibid.*, XVIII, 117–21, which dealt mostly with historical uncertainty.

15. "Le Pyrrhonisme," 236–37.

16. In a letter to a fellow historian Voltaire claimed that in writing *Le siècle de Louis XIV* he had consulted all the available personal memoirs as well as the reports of the intendants, "Voltaire à Jean Baptiste Dubos, 30 octobre, 1738," *Voltaire's Correspondence*, ed. Theodore Besterman (Geneva, 1954), VII, 424–28. More generally his program is set out in "Histoire," *loc. cit.*, and in *Encyclopédie*, VIII, 220–25; J. H. Brumfitt, *Voltaire Historian* (Oxford, 1958), 32–34, 84–86, 98–104, 136–47 *et passim;* H. T. Mason, *Pierre Bayle and Voltaire* (Oxford, 1963), 128–33 *et passim*.

17. Brumfitt, *op. cit.*, 48–70; Paul Hazard, *op. cit.*

18. "Le Pyrrhonisme," 356–61.

19. "Réflexions sur l'histoire," *Oeuvres*, II, 6.

20. The difference in their attitudes to "the great" put a strain on their relations generally and made d'Alembert quite cautious in his dealings with Voltaire. See John N. Pappas, *Voltaire and d'Alembert* (Bloomington, 1962), *passim*.

21. E.g., "Discours préliminaire," 79–80.

22. "Eloge de Leibniz," *Oeuvres Complètes de Fontenelle* (Paris, 1818), I, 228–35.

23. "Sur l'histoire," *Oeuvres*, II, 424–35. For Fontenelle's general approach to the social sciences see Leonard M. Marsak, *Bernard de Fontenelle: The Idea of Science in the Enlightenment* in *Transactions of the American Philosophical Society, N.S.*, 49, Part 7 (1959), 40–59.

24. D'Alembert in general had a low opinion of Leibniz, for the same reasons that made Voltaire ridicule him. See W. H. Barber, *Leibniz in France* (Oxford, 1955), 156–58, 176. Fontenelle was admired but also criticized for superficiality and pliancy, "Eloge de la Motte," *Oeuvres*, III, 137–41.

25. These remarks owe much to a private communication from Professor Roger Hahn; see also his *The Anatomy of a Scientific Institution: The Paris Academy of Sciences 1666–1803* (Berkeley, 1971), 35–57.

26. Gusdorf, *De l'histoire des sciences*, 55. An unpublished paper by George A. Kelly, "The History of the New Hero: Eulogy and its Sources in Eighteenth-Century France," expands on this challenge to religion.

27. *Causeries de Lundi* (Paris, n.d.), I, 392–94.

28. *Préface de l'histoire de l'académie des sciences, depuis 1666 jusqu'en 1699* in *Oeuvres*, I, II; "Eloges," 176–77, 200–01, 65, 95, 193.

29. Robert McRae, *The Problem of the Unity of the Sciences: Bacon to Kant* (Toronto, 1961), 69–88, 107–22.

30. "Eloge de Montesquieu," *Oeuvres*, III, 499.

31. *Réflexions sur l'histoire* in *Oeuvres*, II, 7; "Mémoires et réflexions sur Christine, reine de Suède," II, 120.

32. *Elémens de philosophie* in *Oeuvres*, I, 127–28; "Apologie de l'étude," *Oeuvres*, IV, 9–10.

33. "Lois (Esprit de)," *Dictionnaire Philosophique*, XX, 1–15; "Commentaire sur quelques principales maximes de L'Esprit des Lois," XXX, 407–64; Brumfitt, *op. cit.*, 116–21.

34. Unpublished letter quoted in Thomas L. Hankins, *Jean d'Alembert: Science and the Enlightenment* (Oxford, 1970), 81.

35. *Réflexions sur l'histoire* in *Oeuvres*, II, 7.

36. "Eloge de Montesquieu," *Oeuvres*, III, 448–49.

37. "Causes Finales," *Encyclopédie*, II, 789–90.

38. Montesquieu, in fact, shared many of d'Alembert's concerns about causality in history and psychology, e.g., "Essai sur les causes qui peuvent affecter les esprits et les caractères." *Oeuvres Complètes*, ed. A. Masson (Paris, 1955), III, 397–430. But this essay remained long unpublished.

39. "Climat" and "Caractère," *Encyclopédie*, III, 533–36.

40. "Elémens des sciences," *Encyclopédie*, V, 491–97. This is a truly splendid essay, a summing up of d'Alembert's entire philosophy. Why he changed his mind about Montesquieu is not clear, but it was not merely because of the latter's anticlericalism.

41. "Mémoires et réflexions sur Christine, reine de Suède," *Oeuvres*, II, 119.

42. "Apologie de l'étude," *Oeuvres*, IV, 7–9.

43. "Erudition," *loc. cit.*; "Discours préliminaire," *Oeuvres*, I, 55–56, 61–62, 75.

44. "Mémoires . . . sur Christine," *Oeuvres*, II, 119.

45. "Histoire ancienne," *Oeuvres de Condillac* (Paris, 1798), IX, 20.

46. "Eloge de Montesquieu," *Oeuvres*, III, 450–51.

47. "Réflexions sur l'histoire," *Oeuvres*, II, 1; "Essai sur les élémens de philosophie," *Oeuvres*, I, 127; "Discours préliminaire," *Oeuvres*, I, 79–80.

48. "Collège," *loc. cit.*

49. "Réflexions sur l'histoire," *Oeuvres*, II, 1–3; "Apologie de l'Etude," IV, 5–8.

50. "Réflexions sur l'histoire," *Oeuvres*, II, 5; "Discours préliminaire," I, 36–37.

51. "Elémens des sciences," *loc. cit.*; "Essai sur les élémens," *loc. cit.*, I, 168–74, 346.

52. The *Encyclopédie* explicitly refused to concern itself with these topics. "Préface au troisième volume de l'Encyclopédie," *Oeuvres*, IV, 389. D'Alembert used this occasion to insist that usefulness, not just certainty, must be a standard in selecting the subject matter for discussion (*ibid.*, 391).

53. *Ibid.*, and esp. "Discours préliminaire," *Oeuvres*, I, 63–78.

54. "Elémens des sciences," *loc. cit.*; "Essai sur les élémens," *loc. cit.*, *Oeuvres*, I, 123.

55. Gay, *op. cit.*, II, 385.

56. "Discours sur les origines et les fondemens de l'inégalité, parmi les hommes," *Oeuvres complètes* (Paris, 1964), II, 132–33.

57. "Discours préliminaire," *Oeuvres,* I, 81–82.

58. *Ibid.,* 78–79; "Réflexions sur l'usage et sur l'abus de la philosophie dans les matières de goût," *Oeuvres,* IV, 396–97; "Essai sur les élémens," I, 121–23. See generally René Wellek, "The Price of Progress in Eighteenth Century Reflections on Literature," *Studies of Voltaire and the Eighteenth Century* (1976), 155, 2265–84.

59. It was an expression of this faith that led d'Alembert to argue that the people should be told the truth about religion. Voltaire considered it too dangerous, but d'Alembert thought that it could and should be done with tact and slowly. See Lester G. Crocker, "The Problem of Truth and Falsehood in the Age of the Enlightenment," *Journal of the History of Ideas,* 14 (1953), 575–603.

60. "Apologie de l'étude," *Oeuvres,* IV, 10.

61. "Essai sur la société des gens de lettres et les grands," *Oeuvres,* IV, 341, 348–50.

62. "Eloge de Bernoulli," *Oeuvres,* III, 354.

63. "Elémens des sciences," *loc cit.;* Ronald Grimsely, *Jean d'Alembert* (Oxford, 1963), 222–45; Hankins, *op. cit.,* 104–31; Keith M. Baker, *Condorcet* (Chicago, 1975), 99–109. D'Alembert also believed that there were stable standards of beauty and taste even if only very few people could ever grasp them; see Dennis F. Essar, "The Language Theory, Epistemology and Aesthetics of Jean d'Alembert," *Studies on Voltaire and the Eighteenth Century* (Oxford, 1976), 106–12.

64. "Essai sur les élémens," *Oeuvres,* I, 173–76; *L'abus de la critique en matière de religion,* I, 553.

65. "Portrait de l'Auteur, fait par lui-même," *Oeuvre,* I, 9. "Essai sur les élémens, *loc. cit.,* 127–28.

66. E.g., Arthur M. Wilson, *Diderot* (New York, 1972), 431.

67. "Certain/Certitude," *loc. cit.;* Gay, *op. cit.,* II, 379; and Mason, *op. cit., passim.* For Prades see "Certitude," *Encyclopédie,* II, 845–62.

68. "Essai sur les élémens," *loc. cit.,* 167–68; Baker, *op. cit.,* 231–35.

69. Grimsely, *op. cit.,* 113, 293; John N. Pappas, *Voltaire and d'Alembert,* 33–41; *Essai, op. cit.,* 137–50.

70. Condorcet, "Eloge de d'Alembert," *Oeuvres de d'Alembert,* I, i–xxviii.

71. "Doutes et Questions sur le calcul des probabilités," *Oeuvres,* I, 451–66. "Essai sur les élémens," *ibid.,* I, 157–80; Hankins, *op. cit.,* 146–49; Baker, *op. cit.,* 171–80.

72. "Eloge de Bernoulli," *Oeuvres,* III, 358.

73. "Réflexions sur l'inoculation," *Oeuvres,* I, 467–514.

74. Condorcet, "Eloge de d'Alembert," *loc. cit.,* xx–xxi.

75. "Eloge de Montesquieu," *Oeuvres,* III, 448–49.

76. "Réflexions sur les éloges," *Oeuvres,* II, 152; "Eloge de La Motte," *Oeuvres,* III, 171–74.

77. "Réflexions sur les éloges académiques," *Oeuvres,* II, 150–53.

78. "Eloge de Saint-Pierre," *Oeuvres,* III, 255–58, 262, 274–75.

79. "Eloge de Bernoulli," *loc. cit.,* 164, 338.

80. "Eloge de Dubos," *ibid.,* 208.

81. "Eloge de Fléchier," *ibid.,* 325.

82. "Eloge de Massillon," *ibid.,* 223.

83. "Eloge de Perrault," *ibid.,* 238.

84. "Histoire ancienne," *Oeuvres*, IX, 3–6, 20–22. Isabel F. Knight, *The Geometric Spirit* (New Haven, 1968), 224–25, 267–69.

85. Locke, *Essay, ed. cit.*, Bk. II, Ch. X, *Works*, I, 137–43; "Discours préliminaire," *Oeuvres*, I, 51, 103–04.

86. Nelly N. Schargo, *History in the Encyclopédie* (New York, 1947), 141–53 *et passim*. Lynn Thorndike, "L'Encyclopédie and the History of Science," *Isis* 6 (1924), 361–86. For the extremely technical and definitional character of d'Alembert's contribution see John Lough, *Essays on the Encyclopédie* (Oxford, 1968), 230–51. More generally, Jacques Proust, *L'Encyclopédie* (Paris, 1965), 106–41.

87. "Essai sur les élémens," *Oeuvres*, I, 337–42; "Discours sur l'expulsion des jésuites," *ibid.*, II, 15–27; "Essai sur la société des gens des lettres," *ibid.*, IV, 337–39; "Description du Gouvernement de Genève," *ibid.*, IV, 411–15.

88. Peter France, *Rhetoric and Truth in France, Descartes to Diderot* (Oxford, 1972), 96–112; Ralph S. Pomery, "Locke, d'Alembert and the Anti-rhetoric of the Enlightenment," *Studies of Voltaire and the Eighteenth Century*, 154 (1976), 1657–75.

89. "Discours préliminaire," *Oeuvres*, I, 43–53.

90. Hugh M. Davidson, "The Problem of Scientific Order Versus Alphabetic Order in the Encyclopédie," *American Society for Eighteenth Century Studies*, 2 (1972), 33–49; Hankins, *op. cit.*, 105–08.

91. "Discours préliminaire," *Oeuvres*, I, 40–42, 48. "Essai sur les élémens," *ibid.*, 123–26; "Dictionnaire," *Oeuvres*, IV, 494–95, 500–01.

92. "Elémens des sciences," *loc. cit.*

93. "Expérimental," *Encyclopédie*, VI, 299.

CHAPTER SEVENTEEN

Bergson and
the Politics of Intuition

Political theory is not an independent realm of thought. Ultimately it must always refer back to some metaphysical presuppositions of *Weltanschauung* that is not in itself political. This does not imply that every metaphysical position entails logically necessary political consequences. But it does mean that implicitly or explicitly political theories depend on more general religious, epistemological, and moral considerations. This condition of political thinking serves to explain much of the narrowness of contemporary political theory. For the dominant currents of philosophy neither can, nor wish to, provide a basis for political speculation, which is increasingly regarded as an undisciplined form of self-expression. On the other hand, the naive hope that political studies might fruitfully emulate the methods of the natural sciences, and so share their success, has all but evaporated. The result is that political theory is now concerned to insist on its own limitations, to be critical and even negative in character. This is not a new thing. The lack of philosophical inspiration combined with the decline of "scientific" aspirations has plagued politically sensitive minds at least since the very beginning of the present century. And, from the first, one of the responses to this frustration has been the effort to escape philosophical difficulties by grasping at intuitive short-cuts to truth. The most remarkable of these flights to intuition was political Bergsonism. Moreover, this is not an entirely closed chapter in the history of ideas. Even if Bergson no longer enjoys his earlier popularity, he is still widely read, especially in America. Again, the recent vogue of existentialist "politics" points

This chapter is reprinted with permission from the *Review of Politics* 20 (1958): 634–56.

to an analogous trend, while the penchant for "action," which is inherent in intuitive politics, is as strong as ever among French intellectuals.

These considerations alone lend continuing interest to Bergson and
his followers. There is, however, another issue that merits attention.
In recent years there has been a concentrated attack upon "scientism." It has largely been conservative, inspired by fears of social engineering and its totalitarian possibilities.[1] As such it is more in the
nature of a critique of contemporary thought in terms of the religious
or philosophical principles of earlier times. It cannot in any way be
regarded as a genuine renovation of political thought. Bergson and
his followers, however, did try to create a political philosophy on the
very basis of "anti-scientism." It led them to conclusions which are
wholly abhorrent to the contemporary critics of "scientism." Nevertheless, as the only attempt to make "anti-scientism" the essence of
a new philosophy, Bergsonism is of continuing interest—if only, perhaps, as a warning.

Bergson was not primarily a social philosopher. Indeed much of
his work explicitly excludes any consideration of the social world in
an effort to reach intuitively the truths that lie in the inner being of
man. Yet this essentially personal and poetical philosophy had its
most serious repercussions in the realm of social theory. And this was
all but inevitable; for Bergson alone in his time seemed to offer a
philosophic alternative to the then universally popular worship of
"scientific" ideas about society. In our own day the sudden popularity
of existentialism has much the same escapist motivation. In any case
not only Sorel and the syndicalist movement, but such distinguished
minds as William James and Charles Péguy grasped at Bergsonism
as the last hope of a desperate age. What then was the essential character of Bergson's thought; why did it have so enormous an influence;
and what were the political ideas that it sponsored?

Bergson was not a philosopher's philosopher. Both in origin and
in expression his ideas were essentially literary in character. His place
is among that long line of French essayist-philosophers which
stretches from Montaigne to Sartre in our own day. As such he has
always aroused misgivings among more strictly technical thinkers.
Today most readers would probably concur in Lord Russell's early
verdict that he was simply a poet in prose, heaping image upon image
without much philosophic meaning.[2] This was, moreover, not an accidental feature, a matter of careless expression. His method was an
integral part of this thought. For Bergson was in every sense a romantic thinker—if that term is taken in its broadest sense. Certainly he

did not borrow directly from the early German romantics such as Schelling, though his affinity to them has often been noted.[3] Rather, the cast of his mind was essentially similar to theirs. His romanticism is to be found above all in the fact that his entire philosophy is an effort to provide an aesthetic substitute for a lost religion and an emotionally unacceptable science. In line with this pervasive aim he made a constant effort to limit the functions of reason and intelligence and to substitute "intuition" for them. And Bergson's intuition was just that quality that Coleridge had called the "creative imagination." The supreme model for all human activity was artistic creation, and the artist was a god among men. Individuality, originality, and creativity, these were the highest qualities for Bergson no less than for all romantics. Now this aestheticism is the positive aspect of his as of all romantic thought. And it was the aesthetic conception of man that had to be guarded against the scientific approach to human nature.

Unlike many other romantics, Bergson was not an *homme revolté*, enraged by an inevitably philistine world. The tenor of his writings is remarkably gentle. Nevertheless, the final impression left by his works is that, except for aestheticism, he had no positive conceptions, that he was the philosopher of moods, not of ideas. It was in his attacks upon the modern heresies, upon materialism, positivism, and relativism, upon all determinism in ethics and history, that he was most cogent. His positive ideas, his "substitutes" for science, amount to little more than nicely phrased metaphors. But, for all that, Bergson was not just "anti-scientific," as many other romantics, notably Nietzsche and Sorel, have been, simply scorning science and scientists as purposeless and disagreeable. He quite explicitly noted that he valued modern scientific inquiry and knowledge. What he did dislike was "scientism," or the effort to transfer the methods appropriate to the natural sciences and to mathematics to philosophy in general. His great design was to liberate philosophy from its subordination to science. Above all, he resented the Spencerian habit of imposing the data of biology upon social theory and psychology. For Bergson science and philosophy were "two ways of knowing"—opposed to each other yet complementary.[4]

If Bergson was not crudely anti-scientific, neither was he a simple irrationalist, who proposed to "think with his blood," or to prize instinct at the expense of the mind. Intuition too was, for him, an expression of the mind's activity, a way of apprehending truth.[5] Indeed, he saw in the work of the intelligence itself a contrast between critical and inventive impulses.[6] The whole history of philosophy, in fact, seemed to him to illustrate this division. For, in spite of the preponderance of rationalists among French philosophers, there had always been thinkers inspired by the "ésprit de finesse," of whom Pascal was the greatest.[7] It was the defense of this tradition against what he, rather archaically, could still regard as the "geometric" spirit in science and philosophy, that he saw as his main task. The revival of philosophy, in fact, involved first of all the transformation of philosophical thought itself. And this change was ultimately profoundly anti-intellectualist, if not irrationalist, in character. Neither reason nor analysis were to dominate philosophy. Thought was to become "creative." "Invention and renovation," not explication, were to be its objects. True understanding was participation in the creative process, an intuitive sympathy with life, something like an artistic effort.[8] Above all, it is not reflection but reliving. It was this aspect of Bergson's thought that particularly attracted William James. Schooled in the sciences, so obviously endowed with common sense, James longed for a philosophy that would also permit the imaginative, and even mystical, side of his nature to express itself. He, like Bergson, wanted somehow to *feel* reality, not just to describe its appearance, to analyze it. "Intuitive sympathy with a thing," he noted, in a Bergsonain vein, "alone is the way to *really* know it." Bergson, he gratefully acknowledged, had led him "to renounce the intellectualistic method and the current notion that logic is an adequate measure of what can and what cannot be."[9] "Conceptual logic," that is, analytical reason, no less than science, was to be assigned a very limited scope.

Logic, moreover, was for Bergson and James part of the strangling hold that "ready-made" concepts have upon our minds. To penetrate the truths of inner experience, to be able to participate in "the ocean of life" is possible, only if we can free ourselves from ideas imposed upon us from without.[10] Above all, Bergson insisted that the symbols and conventions of society, and especially society's instrument, language, must be shaken off. For they cast "a veil" over our individuality and hide it from us.[11] Only if we "turn away from the social vision" of reality can we hope to penetrate it by an original insight.[12] And here the real weakness of philosophy as intuition reveals itself. For an inner apprehension of truth that is ineffable, unobstructed by the bonds of logic or communal expression can hardly be called philosophy. The incommunicable may or may not have its place in poetry, but what is a philosophy that cannot be uttered? It is pointless. In fact, it is non-existent.[13] At least it is very hard to conceive of this as "the search for wisdom."

Romantic and aesthetic urges, however, inclined Bergson to conceive philosophy as a form of artistic endeavor. Indeed, all genuine reality was a process of growth and invention and the artist as a creator participates in reality as he creates it. It is thus that he, above all others, becomes the revealer of truth and so the best model for the philosopher. As to the nature of true reality, however, we are left in the dark. A process cannot be defined. But by analogy—if only a verbal one—creativity could be achieved in other realms than that of art. Morality, religion, and philosophy by following the example of artistic creation might also reach that end, though it is never explained just how this is to be done. For the very possibility of such a thing is an intuitive insight—inexplicable and incommunicable. Even James was satisfied to rest here, noting only that philosophers were *like* poets in that both were "path-finders."[14]

With this general nexus of ideas Bergson prepared to attack all "mechanistic," that is "scientific," theories of evolution. To him the social application of Darwin's theories was not of primary interest, nor did their departure from the *Book of Genesis* concern him. What disturbed him was that Darwin seemed to deny man's powers as a creator, as an inventor of new things. Not only *should* man be creative, he *was* in fact *homo faber*, and his status as such in the universe was not to be denied. Actually, Bergson was not really discussing the same thing as the biologists. He was not really competent to deal with the biological development of animal species. *Creative Evolution* is a defense of man, the creator, against every theory of man as a mere creation. To this was added a generous dose of mysticism. All life is a creative stream which constantly brings something new into the world. Until the appearance of man, life battled vainly against dead matter, but in human consciousness the victory of life is manifest, since consciousness itself is a form of creativity, participating in life and promoting it by acts of will and genius.[15] Because man is creative and free he is "the terminal point" of one of nature's great efforts, for he alone is capable of giving life a direction, rather than merely submitting to the laws of nature.[16] Now true creation cannot be accidental, and it was this element in Darwin's theory of natural selection that Bergson particularly disliked. On the other hand, teleology or "radical finalism" was equally objectionable, since it limited creativity by setting up a preordained end for man and nature. Lamarck, too, was wrong, for he slighted the uniqueness of man and of human history. How could we identify ourselves with our ancestors, asked Bergson, if we differ as radically from our predecessors as the theory of the inheritance of acquired characteristics would have us believe?[17]

At the root of all Bergson's objections to the various competing theories of evolution was the fact that they tried to be rational, and not intuitive, apprehensions of man's development. Aesthetically conceived, man is the high-point of the universal spirit of creation, for he himself is a creator, not the product, but the conscious participant in the evolutionary process.

The wonder today is that this poetic "answer" to science should have aroused such widespread and intense enthusiasm. "O my Bergson you are a magician, and your work is a marvel, a real wonder in the history of philosophy," William James wrote after reading *Creative Evolution*.[18] Even odder, perhaps, is the fact that both Bergson and James conceived this to be a contribution to the theory of knowledge. Only George Bernard Shaw seems at once to have grasped that here was essentially an attempt to build a substitute religion with strong social implications. Though he never mentioned Bergson, he clearly thought of creative evolution in very similar terms, and more clearly than anyone else he realized what cultural and emotional needs this philosophy satisfied. If he was somewhat hasty in proclaiming creative evolution "the religion of the Twentieth Century," he was more acute than Bergson in recognizing the notion for what it was—a religious effort springing from social and aesthetic discontent.[19] Like Bergson he saw in creative evolution the possibility of infinitely extending the powers of the creative imagination, "an aesthetic striving." He too envisaged evolution as culminating in the victory of the creative spirit, of the effort "to disentangle . . . life from the matter that has always mocked it." But Shaw freely proclaimed that as an artist it was his "natural function" to be "the iconographer of the religion of my time" and his play about creative evolution was meant to fulfill that duty. Religion, moreover, for Shaw had a primarily social import. His greatest objection to Spencer and Darwin was the notion of the survival of the fittest. Comparing Darwinism to Christianity, he wrote with his usual acerbity.

> Miserably as religion had been debased it did at least still proclaim that our relation to one another was that of fellowship in which we were all equal and members of one another before the judgment-seat of our common father. Darwinism proclaimed that our relation is that of competitors and combatants in a struggle for mere survival.[20]

Spencer was repulsive to him on both humanitarian and aesthetic grounds. Like Bergson he particularly disliked the notion of purposelessness in human evolution. Moreover, for anyone concerned, as

Shaw was, with the re-creation of social relations Spencer was an obvious enemy, especially when he saw that the spirit of "scientism" flourished nowhere more than in Fabian circles. Sidney Webb's celebrated contribution to the *Fabian Essays* contains a fulsome tribute to Spencer and his "scientific" approach to social questions.[21] Now the subordination of individual creative effort to the social organism is no less complete in Spencer's than in Marx's theory. Both ultimately stifle the generous impulse in socialism, for the faith in historical inevitability and social necessity replaces the active will of living, individual men and women. Both deaden the spirit of active faith, which Shaw valued so highly.

In the struggle against Spencer, and, indeed, against all "scientism," it was the status of man as creator that was really at stake. And this Shaw saw far less clearly than Bergson and James, for he was no individualist. It was William James who in discarding Spencer went to the heart of this issue.[22] Evolution in history implied a denial of individual greatness. It was an "oriental fatalism." Moreover, the very existence of men of genius made it folly to speak of laws of history. Social change could not, James insisted, occur irrespective of individual effort and initiative.[23] Bergson, too, rejected so-called laws of history. History is the realm of freedom and "the future of humanity (is) indeterminate, precisely because it is on humanity that it depends: . . . ahead of us lie only possibilities or probabilities." If he saw any regularity in history it was a movement of oscillation, of each generation reacting against its immediate predecessor. Progress as a law was, of course, inadmissible, but Bergson did not belong to that school of pessimists who, having lost their faith in the "law" of progress, turn bitterly to a belief in historical cycles or inevitable decline. Progress was likely, but not certain.[24]

Unfortunately Bergson did not rest with this temperate rejection of historical determinism. He was far more radical than that in his departure from "scientism." To him the law of causality applied to history and psychology seemed as serious a denial of human creativity and freedom as the notion of supra-personal social change. As usual, he attacked not only the substance, but also the method of the "mechanists." Not only had Spencer ignored the mystical element of "duration" in evolution, the living consciousness, but he had looked at evolution only as something already completed and fully comprehensible in terms of causes and effects. And this, moreover, led him to believe that the future was predictable, the determined product of past events. To this Bergson opposed the notion of evolution as a free creative act and of history as a living stream, unpredictable and impenetrable to causal analysis. History and evolution are outbursts of creative energy like artistic creation whose final result cannot be known and whose course follows no premeditated course. They are processes that produce possibilities, not realities. That the very idea of such an originality and indeterminism should revolt the intellect Bergson was quite ready to admit.[25] To him, however, the fault rested with the intelligence and with the operations of logic. The historian like the philosopher must become an artist, as both seek to re-invent rather than to explain.[26]

From this point of view not only Comte's vision of a science of society that knows the laws of all past history and can also predict all future events is absurd, but all historical writing that depicts the past in terms of selected causes and effects is false. Now every practicing historian knows that his selection of "causes" is always somewhat arbitrary.[27] It is equally obvious that what seems to us causally significant in the past may not have appeared so at the time of its occurrence, and, similarly, we cannot tell what will seem particularly important in our own time to future historians.[28] Again historical and social knowledge is never complete, but it is of necessity causal knowledge. Change cannot be described or discussed in any other terms. To communicate historical knowledge inevitably means a causal accounting. Bergson, however, like Herder before him, was not concerned with the dissemination or explanation of historical data, but with intuitively experiencing history. A causal analysis of the past was a modification of the past by the present, he complained. And this fault he felt was inherent in all *ex post facto* explanations by means of causes selected to account for later effects. The sin of "mechanical" philosophers of history is to see "the future and the past as calculable functions of the present." For the causes they regard as binding the present and determining the past appear so only from a fixed vantage point in time. Immersion in the "stream" of life, however, obliterates these coercive concepts and frees history and the historian from their limitations.

Now as a critique of historical writing this is nonsense.[29] Even as a philosophy of history it is weak; for it is a denial of determinism, which is followed by no constructive substitute. History ceases to be communicable and the course of events is firmly declared to be out of reason's reach. History is an experience, free, causeless, and unintelligible. His real difficulty with causality was that he assumed that once causality is accepted as a sufficient explanation of the entire past it is a "law" that also binds the future and makes it, potentially at least, totally predictable. This belief was of course almost foisted upon him by the positivists, particularly Comte. That is why Bergson attacked so bitterly "retrospective" logic as a method of speculation about history and evolution. But he went too far in his efforts to defend man's freedom to create his future. If it remains valid that the future of man cannot be studied in the same way as his past, Bergson's indeterminism succeeds only in rendering both past and present impenetrable.

The confusion of indeterminism, freedom, and creativity in Bergson's philosophy of history and evolution is even more glaringly apparent in his ideas on individual freedom. Yet it was particularly for this part of his philosophy that his early contemporaries admired him. And again it was the aim, the saving of *homo faber,* that animated the entire theory. If we are to be creative, "the artisan of our future personalities," we must not be explained away as the effects of either society or biology.[30] The old argument about the freedom of the will resolved itself for him in the insistence that human volition is indeterminate, unforethought, and unpredictable. At its worst this notion means that the very absence of rational purpose is the true mark of freedom.[31] In its more positive aspect it is only the identification of originality with freedom, which is typical of romantic thought. Indeed, Bergson's romanticism is nowhere expressed more clearly than in his conception of freedom. For him, as for most romantics, freedom is to be found in self-revelation, in acting on an impulse that rises from the innermost, unique, purely individual core of one's personality. "(We) are free when our acts spring from our whole personality, when they express it, when they have that indefinable resemblance to it which one sometimes finds between the artist and his work."[32]

Free actions, moreover, are not only personal, they are distinctly nonrational. They occur on those rare occasions when we act in defiance of reason and calculation to follow some inner urge of our hidden self.[33] Above all, freedom can only be felt, not discussed. Definition destroys freedom. It is mysterious, as is the entire process of creation. There is not one concrete example to illustrate this experience of freedom. And one critic has, indeed, been led to argue that this is not human freedom at all.[34] Certainly a form of freedom that defies discussion is not in the realm of social activity. In everyday life freedom depends on the number of genuine alternatives of action open to the individual, not on the possibility of creating a new, future self out of nothing, nor on the occasional moment of self-expression.

It should be obvious that this entire philosophy does not have any direct political implications. Indeed Bergson never wrote on social subjects before the First World War. It was only during that crisis that he made a statement on political matters. Interestingly enough, he followed his usual method of metaphorical discussion on that occasion. France he represented as the force of creation and life, Germany as that of inorganic matter.[35] The War was thus only an instance of the great conflict of the entire universe—which does not do much to explain the events of 1914. And this is not accidental, for, as we saw, Bergson's method as well as his entire stock of ideas was designed to make social and historical analysis all but impossible. Until the thirties he, moreover, gave no further hint about his ethical and political beliefs.

In view of these considerations it is all the more remarkable that in the years before the War he was regarded as the philosophical patron saint of French syndicalism. The editors of its chief organ, *Le Mouvement Socialiste*, actually described themselves as "the Bergsonian left." The exact meaning of this title was, however, none too clear even to its authors. Consequently, in 1911 they sent a questionnaire to several leading philosophers asking their views on the political implications of Bergson's philosophy. There was no trace of agreement among their correspondents. Some answered that there was no political meaning to be found, others saw at most a trend toward some religion of feeling or toward Catholicism in his ideas.[36] Even the greatest of the syndicalist thinkers, Georges Sorel, an avowed "Bergsonian," at one point admitted that his real debt to the philosopher was limited to borrowing his "phrases," but this, as we shall see, was not his usual position.[37] Certainly among contemporary observers Bergson's "irrationalism" was regarded as the very basis of Sorel's politics of violence.[38] It is, of course, always hasty to assume that a description of the processes of nature should also set a standard for political life. There is actually nothing in Bergson that suggests a preference for blind action in society. However, the theory of indeterminism, the notion that we are free when we do not plan or consider our actions, lends itself very well to just such an interpretation. The problem of thinking in metaphors, as Bergson did, is that it leaves interpreters free to extend their meaning to any subject and in any way that they wish without seeming to violate the intentions of their originator. And this is just what Sorel, and, to a lesser degree, Charles Péguy, did. In short, here was a new religious and philosophical inspiration for politics.

It is not in the realm of logic that the reasons for Bergson's instant political appeal must be sought. It is rather in the intellectual mood of France in the years before the First World War that the answer is to be found. The disillusion of the Dreyfusards, the increasing respectability of socialism, the apparently universal complacency, the popularity of Comte's and Spencer's "scientism" all combined to render desperate those restless spirits that longed for a stirring faith to lift them above an uncongenial society. And their desperation was increased by the absence of a viable substitute for the political and religious passions of the past. The romantic mood of that time very clearly had its roots in a social and ideological sense of lostness.

In these circumstances, anything, even Bergson's rather unpromising philosophy, could be grasped as an instrument of salvation. For some, notably Péguy, it was primarily a road to Christianity, but for others, such as Sorel, it could provide a sufficient basis for a new revolutionary movement of both political thought and action. Above all, Bergson, however remote his speculations, was hailed as a liberator by all those who detested rationalism and materialism but could see no acceptable intellectual alternatives anywhere about them. Thus Joseph Lotte, Péguy's Catholic friend, could write that under Bergson's influence "the framework of Taine's *scientisme,* Renan's intellectualism, Kant's moralism was shattered to bits as far as we were concerned. It provided an escape from determinism."[39] And again, Péguy, even after his conversion to Catholicism, continued to feel a powerful need for some vital social faith suited to contemporary circumstances. Protesting against the placing of Bergson's works on the *Index,* he noted that "everything taken away from Bergson will go to Spencer, and not to Saint Thomas." For Saint Thomas belongs irretrievably to the dead past, while "it was Bergson, and no other, who freed us from that metaphysic of the modern world that poses as physics."[40] Bergson had shown him the path he had long yearned for, away from materialism, determinism, mechanism, associationism, and intellectualism. Sorel too was initially drawn to Bergson as an opponent of Spencer. No one detested the application of biological data to society more heartily than Sorel. Indeed, like Nietzsche, he went further than Bergson, and extended his dislike to science and to scientists in general.[41] As a natural revolutionary, moreover, disappointed by the peaceful course of socialist politics, Sorel found a special significance in Bergson's scorn for "mechanistic" thought. For one thing, it meant that revolutions were not, and could not be, "scientific" in the Marxian sense, but had to be "creative." To wait for history to follow its "laws" was suicidal. The faith in progress, similarly, was absurd, based on a false intellectual-ization of history.[42]

Bergson's idea of freedom, also, found its political analogy in Sorel. Freedom in politics, too, is creativity, and is characterized by the absence of premeditation. In short, in keeping with the aesthetic analogy, political creation and freedom, like that of the artist, must emerge from some blind, nonrational inner impulse. Enthusiasm and moral fervor were to replace all political discussion. Unmotivated action was to take the place of conversation and planning.[43] If we were "artists in institutions," society was a work of art, and social action nothing less than the building of an imaginary world. And this, like all true artistic work, was intuitive, not intellectual, active, not contemplative.[44] Sorel's favorite idea, the general strike, was nothing but an inspiration, an emotional impetus for creative action in politics, or, to be exact, away from politics. For all action related to the state is rational and so sterile.[45] Thus, the positive aspect of Bergson's philosophy, the love of creativity and self-expression, remained intact in Sorel's social version. The negative side, the rejection of logic and causality, of the whole work of the intellect, was not only retained but given a new meaning.

Bergson's effort to expunge causality from historical thought was not particularly successful, as we saw. To Sorel, however, it was the most vital part of Bergsonism, the part best designed to serve his revolutionary irrationalism. "Causes," he remarked airily, "are genii."[46] The least attractive aspect of Marxism, the notion that intellectual life is somehow a dependent effect of economic causes, could thus be dismissed as a mere superstition.[47] More important to Sorel, however, was that history could be regarded as inscrutable, and political plans and predictions for the future as impossible. All utopias could be dismissed as empty intellectualist fancies.[48] Purposive social change, in fact, was an illusion. The alternative to Marxism, in short, was most definitely not reform. For Sorel was above all a pessimistic revolutionary. Very much unlike Bergson, his chief inspiration was hatred for the present. And what distinguishes him from most other revolutionaries was that he was not at all concerned with a better future, or indeed with improving society in any way. What he longed for was a display of heroism to destroy the present. Beyond that he did not look. That is why he never stayed long with any political group or persevered in any one set of beliefs.[49] His most famous contribution to political thought, the general strike, was for him not a program, not a means to any social end, but only a display of destructive purpose and an emotional rallying point for the heroic impulses that he saw lying dormant in the labor movement. Any scheme for reform, however, he rejected as intellectualist optimism, a detestable manifestation of the notion that what is logical is also workable, a part of the false faith in progress.[50] Aimlessness was for Sorel an end in itself. It was to him both the truth about history and the answer to all political projects and theories.

If the future was to Sorel the "mystery of mysteries," it did not quite mean that men are doomed to total ignorance of social life.[51] Though reason and logic can never hope to penetrate it, one may have an intuitive feeling for the nature of social reality. Thus the general strike is not a prediction of some logically necessary future event, nor a proposal, but "a profound intuition of the working class movement."[52] Indeed, socialism appeared to him in the form of a Bergsonian truth. The workers express in the general strike, he wrote, an "intuition of socialism that language is not able to give."[53] The difference between Sorel and Bergson here is, of course, that the latter felt that the deepest truths *were* ineffable, while the former thought that they *ought* not to be discussed, but to be expressed in direct action. For action to Sorel was the social representation of intuitive knowledge—an innovation in Bergsonism that was almost inevitable once it was made to serve ideological ends. The real question is whether intuition as such can have any meaning in the study of society, or are Sorel's Bergsonian analogies meaningless? Is there any sense in the notion that socialism must be seen in a Bergsonian way, that "it must be grasped intuitively as an entity, a flow"?[54]

On the whole it seems an empty play upon words. Yet Sorel was by no means the only one to succumb to this danger of Bergsonism. Charles Péguy as he sought to escape from "scientism" fell into the same rhapsodic habit. The way to understand political, economic, and social matters, he insisted, is not by manipulating statistics, but "by taking a few simple facts and penetrating them with an ever-deepening intuition." The doctors with their tables know nothing; only personal, direct experience matters, and this, he admitted, was "incommunicable and inimitable." Nevertheless, to him it was "the great rule in all method."[55] In short, social science was to become personal—in the same incoherent fashion that we already observed in romantic history.

If Bergson did not share his disciples' enthusiasm for an ineffable sociology, it remains true that they followed him in one important respect. They too used analogies as a substitute for explanation. That this did not lead them always to the same ends is not astonishing, since analogies can produce anything that the imagination desires.

The one great departure from Bergson was in applying his images so directly to social categories. The differences that this engendered become most obvious in the conflicting conceptions of heroism and of myths that Sorel, Péguy, Bergson, and James held. All, as true romantics, were deeply devoted to the dream of heroism. All wanted to see a revival of the heroic spirit in the modern age, but for Sorel and Péguy heroism was essentially a social quality, while for Bergson and James, though they saw the need for heroism in society, it remained an individual, even a mystic manifestation. Again both Sorel and Péguy valued myths or mystiques as political religions, while for Bergson myths were a debased aspect of religious life just because they served social ends.

To Sorel myths were necessary as an emotional stimulus to heroism. And heroic and creative action was in his eyes above all nonrational. The value of a myth rested in the fact that it secured the believer against refutation.[56] The general strike was his idea of the perfect revolutionary myth because it was not a scheme, but "a body of images" moving men to action, a means of imposing their collective strength upon the present in purposeless self-expression.[57]

Péguy's attachment to the great political "mystiques" was based not so much on a wish to destroy the imperfect world of the present as on a wish to salvage faith, any faith, as such. But if he did not share Sorel's bitterness, he too was animated by a hatred of the practical everyday world, and this surely was inherent in all Bergson's thought as well. Nor was Péguy complacent about the present. He had a sense of the precariousness of civilization that is reminiscent of Burckhardt. What he dreaded about the modern age was the barbarism of those who believe in absolutely nothing, who have neither political nor religious faith.[58] Politics he disliked just because to him it inevitably meant a cheapening of some mystique.[59] If, unlike most French Catholics, he did not look back to the monarchy, but accepted the Republic, it was the mystique of republicanism, the fervor that had established it that he loved, not the actual institutions of modern France. The crucial experience for him was the Dreyfus Case. The mystique of the Dreyfusards at the height of the battle had been his deepest political emotion, and its degeneracy into parliamentary tactics his greatest disappointment. No less disturbing had been the decline of Jaurès from a social prophet to a politician and orator. These experiences served to inspire a permanent disgust for all politics in Péguy. And what he hated in political life was ultimately just what Sorel disliked, the commonsensical, reasonable bargaining for limited

ends.[60] Péguy wanted an inspiration and a religion, and it never occurred to him that political life was not a suitable place for such emotions. Consequently he, like Sorel, made social irrationalism an end
in itself. It was an escape from both "social science" and practical
politics, as well as a convenient way of defying all powers that be,
without having to offer any substitute.

Bergson was an infinitely wiser romantic. If like Péguy he saw a
glaring contrast between the purity of mystical experience and all
social reality, he never tried, like the former, to introduce pure belief
into the realm of social life, to which, by definition, it was foreign.
He never confused myth and mysticism as Péguy did in his glorification of political mystiques. To Bergson myth was merely the social
function of religion and essentially primitive and uncreative in character. Mysticism, on the other hand, was participation in the very
stream of life, a sharing in the creative principle of the universe.
Myths, however, are the work of the intellect. They serve to quiet
that unrest that intelligence itself creates when it realizes the inevitability of death. Myths organize worship, they are necessary for social
cohesion, and they defend us against the fears and doubts that our
nature abhors. But they remain utilitarian, and social, and as such,
alien to the spirit of mysticism. Above all, myths are "static," not
living and dynamic, as is the creative religion of purely private
belief.[61]

If myths could not be as important to Bergson as they were to Sorel
and Péguy, he too valued the end that social myths were meant to
serve, the revival of heroism. And to this William James heartily
agreed. As to many other romantics, heroism appealed to all these
men as an aesthetic quality, as something beautiful and colorful. To
James and Bergson, however, the beauty of the heroic act was inseparable from the ends it served. To Péguy it was an end in itself, the
living proof of belief in some mystique. And Sorel, alas, tended to
identify heroism with violence. To be sure, he did not admire indis-
criminately every form of brutality. For example, he was certain that
a violent general strike would be free from the blemishes of "idealis-
tic" revolutions. It would be decent, like war, and would not lead to
terror, vengeance, and proscriptions.[62] And one must remember that,
writing before the First World War, he could really have no idea of
what violence and civil war mean today. However, his admiration
of Lenin indicates that the experience of real war did not sober him.

Today this sort of glorification of force seems almost obscene. But
it must be remembered that many people worried about the apparent

decline of the manly virtues in the years before the First World War.
The names of Burckhardt and Nietzsche again come to mind. It was
felt that mankind was gradually slipping into a sheep-like state of
comfortable sleepiness. To the romantic mind, which always tends
to see mankind divided sharply into the creative few and the lazy,
consuming many, it seemed that the total victory of the latter was at
hand. It was just this that made Péguy curse the modern age for positively hating the saint, the hero, and the genius.[63] And in a less extreme way, both James and Bergson were worried by the disappearance of the energetic spirit.[64] But if Bergson regarded conventional
life as inferior to the heroic ethic, he never proposed that conventions
be abolished or even disregarded. And if James longed for displays
of heroic energy he was quite clear in wanting "a *moral* equivalent
of war," not an upsurge of violence.

Unlike Péguy and Sorel, neither James nor Bergson were revolutionaries. Both felt remote from society in some respects, neither felt
the acute romantic loathing for the philistine world. The future that
James foresaw was not so much the faithless desert that Péguy feared,
but an eternity of peace and socialism.[65] Now as a tireless promoter
of peace banquets and other good causes he was by no means disposed to regret this entirely. He was indeed quite appalled by the
bloodthirsty instincts he still saw about him. "The average church-
going civilizee," he wrote, "realizes absolutely nothing of the deeper
currents of human nature, or of the aboriginal capacity for murderous excitement which lies sleeping even in his own bosom."[66] Again
"the rooted bellicosity of human nature" did not escape him. The
"red-blooded party" and those who saw "a religious beauty in war"
disgusted him, especially when they engaged in imperialist adventures. Teddy Roosevelt was his aversion, an overgrown adolescent
spinning "abstractions" about robustness.

Yet no one cared more for robustness than did James. "Pluck"
was the only quality that could "redeem life from insignificance."
However, it could never be admired in isolation. For "if we are all
ready to be savage in some cause" it matters enormously what that
cause is.[67] There was, then, to be no chest-beating for its own sake.
However, peaceful prosperity was softening. We cannot have a "pure
pleasure economy," James protested. A week at Chautauqua bored
him to distraction, and he returned convinced that "security, intelligence, humanity and order" were not enough. And he lamented the
passing of "the higher heroism" and "the old rare flavors." Perhaps
they might be found again in the back-breaking strain of common

labor, but he was not certain.[68] The great need was to preserve the martial virtues by finding something as exhilarating, but not so immoral, as war. And in this Bergson heartily agreed. James's essay on this theme drew the warmest praise from him.

Even after the war he wrote that war was inevitable because "we are made for a life of risk and adventure."[69] Nevertheless he was an enthusiastic supporter of the League of Nations and served as chairman of one of its committees.[70] For Bergson, too, hoped to turn the ardor of heroism to creative purposes. And in the League he saw the one great opportunity for creative political action. However, his conception of heroism was less political even than James's. His real heroes were the "geniuses of the will," the founders and reformers of morality and religion.[71] And just as his entire metaphysic was designed to save the position of the exceptionally gifted man from the forces of physical necessity, so his ethical theory was concerned to place the moral hero above the limitations of his social environment. Such a hero could not be an actor on any political stage, which must necessarily be confining. He was, rather, the man who wants to end all politics, to dissolve "the closed society" and to create that "open society" which embraces all mankind.[72] About moral obligation in general and the moral problems of everyday life, however, Bergson had little to say, except that obligation is felt only rarely when it somehow conflicts with our inclination. He thus dismissed Kant's rationalism as failing to explain morality. To Bergson morality was only a matter of habit, of social conditioning. Kant limited himself to the exceptional case when reason and choice are involved, he claimed. Usually morality is simply convention, the response of one's "social ego."[73] His real concern was with the morality of "aspiration," not that of mere "pressure."[74] There is no avoiding Jacques Maritain's conclusion that Bergson did much to explain moral passions, but little to explain morality itself, and that ultimately he left man caught between "something *social*, infra-rational, and something *mystical*, supra-rational." There is nothing between "the service of society and the call of the hero."[75] And this seems almost unavoidable in any aesthetic morality, which must be indifferent to the commonplace and overwhelmed by the unique instance of greatness.

Creativity is too indefinite a notion to be a standard of judgment in ethics. In political matters it is, if anything, an even more meaningless term. In neither case, moreover, can creativity as such acquire concrete expression in some definable form of behavior. Ultimately any sort of exhibitionism can parade around as creative morality.

That has always been the fate of aesthetic ethics in the various bohemias. In politics it can just as easily mean Sorel's general strike as Bergson's own preference for liberal democracy. Aesthetic criteria unfortunately can have no specific meaning in social philosophy. And this is true even in Bergson's case, though he never indulged in the excesses of artistic politics, accepting sensibly man's social nature, the fact that if "we are in and out" of society, there need be no constant conflict between the hero and society.[76]

The aim of creative politics was not to destroy natural, habitual society, but to rise above it. For by nature we prefer the xenophobic "closed society," and even when we liberalize and humanize political life we remain shut up in conflicting and confining groups. And just expanding these is not enough. The "open society" differs in quality from all known societies.[77] The League of Nations, though he did not overestimate its possibilities, seemed to Bergson a first move toward that society of universal brotherhood. Again, democracy he regarded as the least natural form of society, the one that came closest to the "open society."[78] What the "open society" might actually be like, however, Bergson never ventured to say. Like most of his visions it remained a secret.

Though his political theory suffers from vagueness and impracticality, it is arresting in at least one respect. Most romantic social thought is rigidly elitist. And this is quite natural, since the artist and the creative worker necessarily form a minority in society. If society is to be dominated by the genius and the hero, if it is to serve the creative few, it cannot be democratic. Moreover, democratic government is unsymmetrical and unheroic; it has all those qualities that made Sorel and Péguy hate all politics. Again, democratic theory is deeply grounded in rationalist thought, which is just what romantics most dislike in modern philosophy. The worship of individuality tends to involve a hatred of the masses, and the love of the unique a disdain for the commonplace. Again, those romantics who have gone beyond their concentration on the individual genius have tended to invest some group, a nation, a race, or a class, with the supreme creative grace. The result is almost bound to be illiberal and undemocratic. Bergson, however, almost alone, is a romantic, democrat, and liberal. For all his aestheticism and glorification of the artist, his distrust of common sense and the "social veil" and his sense of the distance between the creative hero and the consuming masses, he remained, in politics, a democrat. In this none of his disciples followed him.

What conclusion can we draw from this survey of an essentially unsuccessful attempt to save historical and social thought from "scientism"? If Bergson's picture of *homo faber* has gone the way of the "rational animal" and the "economic man" it is not because some new and better image has appeared. It is only that creativity as a standard of judgment and a human truth was not enough. It failed as an explanation of human behavior and as an ideal. Again, faith in the "life force" or creative evolution did not succeed in becoming the religion of the century. Born in opposition to the natural sciences, it remained essentially negative. It never interfered with the progress of scientific thought, nor did it supply the positive gratifications of traditional religion. Lastly, indeterminism could not be translated into a philosophy of freedom. For it is social freedom that men yearn for, the opportunity to make effective choices, not the knowledge that their behavior is not subject to the laws of causality. The fact is that an aversion to "scientism," however well founded, is not an answer to the problems of political theory. It is a refutation that does not seem to carry with it any viable proposals for the reconstruction of political thought. Moreover, it is all too easy to confuse "scientism" with every form of accurate research in the social sciences, such as the use of statistics, the exacting examination of institutions and political behavior. Too often the demand for "intuition" is only a desire to indulge in emotional outbursts or in senseless activism. As an antidote to the notions of Comte and Spencer, it may have had its value, but their influence at present is, in any case, negligible.

Aestheticism in politics, on the other hand, still flourishes. For romanticism is endemic in the modern age. It colors all the writings of the various schools of existentialism and the political attitudes implicit in most contemporary literature. Essentially it is rooted in the desire to escape from politics, from the unpoetic realities of everyday social life. It is an apolitical intrusion into the realm of politics, and as such no less uncongenial to those seriously concerned with the problems of political thought and action than is "scientism."

Notes

1. For example, F. A. Hayek, *The Counter-Revolution of Science* (Glencoe, 1952); K. R. Popper, *The Open Society and Its Enemies* (Princeton, 1950); E. Voegelin, *The New Science of Politics* (Chicago, 1952).

2. B. Russell, *The Philosophy of Bergson* (Cambridge, 1914), pp. 15, 24, 33.

3. C. Dryssen, *Bergson und die deutsche Romantik* (Marburg, 1922); A. Lovejoy, "Bergson and Romantic Evolutionism," *University of California Chron-*

icles, Vol. 15 (1913), pp. 429–487; B.-A. Scharfstein, *The Roots of Bergson's Philosophy* (New York, 1943), pp. 4–5, 129–132; H. Bergson, *Creative Mind*, tr. by M. L. Audison (New York, 1946), pp. 33–34.

4. *Creative Mind*, pp. 99–100, 146–149; *Creative Evolution*, tr. by A. Mitchell (Modern Library, New York, 1944), pp. 212–218; J. Chevalier, *Henri Bergson*, tr. by L. A. Clare (New York, 1928).

5. *Creative Mind*, p. 103.

6. *The Two Sources of Morality and Religion*, tr. by R. A. Audra and C. Brereton (Anchor Books, New York, 1954), pp. 44–45.

7. *La Philosophie* (Paris, 1915), p. 7.

8. *Creative Mind*, pp. 17, 102; *Creative Evolution*, pp. 194–195.

9. W. James, *A Pluralistic Universe* (New York, 1909), pp. 262–263, 250–251, 225.

10. *Creative Mind*, pp. 28–29, 57–59; *Creative Evolution*, p. 210.

11. H. Bergson, *Laughter*, tr. by C. Brereton & F. Rothwell (New York, 1911), pp. 150–157; *Creative Mind*, pp. 52, 71.

12. *Creative Mind*, pp. 57–59.

13. Lovejoy, *op. cit.*, pp. 434–435.

14. W. James, *Philosophical Conceptions and Practical Results* (Berkeley, Calif., 1898), p. 4.

15. *Creative Evolution*, pp. 194–203, 261, 287–289.

16. *The Two Sources*, p. 118.

17. *Creative Evolution*, pp. 43–50, 63–64, 71–73, 85–86, 93–96, 99, 113–117, 187–188; *The Two Sources*, pp. 29–30, 82–83, 127. Yet Bergson admired both Darwin and Lamarck, see *La Philosophie*, pp. 9–10.

18. Quoted in R. B. Perry, *The Thought and Character of William James* (Boston, 1935), II, 618. For an account of Bergson's popular success, see Chevalier, *op. cit.*, pp. 60–64.

19. *Back to Methuselah*, "Preface."

20. *Ibid.*, "Preface."

21. Lord Passfield, "Historic," *Fabian Essays*, ed. by G. B. Shaw (London, 1948), pp. 28–57.

22. W. James, *Memories and Studies* (New York, 1912), pp. 107–142.

23. *The Will to Believe* (New York, 1909), pp. 225–226, 232, 242–245.

24. *The Two Sources*, pp. 299, 292–293.

25. *Creative Evolution*, pp. 32–36, 114; *Creative Mind*, pp. 21–26.

26. *Creative Mind*, p. 121.

27. E.g., Marc Bloch, *The Historian's Craft*, tr. by P. Putnam (New York, 1953), pp. 190–197.

28. *Creative Mind*, pp. 21–26, 122–124.

29. *Creative Evolution*, pp. xx–xxv, 17, 43, 105–106, 181–182, 195, 254–256; *Creative Mind*, pp. 12–14.

30. *Creative Evolution*, pp. 8–10.

31. R. B. Perry, *The Present Conflict of Ideas* (New York, 1919), p. 348.

32. Bergson, *Time and Free Will*, tr. by F. L. Pogson (London, 1910), p. 172.

33. *Ibid.*, pp. 167, 169–170.

34. J. M. Stewart: *A Critical Exposition of Bergson's Philosophy* (London, 1911), pp. 254–255.

35. H. Bergson, *The Meaning of the War*, tr. by H. W. Carr (London, 1915).

36. *Le Mouvement Socialiste*, Vol. 29 (1911), pp. 182–183, 267–269; Vol. 30 (1911), 120–123, 266–269; Vol. 31 (1912), 62–64, 132–133.

37. G. Sorel, *De l'Utilité du Pragmatisme* (Paris, 1921), p. 425.

38. See W. Y. Elliott, *The Pragmatic Revolt in Politics* (New York, 1928), pp. 111–113, 115 & 119–120, for an unusually perceptive account of the tenuous basis of Sorel's "Bergsonism." However, see also, R. S. Jaques, "The Significance of Bergson for Recent Political Thought and Movements in France," *Royal Society of Canada*, section II, 1932, pp. 5–12; J. W. Scott, *Syndicalism and Philosophical Realism* (London, 1919), pp. 40, 125–143, 161–163.

39. Chevalier, *op. cit.*, pp. 64–65.

40. Charles Péguy, *Note sur M. Bergson et la Philosophie Bergsonienne. Note Conjointe sur M. Descartes et la Philosophie Cartesienne* (Paris, 1935), pp. 299–300. (My translation.)

41. *Pragmatisme*, pp. 1–2, 123–127, 357–451; "L'Evolution Creatrice," *Le Mouvement Socialiste*, Vol. 22 (1907), 257–282.

42. G. Sorel, *Reflections on Violence*, tr. by T. E. Hulme (Glencoe, Ill., 1950), pp. 57–60; R. Humphrey, *George Sorel* (Cambridge, Mass., 1951), pp. 149–150, 163 & 167.

43. *Reflections*, pp. 144–145.

44. Quoted in R. Humphrey, *op. cit.*, pp. 148–149; "L'Evolution Creatrice," *Le Mouvement Socialiste*, Vol. 23 (1908), pp. 184–194; *Reflections*, pp. 53–56.

45. *Reflections*, p. 277; Humphrey, *op. cit.*, pp. 195–197.

46. Quoted in R. Humphrey, *op. cit.*, pp. 89–90.

47. *Ibid.*, pp. 155–156.

48. Humphrey, *op. cit.*, pp. 99, 153.

49. Humphrey, *op. cit.*, pp. 19–24, 36.

50. *Ibid.*, pp. 95–99, 123–124.

51. Quoted in Humphrey, *op. cit.*, p. 56.

52. *Reflections*, pp. 148–149.

53. Quoted in Humphrey, *op. cit.*, p. 190.

54. *Ibid.*, p. 194.

55. Charles Péguy, *La Republique notre Royaume de France, Textes politiques choisis*, ed. by Denise Mayer (Paris, 1946), pp. 182–185. (My translation.)

56. *Reflections*, pp. 59–60.

57. *Ibid.*, pp. 144–145.

58. *La Republique*, pp. 151–152, 225–227.

59. *Ibid.*, p. 237.

60. *Ibid.*, pp. 185–191, 238–247, 322–324.

61. *The Two Sources*, pp. 118–140, 152–153, 204–208.

62. Humphrey, *op. cit.*, pp. 186–190, 120–121; Sorel, *Reflections*, pp. 301–302, 303–311.

63. *La Republique*, pp. 298–301, 231.

64. Perry, *Thought and Character*, II, 632–633.

65. *Memories and Studies*, pp. 286–288.

66. Quoted in Perry, *Thought and Character*, II, 317.

67. *Memories and Studies*, pp. 300–301; Perry, *Thought and Character*, II, pp. 270–271, 289–290, 299, 306–318.

68. *Memories and Studies*, pp. 287–288; *Talks to Teachers on Psychology* (New York, 1915), pp. 265–301.

69. Perry, *Thought and Character*, II, 632–633; Bergson, *The Two Sources*, 285.

70. *Ibid.*, pp. 287–288; Chevalier, *op. cit.*, p. 72.

71. *The Two Sources*, pp. 50–52, 58.

72. *Ibid.*, pp. 30–39, 68, 269.

73. *The Two Sources*, pp. 12–30, 85–97.

74. *Ibid.*, p. 50.

75. Maritain, *Ransoming the Time*, tr. by H. L. Binase (New York, 1941), pp. 93–95.

76. *Laughter*, pp. 44–47.

77. *The Two Sources*, pp. 29–33, 56–58, 266–268.

78. *Ibid.*, pp. 281–288.

CHAPTER EIGHTEEN

Nineteen Eighty-Four: Should Political Theory Care?

The original title of George Orwell's novel, *1984,* was *The Last Man in Europe.*[1] If he and his publisher had not renamed it, I would not be talking about it today, and neither would the other members of the American Political Science Association. None of the conferences, symposia, or seminars devoted to it would have taken place. All those anthologies about it would not have been published and the Clarendon Press would not have brought out an elaborate, scholarly, annotated new edition costing $25 this year. I know that counter-factuals are tricky, but this is scarcely guess-work. To speculate more boldly, one would suppose that *Animal Farm* would still occupy its present place in the junior high school curriculum, and that a biographical memoir of Orwell would have appeared because such books about other men of letters among his contemporaries are written regularly. It is, however, not at all clear that *The Last Man in Europe* would or should be read more often than Koestler's *Darkness at Noon,* or that Orwell's journalism would be much quoted now. Clearly the orgy of reminiscences and commentaries that have been encouraged because this is indeed the year 1984 ought to interest a social psychologist, but there is nothing much for me to say about it. The truth is that by changing the last two digits of 1948 around, Orwell set a date close enough to create expectations and so allowed all the fears that his book expressed and illustrated to acquire a mythic force. Here was a fable about what one could imagine simply by projecting terror one already knew into the near future. *1984*

This chapter was previously published as "Nineteen Eighty-Four: Should Political Theory Care?" in *Political Theory* 13 (1985): 5–18. Copyright © 1993 Sage Publications, Inc. Reprinted by permission of Sage Publications, Inc.

therefore always had an urgency that the same book under its first title could never have achieved. It became more than a satire. It was also a prophecy to which everyone could attach any fear whether that be technology, government surveillance, mind-control, consumerism, perpetual war, totalitarianism, or the decline of English, to name only the most common. In all cases, however, it is assumed that people in the Anglo-American world now must enjoy less freedom than they did at some unspecified period in the past. What we may observe in this year's rituals is presumably a purging as well as a reenacting and reenforcing of these fears.

It might be said by a Platonist that it is our first duty as political philosophers to pit the powers of reason against these frenzies and that we should only care about *1984* in order to dispel these mindless manifestations. It is not a trivial point, but it is also true that those who denounce the poets are also much given to quoting and using them to illustrate and illuminate philosophical propositions. *1984* can be put to a use, therefore, that is still worth investigating. To this it might be objected that even though fiction and drama have their place in our discourse, why bother with this particular book? Does it not reveal a false concern for relevance, a spineless effort to seek an audience by discussing topics selected and made familiar by the newspapers? Does philosophy really have to rely on the daily press for its substance? If that is what the "relevance" means, we do not need it. Why now, in short? If we were discussing *The Last Man in Europe* we could have done it just as readily in 1983 or left it until 1986. Is there really any good reason why we should care about *1984* especially now? If it were a question of this book at this moment, we should, perhaps, talk about something else. There is, however, more at issue than that. It is one of the many tasks of political theory to make unstructured beliefs and notions more coherent by relating them, critically and analytically, to the most comprehensive categories of rational thinking. It is a classifying function. We make ideas intelligible by placing them within the existing body of philosophical frames. As a satire, *1984* is, in any case, about attitudes and illusions rather than about characters, so that it particularly lends itself to being interpreted in this way. Assuming that there is no smoke without a fire, and given the vast popularity of the text, we have almost an intellectual obligation to see how it can be read rationally rather than used as an occasion for collective flagellation. In short, we may be able to use *1984* and books like it to give them a more rational character, and in doing so enliven theory itself.

Whether *1984* is an accurate prophecy and why it has become so popular are not questions political theory can answer. We must leave that to more empirical disciplines. Political theory need not waste its time on vague speculations about matters of fact. Again, however, that does not make *1984* of no concern to us at all. It raises real questions. How, for instance, should we deal with this or any effective piece of political literature or rhetoric? What topics are raised, and what might their significance for our knowledge and judgment be? We can simply begin by taking *1984* as an example of rhetoric and of the uses of imaginative literature for political theory. First, what sort of book is it? It is not a prophecy at all, in fact. Orwell meant it to draw out the logical implications of the thinking of his fellow intellectuals who were blind to the character of Stalin's and Hitler's regimes, and in some cases equally uncritically devoted to the more authoritarian aspects of Roman Catholicism.[2] It was not a prediction, but a savage satirical malediction on his contemporaries. In the course of this, Orwell does raise questions of real interest about the artificial and the natural, the state of intellectuals in society, and how one can write intelligently about the politics of cruelty and fear. These are surely matters that have always been important to political theory, and by recapturing them imaginatively, we may avert theory's worst fault: that is, to talk in a vacuum and about nothing at all, to heap words upon words that have no bearing on anything or anyone who has ever lived and spoken in the actual world. I do not in any way underestimate the value of interpreting the canonical writings of the past nor of the philosophical analysis of political concepts— far from it. But we can and ought to do more, to tell stories about how ideas are incarnated in experience, and this can be done by relying on fiction no less than on historical narrative. The difference is after all not between the real and the imagined, but between different ways or alternative rules of representation. Both tell stories about what can occur and about people who are more or less recreated for us here and now. We also have stories to tell and unless we are prepared to imagine what it is like to live in the political worlds we dissect so abstractly, we may lose touch with the concrete altogether. So, because it is so evidently here, we may as well look at *1984* to consider the relations between political theory and literature, and of philosophy and the imagination.

The satirical novel especially, which uses fantasy to dispel illusion, is of course closest to us and perhaps more capable than any other form of literature, scientific or speculative, of making us see things as they really are. We may no longer care much about the sins of Sir Robert Walpole but *Gulliver* is our contemporary because his creator permits us to deal with irrationality and our reactions to it in one of the few ways open to us, caricature, which brings that experience closer to us than does the depersonalized discourse of philosophy. We recognize the actual in these hateful pictures of the possible. The awful possibilities embedded in the actual have to be teased out for us to get a sense of reality. I do not mean to suggest that *1984* is another *Gulliver's Travels,* or that Orwell was a Swift, but he did write that sort of fiction, and its significance for us is in its bearing on the worst immediate as well as enduring implications of humans governing and being governed.[3] What would it be like to live in a wholly human-made world? What indeed are our experiences of the artifacts of politics already? How are they to be represented? What would a world in which all thinking was really ruling-class ideology involve? After all, many theorists claim that this is so always. What would writing about the past and present really amount to if that were indeed the case? It takes real imagination to cope with such propositions and *1984* in fact does that. It is also about the perplexities of skeptics.

What were the ideas and qualities of mind that Orwell brought to *1984? The Collected Essays, Journalism and Letters* reveals a less than first-rate intelligence and an enormous moral self-confidence. He wrote about a vast number of forgotten books and his reviews of these are not memorable. There is no evidence that he knew much about history or economics, though he pronounced on both. What comes across most of all is a ferocious passion for honesty. "The worst thing that can be said about a work of art is that it is insincere," he wrote in an essay on literature and totalitarianism.[4] He thought of himself as primarily an artist determined "to make political writing into an art" and "to fuse political purpose and artistic purpose into one whole."[5] Honesty as the creed of art compelled him to tell what he had seen in clear English, for abuses of language were in his view the way in which dishonesty worked. No one, moreover, was in his view more reprehensible in this respect than the English fellow-traveling intellectual establishment. The right might be a lot of incompetent "stuffed shirts" inclined to fascism, but the left was incurably dishonest. In contrast to these, Orwell idolized the "ordinary man," decent, not puritanical, patriotic, even a bit xenophobic, but not basely power worshipping.[6] Neither in his essays nor in *1984* does "the ordinary man" ever appear as an individual. He is simply a type and mostly a victim. The inclination to idealize this figure misled Orwell's judgment quite extraordinarily. He was among the first to recognize the dangers of Nazism and he even admitted that in this respect the intellectuals whom he despised had been right all along. Nevertheless, in a 1940 review of *Mein Kampf* he admitted that he had never been able to dislike Hitler. There was something "deeply appealing about him." Here was an underdog whom life had treated badly. Moreover, Hitler understood the "falsity of the hedonistic attitude to life" and "the values of patriotism and the military virtues."[7] Orwell not only failed to notice Hitler's hatred of all the weak and vulnerable of the earth, he also did not seem to recognize that "ruthlessness" was Hitler's favorite word of praise. Orwell saw only one of his "ordinary men," whom he believed sacrifice themselves because they know that they are part of an organism greater than themselves.[8] Still, he was a socialist who deeply believed in making life comfortable for everyone. That was hardly heroic. Was he just confused? Probably, but his hatred of his own kind, the eccentric and extremely self-aware literary men, those radical intellectuals, reduced him to inventing an "ordinary man" who was simply the obverse, the very opposite of this, his own crowd. Intellectuals he loathed as bigots, unpatriotic, lying and disloyal. They lied about the treachery of the communists in Spain. They were Machiavellian wreckers. Finally, they were unable to face facts, as they fell for every prefabricated ideological power-fantasy. The intellectual who cannot abide intellectuals is not an uncommon type, of course, but what sets Orwell apart is that he translated this contempt into a vision of a society governed by these objects of his scorn. The totalitarian state he projected was neither Stalin's nor Hitler's entirely. The Inner Party that dispenses Ingsoc and rules Airstrip One in *1984* is made up of radical Anglo-American intellectuals. It is a government composed of people not unlike Thrasymachus. Their chief mark is that they are untrustworthy.

Of the political literature that Orwell reviewed, only three authors stand out. Bertrand Russell's *Power,* Friedrich von Hayek's *The Road to Serfdom,* and two of James Burnham's books.[9] He agreed with Hayek that a command economy had totalitarian dangers, but thought that pre–World War Two capitalism was dead and that a democratic socialist nationalized welfare economy was possible and politically safe. In this Orwell never changed. He remained a faithful member of the Labour Party and he was very careful to explain that *1984* was not directed at it or its programs.[10] It was the party of the people, not of the intellectuals. That's why he did not regard *1984* as an account of the inevitable. It was precisely Burnham's Marxist fatalism that he disliked. That is also what set his novel apart from Huxley's *Brave New World.* Huxley, in fact, wrote Orwell to say that the "sadistic" phase of the new order was only temporary and that it would necessarily be succeeded by something more efficient like his own technological nightmare, unless, of course, we just blew ourselves up in an atomic war.[11] Huxley clearly felt uncomfortable about all that cruelty, but then he misunderstood the political intent of *1984*. Cruelty and especially the denial of reality, lying, were what made up the political order of *1984*. It would be more stable than Russell, whose book Orwell admired, had believed possible. Orwell came to give power its due. His first criticism of James Burnham's works had been that they did not explain why men want power or the ends to which power-holders aspire. Burnham assumed that political power is desired for itself, a proposition that Orwell found very hard to credit. The revelations of Stalin's and Hitler's rules finally convinced him that Burnham had been right, but he continued to reject the latter's indifference to the political strength of the ruled and his refusal to offer any alternative to the empire of the managers. Nothing is inevitable, but power in *1984* reflects Burnham's views. The proles are loyal to each other but wholly demoralized and apolitical. The Inner Party enjoys the exercise of power for its own sake. Orwell was now as ready as Burnham to tear away the ideological veils of the intellectual classes, and indeed, to expose pretense is always the primary aim of satire. Unlike Swift who, in spite of his far deeper misanthropy, did have a moral center from which he spread his contempt, Orwell in *1984* had none, at least in the novel. In *1984* there is eternal war among three superpowers, just as Burnham had predicted, and there is endless unabating misery, but even the memory of better times is being destroyed. This is what Burnham's scenario would be like if it came about, but Orwell did not regard it or any grand historical design as plausible. Indeed the mechanistic rigidities of their theory of history made Marxists blind to what was before their very eyes: the rise of fascism.[12] Their predictive failures had cost them much, and those ex-Marxists like Burnham who maintained their old fatalistic habits of thought would do no better. It is, however, one of the characteristics of *1984* that even by the grim standards of political satire it is despairing. Trust, Orwell's supreme virtue, lies in the dust among the proles who neither can nor will alter their miserable existence on Airstrip One.

To the very end, Gulliver at least knew what a rational being was like. In *1984* the possibility of saying $2 \times 2 = 4$ because one knows it to be true is lost. The plot is largely the story of how this last impulse to speak the truth is destroyed. It is not really just about totalitarianism but rather about the practical implications of the notion that language structures all our knowledge of the phenomenal world. For if it be so, the manipulation of language can determine readily all of what we hold to be true or false. The truth shall not make us free because meanings are infinitely alterable, and one who dominates the language we speak rules us utterly. Freedom and justice are illusions. Even the knowledge of the illusory character of belief is an illusion. That is, of course, a well-known argument against skepticism. It is said to be circular, but in practice it does not matter for there is no exit from the circle.

1984 is then a cognitive nightmare. Only the Thought Police are efficient or important in Airstrip One. The Inner Party makes the control of mental life its chief policy. The Outer Party, who serves its purposes, unlike the proles who only produce, must be composed of people who have internalized every control mechanism. Each member is wholly isolated so that each one can respond directly and exclusively to the signals, that is, the linguistic stimuli, issued from above. The thing to be feared most is any sign of "thought crime," any gesture of deviance, for it can lead only to vaporization. Fear, hatred, and pain are the permitted responses and they are forthcoming upon demand. No science fiction devices are needed for this degree of control. Orwell knew as much as we do now about torture and cruelty as a systematic form of control. Effective as these are in achieving abject submission, however, they do not yield total power. For that, rulers must be the masters of language, for it is language that creates thought. Hobbes had made that point long ago, but Orwell saw the politics of this thought in a new light, as a deliberate program to achieve uniformity and instability, not just the obedience and security for which Hobbes had hoped.[13] "Newspeak" creates and destroys truth. The only alternative is many tongues, and that is what the Inner Party fears and ultimately destroys.

Next to Winston Smith, the hero of *1984*, there works one Syme, soon to be vaporized. His job is to destroy the English vocabulary and to reduce it to as few words of Newspeak as possible. The way that is done is to put out a constant series of new editions of the basic dictionary, each one with fewer words and more compounds than the previous one. The whole notion of goodness and badness will eventually be covered by six words. The vague and useless shades of meaning that were Oldspeak will be eliminated. Most of that was just "quack quack." The "quacks" were politically dangerous because they carried the memory of another life, as Smith knows, to his cost. At a different level, this is also a response to the implications of Ayer's *Language, Truth and Logic,* which had become quite a bestseller since it had appeared in the thirties. Newspeak is the proper language of people who think only empirical propositions make sense because these can be verified, though never with certainty, in terms of experience. Logically necessary statements such as $2 \times 2 = 4$ are all tautologies, and moral pronouncements are expressions of personal emotion.[14] This is exactly what Winston's torturer, O'Brien of the Inner Party, explains to him. The tautological and expressive are clearly not part of the truth and the empirical is manipulated by language as may be necessary. The question is: who governs, who "verifies," who decides? And so O'Brien tells Winston that it is not "solipsism" to say that he decides on what is true and false, for he does not act as an individual. It is not in his view what we would now call nihilism, far from it. He knows that convention rules our perceptions and that truth is collectively accepted verification. He also knows that it can be managed, but only by the undying, collective Party acting as a whole.

The masters of language and of convention are obviously also the lords of historical memory. Traditions are inventions, and history is a story. Partly, Orwell's account was an accurate report on what was going on in Soviet Russia and among Anglo-American fellow travelers who adapted readily to every twist and turn of the Party line, like the Outer Party journalists and literary hacks. They hated when they were told to, forgot what they were supposed to eliminate, and discovered whatever was presented to them. Memory is just as artificial, Orwell discovered, as language. Winston's job is to manufacture past events. In some cases, he invents people altogether like one Comrade Ogilvie. At other times, he makes up reports that he knows contradict stories that he made up earlier. At first, he thinks that some of the contradictory evidence is just false, but he soon realizes that all the earlier statements of "fact" were also constructed. All statistics are equally fabricated, as are photographs and reports. History is not, as Orwell and we know, raw experience. It depends on authority for its credibility and for us the rules of evidence legitimize that. For the Inner Party, there are no rules; it is openly a question of power for O'Brien. The important point is to adjust the minds of people like Smith. They ought to be certain at every moment, to believe that there is no other reality than the one that is created for them. Indirectly they even help make it so. Winston grasps readily enough that he "who controls the past controls the future and who controls the present controls the past." The trouble is that he cannot give up his sense of an enduring personal identity and his private memory. That is why he is tortured and broken by the Inner Party.

If the issue at all times is "who rules" in *1984,* its bearing goes well beyond what is ordinarily meant by governing. One aspect of Stalin's and Hitler's methods of governing is always hardest to credit: its cruelty. That is why *1984* is not just about the end of truth. As satire, it is intent upon undressing and exposing the implications of fellow-traveling dishonesty. It is also about one of the realities they denied: cruelty. Torture had made its reappearance in Europe after more than a hundred years of abeyance, and Orwell intended to make his readers see and feel what physical cruelty was really like. Needless to say, his critics at once psychologized him. It was all the fantasies of a man dying of tuberculosis, as Orwell was when he wrote *1984.* We know better, and it is the gift of literature to theory that it can bring home this ultimate political irrationality about ruling and being ruled. When the British Army liberated Belsen, a reporter wrote up the operation that led up to its occupation in calm journalistic prose; he then went on with "it is now my duty to report something that is beyond human understanding." We are of course quite used to it by now, but Orwell clearly had every reason to feel that he "had a duty" to make cruelty understood. The sheer physical brutality and the misery of daily life in a perpetual war world where power is exercised not only for its own sake but without alternatives or challenges was his ultimate theme or, let us say: pain.

As he accepted the corruption and violence of the Inner Party as a given, there is little about the psychology of fanaticism or belief in *1984.* The Outer Party consists of automata, who are crushed when they wake up momentarily, and the Inner Party is not composed of "true believers." This is already a postideological totalitarian regime. *1984* is not a psychological novel in any case. It is about brute political power and its expressions, not about the subtleties of personal bonds between superiors and inferiors and the inherent attractions of authority. To be sure, Orwell did have a sense of its irrationality. Winston clearly is attracted to O'Brien, the Inner Party cynic who leads him on and then tortures him. O'Brien, as his name might lead one to expect, resembles a Roman Catholic rather than a more recent ideologue. He not only gives Winston his first glass of wine but eventually tells him, "you lacked humility and self-discipline" when he applies the instruments of torture to him. It is he who finally explains to Winston that there is nothing wayward in the creation of reality. It is done collectively and inevitably; the Party is eternal, its members only perish. At first, Winston thinks that he is in the hands of an omniscient lunatic, but he learns to love even Big Brother, and to see that he who creates the laws of nature is not, by definition, a lunatic.

What does, however, distinguish this particular despotism from other kinds of domination by fear is that it realizes the fullness of power by constant change. It alone acts in the knowledge that there is no reality outside human consciousness and that humans, being totally malleable, are most perfectly ruled if nothing is constant, if the world is put into perpetual motion. That brings the artificiality of everything home to all. Winston is finally converted to this state of affairs by the power of love.

What Winston loses when he learns to love Big Brother is "natural skepticism." In its stead he acquires the "artificial" skepticism of O'Brien, the man who creates men and events. Until he is transformed, Winston has a questioning mind, a sense of his own ego. It is not as strong as that force of nature, Julia. She is the supreme natural skeptic. She never attends to the party line, scoffs at everything, and is not taken in by any official utterances. She is the personification of unreflective honest feeling and unbelief. It is she who brings Winston out to the countryside, to sex, and to love. This is, of course, the true natural world of feeling. She is not in the least interested in the difference between truth and falsehood that so torments Winston. All she wants is natural gratification, and this is the real obverse of the artificial world that human power has created. Nature is instinct and Winston longs to believe that it survives among the proles. In the end, of course, the Inner Party teaches both of them their errors. They abandon nature and whatever their powers of feeling may have been; they are no match for a natural order that has been created by intelligent beings. What we do have here is the conflict between two kinds of skepticism, one natural, free, and self-generated, the other artificial, cerebral, and dominating. It is the difference between refusing to believe and inventing reality.

We have heard much of this before. The contrast between the authentically natural and the fraudulently artificial, the spontaneous people and the speculative intellectual, the oppressiveness of a socially determined reality and the freedom of instinctual self-creation, the rational and emotional: All of that is in Rousseau. *1984* is decidedly the product of a Rousseauist imagination, but with a difference. Orwell remained a skeptic, a champion of diversity and of the complexities of an uneasy, doubting, self-assertive mind. Rousseau fled to a dreamworld where the state was rich, the citizen poor, where individuality could shed its burdens and collective wills were indeed triumphant. The satirical consciousness is different. It can expose fraud without substituting any new illusions, but it is clearly not up to creating a coherent political theory. *1984* illustrates theory, it mocks it, and it does more: it forces its readers to recognize that even doubters and skeptics can be just as dogmatic as the most besotted believers.

Thus far, I have said relatively little about Orwell's picture of totalitarianism. *1984* is among other things the story of a society in which the ideology of the ruling class is indeed hegemonic. This is something thrown into the faces of his adversaries, for it shows not only what a society in which this is the case would be like but also that Great Britain was not, in fact, such a society in 1948. It was shabby, drab, and exhausted. Its intellectual classes were up to no good, but its proles were not yet crushed. If the theory of ideology either in Burnham's or the Marxist version were accurate, then it would be something like Airstrip One with its thought crimes and vaporizations. Again, it is as a creative dramatization of the implication of current ideas that this novel does most for political theory. And this is its feature that most recommends it to our attention. If ruling class ideology really is all there is, then O'Brien will be there to see to it that this ideology replaces every other vision of reality and every alternative claim to credibility. Such a state of affairs is of course quite possible; Orwell had Soviet Russia and the Third Reich before his eyes. Even there, as in *1984,* members of the Outer Party, professional intellectuals all, are prone to ideology. Winston, quite unlike Julia, desperately wants to believe in a political creed of some sort. There is every reason to suppose that if he were put in O'Brien's place, he would be no less cruel. In fact he says so in a moment of rebellious fervor. Orwell had come to think that if it were not Soviet Russia, his fellow intellectuals would grasp at something else, some other "external paradise."[15] They were not really interested in any actual place, certainly not England, and not Soviet Russia, which was just an object of belief. This is hardly new. It is not that Orwell had any profound ideas about the relationship of ideology to politics or about the political psychology of intellectuals. What he was able to do is to show what it would be like to be ruled by them and to live in a world wholly structured according to the ideas fashionable among them in 1948.

Because he was so overwhelmingly interested in intellectuals and their chief vice, dishonesty, Orwell spent little time on the relationship between Big Brother and his followers. It might have forced him to a less idealized view of the proles. In any event, mass-theory was no part of his scenario because his "ordinary men" were not the Marxist proletariat and therefore did not have to be excoriated when they failed to live up to a set of wholly ludicrous expectations. Nevertheless, Big Brother was not just a mock-up, and the erotic relationship between leaders and followers, gurus and disciples, is a very real one. It cannot be said that our understanding of these phenomena has been greatly enhanced since Freud wrote *Group Psychology and the Analysis of Ego* in 1921, but Jonestown did happen and its perpetrators and victims were not intellectuals, even though we know that intellectuals are no less gullible than other people.[16] Anyone who teaches at a university knows that there is both a supply of prophetic teachers and an even greater demand for their relieving services. Of all this Orwell has little to say—except as it manifests itself in a belief in an omnipotent Big Brother who may not exist, but can win Winston's love. For Winston does end by fixing his devotion on this idol when he has been pulverized by O'Brien. Hitler, Stalin, and Mao and all the others were, however, real enough, not just pictures on every railway station. In this respect, Orwell illustrates the weakness of a populist political imagination. That also is not an insignificant message to political theory. It raises one of its more urgent general questions: what exactly should the relation between political theory and psychology be now, and do we have anything like an adequate political psychology available or even in the making? If nothing else, *1984* can and should stimulate questions that are the first task of political theory to ask.

There is one other contribution that *1984* can make to the idea of totalitarianism, and that is contextual. It is important in the history of political ideas to understand the circumstances under which specific conceptions were developed. It is often said that totalitarian government, as an ideal type that embraced the practices of both Stalin's Russia and Hitler's Germany, was the creature of the Cold War. It was, it is charged, a crude effort to transfer the hatred aroused by Nazism to the new enemy, Soviet Communism, and that this was done simply by amalgamating two quite different regimes.[17] As for the uniqueness of their practices, that was just mystique, an ideological plot to integrate the intellectuals into the capitalist order. There is much to be said for getting one's dates right. The fact is that the idea of totalitarian rule as a unique and new phenomenon arose among social democrats, who realized that Marxism had nothing to contribute to their understanding of Nazi Germany especially, as well as Soviet Russia, and they did so long before the Cold War, by 1940 to be exact. It was not Djilas, but Rudolf Hilferding who discovered "the new class" just before he was killed in 1941. He then wrote two essays about what he called "state capitalism" and the new bureaucratic class that ran it for its own benefit in both the USSR and Nazi

Germany.[18] Socialists found this idea hard to accept. In his *Behemoth* in 1941, Franz Neumann, still orthodox, rejected Hilferding and insisted that Nazi Germany was a capitalist state and that there was no hope, the regime was omnipotent, and inner resistance futile. In this he was just like Orwell. However, he also asked the crucial question: Was the Third Reich a state at all or was it something else and quite new? After all, it did not have a legal system or rules of legitimization.[19] Clearly the ideal type that Weber had proposed was out of date, and a new and unique formation was recognizable. This was not the old despotism either, as Orwell saw just as clearly. Eventually, Neumann came to accept the primacy of politics and his cry was that of an entire generation of social democrats: "Machiavelli's theory now becomes really true for the first time."[20] That was a thought he had long resisted and it came to him entirely out of his growing understanding of the Nazi episode. Orwell was there before him because he had chosen to speak the truth about Spain, long before the Cold War. Corrupt and inefficient as it was, Hitler's new order had closed the space between government and civil society. *Behemoth* had replaced *Leviathan*. It was obviously so in Soviet Russia as well. This is a rough sketch of the origins of the idea of totalitarianism, and Orwell's part in the socialist context within which it arose. If the theory had a single author, it was Hilferding. And we should care about *1984* and books like it to see how ideas "fit" in history. Political theory is not subject, as it is often said, to the forces of some external reality. It is itself a part of general intellectual crosscurrents, of the languages of the republic of letters, and of the divisions within it. "Climate of opinion" is far too vague a phrase to be useful. It is by attending carefully to all imaginative and scholarly literature that one can establish the historical identity of ideas. So Orwell helps us to recreate the intellectual groans of democratic socialism in its darkest hours when it was compelled to recognize totalitarianism.

There are then good reasons not to care about *1984*, but better ones to take *The Last Man in Europe* seriously. It illustrates, dramatizes, personalizes, and raises the questions that political theory asks and the ideas it suggests. It even helps us to tell our stories, and indeed may even help us to decide what story to tell and how to go about it.

Notes

Author's note: This article was delivered to the annual meeting of the American Political Science Association, Washington, D.C., August 30–September 2, 1984.

1. Bernard Crick, "Introduction," to George Orwell, *Nineteen Eighty-Four* (Oxford: Clarendon Press, 1984); George Steiner, "Killing Time," *The New Yorker,* December 12, 1983, pp. 168–87.

2. Sonia Orwell and Ian Angus (eds.), "Letter to Francis A. Henson," *The Collected Essays, Journalism and Letters of George Orwell* (New York: Harcourt, Brace & World, 1968), 4: 502 (hereafter CEJL). For his views of Catholics, see Crick 1984, and e.g. "Notes on Nationalism," CEJL, 3: 363–366, and "The Prevention of Literature," 4: 61–63. See also William Steinhoff, *George Orwell and the Origins of 1984* (Ann Arbor: University of Michigan Press, 1975), pp. 63–71 and 43–54.

3. Orwell's essay on Swift is a mediocre criticism of Swift's Tory anarchism. CEJL, 2: 205–23. On Orwell's own satire see George Kateb, "The Road to 1984," *Political Science Quarterly* 81 (1966), pp. 564–80.

4. "Literature and Totalitarianism," CEJL, 2: 134.

5. "Why I Write," CEJL, 1: 6–7.

6. See generally, "Charles Dickens," and "Inside the Whale," CEJL 1: 413, 460, 501–504, and "The Lion and the Unicorn," CEJL, 2: 59, 63, 69.

7. CEJL, 2: 12–14.

8. "Notes on the Way," CEJL, 2: 15–21.

9. CEJL, 1: 117–199, 4: 160–181, 313–326.

10. See "Letter to Francis A. Henson."

11. Sybille Bedford, *Aldous Huxley* (New York: Alfred A. Knopf, 1974), pp. 490–491.

12. "Prophecies of Fascism," CEJL, 2: 31.

13. Michael Oakeshott (ed.), "And where speech is not, there is neither truth nor falsehood," *Leviathan* (Oxford: Basil Blackwell, 1947), 1 chap. 4, p. 21. See also 2 chap. 29, pp. 210–12.

14. Crick, "Introduction," p. 79, notes the affinity and suggests it was part of the climate of opinion in which Orwell lived, though he did not know and may not have read Ayer's book.

15. "London Letter," CEJL, 3: 382.

16. This point is raised very ably in Robert C. Tucker, "Does Big Brother Really Exist?" in *1984 Revisited,* Irving Howe (New York: Perennial Library, 1983), pp. 89–102.

17. See e.g. Benjamin R. Barber, "Conceptual Foundations of Totalitarianism" and the literature cited there in C. J. Friederich, et al., *Totalitarianism in Perspective* (New York: Praeger, 1969), pp. 3–52.

18. Rudolf Hilferding, "State Capitalism or Totalitarian State Economy," and "The Modern Totalitarian State," trans. Morris Watnick, *The Modern Review* 1 (1947), pp. 266–271 and 597–605.

19. *Behemoth* 2nd ed. (New York: Oxford University Press, 1944), pp. 223–228, 467–470.

20. *The Democratic and the Authoritarian State* (Glencoe, IL: The Free Press, 1957), p. 267.

CHAPTER NINETEEN

Rethinking
the Past

I n a celebrated essay Friedrich Nietzsche once wrote that there
were three kinds of history: the monumental, the antiquarian,
and the critical. Hannah Arendt was what he called a monumental historian. At its best, monumental history is addressed to political
actors, to remind them that great deeds were performed by notable
men and that what was once feasible is at least possible again. The
past is presented as a storehouse of politically useful knowledge
which one ignores at one's peril. Every act and event worth remembering at all carries an appropriate lesson within it, and to reveal
that meaning is the task of such a historian. History can thus serve
the present rather than bury it under the weight of the past. Like
Nietzsche, Miss Arendt deeply appreciated the vivifying possibilities
of monumental history, and she admired Polybius and the later Roman historians who were its masters. Moreover, warned by Nietzsche, she managed to avoid the errors to which they were chronically
prone. They tended to live by false analogies and also to stress effects
at the expense of causes. Miss Arendt avoided these pitfalls because
she was a philosopher, that is, constantly and completely self-aware
and self-correcting. It made her unique among monumental historians who are, as a rule, so pragmatic that they are not only distrustful
of reason in politics but of speculative thought in general. That was
their undoing. Miss Arendt's aims were intellectually more ambitious
than theirs. She also, as Nietzsche said of them, meant to recall "archetypical truths" and to "repair broken molds." However, she did
not, as they did, merely want to move people to action. She had no

This chapter is reprinted with permission from *Social Research* 44 (1977): 80–90.

intention of abandoning the work of philosophy, which does not tell people how to behave but how to think. "The human mind," she wrote, "stands in need of concepts if it is to function at all . . . its foremost task [is] the comprehensive understanding of reality and the coming to terms with it." Philosophy finds its purpose in this endeavor. It does not try "to offer solutions or to give advice." Even as a monumental historian, philosophy was, for her, a harsh disciplinarian, allowing her at most "to encourage sustained and closer reflection on the nature and intrinsic potentialities of action," which is not exhorting, preaching, or directing conduct.

Monumental History

It was, then, one of Miss Arendt's distinctions to be able both to analyze monumental history and to practice it. In *Between Past and Future* she did the critical work, in *On Revolution,* the creative. As a result, she could recognize far more clearly than Nietzsche, who only thought about it, what monumental history must do. Its difficulties are very great, but it is not in danger of losing sight of the present. The most immediate problem is how to remain credible in the face of critical history. Monumental history uneasily, but unavoidably, must live with and yet also offend critical history. By critical history I mean the scholarly discipline that concerns itself with the explanation of the changes that occurred within a given frame of time and which still pursues, though with diminishing self-confidence to be sure, Ranke's ideal of recreating in words "what really went on" in the past. The critical historian can be true to his vocation only by justifying his every statement by reference to such evidence as our ancestors, in writings and artifacts, chose to leave to us. He therefore remains our best judge of what may and may not be validly said about the men and events of the past. This is extremely inconvenient for the monumental historian, whose aims are quite different, but who must depend on critical history if he is to be at all convincing. To put it bluntly, how many omissions and exaggerations, how many unmentioned qualifications, nuances, ifs and buts can the monumental historian get away with and still avoid total devastation by critical examination? Miss Arendt was perfectly aware of the difficulty and, by implication at least, acknowledged that there was no solution to the conflict. What she said of the Roman historians applies to her also. They were not in the least interested in the process of change per se, and while they were not unmindful of "causes" and "contexts," these were not their main preoccupation. To teach lessons requires one to draw the general implications out of the particular event. The specific and peculiar are ignored to a degree. However, that does not mean that she was blind to the real worth of critical history. She strongly objected to functional sociology, which scorns the sources and the specifics of the critical historian. She merely followed the imperatives of her journey into the past. Her only direct criticism of critical history was its claim to be "value free." That, she charged, only covered either passivity or triviality. True impartiality, which is a higher sort of integrity, is the ability to judge all parties in a conflict fairly, showing neither anger nor favor. She attributed this admirable self-control more to Homer and the Greek dramatists than to modern professional historians. For quite justly she wanted to remind the latter that they in turn depended on monumental history to teach them what deeds and events were great and interesting enough to be worth remembering at all. And any kind of history has a present bearing. But that does not lessen the distance or even hostility between the two kinds of history. It just cannot be reduced. Wisely she did not try, for she counted the ability to live with intense and insuperable intellectual tension a mark of wisdom.

There is no point in denying that Miss Arendt, like every other monumental historian, on occasion made remarks about the past that, strictly speaking, were just not so. These were mostly matters of overemphasis or silence, but they were not casual mistakes. They arose from the purposes and style of argument of monumental history. It has always dealt in opposites. Indeed, there is a streak of Manichaeanism in its very structure, quite as evident in the ancient historians as in "the divine science" of John Adams, whom Miss Arendt admired so much. From the theory of regimes to American constitutional theory we find studies in contrast. Monarchy/tyranny, aristocracy/oligarchy, democracy/ochlocracy, the rule of law/the rule of men, and free government/despotism. To these couples Miss Arendt added at least two, classes/masses and spontaneous/professional politics. Monumental history cannot possibly dispense with this scaffolding. For to praise is also to blame. One can debunk without admiring, and Miss Arendt detested the mentality, both servile and mean, which cannot see anything beyond itself. To acclaim the superior, one must necessarily despise the inferior. The good regime and the great man are threatened by, even as they reject, their opposites, the bad and the petty, in government and in individuals. Monumental history generally, and Miss Arendt particularly, teach us how to praise and, by implication, how to condemn. That is, perhaps, why she finally felt so great an affinity for the epic poets, especially for Virgil.

Founding Fathers

In Virgil she found the most perfect telling of the one political myth which she thought still might have some life in it: the myth of founding new polities. Monumental history has always celebrated the deliberate acts of lawgivers. Polybius extolled Lycurgus, and Machiavelli Romulus and Numa. She came upon them in the course of a rather despairing search for a lost treasure, "the spirit of the revolution." On the way she reviewed all the political virtues which the modern age has abandoned, foremost among them tradition and authority. Both of these were the distinctive political contribution of the Romans, for whom they were quite inseparable in practice. Authority was for them less pressing than the commands of power, but more obligatory than mere advice. Its weight was derived from the respect due to the established and wise who possessed authority, not as a personal quality, but because they followed the standards, offices, and examples set by their ancestors, especially the founders of the republic. Piety was a direct rebinding (*re-legare*) of the present generation to those of the remotest past. Tradition, the sacred memory of ancestors, authority, the imperatives for conduct they set, and religion, the belief that this linking of present and past was a duty that ensured political success, were thus indivisible. To be sure, the Romans were often quite indiscriminate in their constant hearkening back to their earliest days. St. Augustine's sarcastic comment on Sallust, that if the first Romans were really the best, then the rape of the Sabine women must have been Rome's finest hour, was nothing if not to the point. Miss Arendt must have had that passage in *The City of God* in her ears, for she was highly selective in her choice of founders and in the tribute she paid them. Indeed, she tended to identify false piety with that mindless conservatism which believes in an unbroken chain of tradition and does not, after two hundred years, recognize the futility and nostalgia of its rhetoric. To bring authority and tradition, now utterly dead, back to some sort of life would require a complete spiritual refounding, as Virgil saw. True Roman foundings were not seen as original creations, but as returns to foundations. A refounding was therefore what Miss Arendt had in mind, something both radical and traditional. Only the revolutionary spirit, however feeble, she thought, might still remind us of this saving possibility.

The revolutionary spirit was for Miss Arendt obviously not a random form of rebellion. It was strictly the aspiration to freedom, to "public happiness." That is far less the release from this or that limitation on one's will or pleasure than the possibility of playing one's part on the public stage together with one's fellow citizens. The object of the revolutionary spirit is to perpetuate itself by founding a polity in which political participation is continuous and normal. Only once, in fact, in its long, two-hundred years of effort, has the revolutionary spirit succeeded in the act of founding—that was in America. The Founding Fathers were indeed able to build a new polity and to create enduring institutions out of their own superabundant political energies. Their fellow revolutionaries in France were diverted from their original task, the pursuit of freedom, and lost everything. Because of the prevalence of grinding poverty in Europe, the spirit of the revolution was at once confused and dissipated by the politics of pity. Compassion for the suffering of the poor became the true test of revolutionary zeal, and since the passion was doomed to frustration it soon turned into rage. The terror was the expression of this explosive sentimentality, which has haunted and destroyed every one of the subsequent revolutions. Only the American Founding Fathers, living in a land relatively free of misery, could and did ignore the "social question" and avoided political pity. Again, nationalism did not overtake them, for they did not have to find a new absolute principle to assert against an absolute king. King George was, after all, only a limited monarch, and it took no superhuman strength of mind to replace him with a republic that knew no sovereignty. Finally, the Americans did not become professional revolutionary organizers, determined to replace the local and spontaneous public life of the town and locality. Even had they wanted to, they could not have succeeded. Nevertheless, they failed just here, not by acts of repression, but out of indifference. They provided magnificently for the continuation, through unbroken interpretation, of their constitution. Judicial review keeps the founding Ten Tables alive, as it were. The spirit of the revolution, participation, was however allowed to wither and decay. Only Jefferson even worried about it. That is why he wanted every generation to reenact the founding, to make a new start every twenty years, and why he called for local, ward self-government. It all came to nothing, just because representative party government worked well enough. Because the Founding Fathers had done their work so well, their heirs did not feel called upon to make comparable efforts.

There is, of course, something eccentric in this retelling of the story of the American founding. Total silence covers its failures, the fact that a long and bloody Civil War had to be fought to remedy its defects and to refound and complete it. It was not all quite such a bland success story, after all. However, Miss Arendt was not intent upon writing our constitutional history but upon shaking us into taking a new look at our founding. The habitual reverence for the constitution ought to be rethought in terms of a less placid emulation of the spirit rather than of the letter of the founding document. To think anew about the revolutionary spirit means to consider freedom again. Revolutionary freedom manifests itself in the spontaneous organizations of ordinary people, such as the revolutionary societies of France in 1789, the soviets in Russia in 1917, the *Räte* in Germany in 1917, and the councils in Hungary of 1956. These are always put down ultimately by the party organizers, the professional revolutionaries who are neither founders nor liberators. Yet a real founding *did* once take place out of the spirit of the revolution, and to remember it and praise it is the task of monumental history as Miss Arendt saw it. To recall it is to force one to reconsider the revolutionary tradition, not as upheaval only, but also as the possibility of founding polities and of rebinding men authoritatively.

By talking about foundings in this way Miss Arendt meant to invite us to think about history in a special way. The founding is an arbitrary act in two ways. First, it does not depend on any prior rules for justification. Its principle is its own justification. The structure and the spirit of the laws that arise from it justify, and indeed sanctify, a successful founding. It is, second, arbitrary not only normatively, it is also an unforeseeable and irregular interruption of the ordinary course of history and political life. It is a possibility that suddenly breaks in upon the usual sequence of events. It was not Miss Arendt's purpose to follow Nietzsche's call to "life" by a general mythologizing of experience. That was quite foreign to her. Nevertheless, it was for the sake of the present that the necessity of rethinking the past seemed so urgent to her. If the idea of a founding is something like a political myth, it is not itself fanciful. On the contrary, it was meant to fortify us against a very actual and quite specific danger.

Revolution and Tradition

It was in the course of her studies of totalitarianism, Miss Arendt tells us, that she became convinced that the notion of history as an inevitable process contributed materially to the mentality of totalitarian leaders. What was so new about them and their regimes was the belief that anything at all was possible. If history is a process like those taken to be observable in nature, it is clearly subject to technological control. If you know the right technique, you can do anything with—and to—people. It opens the door upon the boundless, and this absence of limits induces the power orgies of the leaders just as it settles the masses in their sense of being helpless and even superfluous. By treating both nature and society as fields open only to technical operation, Miss Arendt argued, even free men exile themselves from their world, since the reliable contours which were once provided have been destroyed. It is therefore hardly astonishing that she resorted to so different a way of considering the past. It is selective, dwelling only on those moments that have a constructive present bearing, and it emphasizes the avoidable in contrast to the inevitable. Not that there were all that many possibilities. Far from it. In fact the spirit of the revolution and the founding were no more than grounds for hope and guideposts in a new exploration of the past— both on highly traditional lines. They had their origin, as we saw, in a historiography far older than that of the nineteenth century. It was not yet concerned with vast impersonal forces, or with the prediction and management of the remote future. On the contrary, it encouraged the present generation to act well, because its predecessors had once done so. Miss Arendt's appreciation of this oldest of historiographies and the support it gives to both authority and tradition arose out of the belief that the subsequent theories of history, from the belief in inevitable progress onward, were hostile to the spirit of freedom. At their worst they could nourish totalitarian fantasies. Even without these, the decay of authority and tradition make it all but impossible to grasp reality, much less teach the young to face it. Without an education in reality, they are ready for the reign of artificial, menacing pseudorealities. Not the least task of politics is to aid education, but only indirectly, by providing the stability it requires. Stability, however, was not an end in itself for her. It was to secure the reality principle and nothing more. The real end of politics was freedom, the survival of the revolutionary spirit, participation, the "public happiness."

There is something paradoxical in uniting revolution and tradition in this way. Are they not natural opposites? Not any longer, for by now we have a long history of revolutionary activity, and a tradition can, therefore, be constructed out of it. To be sure, it is one of almost complete failure. Even its one success, the American founding, proved unkind to the spirit. A memorable series of heroic failures is, however, better than no remembrances at all. Monumental history salvages whatever can still be praised, and cultivates whatever can still be found at hand to nourish us in a very dry season. This is a service to a reality that indulges in no illusions about the distant future, but reconciles us to a living past and teaches us to concentrate on the best conceivable present. Finally, and perhaps most important of all, the odd and startling joining of revolution and tradition is a philosophical strategy, the oldest one of all, in fact. It is the original and lasting task of philosophy to make the familiar seem unfamiliar, to shake one out of the spiritual lethargy of the commonplace. Philosophy shows one that one does *not* know all that one had believed one did know. Theoretical reasoning is a recovery of the ability to be astonished, to wonder. Only inventive philosophies can stir one to that state of awareness. It is far from easy. That is why Miss Arendt spoke of her essays on historiography as exercises. They were partly meant to be the intellectual equivalent of push-ups, especially for those who had avoided any sort of intellectual exertion, and they were also tentative, for speculative thought is bold without becoming dogmatic. It explores, it tries, and it expects.

It was Miss Arendt's choice to place herself, as it were, between the philosophers and the poets. She knew all of Plato's warnings against the latter, but she paid no heed. To write epic history—indeed, any history—one must make one's peace with the masters of tragedy. Nevertheless, political philosophy and history, even if they move within the cave of our actual world, are neither poetry nor mythology, even if occasionally they use these. Miss Arendt did not choose to look beyond politics for political enlightenment. She may well have been tempted by that path to the sun, but she resolutely turned her back upon it. Her book ends with a reaffirmation of the principles of Kant's third *Critique*—and quite properly so. Politics ought to be an expression of the faculty of judgment. As such it is the appeal of the disinterested spectator to all others who strive to be impartial. Their enlightened common sense must be assumed to yield universally acceptable standards, and it is in terms of these that we judge and try to persuade each other. That raises us above the squalid egotism of personal self-display in art and manners. We have taste when we willingly join in the best judgment of our peers, and we are free when we engage in unbroken political argument with them. This is the link between politics and philosophy then—the faculties of judgment and persuasion. It is, as Miss Arendt acknowledged, the core of that humanism that also had its origin among the

Romans. To believe in this sort of universal common sense is evidently an act of rational faith. It is a necessary one if one is to write monumental history for free people. Miss Arendt therefore quite deliberately ended her speculative journey into the past here, with Kant. It ensured the sanity of her enterprise, and it gave it a great and quiet dignity.

CHAPTER TWENTY

Hannah Arendt
as Pariah

Hannah Arendt wanted to be and actually was a "representative" woman, in the Emersonian sense of the term: someone who both mirrors and communicates to the world at large the spirit of her people. To represent the German Jews she had to be neither particularly good, admirable, nor typical, but rather the articulate embodiment of their aspirations, general character, and in this case also their end. She indeed groomed herself for the task, because even before she had to leave Germany she began to write the life of Rahel Varnhagen, née Levin, and she kept revising this favorite of her own works for more than twenty years. Rahel was a member of the first generation of emancipated Prussian Jews and experienced all the ambiguities and difficulties of their situation, being first celebrated and then shunned by her gentile friends. Arendt deeply identified with Rahel as their common world was coming to an end, but she was also quite critical of Rahel's moral cowardice and her frantic assimilation that ended in baptism, when she married Varnhagen. It was as if Arendt were warning herself not to lapse into Jewish self-hatred. Heinrich Heine eventually saved Rahel from this blight, as Arendt learned to save herself. Characteristically, from this very first look at their situation Arendt blamed the German Jews for many of their own troubles. There was much pride in that severe judgment. It was a deliberate refusal to play the passive, pitiable victim. As an expression of public rigor and of an enduring hatred of pity, this was quite in keeping with Prussian customs, but it was meant also to stop the German Jews from thinking of themselves as helpless pawns in

"Hannah Arendt as Pariah" by Judith N. Shklar first appeared in *Partisan Review* 50, no. 1 (1983): 64–77.

other people's games, without self-respect or the esteem of others. Arendt was to return to this theme over and over, often at considerable cost to herself and others.

It was in writing about Rahel that Arendt also came to divide the German Jews into two types, "the parvenus" and "the pariahs," and again she stuck to this notion for the rest of her life. Pariahs are outcasts who develop an intense sense of personal honor and pride in their status as aliens. They do not deign to toady to the hostile majority. That is what Rahel should have done from the first. Instead, even before her marriage, she was for many years a parvenu, who tried to be accepted by gentile society, that is, to become "an exceptional Jew," that proverbial "best friend" of every anti-Semite. The choice of the word parvenu to describe this humiliating behavior is not insignificant. It is *the* classic snob word, which is thrown at the *bourgeois gentilhomme* by the aristocrats whom he tries to join, and at the "new rich" by those who have inherited their money. The parvenu is a universal figure of ridicule and contempt. That she should have used that word for assimilated Jews tells us a good deal about Arendt. The pariah is so sure of her superiority that she no longer wishes to make efforts to join the larger society. She has, in fact, absorbed the attitudes of its upper class so completely that there is no impulse for her to rise from her actual condition. Who, after all, goes back further than "the people of the Book"? It is, nevertheless, startling to find assimilation condemned, not as false and foolish, but as vulgar. That it was useless was clear in many ways even to Rahel, who, a pariah at last, was left with nothing but her love of German literature, just as Arendt was able to salvage only her exceptional German *Bildung* when she was driven from her country in 1933.

Arendt was born in Königsberg into a complicated Jewish community. There were orthodox and also unbelieving Jews with radical political ideas, like her parents. There were Jews who thought of themselves as German citizens of the Hebrew faith, and there were Zionists. There were Jews who had recently come to the city from Eastern Europe, and others who had lived there for more than a century. There were baptized Jews, and Jews who made a point of emphasizing their Jewishness. With the exception of piety, Arendt was touched by all of these manifestations at one time or another. There was little overt anti-Semitism in Königsberg, but those born Jewish knew it, and Arendt's mother was especially firm about brooking no slighting remarks. Arendt clearly thought that neither her parents nor she were assimilated Jews. By that she seems to have meant that they had no intention of being baptized and that they openly declared their

Jewishness. This was no less than their personal duty—or one should say, *Pflicht,* because it has so much more weight, especially in Prussia. By East European and even American standards Arendt was, of course, completely assimilated, a view she always found incomprehensible. That was because she clung to the bizarre notion that being Jewish was an act of personal defiance and not a matter of actively maintaining a cultural and religious tradition with its own rites and patterns of speech.

Arendt did not get any Jewish education, but what she *did* receive was *Bildung,* and of that the best—gymnasium, private tutors, and finally a brilliant university career ending with a Ph.D. thesis on Saint Augustine. By then she had done it all: Greek, Latin, philosophy, literature in every form, and all of it so completely absorbed that it was for her, and her kind, part of the natural self. At this time she also became an ardent Zionist, which had since Herzl's day appealed to those assimilated Jews who wanted Israel to be a nation like all the others. For her mentor Kurt Blumenfeld and her, Zionism was also the solution to the "Jewish Question," as the influx of unwelcome *Ostjuden* was called. Zionism was to make the Jews a single people, especially by settling the East European Jews in what is now Israel. By 1933 there really was not much choice left. Zionism was now a necessity, not one option among others.

The details of Hannah Arendt's life can be found in the biography, *Hannah Arendt: For Love of the World,* by Elisabeth Young-Bruehl, which appeared less than ten years after Arendt's death. Young-Bruehl not only vividly remembers Arendt, she was also able to talk to many of Arendt's oldest friends, and just in time, because many have died since she interviewed them. These people shared their recollections and letters freely, it seems, and the outcome is a rich and detailed biography, with all the strength and weakness of a memoir written by an admiring friend. The disadvantages of haste are that some important documents and correspondences are not yet available and that Arendt, to some degree directly, and indirectly through her friends, was able to choose what would be and what would not be revealed. There are therefore some incomplete details and omissions. The book is also often repetitious. Nevertheless, anyone who might in the future write another life of Hannah Arendt, or the history of the last generation of German Jews, will gratefully rely on this volume.

Young-Bruehl tells the first part of Arendt's story exceptionally well. She might have said a little more about the impact of the First World War, which hit Arendt and her widowed mother very hard. We know from *The Origins of Totalitarianism* that Arendt herself was fully aware of the moral and cultural debasement that followed the war. The universities were a moral chaos, respect for learning was eroded, and the veterans were bitter and cynical. The best people began to ask why all those young men had continued to go to places like Flanders Field; why had they not refused? The memories of these years remained with Arendt for the rest of her life. So also, at a very different level, did the preoccupation with death, the void, the absence of all standards and realities, in short the condition of "nothingness."

Who can doubt that Martin Heidegger's *Sein und Zeit* must be read as a long meditation upon the moods, experiences, and intimations of that protracted horror? When Arendt eventually came to describe the alliance between "the mob" and "the déclassé élite" she was drawing Heidegger's portrait, for not only had he joined the Nazi Party, but he did so out of a long-held loathing for the pseudo-solid world of the bourgeoisie and its hypocrisies, which veiled the suffering of the soldiers with sentimental talk. That he was not just a member of the elite but a genius, and her loved and admired teacher as well, did not make these betrayals easy to bear. She did, however, have a very clear grasp of the origins of Heidegger's conduct in the trenches, and the worst she ever said of *Sein und Zeit* was that it was egoistical. Eventually she found it easy to forgive Heidegger. She had always seen through the cult that surrounded him, knowing perfectly well that none of his admirers had a clue to what he was saying. That, in fact, is still the condition of the thriving Heidegger industry. Arendt, however, not only understood him, she was and remained under his philosophical spell.

Philosophy was for both of them an act of dramatizing through word play, textual associations, bits of poetry, and other phrases their direct experiences. It was "passionate thinking." In this post-Nietzschean activity there is no pretense about pursuing the truth or any other end. Thinking is its own reward and purpose, and to outsiders it seems a random response. Only those who shared a *Bildung* and a culture could decipher it, its myths and many puns. It is also completely arbitrary. Nothing could, in any event, be more remote from either Anglo-American philosophy or traditional Continental idealism.

These philosophical habits were perfectly well suited to Arendt's political experience after the rise of Hitler. She kept them when she moved away from Heidegger and acquired other teachers, such as Karl Jaspers. By then there was only one possible form of politics: resistance, at first to fascism and then to all authorities, even in Paris.

For the condition of the refugees there was a perpetual "Catch 22": no job without a work permit, and no work permit without a job. Arendt did find employment with several Jewish agencies and worked especially for the Youth Aliyah. She even tried, briefly, to learn Hebrew, "to know my people," but she did not get very far. She spoke no Yiddish either. She did, however, get to know a lot of Communists, thanks to both of her husbands. Traces of Marxian class analysis remained fixtures in her work, and not surprisingly, because hating the philistines and the bourgeoisie was built into her *Bildung.* Indeed Marx was one of the few philosophers of whom Heidegger spoke with some respect. At any rate a revolutionary cannot be a parvenu and, in fact, Arendt retained an abiding faith in the civic virtues of the "real" working class in contrast to "the mob." It was one of her many ahistorical fantasies.

When she arrived in America her refugee life continued under new circumstances. She managed to eke out a living by working for various Jewish agencies, papers, and publishers, and she remained involved in Zionist politics. I am not quite sure I know, after reading Young-Bruehl, what she supported, but she was certainly at odds with all sides of the American Zionist movement. From the first one gets the impression that pariah status demanded that she remain apart from all "establishment" organizations, even if they were Jewish. Eventually she joined Judah Magnes's party, which hoped for a federal binational state in Palestine. At all times it was a matter of great importance to her, however, that the Jews remain a European people, and that Israel be composed of both native-born and Diaspora Jews. She was also involved in the more typical forms of émigré politics, particularly a quarrel with the unspeakable Theodor Adorno over the disposition of the manuscripts that Walter Benjamin had entrusted to her before he killed himself.

Someone ought to write a study of émigré politics some day, beginning with the American Tory exiles in London after the Revolution. These politics are so dreadful because they consist entirely of recriminations, for nothing new happens to émigrés, there is no one to persuade, no followings to be organized, and no offices or measures to be pursued. There is no future, only a past. Exile does nothing for one's character. It is a very desperate condition. We know from the history of nineteenth-century immigrations to America that the suffering of the newcomers was dreadful. Their unhappiness was due less to material deprivation, since many had never known comfort, than to homesickness and loneliness. The German Jews in New York in the 1930s and 1940s were able to form little "tribes," as Arendt called her old friends, from among their fellow exiles and so they were not isolated. Only their homesickness, aggravated by worry about friends who did not get out, was overwhelming. It is something that has to be experienced to be understood.

Homelessness, however, has its political dimensions, and one of Arendt's best early essays dealt with statelessness. Her argument, based on her own experience and that of other refugees in France, was that in a world of nation-states, human rights are meaningless apart from citizenship. The only fundamental right of man, therefore, is the right to be the legal citizen of some state. Without that nothing else is possible. This, however, is not a call for an organic community or nationality, but for citizenship as a legal and political entitlement, not an accident of birth. The distinction is theoretically very important, but it was also one of her blind spots. By the time she wrote *The Origins of Totalitarianism* she had made up her mind that nationalism was a thing of the past—it was dead and not to be confused or compared with the living ideologies of the age. This notion, which her Marxist inclinations reinforced, was immune to evidence; nothing could persuade her that nationalism was still a very great force in the present. On this point, I speak from personal experience. As one of her friends, Erich Heller, was to note, when Arendt was wrong she "exploded into wrongness."

Young-Bruehl tells us that Arendt had a hard time organizing the book that made her famous, and indeed *The Origins of Totalitarianism* consists of three detached parts. It is also mistitled since *origins* suggests an historical account of social changes from their first beginnings onward. Like most readers, Young-Bruehl, however, finds Arendt's approach to history confusing. And well she might. Arendt never showed the slightest respect for historians. She called the heirs of Ranke "eunuchs" because of their striving for objectivity. The representation of the past through the chronological arrangement of all the available evidence struck her as trivial. She had no interest in explaining how something came to be, step by step. What she found valuable was "the unpremeditated attentive facing up to and resisting of reality," which was Heidegger's response to *Geschichtlichkeit*. With bits of history, literature, biography, and a lot of personal imagination and speculation, she set out, and in fact managed, to create an enveloping sense of the world of anti-Semites and Jews, and of the imperialists and their victims. This indeed is Nietzschean history, not as piety, political advice, or science, but in the service of the social imagination, if not of "life."

The last part of the book is not an account of what actually went

on in the Nazi and Soviet concentration camps—one need only compare it to any reliable historical work on the subject. What she does
offer is quite different. It is an illustration of the post-Nietzschean
world of "nothingness." The camps are the places of terror with no
exits, where nothing normal remains. They are reality inverted. To
outsiders this world may look insane or like the hell of Giotto's *Last
Judgement,* but that is obtuse. The camps' world, "inside," proves
"that the power of man is greater" than conventional people care to
admit. In fact, of course, human power is all there is. We create our
own knowable world and every standard in it. For God does not
preside over anything. This world, moreover, re-creates itself, for everything in it is superfluous, and omnipotent man creates superfluities
to be discarded and repeated, over and over again. Hell remains well
stocked. Common sense can never grasp, and utilitarianism is only a
barrier to recognition of, this reversal of all values. This is not merely
Dante's *Inferno* without God, it is also an echo of Zarathustra, who
already talked of men as pebbles to be kicked aside—except there is
no hope of any superman now. For the world of terror that omnipotent man has created is also a world of necessity, of "iron" laws of
nature and history and with its own "icy logic." Ideology has made
and maintains this void in the absence of "Being." Such, then, is our
disorder when we must give up the very notion of truth and our
search for it. This indeed is "history" as facing and resisting reality.
For Arendt the totalitarian world was a philosophical nightmare of
which the actuality of the camps was the expression.

   If the last section of *The Origins of Totalitarianism* was an exercise
in post-Nietzschean philosophizing, the book also made a serious
contribution to political theory in the tradition of Montesquieu and
de Tocqueville. Arendt's analysis of totalitarianism as a new and
unique type of rule was a real addition to the theory of regimes. The
importance of superfluous populations also goes far to explain geno-
cide. One need only consider the American Indian. For superfluous
peoples were for Arendt both a surrealist vision and a perfectly
straightforward historical explanation of some imperialist encounters. It ought, finally, to be stressed that although Arendt insisted on
the gulf that separated totalitarian from authoritarian regimes, she
would not have approved of the current use of that distinction. It
would, one suspects, have distressed her to see her work become an
ideological weapon of any kind, but especially one wielded against
the support of human rights abroad. Her own career as a cold warrior
came to an end in the sixties. She was always fiercely anti-Soviet,
knowing what that regime was since the Moscow Trials, but she

could not bear most ex- or anti-Communists. Only those German *former* Communists like her husband, who had quit the party very early, could count on her respect, as Young-Bruehl carefully explains.

Of all the sections of *The Origins of Totalitarianism* the one on the theory of mass society was the least original and the most superficial, as well as the most popular. Its classic exposition had already appeared in Emil Lederer's *The State of the Masses,* to which Arendt failed to acknowledge a very obvious debt. In post-Marxist speculative sociology, the failure of the proletariat to appear and the success of fascism meant that class society was dead and had been replaced by an undifferentiated "mass," which was easily held together by hate ideologies, propaganda, and terror. The nonsociety of these disoriented individuals was the inevitable successor of class society as Marx had seen it. The American spin-offs from this were numerous. The consumer society, McCarthyism, mid-mass conformism, and even the populist tradition in American politics were squeezed into this essentially Marxist vision. For no one could say a good word for the middle class. Mass theory became at most a rather crude weapon in the hands of various local old-left radicals, who wanted to take one last whack at America. As for *The Origins of Totalitarianism*—it remains enormously interesting and must surely become a primary document in the intellectual history of the middle years of this century.

Arendt's next book was the first non-Jewish and the most German of her American writings. By the mid-fifties her *Bildung* had reasserted itself. She had brushed up her Greek and she had picked up the surviving pieces of her German past, including Heidegger. She wrote to her husband that her first visit to Karl Jaspers in Basel in 1949 was "like coming home." She returned to Germany often from then on. Being "back home" revealed some not unexpected layers of thought and feeling. In keeping with the oldest traditions and the purest ideals of German *Bildung* she worshiped ancient Greece. No one ever had a worse case of Athens-worship than Arendt. The passionate longing for that lost culture was the deepest impulse of romantic poetry and of that quest for "spiritual" liberation, especially in a society as unfree as the Germany of Schiller, Humboldt, and Heidegger's loved Hölderlin. In addition to this classicism she appears to have been drawn to Roman Catholicism in those years. Perhaps remaining unbaptized or a pariah was a real struggle for her. She was often in the company of her old Catholic friend, Waldemar Gurian, a liberal baptized Jew; lectured for several years in the neo-Thomist atmosphere of the University of Chicago; and published a great many of her essays in *Commonweal* and in Notre Dame's *Re-*

view of Politics. One would like to hear more about her Chicago associations than Young-Bruehl tells us.

In any case, we know that her first introduction to philosophy came from the Catholic theologian Romano Guardini and that she attended many courses on Christian theology, always making sure that there would be no anti-Semitic talk. Her Ph.D. thesis was on Saint Augustine's concept of neighborly love, considered philosophically, not theologically. It was, nevertheless, a study of a Christian thinker who regarded love as an expression of man's relation to God. In *The Human Condition* the medieval Church is seen as the great preserver of classical values, and Jesus as one of the great heroes of the "active" life. Eventually she wrote a cloying and sentimental essay on John XXIII, "The Christian Pope." This, as well as the preoccupations of *The Human Condition* and of some of her subsequent essays, may well have contributed to her remoteness (in the very middle of Manhattan!) from the actual life of American Jewry. Remote may be too feeble a word, for *Eichmann in Jerusalem* is set in a cultural vacuum.

The Human Condition is likely to remain Arendt's most widely admired book. It is very closely modeled on Hegel's *Phenomenology* and its main arguments owe much to his *Lectures on the History of Philosophy.* This debt is passed over in silence and Hegel is presented only as one of the precursors of Marx's philosophy of history, an enterprise that Arendt thought political theory should abandon, although, in fact, *The Human Condition* itself belongs to that genre. The argument is a "then" and "now" contrast, the ancients against the moderns. In Greek thought and practice, labor, man's natural effort to survive, was despised. Fabrication—the creation of artificial objects out of nature—and action—the realm of human exchanges and of history—were separated from labor and placed on a higher level. At the top of the moral hierarchy was contemplation, man's highest end. This view was adopted by Christian theologians and philosophers, though their contempt for the world was more intense. This hierarchy also set apart the lowly "private" sphere of the laboring household from the "public" sphere, where human activity took place. "Making" and "acting" were also kept apart, as they are not today. Indeed "modern man" has turned all this upside down to disastrous effect. "Making" social life is to fabricate utopias. Above all, the dignity of labor has devalued activity, so that private life has now all but eliminated public space and silenced public man. Only artists still create and only scientists act in the present world. The task now of political theory, therefore, is not to return to the old primacy of contemplation, but to put action in its place, so that public life will stand above private labor.

It is not surprising that Heidegger hated this book. It was Arendt's explicit rejection of his "nihilism" and more especially of his search for a pre-Socratic and also radically anti-Christian ground of thinking. It is not irrelevant that Heidegger was a very lapsed Catholic. Not only did Arendt here seem to turn away from the priority of poetry and the need to devise new myths, she had also taken up a philosophical tradition that Heidegger had long since declared bankrupt. And indeed after she had finished *The Human Condition* Arendt came to share the outlook of her other teacher, Karl Jaspers, and so in due course turned to Kant, especially the *Critique of Judgement,* for guidance in her later political reflections.

Arendt's own political dream remained tied to the polis. In spite of what Aristotle tells us, she was never very clear about what went on in that blessed "public space." In fact, we know that there was ferocious fighting between rich and poor and over who would conduct the next interpolis war, and in what manner. These unpleasant facts are rarely mentioned by those advocates of participatory democracy who became her disciples. She herself tended more toward a Kropotkin-type anarchism of which the polislike kibbutz, the primitive Soviets, and the workers' councils of the Hungarian uprising were the historic illustrations. But she also appreciated American democracy, though it cannot be said that she understood it particularly well. She was, among other things, prone to prophecies of early catastrophe. Whenever something unfortunate occurred she thought that the end of the republic was near. (One does not forget Weimar easily.) Her admiration for the work of the men of 1787 was also exaggerated, because she came to think of them as classical models of civic virtue, latter-day Catos. That is how she came especially to regard John Adams, who feared both the "many" and the "few," the "masses" and the "elite." Even Jefferson passed muster because he wanted our politics to remain local. All this appeared in *On Revolution,* which compares the American to the French Revolution much to the disadvantage of the latter. Like Mandeville and many other eighteenth-century liberals, Arendt discovered that pity is out of place in politics, and that to cure "misery" is to overstep the bounds of the "public" into the "private," which, she claimed, was what led the Jacobins astray.

The only really interesting thing about this embarrassing book is that it is a new version of Friedrich Gentz's comparison of the two revolutions. Arendt had written an essay on him before she left Germany, and she drew an extremely unflattering picture of him in *Rahel*. He had been one of the several hollow men who had betrayed poor Rahel. If this was Arendt's revenge, one must regret it. Arendt's later articles on American politics read like dutiful efforts to remain a "committed intellectual," a stance she greatly admired, especially among the French. Her best essays were wonderful biographies, most of them on women, especially Rosa Luxemburg and Isak Dinesen.

Many writers love to cover trials, which seem to inspire the best novelists. In our time Rebecca West and Sybille Bedford have been notable courtroom reporters. And so Arendt decided that she too would write up a trial—Eichmann's. She wanted to get a good look at a Nazi murderer and she intended to discuss, as in fact she did, some of the great puzzles raised by the trials of war criminals. How should one assign responsibility for acts committed by public agents, not on their own initiative, but as members of governmental organizations? Who can try such people? These are not minor issues in contemporary political theory. Arendt had nothing very new to say about them in *Eichmann in Jerusalem*, where they are discussed in a derivative and amateurish way. Legal theory was not her forte. As for the banality of Eichmann's evil, it was really only a return to a point she and many others have made about the Nazi regime: there was a complete disproportion between its causes and its consequences. To look at any of the defendants at Nuremberg and at the Europe in which they were being tried gave one a far more vivid sense of the distance between them and what they had brought about than did Eichmann in his glass booth in Jerusalem.

What Arendt really did in *Eichmann in Jerusalem*, however, was to assert her pariah status in an outburst of self-centered "resistance to reality," this time in defiance of her own people. Why, she asked, had the East European Jews not behaved like Homeric heroes? Why had they not resisted the Germans more courageously? Why had they contributed to their own destruction? Why had they left no gallant myth for us? All this in spite of the fact that she knew perfectly well that, while Eastern Jews might have made minor difficulties for the Germans, they never could have averted their doom. Only the Allies could save them. One had to be educated, rich, or at least have connections like Arendt (and my parents) to get out of Europe at all. Only a fraction of the "elite"—and not a large one—could hope to leave Eastern Europe at any time. For one of the happy few, in the comfort of New York and in the pages of the *New Yorker*, studded with ads for luxury goods, to ask those "questions" was shocking. The articles, moreover, displayed an extraordinary ignorance. Arendt generalized wildly about the infinitely complex and diverse communities of Eastern Europe, about whose history and structure she knew exactly nothing. To be sure, there had been class conflicts in those societies, and after the anguish of the Final Solution they flared up with bitterness and violence among the survivors in Israel. These also Arendt subjected to the simplicities of her theory of assimilation. The final truth about who did what in Hungary, and what the various Jewish Councils did and did not do during the Nazi era, may never be fully known, but even Young-Bruehl is less than certain that Arendt knew what she was talking about. Truth was not her object.

The reaction from many American Jews was predictable. That Arendt did not anticipate it and was utterly surprised by their anger only shows how divorced she was from local Jewish society. Indeed, apart from a few New York intellectuals, she did not really know any American Jews and she had long ceased to take part in Zionist organizations. But there was more than ignorance and dissociation in her book. There was no particular reason to publish it in that place and at that time. It probably gave no comfort to anti-Semites, as some charged, but it caused pain and justified rage. She meant to inflict the first and need not have been astonished at the latter. At best one can say that she was consistent, because she had always seen Jewishness as the personal acceptance of a fact, and not as a communal way of living. *Eichmann* was, however, not her only lapse into uncomprehending arrogance. Her obsession with pariah status had three years before *Eichmann* provoked her into scolding those black parents who had sent their children into forcibly integrated schools in Little Rock. They ought not to expose their children to its humiliations, she argued, and in any case legal and political rights ought not to be coercively extended into the "social" sphere. Her ignorance of American post–Civil War history, of racism, of constitutional law, and of Southern politics was total. That did not deter her from writing an essay to advise and belabor the blacks in Little Rock. Her essay might, in fact, have been of real use to racists, but fortunately it was published in a radical journal, *Dissent,* which neutralized the mischief. Characteristically she changed her mind about the black parents when Ralph Ellison explained to her that they were not parvenus after all, but were heroically sacrificing their children to the future of black America. This sordid episode is, in some ways, a better illustration than *Eichmann* of the fantasy world into which her private responses had led her.

In spite of all this, the American Jewish establishment *did* overreact. The charge of anti-Semitism cannot hold; even disloyalty is too harsh a judgment. Her idea of what a Jew should be was disastrous, but it began as an honorable reaction to the realities of German-Jewish life. Her American-Jewish critics, even before *Eichmann,* were also too sure that there was only one way to be a good Jew: theirs. There was a disproportion between her awful book and the outbursts that it evoked, the most violent coming neither from Israelis nor Jews of European origin, but from American and English Jews who felt more directly attacked by it. They were certainly far too quick to say "anti-Semite" when they felt affronted. In truth, relations between the German and American Jews had long been simmering. The guilt that many American Jews felt for having done less than they might to help the Europeans played its part; hence their subsequent over-identification with the real victims. There were also very real cultural tensions. The anxieties of Jews in a pluralistic, multi-ethnic, demo-cratic society with fresh memories of the Depression were not those of Jews from unitary, class-ridden, authoritarian societies with fas-cism to frighten them. Moreover the hope, which Arendt shared, that the conflict between *Ostjuden* and *Yeckes* would go away was real-ized only with the final disappearance of the German Jews. When they came to America they were uncomfortably unlike any other first generation of Jewish immigrants. They were well educated, had been well off, were rarely observant, and knew no Yiddish. They were strangers to the language and the rituals of everyday life that make American Jews a cohesive community. The two were at different stages of assimilation. The Germans often felt repelled by even the most welcoming American Jews, and stuck to each other or to soli-tude. (I knew a man who went to the zoo constantly, because it seemed more familiar than the rest of the Bronx to him.) Finally, the German Jews often did very well very quickly in America. These newcomers often found it easier to succeed in the professions, in sci-ence, and in academic life than their long-suffering American peers. Were these Germans genuine *Jews,* or was their ability to get on in the gentile world not a sign of their innate disloyalty?

Even their attitude to America was at first a puzzle. They did not plan to stay. Only the Final Solution finally convinced them that they had no *Heimat* in Europe. That Arendt did go back and did choose to find her spiritual home there was probably at the very root of her self-inflicted troubles. Nor can her Hellenism have helped her to be more realistic. Rahel's contemporary, Ludwig Börne, né Baruch, be-gan the German practice of contrasting the Hebrews and the Greeks, and it did neither him nor anyone since much good, least of all Nietzsche's heirs. In spite of all this Arendt's detractors were no more tolerant or generous than she was, and they were, after all, in a far stronger position. They were not the last members of a quickly dying culture. American Jewry is a flourishing community, while German-Jewish culture died with Hannah Arendt.

While all this was going on, Arendt continued to be an enormous success as a teacher at several universities. Her firmness appealed to American students starved for authority. They could also see that her *Bildung* had a depth that could sustain her in a way that their education never would or could. Most of all she had a great deal of personal magnetism and her histrionic talents were formidable. No one who ever heard her lecture in her rasping, guttural, East-Prussian, German-accented English can ever forget that voice. She was always a great presence. When she spoke, *all* of her was *there*.

Young-Bruehl has written a full, if not complete, life of Arendt. She evidently admired her, but the reader is not forced into sharing her view, and can come away neither liking nor agreeing with Arendt. That is the sign of an honest work. It is the story of a Jewish life, lived as she thought a Jew should live, for better or worse. At her death only five members of her once large family were alive. And one is moved by the last photograph taken of her shortly before she died. It is the face of an old Jewess, with two thousand years of sorrow on it.

CHAPTER TWENTY-ONE

The Work of
Michael Walzer

Let me begin by explaining why I agreed to do something as embarrassing as talking about an old and dear friend in public. My reason is that I am quite sure that along with John Rawls, Michael Walzer is by far the most important, the most original, and the most intelligent political theorist in America. And one of the many reasons for the distinction of Rawls and Walzer is that both write about concrete phenomena in a language that is clear and open to any careful reader.

Walzer's range is also extraordinary. He has written about Puritan revolutionaries, political obedience and disobedience, just war theory, justice and equality, about interpretation, and in short about every significant place where personal moral experience and politics meet. In all these works there is beneath an admirable eclecticism a constant set of themes, above all the conviction that intellectuals are duty-bound to articulate the deepest beliefs and concerns of their fellow citizens, and that political theory is meant not to tell them what to do or how to think but to help them to a clearer notion of what they already know and would say if only they could find the right words. To that end he tells historically grounded just so stories and illuminates his general propositions with copious illustrations drawn from history, poetry, and his favorite political theorists, Hobbes, Marx, and Rousseau. All of this is done with infinite care, is beautifully written, and shows a genuine respect for the independence and dignity of his readers.

Alas, my old and dear friend, having said all that, I must also say

This undated essay has not been previously published.

that the fact remains that since our salad days, we have disagreed, and I shall dwell at length upon those disagreements here. But I want all of you to understand that I shall not say anything that I have not already often said to Walzer, and that for him there is nothing new in my remarks. Indeed, they are but a small part of an argument that has lasted for some thirty odd years. It is a dialogue between an exile and a citizen, and as such it was not born yesterday.

As he says of it himself, Walzer's work is "imminent and phenomenological." This means that it is a relevant and integrated historical and psychological narrative which is familiar and always interesting without ever becoming superficial. It is a tremendous achievement. He has created a political language that by relying on the right examples, drawn from the here and now, has put a new and attractive life into the classical topics of political theory.

Since his very first book, Walzer has been deeply interested in the character and vocation of social critics, especially the intellectuals among them, and in some ways those Puritan radicals remain his models. Most recently he has in *Interpretation and Social Criticism* gone beyond this particular case and worked out a general theory of social criticism as a prophetic enterprise. I want to begin with that project, because it obviously tells us what it is that he is up to. There are, according to Walzer, three styles of political theory and social criticism. One is the way of discovery, the second the way of invention, and the last the way of interpretation. The discoverer acts like an executive official who having either had a divine revelation or made some scientific discovery grounded in new social psychology, such as utilitarianism, acts upon its demands and enforces the rules that follow from the initial act of insight. A theorist who had discovered the secret of historical necessity would thus apply known social truths to the existing order and demand that others follow him. The inventor is more like a constitutional legislator. He thinks things through for himself in a state of mind as impartial, as universal, as objective, and as impersonal as possible. And he asks his fellow citizens to share that exercise, to withdraw for a while from their particular experiences and commitments, and to ask, what would be fair and what would be just for all of us, not as particular persons but as citizens of a possible society. This is not a view from Mars but a radical intellectual experiment that each one of us could undertake to arrive at a view of justice that would satisfy us whether we were among the lucky few or one of the unlucky many in the hazards of life. These two ways of criticizing the actual seem to Walzer defective because he regards them as undemocratic, because they involve escapes from the cave. Of course the critic who has seen the light does return to persuade the cavemen to join him in a journey out of the depth, but he is still a loner. It is especially objectionable to Walzer that these critics seek "a universal cure for all the different social moralities," that in short they do not bend to local custom, preference, and group traditions. Their morality encompasses only the individual moral agent and universal moral imperatives. Cosmopolitan exiles from their place and time, they are remote from ordinary men and women and as such to be rejected. Instead of these elitists, Walzer proposes an interpretive critic more like a judge who reads society as if it were a text and then interprets its immanent values and asserts them against the deviant practices of the present. The text is not an esoteric script, however; it is the "common understanding" of all the members of the society, and the interpretive critic, like an Old Testament prophet, calls the erring multitude to abandon Baal and to return to the law that sustains them all. Why is the prophet a better critic? It might be argued that he is much more likely to succeed if he appeals to beliefs that are commonly shared, even if they have been abandoned. This would be an argument for efficiency, and on the surface it looks convincing, if trivial. It is not, in fact, the argument Walzer makes, for the excellent reason that those prophets ended up being scorned and reviled no less often than every other social critic. So it is not the expectation of success that is at stake here. Rather Walzer wants to argue that the interpreter, the critic from within, is more democratic, because he does not step outside the confines of local values to seek an extratemporal detachment and impartiality. He is also not as manipulative as his two rivals, Walzer claims. There are at least two difficulties with this view. First of all, the interpreter is in his way less accountable to his audience than the detached analytic philosopher. There is no way of checking up on him. This is not what the text means, he says, you have read it wrongly; but I have the right interpretation of its meaning. Meaning, however, is in the eyes of the beholder, that is, the reader. Either you see it or you do not; no rational argument there. There is no slow process of ratiocination, no way of reviewing the accuracy, the coherence, the logical consistency, or the steps of an analysis. That is why scriptural interpretation is the war it has always been. Second, given that there is clearly a conflict between the interpretations that provoked the social critic in the first place, he also must resort to a standard that stands outside the dispute and is not therefore embedded in the local and far-from-shared morality, but which an impartial person would find just or convincing at least. It is a move Walzer in fact often resorts to as well. In short, unless we take "interpretation" to mean that one cannot go beyond the intimations of a given time and place without inexcusably disrupting traditions—Oakeshott's point, which Walzer rejects as too conservative—interpretation is not nearly as earthy and cozy and remote from rational argument as he wants us to think. If it is argumentative, as Walzer thinks it should be, then it is just as likely to be manipulative as any other theory, indeed more so, for the critic will be tempted to appeal to deep sentiments, shared memories, and communal feelings as persuasive techniques. The real difficulty with appeals to communal values and sentiments is that when they conflict, and each side refers to another page of the social text, there has to be some extratextual referee. There must, in short, be impersonal, detached, general standards of interpretation for the judge, and these are what the inventor and the discoverer call moral principles. This is especially necessary in pluralist societies, as Walzer sees them, where there are several competing texts. Surely "we," his favorite characters, want not only to say that Shakespeare and Kant wrote a great text, but we also want to say, as ordinary men and women, "this is unjust" and this is "fair," not just for you and me but for all humanity.

The prophetic political theorist does not in principle seek philosophical foundations for his interpretations of the law. They appeal either to God or, in Walzer's case, to what he calls "shared understandings." He tells stories; he does not argue from first principles to particular instances. The questions of where his parables come from and what they might add up to are best seen in one of his earliest works, but one that is also exceptionally lucid, though in its way as self-divided as all the others. I refer to *Obligations*. The enduring theoretical issues that are raised in that volume concern not only civil disobedience, conscientious objection, and conscription, important and interesting as those are. What is central to these essays is an effort to develop a theory of the relationship between voluntary organizations and the state. Although Walzer fully acknowledges his debt to the English pluralists of an earlier period, especially G. D. H. Cole, he branches out on his own and makes a very distinctive contribution to one of the oldest and newest topics in political theory, the question of political obligation. In the United States the matter has always been treated in terms of the isolated individual facing an authority that might invade the little empire of me. Against that tradition Walzer pits a radically group-centered vision. It is membership in voluntary associations that really shapes our commitments, and it is as members of societies other than the state that we acquire our most fundamental moral characteristics. When we confront the state in protest, we do so as members of distinctive groups, such as sects, churches, or ideological parties, not as simple bearers of a personal conscience. It follows that rights are to be seen as not applying primarily to socially unidentified individuals but to people with recognizable group affiliations. Membership itself, including citizenship in a state, is, however, seen as a matter of consent, and consent is not part of the group story. Nor is it obvious that consent to the law is really like consent to a group when that occurs, especially ethnic, religious, caste, class, and ascriptive associations. We are born into them, in some cases with no choice at all, and in others with very little psychological latitude. We can in principle leave or drop out of the state, but we have no choice at all about who our parents are. Walzer's version of consent has little punch to it. If consent is given at all, it is part of our individual moral biography. It cannot be an actual shake of the hand, the promise to obey and to belong made consciously. Mere authorization of representatives and other manifestations of tacit consent do not suffice to prove that consenting has taken place. There has to be, as there is in a voluntary association, an act of joining. Its equivalent in the modern state is a continuity of little acts that create the expectation of obedience to the law in our fellow citizens and thus constitute a promise in their effect. We are consequently under deep political obligation. The implication is nevertheless that our membership in lesser associations constitutes a prior, more voluntary, and more genuine commitment, and that the state ought to be rather more of a club than it now is. That failing, the state must guarantee the most extensive civil liberties, so that the citizens can at least move freely in performing acts of membership, association, and, one hopes, dissociation, which constitute a life of consenting.

The assumption here is that being a citizen of the state is not intrinsically different from being a member of a club, and indeed that the club is the perfect model for the state, including the bonds of intimacy, common attitudes, and mutual loyalty that members of the same club tend to share. To obey the laws of the state in preference to those of one's club is moreover an act of "selling out," in Walzer's words. It seems to me that there are several difficulties here. First of all, there is a confusion of loyalty and obligation. The two are not at all the same, I think. Loyalty is affective. It is not a considered choice but what we feel for our kin and our club. It is simply an expression of our whole personality. Obligation is evoked by rules whose validity we assess and recognize for a variety of explicit reasons, whether they be prudential or ethical or both. When the state demands loyalty it is looking for trouble, for legislated patriotism is no patriotism at all. Loyalty is either spontaneous or it is thought control, and it is very bad news. So keeping the two apart is a matter of some importance. The second flaw I see in Walzer's case is the tension between an extremely individualistic theory of consent, consent as a series of personal acts that give rise to expectations, as promises do, which is joined to a communitarian view of obligation, and especially of the limits of obligation. The tension between club membership and citizenship is acute. For the citizen all is liberal rights here. But in fact that individualism is a mirage, because we really only act as groupies, as members, as brothers and sisters in a cause. It is membership that structures our personality and that has an unquestioned primacy in our moral and political obligations. There is no question which comes first. The state is simply inferior in the moral and psychological scale here. That is due less to Walzer's contempt for the modern state and his quaint addiction to ancient Athens than to his idealization of voluntary associations. In fact, he recognizes the universality of the state's claim and its dignity as the guarantor of all political and personal rights, but he slips back into a sentimental affection for the "little platoon" at every opportunity. If Walzer had a complete theory, grounded in the history of these associations, his case might be stronger, but as it is he clearly thinks that they are all like Protestant or Reform Jewish congregations or high-minded fraternal labor organizations. Most however, resemble the Teamsters Union, the Ku Klux Klan, and the Anti-Saloon League a good deal more. Moreover, the historical record is grim. During the First World War, for example, the Justice Department delegated most draft administration, spy and loyalty enforcement, and war bond selling to local volunteer groups, and the system of loyalty enforcement they created makes Senator McCarthy look benevolent. Indeed I have come to understand him as the final act of a very sinister history in which the federal government did exactly what Walzer would have it do, delegate its civic tasks to local voluntary associations. It is, finally, no big surprise that the poor, the black, and the injured have looked to the federal government for hope and help and not to the local voluntary or official agencies. That is because the state, even a defective one, is more likely to enforce impersonal rules of justice. Indeed, Walzer agrees that the charity offered by voluntary groups is degrading for the recipients in a way that legislated state benefits are not.

I also think that the notion that voluntary organizations exist in some sense apart from the modern state is as wrong in theory as in practice. It is only the modern state, with its unified legal system, that provides the framework within which voluntary associations can form, and their autonomy is wholly derivative and dependent upon their adherence to the rules of the state. The alternative is, of course, intergroup war, as in feudal Europe and in the multiethnic state everywhere today. Indeed, Walzer might well reflect upon the value of group loyalty either within groups or in the state, considering what nationalism and its xenophobic ethos have cost mankind.

If the consent that the state can get is rooted so deeply in national loyalty, if that is our common understanding, then Walzer has condoned a political view that is both erroneous and violent, for there are no nation-states; all modern states are multinational, and what they need is more citizens with individual rights and a sense of public obligation based on personal justice and fairness to the individual, and less group loyalty. Their consent would not come from the gut, but from a detached calculation, from an ingrained sense of security, and it would come from alienated persons who disliked but did not murder one another. What they would demand is justice.

That brings us to Walzer's finest and most important book, *Spheres of Justice*. It tells two stories. One is the story of what I will call normal distributive justice, that is, impartial fairness among equals in respect to the burdens and benefits of society. This is the story of our shared understandings, because the political community is one of common meanings and, to quote, "shared intuitions and sensibilities," we are told, so that common rules can and do apply. The second story is a pluralistic tale of many incommensurable values and experiences, and also of different and disparate spheres of evaluation and human experience which require, not identity, but a "complex equality," as Walzer calls it, recognizing that we do not distribute love in the same way as we distribute wages, and that we *should* not calculate the interest on a loan on the same scale as the costs of medical care. I emphasize the *should* in the second example, because although Walzer professes to speak for "us" and "our" common understanding, he is in fact very critical of the policies that have governed our Scrooge of a welfare state and our Dickensian medical practices. The "we" for whom he speaks as an insider is not just a critic, he shares the voice of the liberal minority, quasi-populists.

The enemy of any pluralism is monopoly and the domination it yields. The most obvious cases are economic wealth spreading to political office and conversely the expansion of political power into economic and social privilege. These are common enough, and the real interest of Walzer's book is to show how many other such transmutations of advantage there are from sphere to sphere. A pluralist theory of distributive justice must therefore rely on a multiplicity of standards, each within its own fenced-off turf. Need is a readily identified standard at the point of starvation, but it is a highly uncertain measure when the line between needs and wants is crossed. There is merit, so dear to the heart of the successful scholar, but what is merit? An ability to take exams successfully, an abundance of common sense, an ability to understand other people, or a talent for scientific reasoning? There is no easy way to sort all that out. What about distributing dirty work? A good union contract and a snappy uniform turned New York City's garbagemen into satisfied sanitation workers. In San Francisco, a self-organized cooperative firm, composed mostly of Italian-Americans, called the scavengers, did much of the same job, not as unionized state employees but as a private joint venture. They also like their work, because they do it together. Walzer prefers this more communal solution, whereas I prefer the union because it is more likely to include every ethnic group and to insure fairness to all who apply for the job. Unlike the situation with the scavengers, the job is not inherited and membership cannot be exclusionary as it may be in a private concern, however cooperative. But what justice demanded in either case was the abolition of dirty work altogether, for it is a task, like housework, which also need not be degrading if it is not coercively imposed upon women, but shared, done part-time, and as a service to all rather than a chore for one member of the household. Or it might be done for a decent wage by the unionized male and female employees of firms of domestic engineering. Pluralism is very much a way of looking at the world and defining social goods and ills.

To that extent Walzer owes a good deal to Isaiah Berlin's notion of the ultimate incompatibility of fundamental systems of belief and value. Nothing can reconcile paganism and Christianity, for example, and the search for an overarching unity of all ideals is vain and even mischievous because it induces coercive measures to reach agreement. And in spite of his fondness for shared commitments, Walzer is not promoting an ideology of agreement as an end in itself. He is, however, perhaps less sure than Berlin is that the acceptance of philosophical pluralism will necessarily be translated into liberal politics. That is why his book is about distributive justice, not about leaving people to their own devices.

Unlike Berlin's pluralism, Walzer's version is predictably more group oriented in its effects. He treats self-determination as analogous to personal autonomy. Nations are taken to be like clubs, and self-determination is their right. They are entitled to have a government not merely of their choice but one that shares their group identity and their traditional culture. The difficulty is that being governed by people just like oneself, representation as identity, has a history that Walzer does not want to face, but it is responsible for most of the horrors of the twentieth century. Group freedom is not analogous to or like personal liberty, and in this respect it seems to me Berlin has the better sense of what genuine pluralism entails. Many groups are, after all, very repressive.

One of the real gaps in Walzer's case for democracy is his relative silence about representative government, about the way in which it distributes political power and the procedures and laws that structure it. That may be due to his aversion to impersonality and impartiality in social life. It leads to a misreading of *Spheres of Justice*. Walzer is not really indifferent to human rights. Without them there can be no justice and no legitimacy, as he often says. But the fact is that rights create a culture that is a threat to the clubby life of traditional groups. It allows us to move about as we please, socially, intellectually, geographically, and personally. And one cannot have it both ways.

What saves Walzer is his undogmatic and inconclusive style of argument. Consider his argument that a country has a right to control immigration in order to maintain its communal character. In that case the U.S. Immigration Act of 1924 is a model of distributive political justice, for its aim was to maintain the exact proportion of ethnic groups that were in place then. Nor can he fault the New Englanders who did not want to admit a million Irish Catholics to their towns. However, though he begins by apparently siding with the excluders, he bit by bit adds so many qualifications that the borders begin to open up. Still, I am not at all sure I know whether he would or would not have admitted me to this country.

More clear is the matter of money. Its sphere is narrowly circumscribed. It may not buy people, human rights, public office and honors, love, or friendship. All very true, but whether he and I like it or not, money does buy admiration, and that is one of those diffuse goods that moves monopolistically from sphere to sphere, in accordance with the common understanding. Power and publicity are like that too. Our former colleague Henry Kissinger is reported to have said that "Power is the greatest aphrodisiac." He knows what he is talking about, and the psychological limits of separate spheres are therefore severe, and shared mores reject those boundaries.

This brings me to the core of my disagreement with Walzer. What are those "shared understandings" on which everything is based? To be sure, we may speak the same language, but that is no guarantee of sharing. We curse each other and pronounce death sentences upon one another in the same language in which we speak to our friends and fellow club members. Far from sharing a common understanding, the citizens of a modern state are culturally disparate and often deeply hostile to one another as individuals and especially as members of ascriptive groups. A modern state, and that was from the first the great case made for it, not only stands above the warring groups but exists to mitigate by lawful coercion the murderous proclivities generated by racial, ethnic, and religious solidarity. The strong state, as Hegel noted, not only protects, it encourages the freedom of the individual as well as of voluntary associations, but only as long as they submit to a single system of law equally applicable to all. Without it we are reduced to life as it is endured in Lebanon. Walzer's clubs are creatures of a nostalgia that he can afford only because he lives in a constitutional democracy built on Enlightenment principles and not in a suffocating little city-state or in a community of enforced conformity to collective values. That his longing for them amounts to an interpretation of the immanent spirit of his fellow citizens strikes me as absurd. They are here precisely because they wanted to say good-bye to all that.

INDEX

Mathematics: d'Alembert's views of, 304.
See also Geometry
McCarthy, Joseph, 40, 381
McCarthyism, 39, 40, 369
Medici family, 110
Medicine, 273
Mein Kampf (Hitler), 343
Melancholy: and political theory of uto-
pia, 161
Membership: and citizenship, 381
Memory, xxii, 149, 309, 310; and herme-
neutic circle, 76; and myths, 154–156;
party of, viii, 8, 96
Men and Citizens: A Study of Rousseau's
Social Theory, x, xi
Mental cruelty, xv
"Messianism," 170
Metis, the Wise, 135
Michelet, Jules, 111
Middle Ages: and hermeneutic circle, 76
Militarism, 4
Mill, John Stuart, xxiii, 9, 168, 170, 187,
188, 211; Representative Government,
188
"Millenialism," 170
Milton, John, 208, 211, 225, 227
Mind control, 340
Misanthropy, xii, xvi
Misapprehension, 90
Mnemosyne, 149, 152
Moderation, vii, viii, ix
Mommsen, Theodor, 111
Montaigne, vii, xi, xxiii, xxv, 5, 318; view
of animals, 196, 197
Montesquieu, Charles Louis de Secondat,
baron de la Brède et de, xxi, xxiii, 27,
95, 96, 102, 212, 229, 230, 233, 285,
368; Considerations sur les causes de la
grandeur des romains et de leur décadence, 246; on Harrington, 208; and
history, 302, 304, 306, 307, 308; on
intellectuals, 96; and notion of new republicanism, 244–259; Persian Letters,
100; and Rousseau, 249–253; and rule
of law, 21, 22–23, 24, 25, 32; Spirit of
the Laws, The, 100, 245, 246, 247,
248, 257, 300, 301
"Monumental history," xxii, 353, 354–
356, 360, 361
Morality, 333; and freedom, 9
Moral psychology: and political theory,
xi; practical uses for, xv; purposes of,
xiii

More, Sir Thomas, xxii, 162, 164, 175;
utopia of, 175, 176, 181; Utopia, 177,
178
Morris, William, 186, 277
Moscow Trials, 368
Moses, 152, 223, 252
Moses and Monotheism (Freud), 152
Müntzer, Thomas, 162
Murder, 57
Mysticism, 331
Mystification, 90, 93
Myths, 85, 154, 330, 331; of origins, xiii,
133

Napoleon I, 147
Nationalism, 4, 44, 53, 54, 367, 382
"Natural aristocracy," 97, 101, 103, 232;
Adams's view of, 99; Montesquieu on,
100
Natural law, 40, 59
Natural reason, 59
Natural rights: liberalism of, 8
Natural science, 7, 87; and history, 118;
and social sciences, 91–93
Natural selection: Darwin's theory of, 321
Nature: and Pope's Essay on Man, 196–
201
Nazi concentration camps, 368
Nazi Germany, 22, 33, 50, 350, 351
Nazism, 52, 67, 171, 186, 236, 342, 350
"Negative egalitarianism," xvi
""Negative liberty," 10
Neo-Platonic cosmology, 76
Neo-Tories, 225
Nero, 245
Neumann, Franz: Behemoth, 351
Neville, Henry, 222, 226
New Atlantic (Bacon), 177
New England: town meetings in, 286
New Harmony (Owen), 182
Newman, John Henry (Cardinal), 112
New Model, 215
New republicanism: Montesquieu and,
244–259
"Newspeak," 345, 346
Newton, Sir Isaac, 201, 233, 296
New York: German Jews in, 366
New York Times, 19
Nicias, 65
Nietzsche, Friedrich Wilhelm, 7, 116, 133,
138, 155, 197, 319, 332, 358; creation
myth of, 146–152; Genealogy of Mor-
als, The, 147, 148; opinion toward sci-